THE FIGHTING FIRST

The Untold Story of the Big Red One on D-Day

FLINT WHITLOCK

Author of *The Rock of Anzio*

A Member of the Perseus Books Group

All maps courtesy of the author.

Grateful acknowledgment is given to the following authors and publishers for granting permission to quote from their published works:

Blue Spaders: The 26th Infantry Regiment, 1917–1967, edited by John Votaw and Steven Weingarten. Reprinted with permission of Cantigny First Division Foundation.
Bombers and Mash: The Home Front 1939–1945, by Raynes Minns. Reprinted with permission of Virago Press/Time Warner Books UK.
Brave Men and *This Is Your War*, by Ernie Pyle. Reprinted with permission of Scripps Howard Foundation.
The Cannoneer, reprinted with permission of Frank Lindler, editor.
Crusade in Europe, by Dwight D. Eisenhower. By permission of Doubleday, a division of Random House.
Doctor Danger Forward: A World War II Memoir of a Combat Medical Aidman, First Infantry Division, © 2000 Allen N. Towne, by permission of McFarland & Company, Inc., Box 622, Jefferson, NC 28640. www.mcfarlandandpub.com.
My Three Years with Eisenhower, by Harry C. Butcher. Reprinted with permission of Simon & Schuster Adult Publishing Group, copyright 1946 by Harry C. Butcher. Copyright renewed © 1974 by Harry C. Butcher.
No Mission Too Difficult: Old Buddies of the 1st Division Tell All About World War II, by Blythe Foote Finke. Reprinted with permission of Cantigny First Division Foundation, 1995.
Six Armies in Normandy, by John Keegan. Reprinted with permission of Penguin Group (USA), Inc.
16th Infantry Regiment, 1861–1946, by John Baumgartner. Reprinted with permission of Cricket Press, Du Quoin, IL.
A Soldier's Story, by Omar N. Bradley. Reprinted with permission of Mrs. Omar N. Bradley.
News text from the June 12, 1944, issue of *Time*, © *Time* Inc., reprinted by permission.
The Vestibule, by Jess E. Weiss. Reprinted with permission of Simon & Schuster, copyright 1972.

Published in the United States of America by Westview Press
A Member of the Perseus Books Group

Westview Press books are available at special discounts for bulk purchases in the United States by corporations, institutions, and other organizations. For more information, please contact the Special Markets Department at the Perseus Books Group, 11 Cambridge Center, Cambridge, MA 02142; or call (617) 252-5298 or (800) 255-1514; or email special.markets@perseusbooks.com.

Find us on the world wide web at www.westviewpress.com.

A Cataloging-in-Publication data record for this book is available from the Library of Congress.
ISBN 0-8133-4218-X (hardcover)
ISBN 0-8133-4317-8 (paperback)

The paper used in this publication meets the requirements of the American National Standard for Permanence of Paper for Printed Library Materials Z39.48–1984.

Text design by Trish Wilkinson
Set in 10.5-point Minion by the Perseus Books Group

05 06 07 / 10 9 8 7 6 5 4 3 2 1

THE FIGHTING FIRST

ALSO BY THE AUTHOR

Soldiers on Skis: A Pictorial Memoir of the 10th Mountain Division (with Bob Bishop)

The Rock of Anzio: From Sicily to Dachau A History of the 45th Infantry Division

Contents

Dedicated to the men of the 1st Infantry Division
who proved that not even the impossible
was impossible.

Acknowledgments

A BOOK such as this is not the work of one person, although one person deserves the lion's share of the credit: Dr. John Votaw (Lieutenant Colonel, retired), the executive director of the Cantigny First Division Foundation, which operates one of the truly outstanding military museums in the world: the First Division Museum and archives at the Colonel Robert R. McCormick Research Center at Cantigny, in Wheaton, Illinois. Dr. Votaw, over a period of several years, answered all my questions, came up with answers for questions I had not thought to ask, and reviewed several drafts of the manuscript. If every military historian had such an eye for detail and accuracy, then the field's practitioners would be beyond reproach. The days I spent doing research at the Center were among the most satisfying of this entire project. I also want to express my deep-felt gratitude to Dr. Votaw's able lieutenants: Eric Gillespie, director, McCormick Research Center; Andrew Woods, research historian; Kate Giba, archivist; and Tracy Crockett, librarian. All worked tirelessly to uncover many maps, manuscripts, memoirs, photos, and arcane facts that aided me in my research.

A special "thank you" is also due to my longtime friend and mentor, Dr. Richard J Sommers, chief archivist at the U.S. Army Military History Institute at Carlisle Barracks, Pennsylvania, who provided me with hundreds of documents, memoirs, veterans' questionnaires, and a wealth of other material the Institute holds. Words are inadequate to express my gratitude to him for his friendship, which spans over half a century, and his wise counsel as he guided me through the oft-impenetrable hedgerows of history. I also deeply appreciate the help of David A. Keough, chief of manuscript archives at the USAMHI, as well as Jay Graybeal and Randy Hackenburg of the photo archives section, who assisted me in my search for relevant photographs. I am also thankful to Kevin Hymel of *Army* magazine and the staff of the National Archives in Washington, D.C., who went above and beyond the call of duty in their photographic research on my behalf.

A round of hearty thanks goes to all of the veterans (and, in those cases where the veterans were no longer living, their families) for either personal interviews or copies of their written memoirs and photographs. Several of the veterans also thoughtfully reviewed and critiqued numerous drafts of the manuscript. Many others provided their expertise on this subject, including George Gentry, president of the 18th Infantry Regimental Association. I certainly am grateful for Chyrl Zickgraf, daughter of the late Eddie Steeg, for giving me permission to quote extensively from his delightful and hitherto unpublished memoir. I thank Joseph Giove III for the information on Chaplain John Burkhalter. I also thank Pat Spayd, Don Patton, Don Marsh, Donald Van Roosen, Dr. Morey Susman, Lynda Sayers, and Tony Dudman for their contributions, and others who toiled anonymously on my behalf. Their fine eyes for detail corrected a number of errors and misassumptions on my part, and helped provide a more accurate account of what the 1st Infantry Division accomplished than would otherwise have been the case. My good friend Lieutenant Colonel (USA-Retired) Hugh Foster III also contributed his keen military insights to the accounts herein, and I would be remiss if I did not acknowledge his breadth of knowledge of all things military. The efforts of all those named notwithstanding, I take full responsibility for any errors in fact or interpretation.

As an added benefit of working on this project, several of the veterans have become regular correspondents with me, and I thank them for their trust and friendship.

I must also express my appreciation to my agent, Jody Rein, and my editor at Westview, Steve Catalano, whose enthusiasm for this project was most inspiring and kept me going.

Last but not least in the long line of people needing to be thanked is my wife, Dr. Mary Ann Watson, who has encouraged my writing over the years and who has been "without a husband" for long periods of time while I was off exploring battlefields, interviewing veterans, or spending uncounted hours at libraries and in my writing suite in front of the word processor. Her support is inestimable and deeply appreciated.

Flint Whitlock

From all accounts, the 1st Division has been living up to the old World War record.

The dash and precision with which the division carried out its landing and envelopment of Oran awakened memories of other days. . . .

I envy you people and expect great things of you.

—General George C. Marshall,
U.S. Army Chief of Staff

Had a less experienced division than the First Infantry stumbled into this crack resistance, it might easily have been thrown back into the Channel.

Unjust though it was, my choice of the First to spearhead the invasion probably saved us Omaha Beach and a catastrophe on the landing.

—Lieutenant General Omar N. Bradley,
Commander, First United States Army

The success of the First Infantry Division on the beaches, and during the thirty-six days thereafter that it remained in the line, is an outstanding achievement in the annals of military history.

—Major General Leonard T. Gerow,
Commander, U.S. V Corps

There were intimations in print back home that the 1st Division did not fight well in its earlier battles. The men of that division were wrathful and bitter about that. They went through four big battles in North Africa, made a good name for themselves in every one, and paid dearly for their victories. If such a criticism was printed it was somebody's unfortunate mistake. The 1st Division always fought well.

—Ernie Pyle, *War correspondent*

The trouble with the Big Red One is that it thinks the U.S. Army consists of the 1st Infantry Division and ten million replacements.

—Anonymous

Visitor:
Look how many of them there were.
Look how young they were.
They died for your freedom.
Hold back your tears and be silent.

—*Inscription at the*
American Military Cemetery,
Omaha Beach, France

Introduction

THIS IS a book about one American infantry division's role in the biggest amphibious assault of all time. Call it what you will: D-Day, the Normandy Invasion, the cross-Channel attack, Operation *Neptune-Overlord.** The eminent military historian Martin Blumenson once noted that an amphibious operation is the most difficult and complex of all military maneuvers. And no amphibious operation was more difficult or complex than the invasion of Normandy on 6 June 1944. Few amphibious operations have been more critical to the outcome of an entire war, either, than *Overlord.*

Thanks to Steven Spielberg's highly acclaimed 1998 film, *Saving Private Ryan*, a whole new generation now has a clearer sense of the awful carnage that an amphibious invasion—even a successful one—can produce. But neither *Saving Private Ryan* nor its 1960 predecessor, *The Longest Day*, mentioned the 1st Infantry Division's contribution to victory on that fateful Tuesday. In fact, the latter film's screenwriter even took the words spoken by the 1st Division's 16th Infantry Regiment commander, Colonel George A. Taylor ("There are only two

---

*According to a footnote in *The Papers of Dwight David Eisenhower* (page 1,837), "*Neptune* was the code name for the invasion itself. It had a narrower connotation than *Overlord*—that is, the Channel crossing, the seige of the beachhead, and the breakout from the beachhead." The historian Carlo D'Este further explained, "*Overlord* was the code name for the entire operation to liberate Northwest Europe; *Neptune* was the detailed plan for the invasion of Normandy. During the planning of *Overlord,* a code name was assigned to each of the potential invasion sites in France. *Neptune* was the designation given the Caen-Cotentin sector." (D'Este, *Decision in Normany,* p. 68) Hereinafter in this book, the operation will be referred to simply by its common name: *Overlord.*

kinds of people who are staying on this beach—the dead and those who are going to die. Now let's get the hell off this beach!") and gave them to the assistant division commander of the 29th Infantry Division, Brigadier General Norman D. Cota (played in the film by Robert Mitchum). My intent with this book is to give credit where credit is due, especially to the men of the 1st Infantry Division.

This is more than a book about the D-Day invasion, however. It is a history of a remarkable fighting machine known officially as the U.S. Army's 1st Infantry Division, and unofficially as the "Big Red One." It is about the generals and the colonels. It is also about the captains and lieutenants and the sergeants and the privates who did their best to carry out the orders from higher headquarters, even when those orders cost them their lives. It is a story of incredible courage and heroism.

During and after the war, most of the soldiers would not—or could not—share their horrific combat experiences with their parents, wives, or children; civilians simply would not be able to comprehend the terrible conditions under which they lived and the awful scenes they were forced to witness. Only with other veterans would a soldier speak of the unspeakable, for only other veterans would know of the hardships, the fear, the tragedy, and, yes, even the exultation of combat. Besides, each soldier had spent his time in service protecting his country and his family from the enemy. How could he now expose his loved ones to the mind-numbing dangers he felt every minute he was on the front lines? Rather than share, it was easier to keep it all bottled up inside. This, then, is the story the veterans *didn't* tell.

The Allied invasion of the northern coast of France has been called the most important battle of World War II. If successful, it would spell doom for the Nazi regime; if unsuccessful, the war would go on much longer, and perhaps to a different conclusion. Failure, therefore, was not an option.

The site selected for the mightiest invasion ever mounted was a stretch of coastline between the base of the Cotentin Peninsula and the mouth of the Orne River, an area known as the Calvados Coast, in the province of Normandy. From end to end, the Normandy beachhead was sixty miles long. From dawn to dusk on Tuesday, 6 June 1944, those sixty miles were the deadliest, most dangerous place on earth. Along the eastern end of the beachhead, one Canadian and two British infantry divisions stormed ashore at strips of sand code-named Gold, Sword, and Juno. At the far western end, at Utah Beach, the U.S. 4th Infantry Division landed on a shore that was, relatively speaking, lightly defended. The beach in the center of the invasion area, however, a five-mile-long strip of sand and stones code-named Omaha, was quite another story. Here the veteran U.S. 1st Infantry Division, reinforced with two regiments attached from the unblooded 29th Infantry Division, waded ashore into a firestorm of German steel.

The story of the 29th's Omaha Beach ordeal was well told by Joseph M. Balkoski in *Beyond the Beachhead.* Until now, however, what the 1st Infantry Division endured and accomplished has been revealed only in bits and pieces. Here, for the first time, is the story of the 1st Infantry Division, told by the men of the "Big Red One" themselves—specifically the 16th, 18th, and 26th Infantry Regiments and their assigned supporting units. My intention is to concentrate primarily on the experiences of the men in one division during their World War II tour of duty. A number of other books on the Normandy campaign paint a broader canvas and include accounts of the largest amphibious invasion in the history of warfare from a variety of viewpoints: American, British, Canadian, French, and German. These other books (most notably Cornelius Ryan's ground-breaking *The Longest Day* and Stephen Ambrose's monumental *D-Day: June 6, 1944*) have done a fine job in conveying the overall strategic picture. Anyone wishing to explore the wider issues surrounding Operation *Overlord* is well advised to seek out these and other accounts.

Except for the higher-level commanders, the broad view of the strategy and the overall conduct of the operation was denied to the average officer and enlisted man—the latter quite likely a man too young to vote or even drink a beer legally. What he was most concerned about were two burning questions: *Can I accomplish my mission?* and *Am I going to survive?*

Let us go back now to that cold, gray dawn of 6 June 1944. To appreciate what it must have been like for the men in the first-wave landing at the Easy Red or Fox Green sectors of Omaha Beach, picture yourself as a young GI—maybe late teens or early twenties—in a tiny, vulnerable landing craft bouncing over the waves toward the hostile shore. You are loaded down with gear—pack, rifle, grenades, ammunition, steel helmet. With your head below the top of the gunwale, all you can see are the men bunched up in front of you. You are apt to be very seasick. And very scared. All you can hear is the roaring of your boat's engine and the waves slapping against the ramp and the sides of the craft, and the flying-freight-train sound of big shells from naval guns screaming overhead. Your broader mission, as you have been told repeatedly by your officers, is to establish a Second Front, overthrow the tyranny of Nazism, and return peace and freedom to the continent of Europe. This broader mission is the last thing you have on your mind.

As you get closer to shore, you hear—and feel—the concussion of the Navy's munitions exploding in one, long cacophony of noise that pounds an unending drum roll against your eardrums. Your mouth is drier than wool, and you speak—if you can speak at all—only with the utmost difficulty. As the interminable ride continues, you become aware that people on shore are shooting at *you*, with rounds both large and small splashing the water around you, drenching you, and pinging against the steel ramp that is your only shield. Your stomach clamps itself into a state of extreme distress. You may fear that you are about to embarrass yourself by emptying your bowels and bladder right there in your pants; no worry—plenty of your buddies are feeling exactly the same.

Gripping your M-1 Garand rifle so tightly that you think you will leave the impression of your hands forever embossed into the wooden stock, you hear and feel the boat grind into the sand and come to a jolting stop that throws you and everyone in the boat forward. You then watch with unspeakable horror as the ramp begins to slowly and agonizingly descend, a curtain revealing a frightful Technicolor movie full of smoke and fire and ear-ripping explosions that confirm all of your earlier fears. As the noise reaches a crescendo and the ramp drops further, all around you hear prayers murmured by men both pious and agnostic, and your lips join in reciting the familiar litany—"Hail Mary, full of grace . . . pray for us sinners now and at the hour of our deaths"; or "Our Father, who art in heaven, hallowed be thy name, thy kingdom come, thy will be done"; or "Though I walk through the shadow of the valley of death, I shall fear no evil. . . "; or *Schmah yisroael, adonoi elohanue, adonoi echad* ("Hear, O Israel; the Lord is our God, the Lord is One"). You see men touching their St. Christopher medals and fingering their rosaries and making the sign of the cross. Suddenly, the men in front of you are swept forward and you are caught up in a human tide that can only go in one direction. You watch in dumb horror as your officer and non-commissioned officers collapse in an olive-drab, blood-stained heap as the falling shield exposes them to the enemy's fire. You somehow find the courage to step over them and carry on. With your buddies all around you—as frightened as you are—you give one long, terrifying shriek—as much to build up your courage as to act as a relief valve for all the pent-up terror.

Now you are out of the protective shell of the landing craft and into a world the reality of which exceeds your imagination a millionfold, and for which months of intensive training have left you unprepared. Your feet slip on the wet ramp, now under water. Now you, too, are under water, up to your waist or neck in water so cold it numbs everything except the adrenal gland that is still pumping furiously away inside you. A frigid wave splashes you, and you taste salt and oil and blood. If you dare to tear you eyes away from the beach ahead, you notice your fellow amphibians trudging as if in the same type of slow motion found only in bad dreams, toward dry land, pushing through the flotsam of war—pieces of equipment and pieces of men. Geysers of water spring up around you as bullets and shrapnel tear into the surf, and the beach erupts in great volcanoes of sand and fire. You see no enemy at which to shoot, but their unseen presence is felt everywhere. You hear men—most of them boys like you—moaning and screaming in mortal pain and crying out for medics and their mothers.

You try to hunker down as the water becomes shallower—an almost impossible task—so that only your head is a target. Your youthful belief in your own invincibility has been obliterated, and you fear you are apt to obliterated, too, and very soon. You attempt to move quickly but you are weighted down by all your equipment and sodden clothing and the immovability of trapped water molecules. Up ahead, looming above you through the smoke and low clouds, is your objective—the top of the bluffs overlooking the beach. It might as well be Mount Everest, for between you and the top are profuse minefields, mortar and artillery concentrations, thickets of barbed wire, and thousands of men waiting to kill you. You know you will never make it.

You—a 1st Infantry Division soldier, waterlogged, stupefied by the crashing spectacle all around you, and frightened beyond all measure—are now on the sand and trying to run the last few yards across a corpse-strewn beach to what you hope is a place of shelter and safety.

But there is no shelter or safety, for you have just arrived in Hell.

CHAPTER ONE

"An Army That Won't Complain, Won't Fight"

LOUIS NEWMAN had the best seat in the house at the biggest, loudest, most important amphibious assault landing in history. It was a seat he would just as soon not have had.

The twenty-seven-year-old private first class from Brooklyn, New York, a member of Cannon Company, 18th Infantry Regiment, 1st Infantry Division (known as the "Big Red One" from its distinctive shoulder patch designed in World War I), was perched atop the cab of a three-quarter-ton truck that was stalled in chest-deep water about a hundred yards from a beach in France dubbed "Omaha."

Whichever way he swiveled his head, the entire chaotic, horrific panorama of the Normandy Invasion encircled him like the battle cyclorama paintings at Gettysburg and Waterloo. To his front was a prickly landscape of beach obstacles of all descriptions; frightened men wading ashore from landing craft; boats and vehicles wrecked and burning; geysers of water being blasted into the air; and a shoreline erupting with an unending series of violent bursts.

Behind and beside him, warships of all description were firing shells of every caliber over and around him—all accompanied by a stereophonic soundtrack cranked up to eardrum-shattering volume. Above him—most of them unseen above the low, steel-gray clouds—hundreds of warplanes were crisscrossing the leaden sky. Adding to the horror of the scene, bobbing in the water all around his olive-drab, steel island, were the corpses of his fellow invaders, leaking blood. As dangerous as his exposed position was, Private First Class Newman had another problem: He couldn't swim. He had lost his inflatable life belt. His rifle and helmet were also missing. And the tide was rapidly rising.[1]

Private First Class Louis Newman (right), Cannon Company, 18th Infantry Regiment, poses for a photographer in England with his buddy, Louis Lefkowitz, from the Bronx, New York. Lefkowitz was killed in France on 7 June 1944, the day after the D-Day landings. (Courtesy Louis Newman)

While Louis Newman sat pondering his future atop his dangerous perch, a few miles behind him, on board a gray-painted Navy cruiser, General Omar Nelson Bradley fretted like a nervous, expectant father, totally out of touch with the battle he was supposed to orchestrate.

Somewhere in France, a German field marshal by the name of Erwin Rommel was racing back to his palatial command post at La Roche-Guyon, on the Seine between Paris and Rouen, hoping that he was not too late to reverse the tide of a battle that had already spun out of control during his brief, untimely absence.

In a villa in Southampton, England, a bald, grim-faced, American four-star general named Dwight David Eisenhower stood chain-smoking, jingling the English coins in his pocket, and staring at huge situation maps that maddeningly refused to tell him if this invasion, for which he alone took full responsibility, was about to become a stunning success or a crashing, tragic failure.

Across the ocean in America—from where had come so many of the young men who were at that moment engaged in a life-and-death struggle—the war-weary nation was asleep, unaware of the drama unfolding along the northern coast of France. No less than the ultimate outcome of the war in Europe hung precariously in the balance.

Exactly how Louis Newman and 175,000 other American, British, Canadian, and Free French soldiers who were, at that very moment, fighting their way onto the northern coast of Nazi-occupied France found themselves in this situation is a complex story that began several years earlier.

The necessity of invading the European continent as the only way to defeat Nazi Germany was recognized early on by the British. After France fell to the Germans in June 1940, and the British Expeditionary Force sent to provide assistance to the French was sent reeling into the sea at Dunkerque, German dictator Adolf Hitler expected the British to sue for peace; he was not prepared for British defiance. After attempting to mount his own amphibious invasion of Britain, Hitler called it off due to the lack of a proper invasion fleet and the fact that his air force, the *Luftwaffe*, had not gained air superiority over the English Channel during the nine months of the Blitz in 1939–1940. Frustrated, Hitler turned his wrath on the Soviet Union, which he had earlier lulled into inaction with a non-aggression pact.[2]

Although the United States was not yet in the war, American ideas on how to defeat Hitler had begun to take shape during the spring and summer of 1941. With much of Europe under Nazi domination, and Britain and Russia struggling to survive the German onslaught, it seemed obvious to the realists in Washington, D.C., that the United States would not be able to remain neutral much longer. To prepare for the war he saw coming, General George C. Marshall, the U.S. Army's Chief of Staff, asked the War Department to create an assessment on how to defeat the Axis powers. This study, which later became known as the Victory Plan, dovetailed with British ideas and showed clearly that the only way to win the war would be to physically invade the European continent and march into the heart of Hitler's Third Reich.

Before this could happen, however, two main conditions needed to be met: Enough men would need to be trained and equipped for the task, and sufficient shipping would need to be available to transport the men and their supplies to Britain, from which the invasion would be launched and supplied. According to the Victory Plan, the success of such an invasion hinged on eliminating the

German U-boat threat in the North Atlantic; achieving air superiority over enemy-controlled Europe; destroying or disrupting the German economy and war industries; degrading the German military machine on other fronts; and establishing harbors and military bases in Britain.[3]

It was an almost impossibly tall order, especially given the fact that the United States in the summer of 1941 was still a third-rate military power with a small army and obsolete equipment. The grandiose plans of landing in Europe and marching into Berlin would have to wait. The British, on the other hand, now that Germany had called off the invasion in order to attack Russia, began planning an invasion of their own. In September 1941, the British Chiefs of Staff charged Admiral Lord Louis Mountbatten and his Combined Operations Headquarters with studying the feasibility of conducting amphibious operations against German-held Europe. Prime Minister Winston S. Churchill told Mountbatten, "You are to prepare for the invasion of Europe. You must devise and design the appliances, the landing craft, and the technique . . . . The whole of the South Coast of England is a bastion of defense against the invasion of Hitler; you've got to turn it into the springboard for our attack."[4]

Although the responsibility for the invasion soon passed out of Mountbatten's hands, the invasion of Europe became, as one historian observed, "the supreme effort of the Western Allies in Europe—the consummation of the grand design to defeat Germany by striking directly at the heart of Hitler's Reich. One of the last attacks, [Operation *Overlord*] was the fruition of some of the first strategic ideas."[5]

The shock waves from the Japanese bombs that fell on the U.S. military installations in the Hawaiian Islands on 7 December 1941 rudely shook Americans out of their blissful isolationist dreams. With America's military preparedness in a sadly neglected state, the industrial giant began to rise slowly from the enforced idleness of the Great Depression, stoked the cold furnaces of its factories, and began churning out an endless, ever-quickening procession of tanks, trucks, warplanes, ships, rifles, cannon, bombs, bullets, and all the other necessities of war. Whitewashed barracks and canvas camps sprang up practically overnight across the United States to welcome the students, salesmen, farm boys, truck drivers, cooks, clerks, and laid-off workers who were now fledgling soldiers, sailors, airmen, Coast Guardsmen, and Marines, eager to fight for their aggrieved country. There was a war to be won, and almost no American boy or man wanted to be left out of it.

While it was the Japanese who had attacked America, President Franklin Delano Roosevelt had always regarded Nazi Germany as the greater threat; if Britain and Russia fell, the United States would be left to face Germany and Italy alone. It was therefore determined, even before Pearl Harbor, that once the U.S. was at war, the bulk of American military resources would be concentrated against Nazi Germany; Japan, it was felt, could be contained in the Pacific until the European enemies were defeated.[6]

Two weeks after Pearl Harbor, Churchill met with the American Joint Chiefs of Staff in Washington, D.C., at what became known as the Arcadia Conference. There he outlined his strategic concept for the defeat of Germany, which included a naval blockade of Axis nations; the bombardment of German cities, industrial sites, and transportation networks; amphibious attacks against German installations and interests from Norway to the Aegean and Mediterranean Seas; and a final assault on Nazi Germany itself.[7]

As the American war machine gathered steam, U.S. and British planners, with the continual prodding of the besieged Soviet Union, began working together to formulate the invasion of Europe. Churchill, already facing manpower and matériel shortages, and waiting for a United States that had not fully mobilized, was understandably reluctant to invade the Continent alone. The 1940 debacle at Dunkerque was still fresh in his mind. Even fresher were Britain's brave but ultimately failed seaborne assaults in Norway, Crete, and Greece. Trying once more to gain a foothold on the continent, Churchill gave his blessing to a large-scale commando raid at the French port city of Dieppe on 19 August 1942, an operation known as *Jubilee.* Taking part were 5,000 soldiers of the Canadian 2nd Infantry Division, a thousand British troops, two dozen Free French commandos, and about fifty American Rangers. The goal was not to wrest France away from the Germans, or even to be a precursor to a much larger invasion, but simply to gather intelligence about the state of German coastal defenses.

The British quickly learned an expensive lesson. *Jubilee* was anything but a call for celebration; of the 6,100 Allied soldiers who reached the beach at Dieppe, over half were either killed or captured, and the shaken survivors of the nine-hour battle were withdrawn under fire. Dieppe taught British planners two things: a considerably larger landing force was essential, as was a heavy and prolonged air and naval bombardment of the hostile defenses. For Churchill, who, as first lord of the admiralty in 1915 had presided over the disastrous seaborne landing at Gallipoli in Turkey, Operation *Jubilee* was especially chilling. These two signal events—Gallipoli and Dieppe—were to form the basis of his reluctance to send British troops into another amphibious adventure. Churchill's desire, instead, was to nibble at the edges of the Third Reich with his limited forces until the United States could bolster the British effort. He thus proposed postponing any invasion until the periphery of the Reich had been sufficiently reduced. His dynamic mind churning out plans and proposals at a breakneck pace, Churchill saw major attacks against German-controlled North Africa, Italy, the Balkans, and Norway as vital before proceeding with any major invasion of France.[8]

The United States, on the other hand, was not terribly keen on the indirect operations Churchill was advocating. With its growing industrial might, the United States was eager to take the fight to the enemy. If we wait too long, U.S. military advisers argued, the Russians might be defeated, and then the entire German war machine would be free to concentrate on Britain and the United States. Bombing the Reich was fine, but bombing alone would not win the war; it would take troops on the ground, meeting and annihilating the enemy, and marching into Berlin, to achieve total victory.

But where and when to start? Invading the European continent was important as a long-term objective, but certain realities made it impossible in 1942. Facing a two-front war, America was not yet capable of taking on the lion's share of combat in the European/Mediterranean Theater. Until sufficient quantities of men and matériel could be built up in Britain, the two nations could only attempt to break Germany's will to fight and disrupt her war production by round-the-clock strategic bombing of her cities and factories.

The most pressing problem, however, was the fact that German submarines and aircraft were sending to the ocean floor millions of tons of vital, American-made war goods destined for beleaguered Britain and the Soviet Union. Before the millions of men—plus their tanks and guns and planes and trucks and bullets and bombs and gasoline and tires and spare parts and rations and mountains of other supplies and equipment—could be concentrated in Britain, the sea lanes would need to be secured. The navies of both Britain and the United States swung into full action to rid the Atlantic of the U-boat menace, a task that would take time. Until the wolf packs could be defanged and Britain turned into a mighty launching pad for the invasion, some other place needed to be found to engage the enemy.

Among the American divisions being prepared to take the war to the enemy was the 1st Infantry Division, most of whose members hailed from New York and New England. The Big Red One was considered by many to be America's premier Army division, and with good reason. Elements of what eventually would become the 1st Infantry Division could trace their heritage to 1798. The division's predecessors also fought in the War of 1812; the Mexican War of 1846–1848; the Civil War; the wars against the Indians in the Southwest; at San Juan Hill during the Spanish-American War; in the Philippine Insurrection; and during John J. Pershing's 1916 Punitive Expedition against Pancho Villa along the U.S.-Mexico border.

World War I broke out in 1914 and the United States entered it three years later. The days of regiments being the main combat forces were numbered; the exigencies of the First World War required larger units—divisions—made up of four regiments. Thus, before the American Expeditionary Force was sent to fight in France, the Army was reorganized and the 1st Expeditionary Division (soon renamed the 1st Infantry Division) was formed. It consisted of the 16th, 18th, 26th, and 28th Infantry Regiments (when the Army reorganized again in 1940 and the number of regiments in a division was trimmed to three, the 28th was transferred to the 8th Infantry Division).

During World War I, President Woodrow Wilson deployed twenty-nine infantry divisions to France. They fought with a courage and tenacity that shocked the enemy, electrified the Allies, and proved to be the deciding factor in the final victory. And at the head of the list of units that distinguished themselves stood the 1st Infantry Division. It is said that one of the division's artillery batteries fired the first shots of any American unit when it reached the front lines in October 1917; 1st Infantry Division soldiers also became the first American army casualties of the war. The Big Red One was engaged in some of the hardest fighting during the last year of the conflict—battles with names that seared themselves into the consciousness of Americans for generations to come: Cantigny, St. Mihiel, Soissons, Argonne.[9]

The word "infantry" comes from the French—*infanterie*—meaning a soldier trained and equipped to fight on foot. No matter how technologically innovative warfare has become, no one has yet invented a robot to replace the foot soldier, capable of marching long distances in any type of terrain or weather while lugging all his possessions in a pack on his back, and doing battle with the enemy by means of his rifle, grenades, bayonet, knife, and even bare hands.

The key to an infantry division's success is the quality of its personnel and their training. In pre–World War II America, combat skills did not come naturally.

1st INFANTRY DIVISION ORGANIZATION (1944–45)

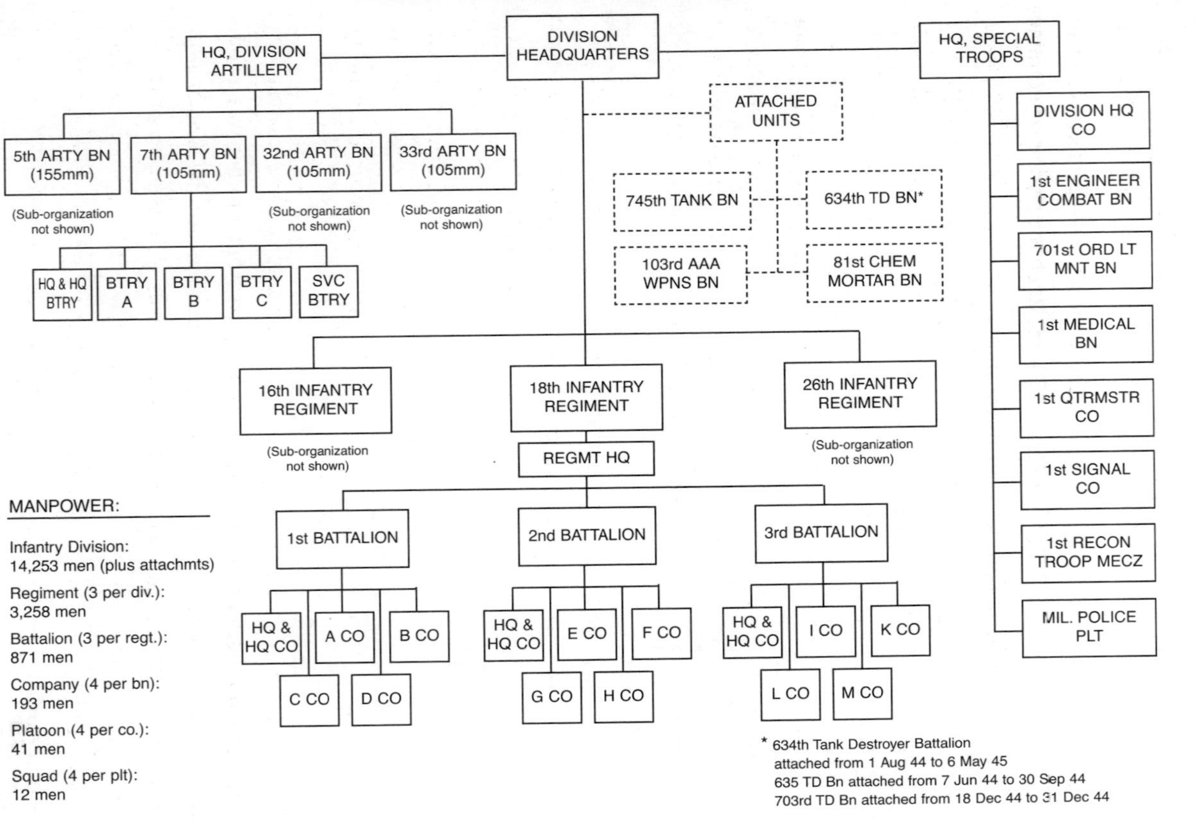

1st Infantry Division Organization (1944–1945)

While some of the recruits (and they were either volunteers or men who had been drafted) may have previously handled rifles in pursuit of pheasants or deer, the vast majority of city-dwelling civilians had no familiarity with firearms. As most families in the 1930s and 1940s were church-goers to some extent, most young men grew up with the commandment "Thou shalt not kill" impressed strongly into them. Thus, turning a recent high-school graduate or young, ex–soda jerk into a trained, disciplined soldier was not easy. It took time—thirteen weeks of basic training, then advanced infantry training—in which the soldier could hone his craft during realistic combat training scenarios and exercises. The young American soldier learned to fire his M-1 Garand rifle with deadly accuracy; to lob grenades; to attack with a bayonet; and to engage in hand-to-hand combat. He learned to dig protective holes in which to take cover while under attack by artillery, aircraft, or tanks. He learned to ignore heat, cold, wet, thirst, hunger, exhaustion, and minor injuries. He learned the limits of his endurance—and was pushed beyond them. He learned to perform not only his own job, but the jobs of those around him, for he never knew when a machine-gunner or mortarman or radio operator might be hit, requiring him to fill in for a downed comrade. He learned how to be a part of a team.

The young soldier also learned to instinctively and unquestioningly obey orders, no matter how dangerous they might be. Conversely, despite the insistence on instant obedience to orders, he was encouraged to think for himself when confronted by unusual situations, and to assume a leadership role when his leaders were killed, wounded, or missing. He learned—no, had drummed into his head—that the most important thing about being a soldier was to accomplish his assigned mission, regardless of the difficulties, discomforts, or obstacles, even at the cost of his own life.[10]

With all infantry divisions having the same organization, the same training, and same broad mission, what set one division apart from another was a combination of factors—mostly the quality of the officers and NCOs, or noncommissioned officers; the sergeants and corporals. The officers of the 1st Infantry Division, most of whom had graduated from the U.S. Military Academy at West Point, New York, considered themselves the best of the breed. Many of the older officers—the colonels and lieutenant colonels and majors—had been in the Army since World War I, and many had seen combat. The same was true for many of the senior NCOs. Between them, they had a wealth of combat experience and knowledge to pass along to the younger officers and soldiers.

Perhaps just as importantly, they would impart their deeply held convictions that the 1st Infantry Division was not just the best damned division in the United States Army, but in *any* army in the world. Therefore, once the U.S. entered World War II, big things were expected from the Big Red One.

In early August 1942, with its stateside training complete, the entire 1st Infantry Division was crammed aboard the converted luxury oceanliner, the HMS *Queen Mary*, and shipped from New York to Scotland. To kill time, poker games broke out all over the ship, and one soldier is reported to have won $28,000.[11] Others also made a killing, including members of the ship's crew, who, according Sergeant George J. Koch, a member of the 1st Reconnaissance Troop, "had a 'field day' and looted our barracks bags, which were in the hold, of personal articles, especially candy, cigarettes, shaving cream, etc."[12]

Upon arriving in Scotland, the division was sent by rail to England, where it underwent almost three more months of advanced training under its battle-hardened commanding general, Major General Terry Allen* and his deputy, Brigadier General Theodore Roosevelt Jr. (who had served with the 1st during the First World War), the oldest son of the rough-riding former American president. Few in the division knew where it would see its first combat of this war; many assumed it would be France, or perhaps even the Soviet Union. Their assumptions would turn out to be wrong.

In the autumn of 1942, the Russians were tenaciously holding out at a city on the Volga River named Stalingrad. The city's namesake needed all the help he could get—and quickly. With Stalin demanding a "second front" to relieve Ger-

*The son of a career Army officer, Terry Allen was born on 1 April 1888 at Fort Douglas, Utah, and later made El Paso, Texas, his home. A stocky five-foot, nine-inches tall, he was described as being "built like an oversize jockey." Never a top student, he had flunked out of West Point but received a commission upon graduation in 1912 from the Catholic University in Washington, D.C. In the Punitive Expedition against the Mexican bandit Pancho Villa along the U.S.-Mexico border in 1916, Allen commanded H Troop, 14th Cavalry. During World War I, he led a battalion within the 90th Infantry Division and was seriously wounded during the St. Mihiel offensive in September 1918. After the war, while at Command and General Staff School in 1924, he graduated near the bottom of his class; a classmate named Dwight David Eisenhower ranked number one. (Terry Allen papers, USAMHI)

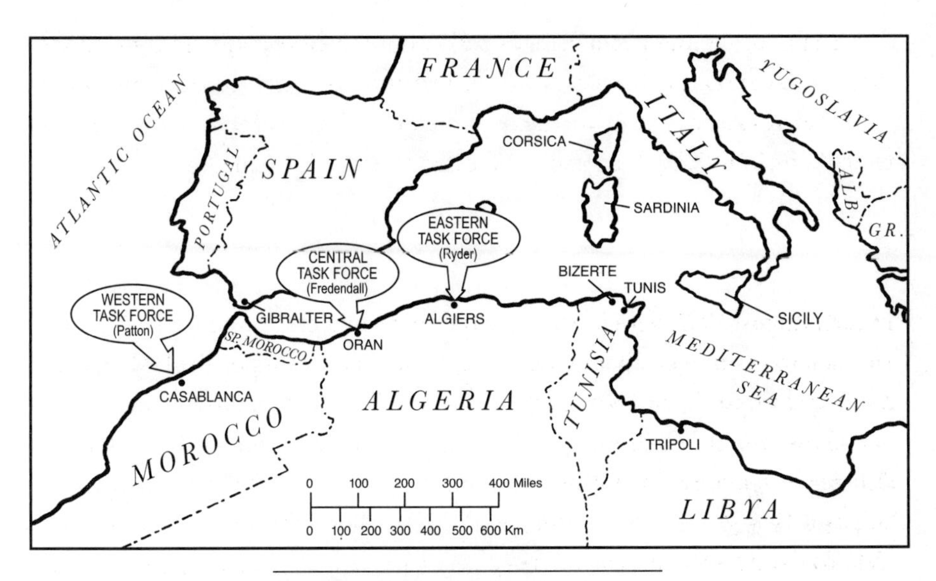

Operation *Torch*—the American invasion of North Africa—November 1942.

man pressure on his nation, the United States agreed to enter the European war through an unlikely door: pro-German, Vichy-French-controlled Morocco and Algeria, from where the United States would reinforce the British who had been battling the Germans and Italians in North Africa since March 1941.[13] Operation *Torch*, as the invasion of North Africa was code-named, would give Americans their first real taste of battle outside of the Pacific. Under the overall command of Lieutenant General Dwight David Eisenhower, 67,000 U.S. troops were poised to begin wading ashore at three points along the Moroccan and Algerian coasts.[14]

In the black morning hours of 8 November 1942, the 1st Infantry Division lay in darkened transports off the unsuspecting coast of Algeria in the Gulf of Arzew, keyed up and ready for just this moment—its baptism of fire—and its young members wondered if they could live up to the reputation established by the "old-timers."

To say that the campaign was a confused mess would be an understatement. The 1st Infantry Division, landing near Oran as part of Major General Lloyd Fredendall's Central Task Force, did well in its initial combat operations, quickly taking the Vichy-French-held cities of Oran, Arzew, and St. Cloud. The fight for

A smiling Terry Allen (front, without helmet) drives through the streets of Oran, Algeria, to the friendly greetings of civilians. (Courtesy Colonel Robert R. McCormick Research Center of the 1st Infantry Division Museum at Cantigny)

Oran was over almost before it began, and the advancing 1st Infantry Division was warmly greeted by the citizens. Terry Allen noted in a letter home, "Our passage through the city was most impressive. The entire civilian population turned out en masse and were hysterically enthusiastic at the sight of the American flag."[15]

Within three days, Allied troops claimed 1,300 miles of coastline, and the British and Americans were soon preparing to push into Tunisia and Libya. During this three-day period, the 1st Infantry Division had been blooded—and bloodied: 94 killed, 251 wounded, and 73 missing.[16]

After this initial success, Eisenhower inexplicably allowed his subordinate, British Lieutenant General Sir Kenneth Anderson, to split up the division and parcel out elements of it as reinforcements for British units. Not unexpectedly, these elements did not perform well, and the only reinforcement that was done was to reinforce British perceptions that the American Army was untrained, undisciplined, and ineffective. On the other hand, the British Eighth Army, under General Bernard Law Montgomery, was doing well. German and Italian forces seemed to be crumbling. By 17 November, even the French forces in North Africa, perhaps sensing which side was eventually going to win the war, had broken with the Germans and turned into American allies.[17]

Brigadier General Teddy Roosevelt Jr., the 1st Infantry Division's beloved assistant division commander. (Courtesy Colonel Robert R. McCormick Research Center of the 1st Infantry Division Museum at Cantigny)

Angry at his division's mounting casualties under British leadership, however, Terry Allen went to see Eisenhower in Algiers to request that his division be reunified under his command; Ike promised to look into the matter, an answer that did not satisfy Allen. Upon leaving to return to his headquarters in Oran, Allen ruffled the feathers of Ike's irasible chief of staff, Walter Bedell Smith, with an offhand remark: "Is this a private war in Tunisia or can anybody get in on it?" Smith was not amused, the division was not reunited, and the remark would later cost Allen dearly.[18]

With the North Africa campaign still under way, Churchill and Roosevelt met at Casablanca from 14 to 24 January 1943 to discuss broad strategy for the eventual invasion of the European continent. General Marshall's staff had already drawn up a plan (code-named *Roundup*) that called for the invasion of France in the spring of 1943, while the bulk of the German army was tied down on the Russian front and before the coastal defenses of France could be strengthened.

Roosevelt, Churchill, and their staffs worked tirelessly to hammer out an agreement that consisted of several major objectives: stepping up efforts to eliminate the U-boat menace in the Atlantic; increasing the bombing offensive against Germany; keeping German troops pinned down in the Mediterranean area with additional operations; providing more material aid to the Russians; engaging in "island-hopping" by the Americans across the Pacific with an eventual invasion of the Japanese home islands; increasing pressure on the Japanese in the China-Burma-India Theater; and proceeding with plans to develop the top-secret atomic bomb.[19]

A number of factors still conspired against a quick invasion of France: a lack of shipping (especially LSTs—Landing Ship, Tank); a lack of trained and/or combat-tested American units (the *Roundup* plan called for forty-three assault divisions); a lack of necessary supplies; and a lack of sufficient air and naval support. It would take more time to overcome these obstacles. Much to the disappointment of many, especially Stalin, the invasion of France was postponed until 1944.[20]

The Americans, meanwhile, stumbled through a series of embarrassing defeats at the hands of Erwin Rommel's *Afrika Korps*, including a devastating reversal at Kasserine Pass in mid-February 1943. Finally, Allen received permission to reunite his division and was ordered to hold the line west of Kasserine. Hold they did. On 23 February, Rommel sent two panzer divisions against the thin line of Yanks, but the riflemen, anti-tank gunners, and artillerymen of the Big Red One, along with American armor and air power, stopped them. The Germans regrouped, returned, and were stopped again. Rommel called off the assault and retreated to lick his wounds; Major General George S. Patton Jr. wrote to his wife, "This has been a great day for the American Army. The 1st Div stopped the famous 10th Panzer cold in two attacks."[21]

In a 3 March 1943 letter to George C. Marshall, Eisenhower expressed his confidence in the 1st Infantry Division's two leaders: "Terry Allen seems to be doing a satisfactory job; so is Roosevelt."[22]

Eisenhower knew he had a problem with II Corps commanding general Lloyd Fredendall, who was disliked by almost everyone, both above and below him. Upset with Fredendall's lack of aggressive spirit (and especially his pen-

Members of the 2nd Battalion, 16th Infantry Regiment, advance through Kasserine Pass on their way to the Tunisian town of Kasserine, 26 February 1943. (Courtesy U.S. Army Military History Institute)

chant for selecting poor subordinates), Eisenhower sacked him in early March and replaced him with the fire-breathing Patton, a fifty-seven-year-old officer notorious for his shocking obscenities, volcanic temper, and demanding, Prussian-style approach to discipline. Believing that slovenly troops were unlikely to be good fighters, Patton sought to bring about a swift change in attitude with a proven method of behavior modification: Hit 'em in their pocketbooks. Patton established strict dress regulations and swooped down on anyone caught violating them. Soldiers could ill afford the loss of pay, so he steeply fined officers and enlisted men alike for breaches of his dress code. Steel helmets and leggings were to be worn at all times, and officers were required to wear ties—even in battle in the desert. It was reported that Patton even flung open latrine-stall doors to see if soldiers had their helmets on while relieving themselves.[23]

Second Lieutenant Harold Monica, D Company, 18th Infantry Regiment, was told that "any officer of II Corps apprehended by the MPs [Military Police] without a neck tie would be fined $25.00. I heard a couple tried it to see if he was serious and were picked up and promptly fined. My tie may have been a little loose, but I had one on."[24]

The harassment worked. Soon, the steel-helmeted, legginged, and necktied soldiers hated and feared Patton more than they hated and feared the Germans. As unpopular as Patton's methods were, the disgruntled troops got the message and began shaping up. Besides *looking* like soldiers, they now began to *perform* like soldiers.

While the American soldiers in general cursed Patton, Allen was worshipped by his 1st Division troops. Unlike the peacock Patton, who always appeared spit-polished from his varnished helmet to his gleaming cavalry boots, Allen was a soldier's general. He stayed with his troops at the front, sharing their hardships. He was also reportedly the only general who slept on the ground, rather than on a cot or a bed. He didn't care that his clothes were wrinkled and his black hair tousled. What he most cared about was making his men the finest soldiers they could be. Between battles, there was very little slack time for the Big Red One; Allen always had some sort of training program scheduled. Because he believed night attacks were safer than daylight assaults, much time and effort was devoted to training the men in how to move and fight in the dark.

It was natural, then, that Patton and Allen would have their clashes. In one of the most celebrated, Patton, while visiting 1st Division headquarters, asked about some narrow trenches outside the command tents. Allen explained that they were for the men's protection from enemy air attacks. To show his contempt for what he thought was cowardice on Allen's part, Patton urinated into Allen's trench. "There—now try to use it," he challenged. Allen's bodyguards audibly clicked off the safeties on their Thompson submachine guns—a not-so-subtle hint that they did not appreciate Patton's disrespectful act toward their commanding officer. Patton evidently realized he had crossed the line and prudently departed the scene.[25]

It was the middle of March and time for a new II Corps offensive, one that Patton felt needed to be a resounding victory in order to finally gain the respect of the British after the mediocre showing of American troops under Fredendall. With Montgomery's Eighth Army engaging Rommel's troops along the Mareth Line in southeast Tunisia, and Alexander's First Army attacking Colonel-General Jürgen von Arnim's Fifth Panzer Army around Tunis, Patton would attack to the south at El Guettar with four divisions: the 1st, 9th, and 34th Infantry and 1st Armored. Patton directed elements of the 9th and 34th Divisions to make a feint toward Faid and Fondouk while the 1st Armored Division headed for Kasserine and beyond. Allen's Big Red One would capture Gafsa, an important road junction and railroad town, and drive through enemy lines at El Guettar.[26]

On 16 March, the II Corps units burst out of eastern Algeria and began hunting for the enemy. The 1st Infantry Division roared into Gafsa, only to discover it abandoned by the Italians. The offense pushed on to El Guettar, twenty miles away. With the help of a Ranger battalion, the 1st held the Kasserine Pass. The Germans were not about to let this valuable piece of terrain go so easily. For the next three days, the 10th Panzer Division hammered the Big Red One, overrunning some positions with its tanks while the Luftwaffe strafed others with relentless air attacks. Yet, Allen's men, supported by artillery and tank destroyers, held fast, refusing to yield. Thirty-two panzers were knocked out and hundreds of infantrymen killed, forcing the Germans to fall back. Eisenhower wrote glowingly to Marshall, "The First Division continues to give a good account of itself." A new reputation for the 1st Infantry Division had been forged.[27]

The war correspondent Ernie Pyle wrote, "For you at home who think the African campaign was small stuff, let me tell you just this one thing—the First Division did more fighting then than it did throughout all of World War I."[28] Pyle also had a particular fondness for the Big Red One's commander. He noted, "Major General Terry Allen was one of my favorite people. Partly because he didn't give a damn for hell or high water; partly because he was more colorful than most; and partly because he was the only general outside the Air Forces I could call by his first name. If there was one thing in the world Allen lived and breathed for, it was to fight. He had been all shot up in the last war, and he seemed not the least averse to getting shot up again. This was no intellectual war with him. He hated Germans and Italians like vermin . . . ."[29] In April, Patton's II Corps, including the Big Red One, was shifted 150 miles to the north behind British lines and prepared for the last battle of the North Africa campaign. But Patton would not be around to command the fight; on 15 April, he turned over the reins of II Corps to his deputy, Omar Bradley, and departed for Casablanca to work on the plans for the next phase of the Mediterranean campaign.[30]

Under Bradley, the 1st and 34th Infantry Divisions, although suffering heavy casualties, prevailed, killing or capturing hundreds of the enemy. With the exhausted, depleted, and starving German and Italian troops now boxed into a corner from which there was no escape, Allied artillery batteries and aircraft

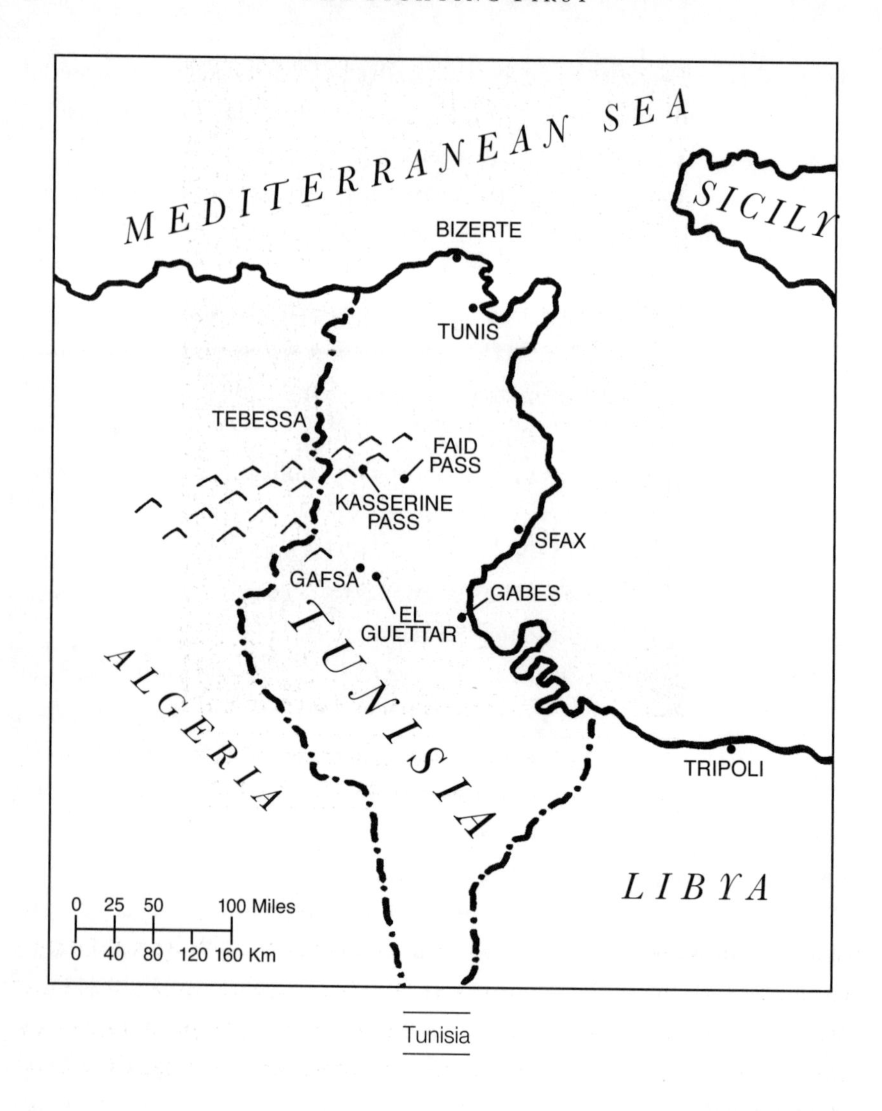

Tunisia

pounded them unmercifully until they surrendered on 1 May. The battle for North Africa was over.[31]

The 1st Division was pulled off the line and trucked back to near Oran, where it recovered from six months of combat and added reinforcements from the States. First Lieutenant Fred Hall of Hudson, New Hampshire, the executive officer of E Company, 16th Infantry Regiment, indicated that the division was not in a particularly jolly mood. "Since arriving in Africa, we had been wearing woolen uniforms. The weather turned hot. The base personnel at Oran were all dressed in summer khakis. We expected to be issued the same uniforms; when

Captain Fred W. Hall Jr., executive officer of E Company, 16th Infantry Regiment. (Courtesy Fred Hall)

we found out we were to continue wearing woolens, it only heightened the resentment between combat soldiers and the [rear-echelon] personnel. There wasn't a lot of recreation. We would go into Oran for a couple of drinks and movies. The atmosphere in the city was sometimes tense between the combat veterans and the service personnel."[32]

Hall may have downplayed the situation. General Bradley had a slightly different view: "While the Allies were parading decorously through Tunis," he wrote, "Allen's brawling 1st Infantry Division was celebrating the Tunisian victory in a manner all its own. In towns from Tunisia all the way to Arzew, the division had left a trail of looted wine shops and outraged mayors. But it was in Oran, the city those troops had liberated on the [Operation] *Torch* invasion, that the division really ran amuck. The trouble began when SOS (Services of Supply) troops, long stationed in Oran, closed their clubs and installations to our combat troops from the front. Irritated by this exclusion, the 1st Division swarmed into town to 'liberate' it a second time." Eisenhower ordered Bradley to get the rampaging 1st Division troops out of Oran. Bradley believed that the 1st's behavior signaled "a serious breakdown in discipline within the division. Allen's troops had now begun to strut their toughness while ignoring regulations that applied to all other units. . . . Despite their [prodigious] talents as combat leaders, neither Terry Allen nor Brigadier General Theodore Roosevelt, the assistant division commander, possessed the instincts of a good disciplinarian. They looked upon discipline as an unwelcome crutch to be used by less able and personable commanders. Terry's own career as an army rebel had long ago disproved the maxim that discipline makes the soldier. Having broken the mold himself, he saw no need to apply it to his troops. Had he been assigned a rock-jawed disciplinarian as assistant division commander, Terry could probably have gotten away forever on the personal leadership he showed his troops. But Roosevelt was too much like Terry Allen. A brave, gamy, undersized man who trudged about the front with a walking stick,* Roosevelt helped hold the division together by personal charm."[33]

Many felt Bradley's criticism of Allen was unjust. Some of it, no doubt, was the result of Bradley's hearing Walter Bedell Smith's side of his brief, sarcastic run-in with Allen. Some of it, too, could be attributed to Bradley's being a teetotaler and finding Allen's reputation as a two-fisted drinker repugnant. And part of the problem was Allen's reputation as a free spirit; while on maneuvers or in a class on tactics at Command and General Staff School, Allen could never be counted on to come up with the "book" answer; his creative mind had already puzzled out several unconventional solutions. But while his personal appearance and manner often marked him as "casual," beneath the rumpled exterior beat the heart of a fierce competitor. An excellent horseman and polo player, Allen was an aggressive type who hated to lose at anything. Some members of his division may have been slightly lax when it came to military bearing, saluting, neatness, and close-order drill, but it was wrong for anyone to regard them as "undisciplined." The men of the 1st Infantry Division were *fighters*, not choirboys, and woe be unto anyone—Allied or Axis—who challenged them or got in their way.[34]

---

*Roosevelt needed the stick for the rest of his life after being wounded in the leg while commanding a battalion of the 1st Infantry Division during the Battle of Soissons in July 1918.

A year later, after the Normandy landings, war correspondent and radio commentator Quentin Reynolds broadcast a tribute to Terry Allen and his men. "Terry Allen used to like to fight [the Germans] at night. We would ask General Allen why. And he gave us profound military reasons, such as that the surprise would be greater. He could sneak artillery up through the night. But when we really pressed him, Terry Allen would admit that he liked to fight . . . at night because his casualties were fewer. The 1st Division had terrific casualties in Tunisia—about thirty percent. The boys hoped that they'd be sent home for a rest. Most of them were Dodgers fans, and they wanted to get home for the 1943 baseball season. At that time, the division was composed chiefly of New York City, Long Island, Pennsylvania, and a few New England men. But then the Sicilian invasion was being planned. Terry Allen sent his men to Oran for a rest. They just about tore that city apart—these kids had been in tough combat for so many months. Terry Allen said to the MPs, 'My boys have had a tough time; let them enjoy themselves.' . . . The 1st was proving itself to be a great division. The boys in the 1st Division grumbled. They wanted to go home. . . . They grumbled and complained, and little, hard-bitten General Terry Allen listened to them. And then he said, with his eyes smiling: 'An army that won't complain, won't fight.'"[35]

On 13 May 1943, the North Africa campaign was declared officially over. There was much rejoicing, and the Americans and British were showered with flowers by grateful civilians from Tunis to Arzew. But Tunis was a long way from Berlin, and between the two cities lay a hot, rocky, volcanic island known as Sicily. There would be plenty of complaints ahead.

About the time the Big Red One was fighting for its life at El Guettar, back in England an unheralded appointment took place. It was announced in no newspapers, was heard on no radio broadcasts. Like much of what happened during wartime, the appointment of British Lieutenant General Frederick E. Morgan to a secret post was closely guarded information. By April 1943, he and a small staff had created COSSAC—Chief of Staff to the Supreme Allied Commander—and to Morgan and the new organization fell the daunting task of drawing up preliminary concepts for the invasion of the European continent. Morgan cautioned his staff to avoid thinking of themselves as *planners* of the invasion; rather, they were the embryo of a future supreme headquarters—SHAEF, the Supreme Headquarters Allied Expeditionary Force—that would coordinate everything needed to put millions of men into France and, ultimately, into Germany.[36]

While the first rudimentary steps were being taken to create what eventually would be known as Operation *Overlord*, the rest of the war against Hitler could not be allowed to wither on the vine. After the Allies had swept North Africa free of the Germans and their Italian partners, it was deemed critical to keep as many of the enemy as possible bottled up in the Mediterranean, where they could not bolster Nazi forces on the Eastern Front or be used to build even stronger defensive fortifications along the French coast. To accomplish this, the British and Americans would need to invade the island of Sicily.

This operation, known as *Husky*, was the largest amphibious operation up to that point in the war, with 181,000 men, 3,200 ships, and 4,000 aircraft taking part. Eisenhower was named overall commander of *Husky*, just as he had been for Operation *Torch*. *Husky* would be a combined Allied operation, with four American divisions, under Generals Patton and Bradley, and six British divisions, under General Bernard Law Montgomery, the hero of the North African campaign, landing on the southeastern corner of the island.[37]

In May, during the planning for *Husky*, Eisenhower told Patton that he was considering sending Terry Allen back to the States for an eventual new job as a corps commander, but Patton wanted Allen and the 1st Division. Despite their often-stormy relationship, Patton had a genuine respect for Allen and the division he led. While Bradley preferred to use the untested 36th Infantry Division (Texas National Guard), Patton insisted on the Big Red One. "I want those sons of bitches," he pleaded to Eisenhower. "I won't go on without them!" He got them.[38]

After weeks of additional training under the broiling Tunisian sun, the grumbling, complaining 1st Division was alerted: Grab your gear, load up. We're going to Sicily.

When one looks at a map of the Mediterranean, one notices that there is an obvious stepping stone between Tunisia and Italy: Sicily. When one reads a guidebook about Sicily, one learns that it is the largest island in the Mediterranean, with an area of 9,926 square miles, or 25,708 square kilometers. One discovers that 85 percent of the land is hilly or mountainous, with Mount Etna, an active volcano, its highest peak at 11,122 feet (3,390 meters). The capital, largest city, and chief seaport is Palermo, on the northern coast. One learns that

German air raid against American ships in the harbor of Gela, Sicily, 10 July 1943. (Courtesy U.S. Army Military History Institute)

most of the Sicilians are very poor, eking out a living through farming the overworked soil. The island is prone to earthquakes, and a hot summer wind from North Africa, called the *sirocco,* leaves the riverbeds bone dry and tempers frayed. One finds out that, owing to its strategic location, Sicily has been invaded, occupied, and ruled by the ancient Greeks, Romans, Carthaginians, Vandals, Ostrogoths, Byzantines, Saracens, Normans, Germans, French, Spanish, Austrians, and the Bourbon Kingdom of the Two Sicilies. One discovers that the Siciliani have very strong family ties, that the people have an ingrained distrust of foreigners and government, and that their code of honor forbids them from reporting to the police crimes that they consider to be private, family matters. One also learns that the Mafia is the de facto government of Sicily.[39]

What the guidebooks don't point out is that, in the summer of 1943, the island was also home to some 365,000 heavily armed Italian and German soldiers just waiting for the Americans and British to invade.

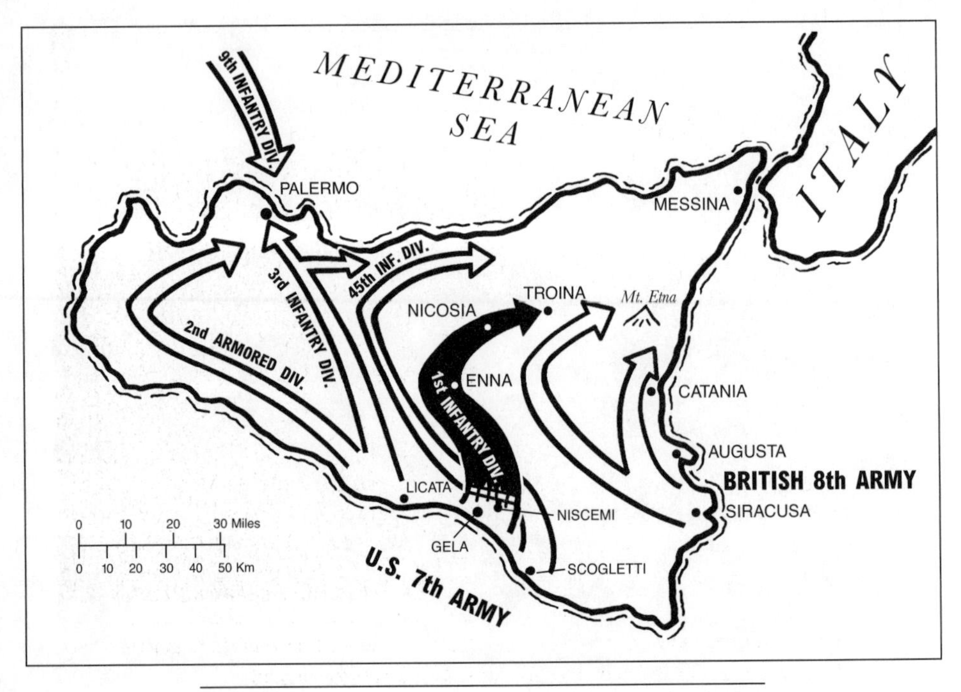

Operation *Husky*—the Allied invasion of Sicily, 10 July 1943

Operation *Husky* began at dawn on 10 July 1943, in extremely rough surf along the southeastern coast. Approaching in LCVPs (Landing Craft, Vehicles and Personnel), eight infantry divisions prepared to disembark onto the beaches and rush inland. Overhead, elements of the U.S. 82nd Airborne and British 1st Airborne Divisions roared in, ready to drop behind enemy lines. Under the aegis of Patton's Seventh Army and Omar Bradley's II Corps, the American assault divisions were the 1st Infantry Division (with a Ranger battalion attached), the 3rd Infantry Division, and the 45th Infantry Division (Colorado and Oklahoma National Guard). The 2nd Armored Division was the "floating reserve" (to be brought in when necessary, while the 9th Infantry Division would remain in North Africa until needed). Five British infantry divisions, plus the airborne, made up Montgomery's Eighth Army invasion force.[40]

After surviving a jolting ride in the small landing craft, the Big Red One hit the beaches near Gela. It was fortunate for the invaders that the coastal defensive positions were manned by Italians. The defenders, caught by surprise, put up only token resistance before either surrendering or retreating. Lieutenant

German armor knocked out by the 1st Infantry Division after a failed counterattack north of Gela. (Courtesy U.S. Army Military History Institute)

Leonard E. Jones, of C Company, 18th Infantry Regiment, laughed: "Italians are the worst soldiers on the face of the earth. They love to be captured."[41]

The next day, the weak Italian defense gave way to a determined German counterattack with tanks—headed directly for the 1st Infantry Division's positions. Thirty panzers and fifty-five truckloads of German infantrymen were spotted coming down the Gela-Niscemi road, attempting to split the invasion force, with virtually nothing to stop them. In the literal nick of time, the 16th Infantry Regiment's Cannon Company arrived and blasted away at the enemy with its 105mm howitzers, knocking out dozens of tanks and sending the enemy fleeing.

Next came the fight for the Ponte Olivo airport, north of Gela. At midnight on 11 July, the 1st Infantry Division moved into the attack and caught the German garrison before it could react; by noon, the airfield was in American hands. The Germans continued for days to mount counterattacks in the hope of throwing back the Big Red One but, no matter how many panzers and truckloads of infantry the Germans employed, they could not stop the Yanks—nor the British, who were also moving inland from their eastern beachheads and overcoming opposition. After hard fighting, the 1st Division moved northward through the mountainous center of the island. By 29 July, despite heavy losses, Allen's men had managed to battle their way just to the west of a town called Troina.[42]

In the meantime, developments were taking place behind the scenes that would have a major impact on the future conduct of the war in Europe. On 19 July, the first Allied bombs fell on two major railroad marshaling yards and an airbase in the city of Rome. This raid, preceded by the Italian army's woeful performance in North Africa and Sicily, brought about a crisis in Italy. Five days later, after the fall of Palermo, an anti-Mussolini backlash erupted. A vote of no confidence by the Fascist state's Grand Council shocked the dictator and he appealed to King Victor Emmanuel III for support; even the king expressed his displeasure with Mussolini's conduct of the war and the affairs of state. Stunned and humiliated, Mussolini had no choice but to resign—and was promptly arrested. In his place, a caretaker government under the aging, anti-Fascist Field Marshal Pietro Bodoglio was installed and immediately proclaimed that the war, and Italy's role in it, would continue (while simultaneously holding secret talks with the Allies that would lead to Italy's capitulation). The Romans, who had once lustily cheered Mussolini, marked the fall of the Fascist government with wild revelry. In Sicily, over 120,000 Italian troops celebrated the news by deserting or surrendering, although some continued to fight alongside German units. Feeling he had been stabbed in the back by Italy, Hitler ordered the evacuation from Sicily of as many German units as possible. The steady withdrawal of German troops across Sicily for the city of Messina—only a mile from the Italian mainland—turned into a raging river of gray-uniformed humanity.[43]

With the 1st and 9th Infantry Divisions sweeping eastward through the center of the island, the 3rd and 45th Infantry Divisions driving eastward along the northern coast, and the British rolling northward along the eastern coast, the likelihood of a carbon copy of the Allies' victory in Tunisia seemed very real. Once Troina fell, the 1st was promised a welcome relief by Major General Manton S. Eddy's 9th Infantry Division.

Troina was built atop a ridge that dominated Highway 120 and the surrounding barren countryside. Considered a natural strongpoint, Troina and its environs are extremely steep, with little room for an attacking force to maneuver. The battle did not go well from the start. For openers, both II Corps and Divi-

Aerial view of Troina, Sicily, where 1st Division troops faced strong enemy opposition for five days in August 1943. (Courtesy U.S. Army Military History Institute)

sion Intelligence had failed to detect the presence of elements of four enemy divisions—all of them seasoned fighters, firmly entrenched in strength in the town and surrounding mountains, and determined to keep open the escape route to Messina. The 1st Infantry Division was exhausted from three weeks of nearly continuous, uphill fighting in stifling heat. The division was below strength, too, due to malaria and the heavy casualties suffered since the landings.

The unsuspecting Americans, advancing from Cerami, were a mile west of Troina when the Germans unleashed a storm of artillery shells that brought the advance to a halt. Three days later, the 1st had crawled only a few hundred yards, all the while taking a severe pounding from German guns that not even aircraft could knock out. On 3 August, Allen launched a night attack by the entire division which very nearly succeeded. The Germans struck back with a fierce counterattack, however, and there the matter stalemated. The fifth day of the battle,

4 August, began with an air and artillery bombardment of German positions, but still the enemy refused to be dislodged.[43] So furious was the battle for Troina on 5 August that Private James M. Reese of the 1st Division's 26th Infantry Regiment was awarded the Medal of Honor, posthumously. Reese, a member of a mortar squad, kept up a steady rate of fire against German attackers at nearby Monte Basilio until enemy fire drove the squad from its position. Down to three rounds, Reese knocked out a machine gun, then inflicted further casualties with a rifle before dying in a fusillade of German fire.[45]

The German defenders had done their job well, having delayed the Americans for nearly a week to allow their units to escape across the Strait of Messina—units that would live to fight another day in Italy. Under cover of darkness on 5/6 August, the enemy began slipping quietly out of Troina and the neighboring mountains. On the morning of 6 August, Allen's men entered the shattered town to find the enemy gone.[46]

The Big Red One had suffered greatly; some of its rifle companies were down to sixty-five men from their authorized strength of 193. Troina also claimed two more casualties—Generals Allen and Roosevelt. While the battle was still raging, a message that was not intended to reach Allen until the battle was over was delivered to him: He and his assistant were to be relieved of command. In the military, being relieved of command is tantamount to being fired. And for the order to come down before a battle was even concluded carried a strong odor of dissatisfaction about the performance of the officers in question.

While the battle for Troina counted as an American victory, Allen and Roosevelt could feel no satisfaction. Although Patton had requested that Allen and Roosevelt be relieved, and Eisenhower (who had personally seen that Allen was exhausted as far back as May) had approved the request, it was Bradley, curiously, who took full responsibility for the action. For his part, Allen later blamed Ike's chief of staff, Walter Bedell Smith.[47]

In his autobiography, Bradley expressed his belief that the two-star general was too close to his men, who would fight like Tasmanian Devils in combat but suffered from an exaggerated sense of self-importance and a lack of personal and unit discipline. Bradley noted, "Among the aggrieved champions of Terry Allen, and he had many, the relief was condemned as completely unwarranted, and some of them mistakenly ascribed it to a pique between Allen and Patton. There were no grounds for their suspicion. It is probably true that Patton irritated Allen, but it was Patton who persuaded Eisenhower to give him Allen for the Sicily invasion. Responsibility for the relief of Terry Allen was mine and mine alone."

Bradley firmly believed that the 1st Division was unable to subordinate itself to the corps mission and participate willingly as part of a larger group: "The division had already been selected for the Normandy campaign. If it was to fight well there at the side of inexperienced divisions and under the command of an inexperienced corps, the division desperately needed a change in its perspective." According to Bradley, "Under Allen, the 1st Division had become increasingly temperamental, disdainful of both regulations and senior commands. It thought itself exempted from the need for discipline by virtue of its months on the line. And it believed itself to be the only division carrying its fair share of the war."

Bradley saw Terry Allen as too much of an individualist, and the division too full of pride and self-pity. Something had to be done. "To save Allen both from himself and from his brilliant record, and to save the division from the heady effects of too much success, I decided to separate them. Only in this way could I hope to preserve the extraordinary value of that division's experience in the Mediterranean war, an experience that would be of incalculable value in the Normandy attack."

Bradley knew that relieving Allen of command, especially after the difficult battle for Troina, would be seen by some as a punishment for failing to take the town quickly, but so be it. He could not replace Allen with Roosevelt, either, for, if anything, Roosevelt was even more popular than Allen and governed with a gentler hand. And he couldn't very well allow Roosevelt to stay on as assistant division commander because, "any successor of Allen's would find himself in an untenable spot unless I allowed him to pick his own assistant commander. Roosevelt had to go with Allen for he, too, had sinned by loving the division too much."*[48]

---

*A millionaire in his mid-fifties, Roosevelt had been assistant secretary of the Navy (1921–24) and governor general of both Puerto Rico and the Philippines, and he had endeared himself to his men with his warm, caring, grandfatherly style. If he thought himself special because he was the son of one of America's most popular presidents, he certainly never showed it. Private First Class Louis Newman recalled two prewar stateside incidents that illustrated the general's easy style: "It was a Sunday and the men were out for the weekend. I was in the mess hall talking to the mess sergeant when Teddy walks in with a pair of pants under his arm, and with his cane. He asked me if I knew anyone who could shorten his pants. I said I would. I was a great fan of his father, and here he is, sitting across from me, discussing his father. We had quite a conversation for about 30 or 40 minutes." Later, Newman found himself standing near the general when the exhausted troops were coming back to camp after a long march. The officers were riding in jeeps but Roosevelt ordered the officers out of the vehicles. Gesturing to the tired, sweating enlisted men, the general said, "*They* walk, *you* walk."

Although failing to acknowledge Bradley's role in the "firing," an officer on Eisenhower's staff noted in his diary on 2 August, "Major General Terry Allen, commander of the 1st Division, and Brigadier General Theodore Roosevelt, his assistant, had been relieved by Patton, the decision confirmed by Ike. The former for 'war weariness,' and to be returned to America, without discredit, under our rotation policy. There he could rest and take another division, as he's an excellent commander. His men love him. . . . General Roosevelt had proved to be a gallant leader of inexperienced troops. He is battle-wise and extremely courageous. Likewise, he had 'had it.' Ike thought eventually his good qualities could be used by later assigning him to an inexperienced division about to go into battle. . . . The 1st Division has been in more fighting than any other outfit in this operation, and General Allen simply became fatigued to such a low ebb that he was unable to afford the inspiration and the leadership, as well as the imagination and discipline, that are necessary for a divisional commander."[49]

On 7 August 1943, the day after he was officially relieved of command, Allen wrote a farewell message to his men: "To all members of the 'Fighting First:' In compliance with recent orders, Major General Clarence Huebner, who fought in this division with great distinction during the last war, has been designated as Division Commander. I feel most fortunate to have been your commander during the proceding [sic] year. You should be proud of your combat records. . . . You have lived up to your battle slogan, 'Nothing in hell must stop the First Division.'"

Allen then received the Distinguished Service Medal and departed for the States.* He apparently bore no bitterness toward Patton. In fact, in a 14 August letter to his wife, Mary Frances, he noted, "My change of assignment orders were a great surprise. . . . Patton was most kind and cordial and thoroughly appreciative of what the division had done. Said the division had carried the weight of the attack in Sicily."[50]

Omar Bradley had already selected a new commander for the Big Red One, a general who was Allen's polar opposite. "As Allen's successor in the 1st Division,"

*After returning to the States, Allen was given command of the 104th Infantry Division, which would later distinguish itself in Europe. Replacing Roosevelt at the same time was Colonel (soon to be Brigadier General) Willard G. Wyman, who would also become a legend within the division and the Army.

Bradley noted, "we picked Major General Clarence R. Huebner, known to the army as a flinty disciplinarian. Huebner had enlisted in the army as a private in 1910 and was commissioned before World War I. He was no stranger to the 1st Division, for he had already worn its patch in every rank from a private to colonel. In returning to command the division, however, he had come from a desk in the Pentagon,* an assignment which did not tend to ease his succession to Allen's post. On the second day after he assumed command there in the hills of Troina, Huebner ordered a spit-and-polish cleanup of the division. He then organized a rigid training program which included close-order drill.

"'Keerist—' the combat veterans exclaimed in undisguised disgust, 'here they send us a stateside Johnny to teach us how to march through the hills where we've been killing Krauts. How stupid can this sonuvabitch get?'"[51]

Although Clarence Huebner's resumé was impressive, everyone wondered—did he have what it would take to replace the beloved Terry Allen and turn the exhausted, self-pitying 1st Infantry Division into the hardened steel needed to crack Hitler's Fortress Europe?

---

* Partially true: Huebner *had* been at the Pentagon but was later assigned to British General Sir Harold Alexander's operational staff before being appointed the 1st's new commander. So outspoken and critical was Huebner that Alexander could hardly wait to be rid of him. He became available to Bradley on 25 July 1943. (Butcher, p. 349; and D'Este, *Bitter Victory*, p. 469)

CHAPTER TWO

"Overpaid, Oversexed, and Over Here"

MOST OF the stunned members of the 1st Infantry Division were livid at the change of commanders. Omar Bradley shrewdly noted that "Huebner knew what he was doing, however unpopular his tactics might be. From the outset he was determined to show the division that he was boss, that while the 1st might be the best division in the U.S. Army—it nevertheless was *a part* of the army, a fact it sometimes forgot. Fortunately, the animosity did not perturb him. He had ample time, he reckoned, to win the division to his side. A more sensitive man than Huebner might have cracked under the strain, for it was not until after the Normandy invasion, one year later, that the last resentful adherents to Terry Allen conceded Huebner the right to wear the Big Red One. When he finally left to command a corps [V Corps], they missed him almost as much as they did Allen."[1]

Born in Kansas on 24 November 1888, Clarence Ralph Huebner was no stranger to combat. In April 1918, as a captain in command of a rifle company in the 28th Regiment, 1st Infantry Division, Huebner was wounded at the torn-up French village of Beaumont, between Toul and St. Mihiel. After recuperating, he and his company were back in the thick of fierce fighting at Cantigny. When his battalion commander was killed, he took command, earning a promotion to major and the Distinguished Service Cross. His citation read, in part, ". . . although his command lost half its officers and 30 percent of its men, he held the position and prevented a break in the line at that point."

In July 1918, Huebner led his battalion in the Aisne-Marne offensive, where he was again wounded and gained an Oak Leaf Cluster to his DSC.* He returned to

---

*The addition of an Oak Leaf Cluster to any medal is the equivalent of being awarded the same medal again.

Major General Clarence R. Huebner, the 1st Infantry Division's new commanding officer. (Courtesy Colonel Robert R. McCormick Research Center of the 1st Infantry Division Museum at Cantigny)

duty to lead his men in action in the Saizerais sector (August), St. Mihiel offensive (September), and the Meuse-Argonne offensive in September and again in November. In October, he was promoted to lieutenant colonel and given command of the 28th Infantry Regiment. As one historian has written, "When the war ended, Huebner was one of the most highly decorated officers in the army. In less than a year, he had risen through the ranks from lieutenant to lieutenant colonel, and had commanded at every level from company to regiment. Huebner was fully tested in World War I. He was an officer of proven courage and leadership abilities." In addition to the DSC with Oak Leaf Cluster, Huebner received a host of other honors: Distinguished Service Medal, Silver Star, Purple Heart with Oak Leaf Cluster, the French Legion of Honor, French Croix de Guerre, and the Italian War Cross. Huebner was a true American war hero.

Even so, it would be years before the pro-Allen contingent would accept him as "one of theirs."[2]

Huebner himself wrote, "To me, it was a return home: a return to the Division I had served with in peacetime, which included the regiment where I had learned the first lessons of soldiering and with which I had served as a young officer through the great battles of the First World War. It was a homecoming to the organization I had watched with pride in its earlier actions in North Africa."[3] If anyone was more qualified than Terry Allen to lead the Big Red One, it was Clarence R. Huebner.

According to Associated Press war correspondent Don Whitehead, Huebner had "a kindly face and direct blue eyes that twinkled with humor. I judged that he was in his early fifties. He was physically fit and there was an air of confidence about him that I liked."[4]

But, like a stepfather trying to win the affection of his new children, acceptance of Clarence Huebner was slow in coming. The attitude of Lieutenant Joe Dawson, 16th Infantry Regiment, was typical of the 1st Division men at the time. On 6 August 1943, Dawson wrote to his family: "Terry left tonight and with him went a record unequaled by any general officer in the divisions of the U.S. Army. We've been through a lot and we all feel keenly his going . . . I should like to be with him. Our new C.O. is a grand soldier of the old school from all accounts, but I'll reserve judgment till I see him in action."[5]

Dawson later added, "We had the most wonderful leader in Terry Allen, whose absolute capacity to inspire an esprit de corps as no other man I've ever known and was loved by everybody in the division because of he being a soldier's soldier. . . . [M]any of us felt a letdown at first because everyone knew Terry, and not only respected him but loved him, and he was a great morale factor. General Huebner came in and he faced a problem. He realized the problem, and he was smart enough and shrewd enough to take some people into his confidence and say, 'I've got to become the commander of the 1st Division, and it's going to be tough because I've got to follow a man who has been outstanding, but I've got to lick it; I've got to stamp myself as being *the man*.' And what did he do? He did it the most incredible way I could ever possibly conceive. . . . [W]e were battled-seasoned veterans by that time, and so Huebner . . . insisted on everybody from the division staff down to the lowest private in the ranks to learn to hand salute and the manual of arms and close-order drill. We had said, 'Why, those are superficial non-entities; we're combat men, we're veterans.' And we hated him at first. I say that categorically because I came to love him just like everybody else did when we learned who he was and what he was and how great a man he really was. But that first time was something to behold."[6]

Others more quickly recognized Huebner's outstanding qualities. Colonel James K. Woolnough, executive officer of the 16th Infantry Regiment (and later commanding general of the 99th Infantry Division), had nothing but the highest regard for Huebner. "He was the greatest soldier there ever was. He was a wonderful division commander."[7]

Colonel George Pickett, the 1st's signal officer, had a memorable first meeting with his new division commander. While at the division command post during the fight for Troina on 6 August, he was introduced to Huebner, who "had an aggressive, demanding tone to his voice." Having been under fire and unable to shave for three days, Pickett was upbraided by the general: "In my outfit, *every*one is going to shave *every* day; it only takes this much (holding up two fingers) water. Yes, colonel, that means you, too!"[8]

Lieutenant Fred W. Hall, executive officer of E Company, 16th Infantry Regiment, had his own encounter with the new CG. One day, after the weekly battalion parade, General Huebner pulled up in his jeep next to the battalion staff officers to give a personal lesson in saluting. "The general commented that saluting was an important factor in restoring respect between officers and men and we should be able to salute properly," Hall said. "He then asked [Major Herbert] Hicks [2nd Battalion commander] to salute him, made a minor adjustment, turned to [Captain William] Washington [battalion executive officer], and then to me. I apparently didn't get my hand at the right angle. He explained I should be able to see my little finger out of the corner of my right eye. He then asked me if I could. When I replied no, he said, 'Why not?' I replied, 'I don't *have* a little finger, sir.' (I had lost it as a youngster.) With that, the general drove off."[9]

The island of Sicily was declared secure on 17 August 1943, but 120,000 enemy troops had managed to slip across the Strait of Messina to the Italian mainland. The Big Red One counted its successes: In a little over a month of continuous fighting, it had liberated eighteen towns and captured nearly 6,000 prisoners. In the minus column, the division had lost 267 men killed, 1,184 wounded, and 337 missing—and had their two popular leaders stripped from them.[10] For the time being, the division was allowed to stand down; it would not have to chase the enemy to Italy. That was now the job of the newly formed U.S. Fifth Army, under Lieutenant General Mark Clark, which would launch Operation *Avalanche*, the invasion of Italy, at the Bay of Salerno on 9 September.[11]

Rather than blame Bradley for the ouster of their two popular leaders, many of the men in the division personally blamed General Patton. Allen Towne, B Company, 1st Medical Battalion, was not fully aware of the depth of the anti-Patton feelings that ran through the division. On 27 August, he received an education: "The entire division was summoned to hear an address by . . . Lt. Gen. George S. Patton. Our division had no love for Patton because our first experience with him had been in southern Tunisia when he took over the II Corps. He had decided to instill discipline and had ordered us all to wear ties and leggings while the division was fighting in the African desert. . . .

"We were trucked to a natural outdoor arena formed by a small hill overlooking a level area. Here, a small platform had been constructed. While the 18,000 men were assembling, I wondered why we were there. We had been on alert because it was thought that the surrender of Italy was imminent. There was a tentative plan to land a U.S. division at the Rome airport and help to bring an earlier end to the war. Rumor had it that the 1st Division would be doing this. Did it mean the rumors were true, that we were going to be airlifted to the Rome airport? We knew that the Italians wanted to get out of the war. Or was it possible that some of us might go home? After all, we had been overseas for more than a year.

"The division band played while everyone was assembling. Then an honor guard, made up of a spruced-up infantry platoon, performed a formal rifle drill. Finally . . . Patton came forward, wearing his pearl-handled revolvers and his helmet liner with the three stars. He started his speech by saying, 'You are part of the Seventh Army that was born at sea and baptized with the blood of our filthy enemy. We have killed many of them and will have the opportunity to kill more. That is what our job is. We are here to kill the enemy.'

"It was a real blood-and-guts speech. When he finished, there was complete silence. There was no applause. Nothing at all. My reaction, which was probably shared by everyone, was, *What is this all about? Why are we here listening to this?* Most of us thought the speech was in bad taste. There were very few men who just wanted to kill the enemy. We would rather that they surrender so we could all go home. It was not until weeks later that we found out what the speech was all about. I read . . . that Patton had slapped a 1st Division soldier in

Lieutenant General George S. Patton Jr. "apologizes" to the assembled 1st Infantry Division, Sicily, 27 August 1943. (Courtesy Eisenhower Library, Abilene, Kansas)

a field hospital for being a coward. The man was in the hospital because he had an anxiety state breakdown, probably brought on by malaria. Patton had been ordered to apologize to the men of the 1st Division. That speech was supposed to be an apology."*[12]

Sergeant Bill Faust, a member of Division Artillery headquarters, expressed the division's anger at Patton: "After the slapping incident, to say the men of the division hated him would be putting it mildly. We *despised* him. Him and his Goddamn pearl-handled pistols coming ashore at Gela in his high leather boots

*Patton was in Eisenhower's "dog-house" for two incidents of slapping soldiers in Sicily. On 3 August 1943, while visiting wounded 1st Infantry Division soldiers at the 15th Evacuation Hospital near Nicosia, Patton came across an obviously distraught Private Charles H. Kuhl of L Company, 26th Infantry Regiment. When the soldier admitted his nerves could not take the strain of combat, Patton became furious, slapped him with a glove, hoisted him up by his shirt collar, and literally kicked him out of the tent. A week later, Patton virtually repeated his performance with another "battled-fatigued" soldier from the 13th Field Artillery Brigade. The incidents nearly cost Patton his career. (D'Este, *Patton,* pp. 533–534) and lacquered helmet. His dress would have been more appropriate in a Wild West show. 'Old Blood and Guts' they called him—his guts and our blood . . . ."[13]

Most of the 1st Division men hoped and expected that, following the North Africa and Sicily campaigns, they finally would be permitted to return to some safe, cushy stateside training assignment that would enable them to impart to raw recruits all the combat knowledge they had absorbed in their previous combat actions. It was not to be. Men groaned as rumors began circulating that the division had been selected to take part in another major amphibious assault operation—the toughest one of all—the invasion of Nazi-fortified France.[14]

While members of the 1st Infantry Division griped about their new commander, whom they saw very much in the Patton mold, they added the rumors about their possible participation in a new invasion to their list of complaints. Private Louis Newman, Cannon Company, 18th Regiment, observed, "We weren't exactly happy about being picked again to spearhead another amphibious assault."[15]

As the Allies learned during Operations *Jubilee*, *Torch*, *Husky*, *Avalanche* (Salerno), and *Shingle* (Anzio), a large-scale amphibious assault is the most complicated and difficult of all military operations. Control of the seas and skies and split-second coordination between air, naval, and ground forces are crucial, and sufficient follow-up forces and a well-conceived and executed logistics plan are essential to prevent the invading forces from being forced back into the sea. Only someone with experience in this specialized line of work could be entrusted to coordinate its many complex aspects. While COSSAC's Morgan (and, for that matter, Marshall) was briefly considered for the job of Supreme Allied Commander, it was Eisenhower who was the leading candidate. Only "Ike" had commanded two large-scale amphibious landings. And few had Eisenhower's ability to work with the oft-cantankerous British and engender a spirit of cooperation between factions that often seemed more like adversaries than allies. So, in December 1943, Ike was officially named Supreme Allied Commander of the Allied Expeditionary Force, and his headquarters became known as SHAEF—Supreme Headquarters Allied Expeditionary Force.

Eisenhower gathered the best military brains around him. To make the effort a truly Allied coalition and not just an American-dominated show, Ike named Air Chief Marshal Sir Arthur Tedder to be his deputy and principal coordinator of the theater's air forces; Admiral Sir Bertram Ramsay was made commander of naval forces. Lieutenant General Carl Spaatz commanded American Strategic

The top brass at SHAEF Headquarters (left to right): Lieutenant General Omar Bradley; Admiral Sir Bertram Ramsay; General Sir Arthur Tedder; General Dwight D. Eisehnhower; General Sir Bernard Montgomery; General Sir Trafford Leigh-Mallory; Lieutenant General Walter Bedell Smith, Chief of Staff. Not pictured: Sir Arthur Harris; General Sir Miles Dempsey; Lieutenant General Carl Spaatz. Photo taken 12 February 1944. (Courtesy National Archives)

Air Forces while his British counterpart, Air Chief Marshal Sir Arthur T. Harris, kept his post as commander of the Royal Air Force's Bomber Command. Air Chief Marshal Sir Trafford Leigh-Mallory was put in charge of Allied tactical air support, including the airborne troops. For his chief of staff, Ike retained the acerbic Lieutenant General Walter Bedell Smith; Morgan became Smith's deputy. General Montgomery was made Twenty-first Army Group commander and head of the ground forces going into France. Beneath Montgomery were Lieutenant General Omar Bradley, commanding the First U.S. Army, and General Sir Miles Dempsey, in command of the Second British Army, consisting of British, Canadian, and a small number of French troops.[16]

But where would all these troops land? Since the summer of 1943, Morgan and COSSAC had been considering the options for a suitable location for an invading force of from three to five divisions—45,000 to 75,000 troops. Using a process of elimination, the COSSAC team determined that a fifty-mile stretch of beach along the Normandy coast, between the mouth of the Orne River and the southeastern base of the Cotentin Peninsula, would be the ideal spot. Normandy offered a number of advantages: wide, gently sloping beaches that would allow landing craft to drop the troops in shallow water; except for Caen, no major urban areas that would need to be cleared before the troops could move inland; a good road network behind the beaches; and relatively weak fixed defensives.[17]

When Eisenhower received the COSSAC recommendations, he generally concurred, but realized that three to five divisions would not be enough. Ultimately, it was decided to land five infantry divisions on five beaches codenamed, from west to east, Utah (near La Madeleine), Omaha (near Vierville), Gold (at Arromanches-les-Bains), Juno (near Courseulles-sur-Mer), and Sword (near Lion-sur-Mer). Three airborne divisions (two American and one British) would be dropped behind German lines at both ends of the beachhead to seal off the area from flank attacks and to secure the causeways the Allies would need to drive inland.[18]

As planning progressed, and units were detailed for the operation, the British selected the 50th Division, under XXX Corps, to land at Gold Beach, while two I Corps divisions, the Canadian 3rd Infantry and British 3rd Infantry Divisions, would assault Juno and Sword Beaches, respectively. The U.S. 4th Infantry Division, under the U.S. VII Corps, would land at the westernmost beach, Utah, while the U.S. 29th Infantry Division, under V Corps, would come ashore at Omaha Beach. A smaller force of U.S. Rangers would assault the casemated batteries atop the cliffs of Pointe du Hoc, between Utah and Omaha.[19]

Originally, the 1st Infantry Division was not a part of the American invasion plan. Then, Omar Bradley, as commander of the U.S. First Army, began having second thoughts. "Even before I arrived in England," he wrote, "the 29th Division had staked out squatter's rights on Omaha Beach. . . . It was commanded by Major General Charles H. Gerhardt, a peppery 48-year-old cavalryman whose enthusiasm sometimes exceeded his judgment as a soldier. When *Overlord* was expanded to include Utah Beach, we paired the 4th Infantry [Division] with the 29th as the second assault division. But although both divisions had undergone extensive amphibious training, neither had yet come under fire. Rather than chance a landing with two inexperienced divisions, I looked around for a veteran division to include in the line-up. In all of England, there was only one experienced assault division. Once more the Big Red One was to carry the heavy end of our stick. By this time, the 1st Infantry Division had swallowed a belly-full of heroics and wanted to go home. When the division learned that it was to make a third D-day assault, this time in France, the troops grumbled bitterly over the injustices of war. Among the infantrymen who had already survived both Mediterranean campaigns, few believed their good fortune could last them through a third.

"Although I disliked subjecting the 1st to still another landing, I felt that as a commander I had no other choice. My job was to get ashore, establish a lodgment, and destroy the Germans. In the accomplishment of that mission there was little room for the niceties of justice. I felt compelled to employ the best troops I had, to minimize the risks and hoist the odds in our favor in any way that I could. As a result, the division that deserved compassion as a reward for its previous ordeals now became the inevitable choice for our most difficult job. Whatever the injustice, it is better that war heap its burdens unfairly than that victory be jeopardized in an effort to equalize the ordeal."*[20]

New Yorker Lieutenant Colonel William B. Gara, commanding officer of the 1st Engineer Combat Battalion, remembered the grumbling in the ranks. "When we got through with the Sicilian campaign, the men said, 'we're ready to go home now—we've done our share—get somebody else to do it.' But they took us back to England and started preparing us for the Normandy invasion."[21]

Captain Fred Hall recalled, "Sometime in October, we were alerted that we would be returning to England. It had been a difficult summer [in Sicily]—heavy fighting, heat, bad living conditions, and finally malaria and jaundice [Hall himself had been hospitalized with malaria]. This, along with the fact that most of our [North] African veterans were suffering from malnutrition."[22]

---

*Bradley's account implies that the decision to include the 1st Division in the first wave of *Overlord* was almost an afterthought once the division had returned to England. In fact, the decision had been made shortly after the Sicily campaign had ended.

Second Lieutenant Harold Monica, a platoon commander with D Company, 18th Infantry Regiment, remarked, "We began to think maybe the 1st Division would go home and become training cadre for new units. What daydreamers we were. First Sergeant Benedict of D Company had it right: 'Lieutenant, the 1st Division will be going home when the war is over, not before, and you might as well recognize it. You're here for the duration.' How right he was. . . . In our minds, there was only one reason for this: we had been picked to lead the invasion of Europe. We knew no other outfit could do it, so we came to accept the fact; whether we liked it or not had no bearing."[23]

So, on 23 October 1943, the Big Red One loaded aboard a number of ships in the harbor of Augusta, between Catania and Siracusa, and prepared to sail in convoy from Sicily to England. Before they could depart, however, they became the unwilling recipients of a farewell visit by their nemesis, General Patton. Colonel Stanhope Brasfield Mason, the 1st Division's chief of staff, recalled that the division received "an official notification that General Patton would see us off by cruising around through the anchored convoy in an open launch. Though not mentioned in the dispatch, it took no great imagination [to realize] that General Patton wanted to be seen by all the departing troops. General Huebner correctly sensed this implied wish. Huebner had served with great distinction in World War I, but was comparatively new at our Division headquarters, so he had not acquired a feel of their grudge against Patton.

"General Huebner told me to issue orders that, at the hour specified for the Patton visit, troops would line the rails and give [Patton] a cheer as he traversed the waters of the harbor. Even at that brief time of [my] having served as his chief of staff, he expected and listened rationally to opinions and recommendations that I felt he should consider. In this case, I recommended that he *not* have the troops line the rails. I filled in all the background which led me to believe the troops would neither applaud nor cheer. Sure, they would obey orders and man the rails, but Patton would sail around amidst a silence that would both disappoint and displease him; that he, General Huebner, would be greatly embarrassed if I was right in my surmise. Huebner gave it careful thought but came to the conclusion that I was overly apprehensive. He knew soldier thinking, and he wasn't wrong often as to their reaction. This time he was completely wrong.

"The order to man the rails for the Patton send-off was issued. It included a veiled suggestion as to how (applause, cheering) the troops should show appreciation of the Army Commander's visit to say *bon voyage* to the departing Division.

At the appointed time, General Patton, beribboned and impressive, stood majestically in the center of the open launch as it cruised through the anchored ships. Silence was total. Every ship had its rails solidly lined with soldiers as deep as space permitted. But not a cheer was heard. No applause. Nothing but sepulchral silence.

"When the cruise-around ceremony was finished [and] General Patton via launch had exited the scene, I headed back to our tiny shipboard office space where I would be face-to-face with a very much disconcerted boss. I, therefore, was rapidly schooling myself, in my own mind, to avoid at all costs any major display of an 'I told you so' frame of mind. I found General Huebner quiet, thoughtful, with mixed emotions running all the way from anger and chagrin to a deeply felt embarrassment. I was relieved to see that he intended to let bygones be bygones, holding no one to blame for a regretful outcome of what was in reality a well-intentioned gesture. For my part, I also regretted this ill will being so evident at a time when Patton was most in need of a morale boost. On the other hand, it must be admitted that his former and generally known slurs on men of the 1st Division gave them ample cause to be resentful. In brief, he brought it on himself."[24]

General Patton now became a part of the past, someone to be forgotten. The 1st Infantry Division had more important things to worry about—such as invading and liberating a Nazi-held continent.

On 5 November 1943, after a ten-day voyage of 3,814 miles, the ships carrying the 1st Infantry Division from warm, sunny Sicily landed at cold, gray Liverpool, England.

Lieutenant Harold Monica recalled that, "In the year we had spent in North Africa and Sicily, the build-up of American troops in the UK had been proceeding. So the Services of Supply troops, responsible for the docks, troop trains, etc. and our overall unloading from the ships, wanted to know, 'How's everything back home?' All we could do was laugh, as we were not wearing the 1st Division insignia, and had been ordered not to say where we had been. Why this, I wouldn't have the faintest idea, unless the high command wanted to keep our troop strength in England as secret as possible from the enemy."[25]

From Liverpool, the troops crowded aboard soot-streaked trains and headed to Dorchester, 300 miles due south, and just north of the English Channel port

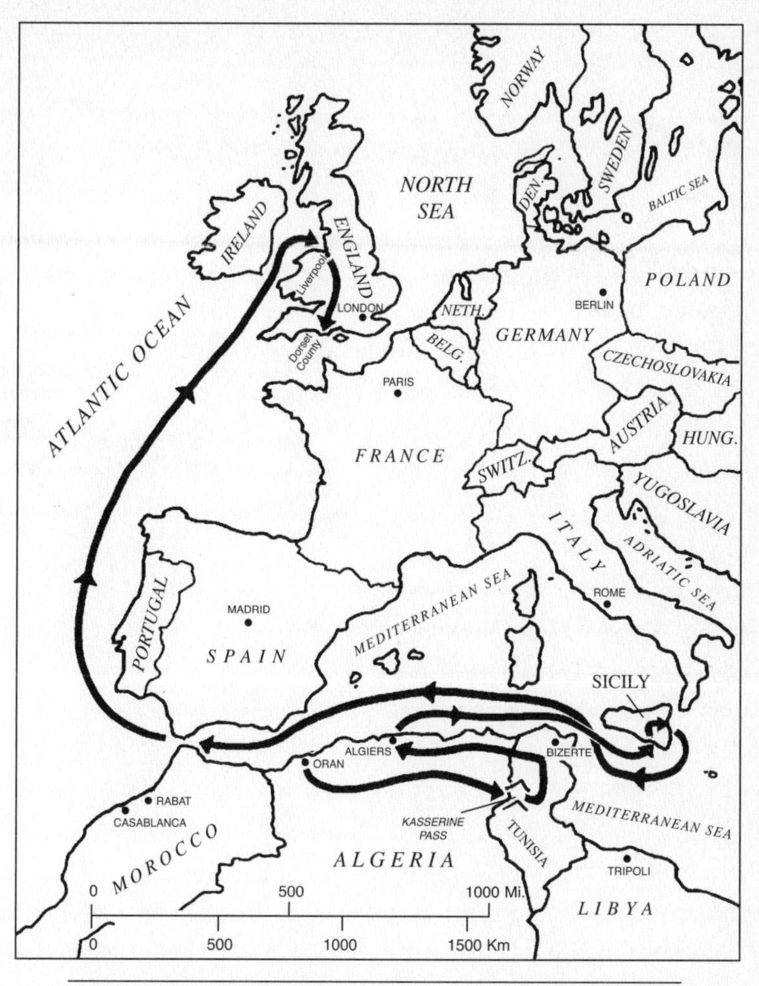

The route of the 1st Infantry Division from Oran back to England.

city of Weymouth.[26] Rather than concentrate the entire division in one location, the units of the 1st were billeted in different towns and villages around Dorset County in southern England—Weymouth, Lyme Regis, Bridport, Swanage, Maiden Newton, Warden Hill, Puddletown, and others. Division headquarters was established in the vicinity of Blandford. The men had varying reactions to their new living conditions. Chicagoan Edward J. Sackley, a private in C Company, 16th Infantry Regiment, recalled that his unit was "way out in the country, living in buildings. Toilets could only be used during special hours. Made no sense at all to me."[27]

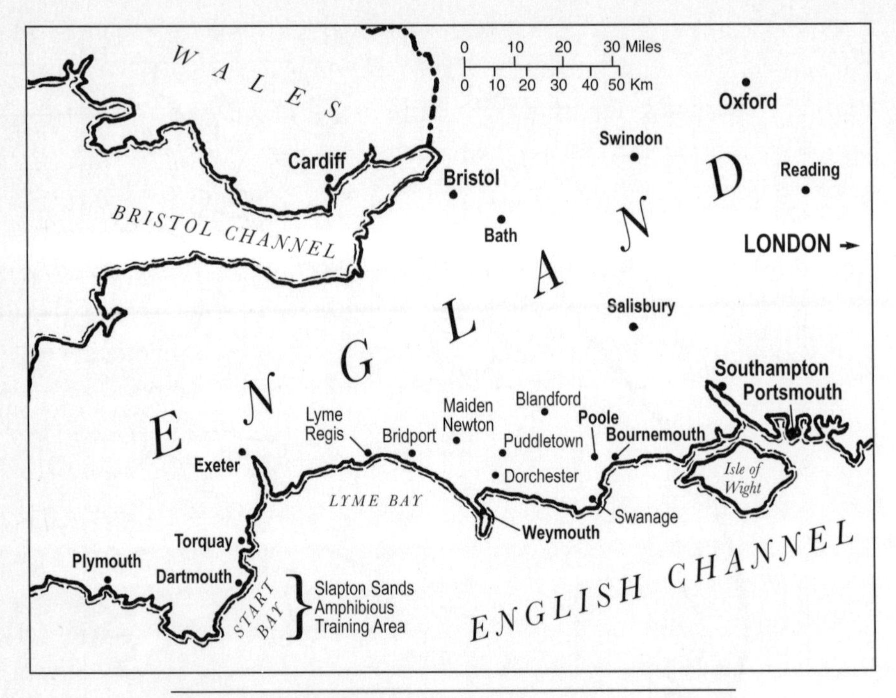

The 1st Infantry Division's principal camps and training areas in southwest England, November 1943 to May 1944.

Harley A. Reynolds, from St. Charles, Virginia, a staff sergeant in B Company, 16th Infantry, said his company was stationed in the small town of Lyme Regis. "The company was billeted anywhere in town that room could be found—small hotels, rooming houses, empty rooms over buildings along main street, and a couple of small Nissen huts vacated by the Home Guard. Lyme Regis was central to various sites [where] we would train."[28]

Harold Monica recalled that, "Due to the proximity of the enemy, we were well dispersed and the largest unit in one place was a battalion. After a little shuffling around, the 1st Battalion, 18th Infantry, settled into Camp Chickerell in Weymouth, right on the Channel coast."[29]

Eddie Steeg, D Company, 18th Infantry, and, at just a shade over five feet tall, one of the smallest men in the 1st (or any other) Division, recalled with good humor, "We arrived back in England and, despite the constant air bombardments, the island was still afloat; apparently, the [barrage] balloons were still doing the job. The weather seemed to be pretty much the same as when we left here just about a year ago and headed for North Africa. I wondered to myself if it ever got any different. Frequent rain and heavy-duty fog seemed to be the order of the day, almost every day. It seemed that not much else had changed since our previous departure. Perhaps the port area looked more crowded and congested than before, if that was possible. We [went] to Dorchester, where our headquarters were located. For the most part, when we were not living on a troopship, we were housed in Quonset huts. The constant rain caused our bivouac area to become a veritable quagmire. When we were not *on* the sea, we were *in* a sea of mud. The fog was so thick at times that it was damn near impossible to recognize the guy standing next to you in a morning reveille formation.

"Needless to say, the comforts of home or the comforts of our previous stay at Tidworth Barracks* were sadly lacking in our new quarters. Our beds were [mattress covers] stuffed with straw. Without available electricity, kerosene lanterns became our chief source of light. Each hut had its own pot-bellied stove and a supply of firewood to supply heat. Sometimes the logs had to be split down to fit the stove. One night, while trying to split some of the logs with the hatchet provided, I missed and sliced the palm of my hand at the base of my thumb. The cut was serious enough to require stitches. I went to the battalion medical hut for a repair job, and had a long wait while the doctor rounded up his medical team to watch and assist him. He explained each step of the suturing process to his associates as they observed under lantern light. He remarked that this wound and the conditions could be typical of what to expect in combat. I didn't get a Purple Heart for this wound but I did hear rumors later that some GIs were awarded one for cutting their hands on a can of C rations. I guess getting hurt or injured on a government-issued item made the difference."[30]

Camp life in England was initially pleasant as the men unwound from their North Africa and Sicily combat experiences. There were football and softball games, movies, real beds, real food (a break from the near-constant diet of C-rations, Spam, and powdered eggs on which the troops had subsisted in North Africa and Sicily), Service Club diversions, and USO shows with such entertainers as Al Jolson, Bob Hope, Frances Langford, Jerry Colonna, Glenn Miller and his Army Air Force Band, and others from the States who brought

---

*Tidworth Barracks, near Salisbury in southern England, had been one of the division's homes and training areas prior to the 1st's 1942 departure for the invasion of North Africa.

Private First Class Eddie Steeg, D Company, 18th Infantry Division, shows off a war souvenir. Note that he is wearing a "liberated" Nazi belt and buckle. Photo taken "somewhere in Germany," 1945. (Courtesy Chyrl Zickgraf)

with them a little touch of home. There were also trips to pubs in neighboring towns and occasional jaunts to London.

As the Big Red One settled into its new quarters in southern England, a flood of replacements arrived and were assigned to combat-decimated units. Many of the newcomers found being accepted by the veterans difficult. One such replacement was Steve Kellman, a former New York University student who had joined the Enlisted Reserve Corps in August 1942. He arrived at the small village of Long Bredy, near Dorchester, where he was assigned to L Company, 16th Infantry. "[The veterans] had been through some tough fighting," he said. "I remember hearing stories about Kasserine Pass, where they got their butts kicked. They were kind of stand-offish and I could understand that; I was a green kid coming in and these were battle-hardened veterans."[31]

Chicagoan and combat veteran Private First Class William M. Lee, D Company, 26th Infantry Regiment, explained why it was so hard for new men to gain acceptance. "The veterans were reluctant to get to know new replacements—you couldn't stand the trauma of death when they were killed. It was easier to ignore them than to accept them. But you did what you could to keep them alive."[32]

Replacement Kellman remembered, "We lived in Quonset huts and they had these little stoves in the center of them to heat the hut. We had to take turns going out and filling the bucket with coke.* One day, the sergeant in my hut said, 'Kellman, it's your turn to get the coke,' and I said, 'I just did it.' He replied, 'That's the trouble with you damned draftees.' That kind of ticked me off, so I said, 'I'm not a draftee—I enlisted.' He said, 'Let me see your dog-tags.' I had serial number 12128614; the first '1' indicated I had enlisted—if you had a '3,' that meant you had been drafted. So that calmed things down. If you did your job, you were eventually accepted. But they didn't welcome new replacements with open arms."[33]

Another new replacement was Private Al Alvarez from Chelsea, Massachusetts, assigned to the 7th Field Artillery Battalion, one of the 1st Division's organic artillery units. The young private was indelibly impressed by a soldier he referred to only as "The Corporal." According to Alvarez, the man's fondest greeting was a bellowing, "I'm your corporal—the lowest non-commissioned officer in this cotton-picking Army! But to you, these two chevrons mean I'm the Rat of God! If you don't believe that, you better be right! I ain't no gypsy fortuneteller and I ain't promising you no tomorrow, so get on the stick today!" The corporal's salty language and seven years of service made him a man to be feared and respected, especially by the callow youth under his tutelage. "At night, his wheezing snores amid the aroma of imbibed vanilla extract emanating from his end of the Nissen hut kept us vividly conscious of his drunken presence. Yet no one dared awaken him during these six months of a 1944 spring training period in Dorchester, England! We marveled every morning how that 'Old Sweat' could be the first up and ready for reveille with the tightest bunk and OD's crisply creased. It's still enthralling to remember his ironing his trousers on his foot locker with a heated mess pan! Then his tattooed arms moved in continuous motion as he spit-shined his boots.

"Here we were, newly arrived replacements assigned to the premier fighting division in the whole U.S. Army: the 1st Infantry Division! Obviously, this crusty corporal, with the two hash-marks on his sleeve fully denoting his six years of hard-bitten service, fully comprehended what was in store for us and what he had to do to prepare us. . . . He was the warrior that we and the military world aspired to be. His constant rowdy belching at our many mistakes during his battery recruit school were always loud, irreverent, and profane, yet invariably

---

*A type of low-grade coal used for heating.

hilarious. 'If I'd wanted to send a stupid SOB, I'd gone myself!' For those who hailed from the great Lone Star State, it was, 'Texas, where more men needed killin' than horses needed stealin.' As for me specifically, he savored this gem: 'You're a lucky SOB. Your name begins with "A," so it'll be inscribed high on the top of the war memorial in your hometown—and the dogs won't be able to pee on it.'

"On the other hand, amid these churlish admonitions, he included truisms I've always respected, remembered, and now repeat: 'Never, ever forget you're the First, and nobody in hell—German, British, or Chinaman—will ever stop us!' Always the boss, which he gutterally explained meant, 'Double SOB spelt backwards,' he delicately pounded in sage combat wisdom: 'It's "duty first," and for us cannon-cockers, it's "support the doughs!"' . . . . He honed my manual-correct military craftsmanship with verbal flames to my posterior: 'Dig your commo pit hole deeper! Protect your radio! Carry "too many" batteries! Commo is more important than you!' We absorbed his basic tenets of battle soldiering: 'Carry two full canteens! Wear three first-aid packets, one with morphine syrettes, on your helmet! Tape wound-powder packets on your equipment!' Believing he was the noblest creation of the devil, we incessantly strived to learn while leaping around like the proverbial third monkey on Noah's gangplank, yet knowing we could never enter this veteran's coterie.

"Not only this infernal corporal, but most of all the other accursed battery NCOs came across as exclusive, eccentric, and maybe arrogant buggers, but they had 'smelled the smoke and seen the elephant.'* Surely, they were narrow-minded, rigid, one-way, and harsh in their crude, incessant discipline, yet they all oozed a distinct 'professionalism.' Certainly, they were 'Old Army' and therefore permitted no evasion of orders. Seemingly always, they were inflexible as they maintained the strict application of their rules. Yet, in some strange way, they formulated in us John-ass recruits, 'the rule of the bunky.' These NCOs would look out for us by teaching us the hard truths. We then would learn to look out for our section buddies, then as platoon mates, and finally as battery members. Thus we bonded and became a military family!

"Fortunately for us 'young soldiers,' The Corporal's extensive supervisory months of comprehensive common-sense, combat-survival skilled training

* A Civil War expression meaning one's initial combat experience.

transformed us technically proficient craftsmen into battle-wise, energetic, enthusiastic, hot-to-trot field soldiers. We could shoot, scoot, and communicate! We were 'The Lucky Seventh!'"[34]

Everyone—whether a freshly arrived recruit or a battle-hardened veteran—was put through months of grueling training. Of the training regimen, General Huebner noted, "The period in England can be compared to that of the normal training of a division in the States. The development of the skills and techniques of our weapons, the training of specialists, and the moulding of our battle teams were the primary requirements. To assist in these aims, we had the services of many combat-wise and experienced leaders who could impart to our new replacements the know-how of battle. . . . There were small-unit problems; the artillery went back on the range for battalion exercises; we rehearsed our coordination in the infantry-artillery-tank team; and we worked on our communications. And with the Navy and the Air Force there was planning and practice, for there was a triphibious landing to be made. Thus passed the days in England: building and re-building and ever looking over the bows of our landing craft."[35]

The England to which the 1st had returned was little changed, except for a huge influx of American and Canadian forces—over 1,500,000 Americans alone by June 1944—who had arrived and taken up residence in the eleven months that the Big Red One had been away. The civilians, however, were suffering greatly from a variety of privations. Having been at war since September 1939, and standing nearly alone against Germany since the fall of France in May 1940, England was looking frayed around the edges. Almost everything was in short supply—gasoline (or petrol, as the Brits called it), cigarettes, clothing, footwear, coffee, and, most importantly, food. The normally spotless British trains were dirty and crammed with uniformed men and women; the roads were mainly the realm of military traffic; and nightly blackouts in London and towns and cities near the coast and within range of German bombers made getting around after dark a hazardous affair.

At first, an air of hostility and suspicion greeted the returning men of the 1st Infantry Division. What really bothered many of the reserved British people (besides the feeling that a bunch of loutish strangers had barged into their homes, taken over, and put their feet up on the furniture) was the brash, condescending, "we're here to save you" attitudes they detected in many American servicemen. Naturally, much resentment, if not outright hostility, was felt by some of the locals, mostly the British men in uniform. The presence of so many newcomers

("Johnny-come-latelys," as they were called) was an intrusion to which the Tommies did not take kindly, especially when the Yanks, in their sharp-looking uniforms and pockets bulging with candy, cigarettes, and cash, became rivals for the affection of the local young ladies. "There was also a great deal of resentment because the American soldier was paid five times what the British were, plus American soldiers got booze and chocolates," noted Lieutenant Leonard E. Jones of C Company, 18th Infantry Regiment. "The Brits thought we were sloppy and undisciplined—with some justification—but the Brits were also reacting to our arrogance and stealing all their girls."[36]

With the supply of alcohol limited or nonexistent on American bases, the Yanks, in their off-duty hours, headed for the local pubs. Of course, when a loud, boisterous group of Americans burst into a normally reserved pub, conflict was bound to arise, and more than one pub was broken up when the two cultures clashed. Thomas R. McCann, a Mississippian and a member of the 18th Regiment's Intelligence and Reconnaissance Platoon, recalled that in Puddletown, where his unit was billeted, "There was some animosity between the British people and the American soldiers. One example was the rationing of alcohol. The Americans would go into the pubs and drink the ration in one night, denying the British their favorite drinks and taking over the pubs."[37]

In an attempt to keep the peace, the U.S. Army issued a flyer to the troops that read, "Not much whisky is now being drunk [in Britain]. Wartime taxes have shot the price of a bottle up to about $4.50. The British are beer-drinkers and can hold it—the beer is now below peacetime strength, but can still make a man's tongue wag at both ends. You will be welcome . . . as long as you remember one thing. The pub is the 'poor man's club' where the men have come to see friends, not strangers."[38]

Some soldiers did go out of their way to make friends with the locals. Denver-born Bob Hilbert, a buck sergeant assigned to K Company, 18th Infantry Regiment, recalled, "Some buddies and I went to Weymouth several times and I met some very fine people. This one lady and her husband who ran the pub where we went—The King's Head pub—were really, really good to us. One day, we were invited into the sitting room of the pub when some British soldiers came in. They started firing off some insults about Americans, and 'Mum' just kicked them right out of the place."[39]

Louis Newman, Cannon Company, 18th Regiment, also spent much of his off-duty time getting to know the English people. He had obtained a pass during Christmas of 1943 and he and his buddies went from one town to another. "I went to London. I would meet girls, go to dances, talk to people. The British people are more reserved—not like Americans. We like to talk a lot. But I got along well with them."[40]

Thomas McCann remembered that many of the English people went out of their way to make him feel at home. "The night we arrived in Puddletown, I met the village policeman who told me we were in Thomas Hardy's country.* He also told me Hardy's first cousin's widow lived across the street from our [Quonset] hut and he would introduce me to the lady. Mrs. Antell was a lady in her seventies, lived in a thatched cottage, and was taking care of a little boy about eight years of age who had lived in London and had been brought to the rural area for safety from the German bombs. She was very nice to me, always had fresh eggs for me (which were rationed). I learned a lot about Hardy; she gave me one of his childhood books autographed, and a picture of Hardy with the former Prince of Wales, the Duke of Windsor. I had my mother send gifts to her and the boy. As I did not care for drinking and pub crawling, I met many of the local people and was invited into their homes." McCann was also invited by the locals to join them for bridge, whist, mahjong, and for Sunday services at their church. As the shower facilities were quite a distance from his billets, the village policeman even told McCann he could bathe at his home any time he wanted. "The British people were very nice to us," he noted. "They allowed us to visit places they would not let their own people visit."[41]

Not all of the American soldiers from the various units were as considerate or appreciative as McCann. After some complaints reached higher headquarters about American GIs making critical comments over Britain's shabby state, another memo reminded the Yanks: "With 45 million people living on a small, crowded island . . . Britain may look a little shopworn and grimy to you. The British people are anxious to have you know that you are not seeing their country at its best. . . . the houses haven't been painted because factories aren't making paint, they're making planes. The famous English gardens and parks are either unkempt—there are no men to take care of them—or they are being used to grow vegetables. British taxi cabs look antique because Britain makes tanks

---

*Thomas Hardy (1840–1928) was one of England's most beloved poets and novelists. His most famous works of fiction included *Far from the Madding Crowd; The Return of the Native; The Mayor of Casterbridge;* and *Tess of the d'Urbervilles.*

for herself *and* Russia and hasn't time to make new cars. British trains are cold because the power is needed for industry. There are no luxury dining cars because the war effort has no place for such frills. The trains are unwashed and grimy because men and women are needed for more important work."

In an effort to further reduce friction between "two peoples, separated by a common language," Eisenhower's staff also advised, "Don't comment on politics. Don't try to tell the British that America won the last war. NEVER criticize the King or Queen. Don't criticize food, beer, or cigarettes. Remember they have been at war since 1939. . . . Neither do the British need to be told that their armies lost the first couple of rounds in the present war. Use your head before you sound off, and remember how long the British alone have held Hitler off. If the British look dowdy and badly dressed, it is not because they do not like good clothes or know how to wear them. All clothing is rationed. Old clothes are good form."

To impress their island's guests, many of the young ladies saved their one good dress and their last precious pair of silk stockings for the big dances and parties held at American military installations, while others demonstrated their creativity with needle and thread by creating fetching evening gowns and dresses from curtains and bedsheets adorned with sequins. Their creations must have paid off, for 81,000 Americans succumbed to wartime romances and married their British sweethearts.

Still, some thoughtless American habits rankled. In her book on life in wartime England, *Bombers and Mash: The Domestic Front 1939–1945*, British author Raynes Minns noted: "At the more stylish dances at American and Canadian bases, girls were regaled with unaccustomed extravagances." Since U.S. storerooms bulged with articles the Britons had not seen for years, "Piles of doughnuts, bowls of sugar, mounds of oranges, novelties like peanut butter, salad cream, Coca-Cola, and *real* coffee astounded the girls," chronicled Minns. "Fruit and tomato juice flowed freely, much resented by those that knew it was shipped 'over here' by the endangered British Merchant Navy. Some girls not only saved their oranges to take home, but scavenged the peel from others' plates for syrups, marmalades, and flavourings. Many were horrified at the waste of delicacies left on GI plates, and, to add insult to injury, GIs were even seen stubbing their cigarettes out on mounds of food. To the British uniformed counterpart, a GI mess meal looked more like a week's rations."

Gradually, the two sides developed a fondness for each other. Despite their own shortages, many British families took in American GIs for Sunday dinners

American GIs stroll through London's St. James Park with a couple of uniformed English girls. (Courtesy U.S. Army Military History Institute)

and special occasions. A Ministry of Food pamphlet reminded the British, "Many of our housewives have sons in the Forces and they know how homesick a soldier can feel far from his home. America is famous for its open-hearted hospitality to strangers. Let us show America that we are hospitable, too. Let us all invite a soldier from overseas to share in the [Christmas] festivities."

When the GIs accepted invitations into British homes, most behaved like gentlemen—and were shocked at the extent of the shortages. Another memo advised the Americans, "If you are invited into a British home, and the host exhorts you to 'Eat up—there is plenty on the table,' go easy. It may be the family ration for a whole week spread out to show their hospitality. You are coming to Britain from a country where your home is still safe, food is still plentiful, and lights are still burning. . . . Remember that the British soldiers and civilians have been living under tremendous strain. It is always impolite to criticize your hosts. It is militarily stupid to insult your allies."

As a consequence of their personal contacts with the English people, many of the Yanks began supplementing their hosts' meager rations out of their own abundance. Some GIs, with access to their mess halls' storerooms, paid back the kindnesses of their adoptive families with "large tins of corned beef, soup, pats of butter, grapefruit, bananas, dried fruit or unfamiliar American cigarettes, as well as soap, not only scented but wrapped." Officers and mess sergeants generally looked the other way, knowing that such thievery was helping the war effort by cementing relationships between the two allies.[42]

Lieutenant Harold Monica was impressed by the resolve of the civilians he met. "I began to appreciate the tenacity and feeling of the British people. No one, especially the Germans, would ever have been on that island without their approval. If the war had gone on for fifty years, they would still be fighting, as they certainly would never have surrendered. Call them 'bulldogs' if you want to; it is certainly appropriate and fitting. Wartime shortages, bombings, and the other inconveniences just seemed to strengthen their spirit. . . ."

He also recalled the efforts that were made to improve British-American relationships. "We had frequent visits to the local pubs in the small farm communities of Puddletown, Piddlehinton, and others. Lieutenant Colonel [Robert] York [a battalion commander in the 18th Regiment] decided we would have a Christmas party and invite our new friends and acquaintances. In these local pubs, the only patrons were the farmers, as women were not allowed. Invitations were extended to various pubs, not just individuals, that all were invited who cared to attend. On the given dates, trucks were dispatched to the pubs and we had 35–40 men take us up on the offer. Orders from Battalion were, 'I don't expect to see any two Englishmen seated next to each other.' Colonel York's orders, we knew, were to be carried out, and we did."[43]

Jim Hunt, then a young boy, had fond memories of when the 1st Infantry Division's 26th Infantry Regiment moved into his hometown of Swanage: "Every hotel and guesthouse in Swanage was taken over by them. To us youngsters, who had only seen or heard Americans on films, they seemed like film stars from the Wild West. They were very kind and generous to us kids. My brother and I sold newspapers to the young GIs in their billets in the mornings before we went to school. Some of them would give us their K rations which contained food that we had never seen before because of the severe rationing. The K ration was a waxed box containing biscuits, chocolate, small cans of ham, eggs, orange and lemon powder, candy, which we call sweets, chewing gum, and cigarettes.

Lieutenant Harold Monica, D Company, 18th Infantry Regiment. (Courtesy Harold Monica)

"Just opposite our school was the Craigside Hotel which billeted part of A Company and, as my brother Kenny and I sold newspapers there, we became familiar faces. Some of them would give us their mess kits to join the queue for the delicious chow they served. We got very friendly with the cook who was known as 'Two Gun.' They loved talking to us kids; they were homesick, and they would tell us all about their families and life as it was back in the States. One of them asked me if I would like to write to his younger sister who lived in Pittsburgh, which I did."*[44]

Jim Hunt was one of thousands of Britons who came to see the 1st Infantry soldiers as who they were—lonely young men far from home getting ready to take part in one of history's most important battles. The derisive phrase, "Overpaid,

* The following year, Jim Hunt received a letter from the GI's sister, informing him that her brother had been killed during the landings at Omaha Beach on D-Day.

oversexed, and over here," was certainly bandied about by some jealous and resentful Britons, but no one could deny that the presence of so many Americans in Britain would soon, it was fervently hoped, turn the tide of battle and bring the war to a victorious close.

Allen Towne, B Company, 1st Medical Battalion, recalled, "During the Christmas week [1943], we would go to a pub in Weymouth and listen to all the latest songs from the States. Most of them were pertaining to the war, and to us they were quite sad. These songs were *I'll Be Seeing You*, *When the Lights Go On Again All Over the World*, and *I Don't Want To Walk Without You*. In particular, the new song, *White Christmas*, sung by Bing Crosby, made everyone homesick. Contributing to our emotions was the uneasiness about the forthcoming battle. We wondered if we would survive the invasion and ever see home again."[45]

Harold Monica recalled a memorable night on the town. Somehow, he had managed to obtain a ticket to the show, *Dreaming of a White Christmas*, that was playing in nearby Bournemouth. On the day of the show, "We loaded up in late afternoon and arrived in Bournemouth before dark. I don't know if the cast was from home or if so-called local talent was used. In any case, it was super and there were tears in the eyes of many. What else could we think about but home—and how sorry we were for ourselves that we weren't there? Like many things—this show included—the best is often saved for last. The show ended, or so it seemed, but one more act was to follow. The curtain went up and who came walking onto the stage?—none other than Irving Berlin in person, and he started to sing. He didn't have much of a voice, but the magnetism of his personality and surroundings put him in complete command of the audience. He did his song and said, 'Please join me.' What a response—it's a wonder the theater walls were not shattered. The return to Weymouth, black-out or not, didn't seem so long."[46]

The long, bloody campaign being waged in Italy had turned into a stalemate, a stalemate that was seriously impacting Allied preparations for the invasion of France. The Americans had never been terribly enthusiastic about slogging through the rugged Apennine mountains, but had given in to the campaign at Churchill's urging. Following the near-disastrous landings at Salerno on 9 September 1943, Mark Clark's Fifth Army became bogged down below the heights of Monte Cassino; the main passageway to Rome was denied to the Allies and an end run behind the German lines at Anzio was being promoted by Britain's prime minister as the only way to break the impasse. The Anzio operation, code-named *Shingle* and scheduled for the end of January 1944, siphoned off many resources that the *Overlord* planners expected would be available to them—especially the LSTs. The two theaters of operation played a game of tug-of-war over the transports, and *Shingle* nearly turned into a disaster for the Allies, due partly to insufficient shipping. Follow-up forces at Anzio consequently arrived in piecemeal fashion, which gave the Germans time to react and, for the next five months, stymie Allied efforts to take Rome.[47]

In England in early February, while the Anzio operation was still in doubt, Eisenhower was formally named Supreme Commander, COSSAC was disbanded, and SHAEF was officially born. Operation *Roundup* was scrapped and in its place was born Operation *Overlord*. Ike's public relations officer, Navy Captain Harry C. Butcher, noted in his diary on 14 February that the Combined Chiefs of Staff had directed Eisenhower to "enter the continent of Europe and, in conjunction with the other Allied nations, to undertake operations aimed at the heart of Germany and the destruction of her armed forces. The target date for entering the Continent is May 31, 1944." He also added, chillingly: "Will the Channel run red with blood?"[48]

Hundreds of problems, from the simple to the simply overwhelming, were laid on Eisenhower's desk. Overriding everything was logistics—the art and science of supplying an army with all the weapons, food, clothing, ammunition, fuel, medical supplies, tanks, trucks, typewriters, and millions of other essential items. Without an unbroken pipeline of matériel from Britain to France, the whole operation would grind to a halt. Creating two massive, portable artificial harbors (code-named "Mulberry" and "Gooseberry") that would be towed across the Channel once the beachhead was secure was just one of thousands of critical tasks on the Allies' "to-do" list.

Obtaining enough landing craft—and getting them to the right ports—was equally daunting. Drawing up loading diagrams so that the right men and equipment hit the right beach in the right order was a monumental headache. Holding the multinational coalition together was also taxing; for example, Leigh-Mallory fretted constantly about the airborne plan and was convinced that the three airborne divisions would be slaughtered. Then there were security problems to worry about; with over a million men poised to invade France, a leak of the time and place for the invasion was all but inevitable. There was also General Charles de Gaulle, the self-proclaimed leader of Free French forces in exile, who refused to cooperate with the Allies. Murphy's Law—if anything *can* go wrong, it *will* go wrong—seemed to hang over the heads of the coalition partners.

Some things, on the other hand, went better than anyone could have imaged. Since Allied intelligence knew through their "Ultra" intercepts that the Germans expected the cross-channel attack to come at the narrowest point along the coast at the Pas de Calais, and continued to build up their forces and fortifications accordingly, the Allies continued to feed the German belief with a brilliant deception plan known as Operation *Fortitude*. SHAEF built a fictitious army, the First United States Army Group (FUSAG), around America's most flamboyant general, George S. Patton Jr., to convince the Germans that any attack on Normandy was merely diversionary and that "Old Blood and Guts" would lead this huge, but nonexistent, force across the narrows.*

With the expenditure of incalculable man-hours, the pieces of the giant jigsaw puzzle known as Operation *Overlord* began to slip into place. The most important consideration—the place of invasion—already had been decided upon by Morgan and COSSAC in 1943. The selection of Normandy was due to a number of factors. First, it was within striking range of air bases in England. Second, it allowed the Allies to disperse their assembled ships and landing craft in ports over a wide area where they were less likely to be spotted by German reconnaissance aircraft—and assaulted from the air. And third, it *wasn't* the Pas de Calais—where the Germans had constructed their greatest fortifications and concentrated the greatest numbers of their best troops.[49]

Nevertheless, Normandy would be no cakewalk. To establish parameters in which the assigned invasion units would operate, five assault areas in Normandy were established. From one end to the other, the entire assault area covered 61.7 miles.[50]

Army planners felt the forces initially scheduled to hit four of the landing beaches were sufficient, but one five-mile-long strip of coast had them wor-

---

*In actuality, Patton would lead the U.S. Third Army once the bridgehead in France had been secured.

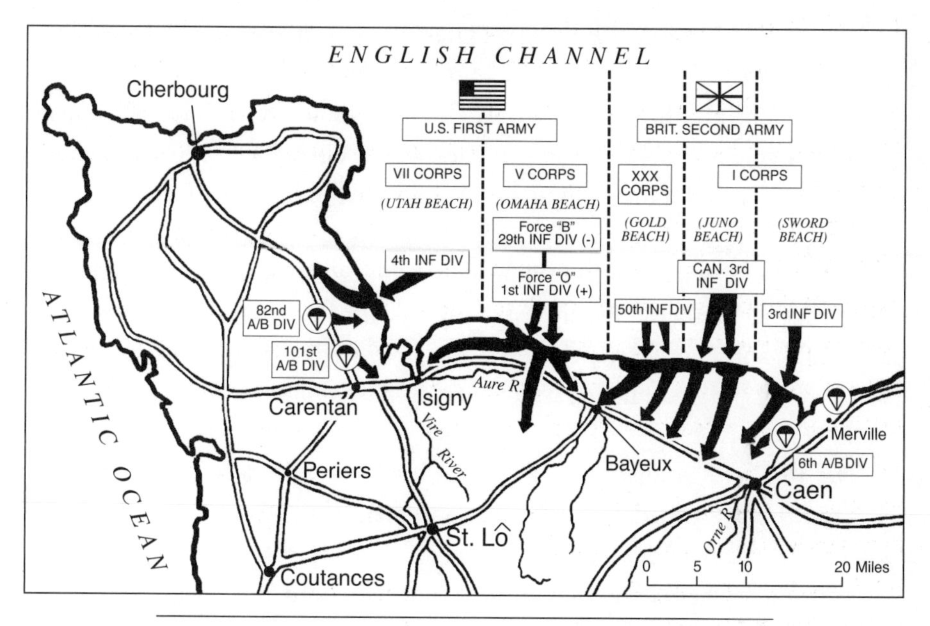

Allied amphibious and airborne landing plan and initial objectives.

ried—the strip marked on maps as "Omaha." Eisenhower and his staff felt that a single, 15,000-man infantry division was insufficient for the task, so it was decided to attach two regiments of Gerhardt's inexperienced 29th Division to Huebner's battle-tested 1st. The invasion plan called for the Big Red One to attack with two regiments abreast: its own 16th Infantry Regiment and the 116th from the 29th. The second wave would consist of the 1st's 18th Regiment and the attached 115th. All these troops in Force O (for "Omaha") would be brought ashore by Task Force O, under the command of Rear Admiral Alan Kirk, U.S. Navy. A third wave, known as Force B, consisting of the 1st's 26th Regiment and the 29th's 175th Regiment under Gerhardt's command, was in Corps reserve and would go ashore at the direction of Major General Leonard T. "Gee" Gerow, commanding V Corps.[51]

Omaha Beach was itself broken down into seven assault sectors. These were, from west to east: Able, Baker, Charlie, Dog, Easy, Fox, and George. These sectors were further subdivided and designated by colors: Green, White, and Red. The 116th Regiment would hit Dog Red, Dog White, Dog Green, and Easy Green beaches while the 16th was landing simultaneously to their east on Easy Red and Fox Green beaches.*[52]

Because the attachments were only temporary, and the regimental combat teams from the two divisions had not rehearsed the operation together, it was decided that the 1st Infantry Division's assistant division commander, Brigadier General Willard G. Wyman, and Wyman's counterpart in the 29th, Brigadier General Norman D. Cota, would go ashore with the initial waves and establish coordination and communication between the units. Once the first two waves had been successful, and Force B came ashore, the two divisions, upon V Corps order, would revert to the command and control of their respective commanders and staffs.[53]

The 16th and 116th Regiments would land side-by-side at approximately 0630 hours,** preceded by amphibious Sherman tanks. The 16th's 2nd Battalion Landing Team (BLT), led by Lieutenant Colonel Herbert C. Hicks Jr., would break through whatever was left of enemy lines and head for Colleville-sur-Mer, some 2,400 yards to the southeast, to establish a blocking position. The 1st BLT, commanded by Lieutenant Colonel Edmund F. Driscoll, would pass through the 2nd BLT to capture the town of Formigny at the important junction of Highways D517 and N13. The 3rd BLT, under Lieutenant Colonel Charles T. Horner Jr., would seize the top of the bluffs and advance toward the village of Ste.-Honorine-des-Pertes. The 29th Division elements would push southward in the direction of Vierville and link up with the 4th Infantry Division, moving inland from Utah Beach.

At 0930 hours, the second wave, comprised of the 1st Division's 18th and the 29th Division's 115th RCTs, still under Huebner's operational control, would hit the beach, leapfrog the initial elements, and drive farther inland. The 18th RCT,

---

*For the invasion, the regiments were organized into regimental combat teams, or RCTs, as described in Field Manual FM 100-5 "Operations": "To insure unity of effort or increase readiness for combat, part of all of the subordinate units of a command may be formed into one or more temporary tactical groupings (task forces), each under a designated commander. In each, the unity of tactical organizations is preserved as far as practicable. In an infantry division, the term *combat team* is usually applied to a task force consisting of a regiment of infantry, a battalion of light artillery, and essential units of other arms in suitable proportion." (Army Field Manual FM 100-5, "Operations," 15 June 1944, p. 5) The abbreviation "RCT" will be used hereinafter, where appropriate.

**The twenty-four clock will be used throughout. For example, "0630 hours" is 6:30 a.m.; "1300 hours" is 1 p.m.; "2130 hours" is 9:30 p.m.

commanded by Colonel George A. Smith Jr., was to dash all the way to the River Aure southeast of Colleville; cross it; take and hold the high ground east of Trévières; then send out patrols some 2,000 to 3,000 yards south of Highway N13. Around noon, presuming that all was going according to plan, V Corps would order Force B—the 1st's 26th and the 29's 175th RCTs—to be landed. The 26th would then head east and link up at Tour-en-Bessin with the British 50th Infantry Division, pushing inland from Gold Beach, while the 175th would drive to the west.[53] It was a very ambitious schedule, and one that depended on everything going right. But, as anyone who has ever been in battle can testify, in combat virtually nothing ever goes according to plan or schedule.

Before the invasion could take place, however, the participating units would have to be trained (or, in the case of the 1st, re-trained) in the science of storming a hostile shore. For this purpose, a number of amphibious training centers were established along the southern coast of England and Wales. These included Rosneath, Falmouth, Salcombe, Appledore, Instow, Penarth, Milford Haven, and Teignmouth. The major training center for V Corps was Slapton Sands at Start Bay, south of Dartmouth, a site chosen because it had many features that resembled the terrain at Omaha Beach.[55]

These practice exercises did not always go smoothly. Landing craft did not always hit their designated beaches at the right moment; essential equipment was lost; and company and platoon leaders lost control of their men. And this was *without* the additional problems that enemy fire and casualties would create. On 28 April, 1944, after observing the 4th Infantry Division run through its paces during Exercise *Tiger* at Slapton Sands, Captain Harry Butcher recorded his private worries in his diary: "I am concerned over the absence of toughness and alertness of the young American officers whom I saw on this trip. They seem to regard the war as one grand maneuver in which they are having a happy time. Many seem as green as growing corn. How will they act in battle? . . . A good many of the full colonels also give me a pain. They are fat, gray, and oldish. Most of them wear the Rainbow Ribbon of the last war and are still fighting it. The 1st U.S. Division is the only experienced American infantry division actually in the assault."[56]

Butcher, Ike, and all the top brass had another major worry: During the night of 27–28 April, a flotilla of nine German E-boats* slipped past the screen of

---

* These torpedo boats were larger than the U.S. PT boat and were called E-boats by the Allies, the "E" standing for "enemy"; the Germans called them *Schnellbooten,* or "fast boats." (Ambrose, p. 32)

destroyers and patrol boats, penetrated the Exercise *Tiger* area, and sank two LSTs carrying 4th Infantry Division men, while damaging another LST. The death toll was tragically high: 441 soldiers and 197 sailors were lost. It was more than the 4th would lose at Utah Beach on D-Day.[57]

The first few minutes of an amphibious landing are the most dangerous for the invaders. Artillery support is in short supply, and tank support is also usually nonexistent. To solve the tank problem, an inventive British officer, Major General Sir Percy Hobart, devised a method of turning thirty-three-ton Sherman tanks into floating fortresses. By waterproofing them, then attaching propellers and an inflatable "skirt," he proved that tanks could "swim" to shore from their launching vessels. While the experiments worked reasonably well in calm water, the practicality of having tanks swim for several miles in the pitching swells of the English Channel was a great unknown.

At H-Hour minus fifty minutes on D-Day, the plan called for thirty-two DD (Duplex Drive), amphibious tanks to be launched from their mother ships approximately 5,000 yards offshore and head for Easy Red and Fox Green, where they would land and operate primarily in support of the 16th RCT. An additional thirty-two DD tanks would be launched simultaneously to support the 116th RCT at Dog Green, Dog White, and Dog Red. It was calculated that it would take the tanks forty-five minutes to swim this distance and reach land. Just the shock value of seeing tanks emerging from the sea—the planners were certain—would be enough to send the defenders fleeing.

There was another aspect of the invasion Eisenhower's team considered: guarding the flanks. While seaborne soldiers were struggling to establish a foothold on the slim beaches, a force would be needed to prevent the invaders from being hit from the side. To protect the western flank of the invasion area from enemy counterattack, the area behind Utah Beach would be secured by the American 82nd and 101st Airborne Divisions, dropped several hours before the amphibious forces hit the shore. As the fields behind the invasion beaches had been flooded by the Germans, the slightly elevated roads, called causeways, running inland from the beaches, would need to be secured by the parachute troops—both to allow the seaborne invaders to dash inland and to keep the German reserves out of the beachheads. On the eastern edge of the invasion area, elements of the British 6th Airborne Division would parachute or glide in behind—or directly onto—enemy positions near Ranville and Benouville to secure the vital bridges over the Orne River and canal to forestall a German counterattack from the east and to neutralize a German battery at Merville.[58]

Never very far from the minds of Ike and his staff was the terrible human cost that amphibious operations exacted. All they had to do was look at the carnage at Dieppe and in the Pacific. Everyone knew about the toll during Operation *Watchtower* on Guadalcanal and Makin Islands in the Solomon chain, east of New Guinea; there, 16,000 U.S. Marines and Army troops spent seven months slogging their way through a green hell against a fanatical, entrenched foe—and lost 3,000 men killed and wounded in the process.[59] Then there was Bougainville Island, also in the Solomons, where the Marines alone suffered over 3,600 casualties before the enemy was beaten and the island secured.[60] In late 1943 and early 1944, the cost of taking the Japanese-held islands and atolls of the Marshalls and Gilberts in the Central Pacific was extraordinarily steep: some 5,000 Americans killed and wounded.[61] Would not the Germans be just as fanatical, just as ruthless, in defending the French coast? How many thousands of young Allied soldiers, sailors, and airmen would be killed or wounded trying to batter down the ramparts of *Festung Europa*—Hitler's Fortress Europe?

Operation *Overlord* was a terribly complex plan that depended upon split-second timing to insure that all elements of it worked in harmony with each other. If any portion of the plan failed, then the entire operation—and perhaps even the outcome of the war—was in jeopardy. While every assault area in Normandy was important, none was more important than Omaha Beach, in the very center of the invasion area. If Omaha Beach could not be taken and held, the Germans could eventually isolate the Utah beachhead, as well as the British and Canadian beaches farther east, and destroy the invaders piecemeal. If the invasion failed, many Allied planners worried that Stalin might conclude a separate peace with Hitler, who would then be free to make his French coastal defenses—his "Atlantic Wall"—even more formidable than they already were. Another Allied attempt at invasion would need to be put off for another year or two—or postponed indefinitely—giving Hitler complete control of most of Europe. The prospect was frightening.

How, then, to insure success? Should green, untried troops be sent into combat in hopes that their eagerness for battle and youthful sense of invulnerability would carry the day—or should war-weary veteran divisions be thrown, once more, into the breach in hopes that their experience would be the telling factor?

In the end, the mantle of responsibility for cracking through some of the most formidable defensive systems on earth was draped across the shoulders of both groups—the veteran 1st and untried 29th Infantry Divisions—the very tip of the Allied spearhead.

CHAPTER THREE

"Rumors Were Rampant"

IT WAS NO secret to the men of the 1st Infantry Division why they were in England. Some, like Staff Sergeant Christopher J. Cornazzani of Brooklyn, an operations sergeant with 1st Battalion headquarters, 18th Infantry, clearly saw the importance of their role in the impending invasion: "Those of us who had survived the war in Africa and on the island of Sicily knew what to expect when we reached the beach. We had memories of two other invasions and the many battles and hardships we had encountered before arriving at this moment in history. If we failed now, all the other battles would have been in vain."[1]

Corporal Dan Curatola, a Pennsylvanian in the 3rd Battalion, 16th Infantry, and a veteran of both North Africa and Sicily, noted that he was "exhilarated at the sense of making history and making progress toward ending the war, but apprehensive of becoming a casualty. I was taking it one day at a time with no real expectation of survival."[2]

"I think we all knew we were going across the Channel," commented Captain Joseph T. Dawson, a seasoned officer from Waco, Texas, and son of a Baptist minister. "We knew this was an interim period. But all of us knew from the very time we landed on the return to England from Sicily . . . that we were preparing for the big showdown." Dawson, who had taken command of G Company, 16th Regiment, in Sicily, was confident that his unit was equal to the task. "The company had been in the hands of one of my closest friends in the war, Ed Wozenski, who was one of the greatest soldiers we had in the war, and he had made G Company an outstanding outfit, so I inherited the best. When I came down there to take over from a man that had achieved not only the respect and admiration but the affection of his men . . . I think I was regarded as an outcast or an outlander by the men. And I made no effort to change their attitude other than to try to ingratiate myself into their confidence. . . . I realized in the earliest days of my career that the only way you could achieve success as a commander was to get the respect of your men, but you had to earn it. I had difficulty in overcoming the fact that I was then a staff officer instead of a combat officer, so that when the training programs would be conducted during the period from the time we came back to England until the D-Day operation, I tried to make my men into a fighting force, physically and mentally, and I didn't spare the horses. And I tried to instill in them an understanding and awareness of the gravity of the situation and the necessity for total teamwork. . . . But in doing so, it didn't necessarily endear me to my men. And I could not do anything about that except to [make a] covenant with God and my own self that I was going to be the one that would lead them when the time came."[3]

With the fixing of the date for the invasion, the diversions for the troops in Great Britain became fewer, and training took on a more serious, purposeful tone. Soldiers—new recruits and old sweats alike—were drilled constantly, both mentally and physically, in everything their commanders thought would save their lives and accomplish the mission. To toughen their bodies, the troops performed hundreds of hours of calisthenics and went on long, fatiguing, blister-filled marches, loaded down with full field gear. To heighten their instantaneous response to commands, the men practiced close-order drill for hours at a time. To help them tell the difference between a P-51 Mustang and an ME 109, or between a White half-track and an Sd Kfz 10, classes in aircraft and armored-vehicle recognition were repeated over and over. To sharpen their shooting eyes, the troops—everyone from the infantryman to the clerk and cook—spent uncounted hours on the rifle ranges improving their marksmanship. To steel their nerves, the men took part in numerous maneuvers conducted using live ammunition. To increase their chances of surviving a poison gas attack, the troops were re-introduced to their gas masks, and were issued woolen uniforms impregnated with an anti-gas chemical agent that felt greasy and smelled foul.*

*First Lieutenant James Watts recalled that the impregnated clothing wasn't the only foul-smelling thing. "We were all told by the medics that we were not to shower for a week before the invasion—we'd have more body heat in the water. I wore the same clothing until D-plus thirty; when I finally took it off, it could almost walk by itself."

To keep officers from being easily spotted and picked off by snipers, saluting at the front was discouraged, and outward signs of rank were removed; replacing them was a white vertical stripe painted on the rear of the helmet to designate an officer and a horizontal stripe to indicate a non-commissioned officer. To ensure the success of the mission (and, as yet, no one in the lower ranks knew the exact nature of the mission, nor when or where it would take place), soldiers were cross-trained in other specialties; riflemen were also taught how to use bazookas or flamethrowers or radios, radiomen learned to be riflemen again, and cannoneers were reintroduced to the M-1 Garand and carbine. Everything that could possibly be done to ensure survival in this most important of battles was being done at a fevered pace.[4]

"If a man went down, you were supposed to be able to take over his job," recalled Steve Kellman, of L Company, 16th Infantry. In addition to being completely familiar with his own rifle, Kellman also learned how to handle a flamethrower—once he learned how to stand up with it. "I was a six-footer and maybe 140 pounds, and when they put that flamethrower on my back, I almost went over backwards. We did that kind of training and we thought that, working as a team, there was a confidence there. If you did what you were supposed to do and were a part of the team, that made it a lot easier." He also noted, "You were apprehensive at the uncertainty of what was ahead of you. The other guys had been through it. But we ran those problems over and over and over again. We had photographs—eight-by-tens or even larger—of the beach we were going to land on. We practiced falling on barbed wire to mash it down so others could jump over it. With your rifle in front of you when you went down, you pressed the wire down and with your heavy uniform and the web gear and all the rest of that, you didn't get hurt."[5]

The rifles, machine guns, grenades, bayonets, flamethrowers, pistols, artillery pieces, and other weapons of war gave many soldiers a feeling of security, a sense that, if their life was in danger, at least they had the means with which to fight back. Three groups of men, however, would make the invasion without weapons. The best known of these were the medics—men trained to ignore their own safety while giving aid and comfort to their wounded and dying comrades in the midst of battle. Another group consisted of chaplains, who would brave the same dangers as the combat troops, minister to their fears, and give last rites to those who were dead or dying. Less heralded but no less exposed to death and disfigurement were the combat cameramen—soldiers assigned to Signal

Corps photographic units whose mission it was to record for posterity everything about war and army life, from the mundane to the molten-hot crucible of combat. Corporal Walter Halloran, a Signal Corps cinematographer from Minnesota, was assigned to accompany the 16th RCT to the beachhead with his 16mm Bell and Howell movie camera; he was destined to capture some of the most memorable pictures ever taken in combat.[6]

To prepare the Big Red One for its most important seaborne operation yet, the first week of May was spent splashing ashore at Slapton Sands, in an exercise named *Fabius I.* Navy Captain Harry Butcher, Ike's public relations officer and old friend, wrote, "I spent from Tuesday noon, May 2, until Saturday the sixth aboard the *Ancon*, largely in the operations room, watching the intricate task of direction of the amphibious landing of the U.S. 1st Division. . . . Yesterday the Commanders-in-Chief met, and Ike decided that D-Day would be Y plus 4 (Y-Day is June 1). On Y plus 4, 5, 6, and 7, the tides are right and the moon is full. H-Hour is yet to be set and may be staggered for different beaches, depending upon the nature and location of obstacles. The type which apparently will cause the most trouble is called 'Element C,' which is a gatelike structure of steel angles at the center. . . . [Unlike Exercise *Tiger*] *Fabius* developed no enemy reaction but we did get a heavy gale. One GI was hospitalized with pneumonia and a second lieutenant was shot accidentally in the buttock. We were 'snooped' by enemy aircraft on at least four occasions. . . . The Germans [have] been actively sowing mines in this area."[7]

Undaunted by the obvious danger from gales, mines, E-boats, and enemy aircraft, the 1st Infantry Division continued to train. Lieutenant Harold Monica, encamped at Camp Chickerell, near Weymouth, said, "A strenuous training program was in full swing covering use of the compass, weapons, tactical problems both night and day, and physical training. Each day started with a five-mile forced march from 0730 to 0830; any man more than a minute slow would be confined to quarters and not allowed to go to town that evening. When the troops found out that Captain [Sam] Carter was enforcing this, there were some interesting sprints to cover the last hundred yards. Somehow, it seemed as if everyone could make it. Who wanted Camp Chickerell when they could go to Weymouth, which was only four or five miles away?"[8]

Roger L. Brugger, from Clyde, Ohio, a private first class in K Company, 16th Infantry, noted, "From January to May, we went through four amphibious maneuvers and basic infantry tactics." Brugger said that the company, which was stationed at Abbottsbury, about nine miles from Weymouth, was divided into six boat sections of about thirty men each. "They had a machine gunner with an ammunition carrier, a 60mm mortar team, flame thrower, bazooka with ammo carrier, Bangalore torpedoes (tubes filled with explosives), pole charges (TNT on a pole), and satchel charges (TNT in a burlap satchel) to be used against pillboxes. The men wore assault jackets rather than a pack and cartridge belt. The assault jackets had several pockets and pouches for ammo and rations; we wore a lifebelt under the jacket. They also wore impregnated uniforms with an antigas compound in the fabric, and carried a gas mask in a rubberized bag."[9]

Fred Hall, now a captain and the operations officer of 2nd Battalion, 16th Infantry, recalled attending a momentous V Corps briefing. "We were officially informed we were to be part of the assault force in the invasion of Europe. I began to spend a substantial amount of time at regimental headquarters, under very tight security, writing the battalion battle order for the invasion. At the same time, we were reorganizing our infantry platoons into assault teams for the Normandy invasion and working on support and logistical plans. The assault teams consisted of about thirty men. Teams were variously armed with flamethrowers to use against pillboxes, Bangalore torpedoes to use to breach wire and other obstacles, bazookas as anti-tank weapons, automatic rifles, light machine guns, and 60mm mortars. This was a potent force. Each team was considered to be self-sufficient to penetrate the beach obstacles, including pillboxes, and with sufficient firepower to achieve its initial objective. The pace of training increased. In February 1944, we went to the Barnstable beaches in west England for assault-team training. We lived in pyramidal tents for two weeks in mud and rain. Later, we participated in amphibious landing maneuvers at Slapton Sands where live ammunition was used to lend reality to the landings. We were now provided with some maps and began to see fly-by photographs of the beach assault area, which was not yet to be identified."[10]

The main focus of the 1st Infantry Division's seven months in England continued to be the practice of amphibious landings. As John Baumgartner, the 16th Infantry's historian, wrote, "Actual landings were made from the type of craft to be used in the projected invasion. Vessels ran inshore under simulated fire, men charged into the water and up the beaches, across obstacles similar to those they expected to encounter in France, and worked their way inland."[11]

There were a number of specialized vessels whose purpose was getting men and matériel onto the enemy shore. The LCT, or Landing Craft, Tank, came in several sizes and could carry from three to nine tanks. The largest craft designed primarily to bring significant numbers of troops ashore was the LCI(L), or Landing Craft, Infantry, Large. This boat was half a football field in length and could carry 102 troops. The smallest craft were the LCVPs*—also known as Higgins boats, after their inventor and manufacturer, New Orleans boatbuilder Andrew Jackson Higgins. It was the LCVPs, piloted by Navy or Coast Guard coxswains, that would bring the first-wave troops to Normandy.[12]

For several weeks, the invasion force practiced climbing over the gunwales of larger ships, climbing down cargo nets (dubbed "scramble nets") draped over the sides of the ships, and descending into the LCVPs, then disembarking from the smaller craft and wading ashore. It was a dangerous business, especially when the sea was rough. Some soldiers slipped from the scramble nets and fell into the chilly sea. Sometimes, soldiers would mis-time their jump from the scramble net and fall into an LCVP that had slid into the low trough of a wave, injuring themselves and often the soldiers on whom they landed. On more than one occasion, soldiers were crushed between the hull of the larger ship and that of the LCVP when a wave caused the two craft to slam together.[13]

Even if one managed to safely enter an LCVP, there was no guarantee that one would exit it without incident. The troops were forever being cautioned to jump diagonally off the lowered ramp, rather than jumping forward, where the boat, caught by a wave, might surge forward and knock the men under water. And other men worried what would happen during the real thing, when the front ramp dropped and exposed them to enemy fire.

The diminutive Eddie Steeg, D Company, 18th Infantry, also recalled that, as the unannounced day for the invasion drew closer, the training became more strenuous, more serious, more purposeful. "Even with all of the prior amphibious training and the two actual landings we had previously experienced under enemy fire, we were still subjected to additional intensive training for what was yet to come. There was no let-up. We spent a lot of time on ships, and sometimes I wasn't sure if I was in the Army or the Navy. It seems that when we were not walking in the water, we were walking in the mud. In one case, however, we

* The LCVP (Landing Craft, Vehicles and Personnel) was the basic assault craft for American amphibious forces in the European and Pacific Theaters. The flat-bottomed, plywood-hulled boat could carry thirty-six troops, or twelve men and a jeep, or 8,100 pounds of cargo, and could run aground and refloat itself. It was open-topped and lightly armored, with just a steel ramp and a quarter-inch of steel plating on the sides. (Ambrose, pp. 43–46)

were in both at the same time. We had made another simulated landing and this time we continued inland for a forced march. We came upon this great-looking green field. It was the richest looking grass I had ever seen. As I stepped on the 'lawn,' I immediately sank down almost to my knees. Of course, my knees were closer to the ground than all of the other company GIs, so they didn't sink as much as I did. We had come upon an English moor covered, not with green grass, but rather with green moss, or peat, as it is called. I was certainly getting my education the hard way."[14]

The infantry regiments weren't the only ones preparing for battle; the 1st's supporting units also got in plenty of practice. Lieutenant Lawrence Johnson Jr., a forward observer with the 7th Field Artillery Battalion, recalled, "In addition to routine individual and unit training, the 7th conducted service practice at the Sennybridge artillery range in Wales and a full-dress invasion rehearsal at Slapton Sands in southwest England."[15]

Al Alvarez, C Battery, 7th Field Artillery, which would be supporting the 16th Infantry, recalled that his unit was always on the go. He reported, "We were constantly practicing assault landings with the [105mm] guns, vehicles, and equipment. Then marksmanship firing, lengthy foot marches, chemical warfare classes, aircraft identification and land mine warfare classes. The all-inclusive and time-consuming boat exercises involved loading and riding LCTs, wet landings at Slapton Sands, reconning our projected landing areas, finally selecting and occupying projected battery sites. Then load and return to camp. Now cleaning of equipment, formations, and inspections, then squeeze in time for eating and sleeping."[16]

Lieutenant James H. Watts was a platoon commander with A Company, 81st Chemical Mortar Battalion—a unit equipped with the 4.2-inch heavy mortar that could fire both high-explosive and white-phosphorus shells, and assigned to support the 2nd Battalion, 16th Infantry. He said, "The original plan was for us to provide mortar fire on the beaches as the naval gunfire lifted. We had been so trained at the Assault Training Center in southwestern England. We had spent months in preparation for this day, beginning with amphibious training in the United States and many maneuvers in England. The decision was later made not to use us in this fire-support role, but we were kept in the early landing waves, as originally planned, mostly about H+50 minutes."[17]

The combat engineers, too, were being primed for their upcoming role in the invasion. Lieutenant Colonel William B. Gara, commanding the 1st Engineer Combat Battalion, detailed his unit's specialized responsibilities: "Engineer troops

Lieutenant Colonel William B. Gara, commanding officer, 1st Engineer Combat Battalion. (Courtesy William Gara)

are highly trained. It takes a lot longer to train an engineer soldier than an infantryman—he's far more versatile. The engineers' job is specifically to do everything possible to advance the infantry units during the attack—remove obstacles, remove enemy mines, knock down walls, remove anything that would in any way interfere with the advance of an infantry element . . . [while] at the same time stand by and be ready to perform combat duty. When on the defense, it's precisely the opposite. The engineers install minefields, erect barbed wire, build walls, and build anti-tank ditches to prevent the enemy from reaching our lines. We are also placed alongside the infantry to serve in combat to defend."[18]

Assisting Force "O" and scheduled to land in early afternoon on D-Day was the U.S. Navy's 6th Beach Battalion. "What the hell is the Beach Battalion?" rhetorically asked one of its veterans, Jerome Alberts. "To start with, they are seamen, as in every naval organization—radiomen, corpsmen, signalmen, carpenters, boatswain mates, coxswains, shipfitters, and perhaps one or two other ratings that I can't think of at the present. . . . We are a small part of an amphibious operation. . . . Our job is running various beaches—through communications, clearing channels, bringing in amphibious craft, and last but hardly least, applying medical attention to those in need of it in the early stages of the campaign. . . .

"We knew pretty well that this was the real thing. We had been briefed; by the way, that means informed of landmarks, shown maps, and told how and where we are going to move. We had been on countless maneuvers, and this was the thing we had been waiting for. After six months of overseas duty, finally it was going to happen!"[19]

Another member of the 6th Beach Battalion, eighteen-year-old Navy corpsman Richard W. Borden, recalled an incident of horseplay that helped relieve some of the pre-invasion tension: "Through the rigors of training, I had endeared myself to my fellow comrades and certainly they to me. I smiled as I thought of my friend Eddie Johnson. He had strung me by the heels upside-down off a tree limb, my fingers six inches from the ground in friendly jest as the crew ambled off to chow—everybody laughing but me. All I had done was threaten to split the tongue of his pet rook (crow). It's crazy, but we had become a fighting unit."[20]

As sharp as most of the troops were becoming, some did not reach the standards their commanders had set. Lieutenant Colonel Francis J. "Frank" Murdoch, the new commander of the 1st Battalion, 26th Infantry, recalled that General Huebner reminded him that "the combat soldier tends to get tired and bored, sloppy about procedures and maintenance, and he may not want to work hard when the pressure is off. . . . Soon after I took over, I called for a showdown inspection, a full layout of equipment in all companies. In general, all companies were in excellent shape except one, where both the equipment and the soldiers were sloppy. So I told them I would re-inspect. When I did so, there was little improvement; the attitude of the company commander was, 'I am a combat soldier, and the hell with this.' [The company commander was relieved of duty.] General Huebner was a stickler for attention to military detail. He emphasized maintenance and zero[ing in] of rifles, and rifle marksmanship. He also had us put in a lot of work on night attacks and night patrolling. . . . During our first exercises in England, I noticed a tendency not to take training seriously, to sort of slop through exercises, and the discipline was not too good. Well, that meant they needed an SOB to get them ready for the landing. When they did

Captain Kimball R. Richmond (left), commanding officer of I Company, 16th Infantry Regiment, discusses the maneuvers being observed by Lieutenant General Omar Bradley (second from left), Brigadier General Willard G. Wyman, assistant division commander, and Lieutenant Colonel Charles T. Horner Jr., commander of the 3rd Battalion. Photo taken 11 April 1944, near Dorchester, England. (Courtesy Colonel Robert R. McCormick Research Center of the 1st Infantry Division Museum at Cantigny)

not do an exercise correctly, I kept them in the field until they did, even if that meant staying out another twelve hours in the cold and wet."[21]

For some soldiers, it only took the occasional tragic training accident to hammer home the deadly nature of their upcoming assignment. "We were on board a ship and making a practice landing at the Dartmouth Naval Firing Ground," recalled Steve Kellman, "when some of the live rounds the Navy was firing fell short near our boat. A fellow in my LCVP was hit and killed. It was quite a shock, and brought the reality of what was ahead of us to the forefront."[22]

For others, the belief that the time for the invasion was drawing near manifested itself by the increasingly frequent appearances by members of the high command. "We started to get visits by all the big brass, like Montgomery and Bradley," recalled Louis Newman, Cannon Company, 18th Infantry, "and our own division commander made a speech to us. We were the most experienced division as far as combat was concerned, and Bradley picked the best people he could get—the most experienced—and we were."[23]

Steve Kellman remembered, "One time, General Montgomery came to address us. He got up on a jeep and said we weren't there to spend a warm winter by the fireside—we were training for the difficult job ahead. The veterans who went through North Africa and Sicily kept saying, 'Why the hell does it have to be *us* again? We've done our share. What about the 29th Division? They've been sitting on their butts in England for two years.' It wasn't that we were shirking the job; it was just that the 1st had been bloodied twice before and we felt that perhaps it was someone else's turn."[24]

Lieutenant Colonel William Gara recalled another encounter with Montgomery. "In mid-April, we get the word to load on busses and trucks—officers only. We have no idea where we are going. About four hours later, we arrive at a theater with officers from all the other 1st Division units. We're milling around in the theater—a lot of smoking, a lot of talking, and then we see a little guy come up on the stage and stand in the middle. Doesn't say a word. Somebody spots him and says, 'That's Montgomery.' He doesn't say anything. There was no yell for 'attention.' He waited for three or four minutes and then the theater was so quiet you could hear a pin drop. He waited for everyone to recognize him. And then he tells us about the plans solely to instill the confidence in these troops that everything has been handled: 'We know what we're going to do—we've been working for months—we have the forces—we have four thousand ships—we have two and a half million tons of supplies for this invasion—we have one and a half million men—we're going to take Fortress Europe and here's how we're going to do it. Fortress Europe reminds me of the department store Harrod's. Everything they have is in the window. We're going to break through the window and find out they have nothing in inventory, nothing in the storeroom. And we're going to go all the way to the Siegfried Line* and we're going to get there probably in late September.'"[25]

---

*The Siegfried Line, formally known as the *Westwall*, was a defensive line of pillboxes, bunkers, concrete tank obstacles, and other fortifications the Germans had constructed to prevent, or at least hamper, an invasion along Germany's western borders.

Despite his overwhelming duties and crushing schedule, General Eisenhower, the Supreme Allied Commander, refused to isolate himself from the men who had been chosen to carry out the invasion plans. Theodore G. "Ted" Aufort, a New Yorker, a veteran of North Africa and Sicily, and a sergeant with Headquarters, 1st Battalion, 16th Infantry, never forgot the day Ike paid a visit to his unit: "About the fourth day in camp, we got a real surprise. General Eisenhower came walking into the area. Everyone started saluting but he insisted that we be at ease. We formed a circle around him. He laid the whole bill of fare on us: we were going to land by sea on the coast of France, a place called Normandy. I know my heart was pounding like crazy; I wanted to know a million details. I guess everyone there did, also. He was way ahead of us and explained that all the officers and NCOs would be briefed and could relay all information to our men. He then saluted us and said, 'Good luck,' turned, and left. No doubt he had many areas such as ours to call upon. Shortly thereafter, all NCOs were called into a large tent for instructions and briefings. There we were told what our objectives were and what to expect on Normandy. And we were also told a lot of men would die."[26]

The exact nature of the operation for which the 1st and the other assault divisions were being prepared continued to be a well-guarded secret. Captain Joe Dawson, who would play a key role in the invasion, recalled that his 200-man G Company, 16th Infantry, was down to 125 men when it returned to England from Sicily. It was quickly brought up to full strength by the addition of replacements. Dawson said, "[General Huebner] was a superb officer and . . . was able to . . . obtain the best talent he possibly could get from the things that were available and the replacement pools. And we insisted on trying to get the men with the highest standards of intelligence and knowledge and ability and physical characteristics, and that was what we did. We filled up . . . with that kind of men."[27]

Philadelphian Ray Klawiter was one of the green replacements who had never before been under fire. A private first class, he was sent to England in January 1944 and ended up in Weymouth in the 18th Infantry's heavy-weapons D Company. Klawiter recalled that General Huebner made a strong impression on him: "We called him General Hobnails—man, he was strict, a real disciplinarian. He believed in a lot of training to get you prepared, and he did a good job in that. The men loved Terry Allen, but they say he was easy." Asked about his state of mind during the buildup, Klawiter replied, "You try to forget what it's going to be like. But when you see the veterans of North Africa and Sicily, they were all

Private First Class Ray Klawiter, D Company, 18th Infantry Regiment. (Courtesy Ray Klawiter)

nerved up because they went through something like that before. So you know it's going to be scary."[28]

Although the soldiers' days were full of training, marksmanship, drilling, cleaning weapons, and maneuvers, there was still time for the diversions that keep a man sane: sports, visiting village pubs, meeting the locals (especially the girls), writing letters home, listening to records, watching movies, and just thinking. To keep his mind off the upcoming invasion, Eddie Steeg, for one, had time to ponder some of life's imponderables, such as "dog tags": "Dog tags. Why were they called 'dog tags'?" he wanted to know. "Because we were known as 'dogfaces'? Why 'dogfaces'? Did the name 'dogfaces' come from the fact that we were issued dog-tags, or did the word 'dog-tags' come from the fact we were called dogfaces? According to my limited research, the gas mask in World War One was called a 'dogface'; hence, a soldier was to become known as a dogface when wearing one, and I assume that everyone with or without a gas mask all answered to that name."

Since Steeg was but five feet two inches tall (or less), he also pondered the size of the equipment he was issued. "My backpack was the same size as everyone else's. Why didn't I have a smaller pup tent, making my load lighter? Why a 'pup' tent? Because we were dogfaces? Why not a 'dog tent'? Were they only meant to shelter puppy-size dogfaces like me?" His questions would go unanswered. As the unknown date for the invasion crept inexorably closer, the usual happy-go-lucky Steeg found himself worrying. "Worry is always there until the action begins, then the sheer fright takes over and all the worry has been for naught. I learned to concentrate on only what I was doing at any particular time. Could I keep up with the rest? Would I pass inspection? Would I stay awake on guard duty? Could I hold another beer? Did I have room for seconds at chow? Plus many other limitless and important things. Still, the thought of the impending invasion of France was a worry that persisted. It just wouldn't go away."[29]

Worry wasn't confined to the enlisted men. While strolling through Weymouth one day, a few weeks before the invasion, Nelson Park, a twenty-three-year-old first lieutenant in C Company, 18th Infantry, from Montebello, California, ran into a former University of Idaho classmate and fellow lieutenant, John S. Kersey. Kersey was in the 16th Infantry and was a veteran of the fighting in both North Africa and Sicily. "As we walked back to our camp," Park recalled, "John told me not to worry about the landing because you simply walked ashore, as he had done in the orderly landings in Africa and Sicily."*[30]

Kersey may have been merely trying to calm his friend's nerves, for the earlier landings had been anything but "orderly." William Gara recalled that, during an amphibious combat assault, "You're very hesitant, you have all kinds of apprehensions. You no sooner land on shore than you see some of the dead of your own people, and you hear people crying, 'Medic! Medic!' It's a hair-raising experience but you get over that rather quickly. You gather your forces; you've been well-trained on what to do."[31]

Like most youth who view themselves as immortal, Al Alvarez, 7th Artillery, managed to maintain a worry-free outlook on the upcoming operation, and couldn't wait to get to France. "I thought I was smart, young, and now, with these 1st Division vets, well trained. I was INDESTRUCTIBLE!!! Bring on those French gals!"[32]

---

*Kersey would be killed during the invasion.

Betting on the day of the invasion became a popular pastime for many of the men. Eddie Steeg remembered, "Rumors were rampant and numerous, and a pool was started to determine the actual date of the invasion. It was decided that the topkick* should hold the money. Then there was a lively discussion as to the best way to protect him to insure a payoff. I suggested that I should hold the money and everyone else try to convince the company commander to arrange for me to stay in England until the shooting had died down and it was safe; then I would deliver the money. Needless to say, this did not go over with a very big bang. It was decided that the topkick would hold the money and everyone would be responsible for his protection until the payoff. Along with some others, I selected July 4th as invasion day. This lottery payoff became the only positive thing to look forward to as we approached the coming invasion."[33]

During what little free time they had, the men would lounge on their bunks in their tents, barracks, and Quonset huts and "shoot the breeze"—talk of their life back in the States and how it was that they ended up in uniform. Staff Sergeant Joseph E. Nichols, from Albany, New York, a member of the 16th Infantry's Intelligence and Recon Platoon, was proud of his family's past service in the Revolutionary and Civil Wars. "I didn't want to be a 'draftee.' I felt honored to enlist and serve my country 'on my own.' Five of us, old school buddies, went together and enlisted. We felt it was the noble thing to do. I couldn't wait to get into uniform. . . . Someone has to volunteer, and I liked to try something new and exciting."[34]

Bob Hilbert, a buck sergeant from Denver, assigned to K Company, 18th Infantry, impressed many new replacements with his unique tale: He had been captured by the Germans in North Africa, but the ship taking him to a prisoner-of-war camp in Germany was bombed and ran aground in the harbor at Tunis. Regaining his freedom, Hilbert went on to fight with the division in the Sicily campaign.[35]

Staff Sergeant William D. Behlmer, Anti-Tank Company, 16th Infantry, recalled he had not minded being drafted. "Somebody had to [fight]—why not me? [I was] young and healthy with no wife or kids and [was] mad about Pearl Harbor."[36]

Louis Newman, Cannon Company, 18th Infantry, had been a shipping clerk and part-time high school student in Brooklyn before the war. He had enlisted

*Slang for the company first sergeant.

in 1940 and joined the 1st, which was stationed at that time at Fort Wadsworth on Staten Island. After a year in the service, he was discharged on 14 October 1941. A week later, he joined the Enlisted Reserve Corps because he was told he might be drafted. On Sunday, 7 December, Newman was taking a nap during his lunch period at the Department of Mental Hygiene of the State of New York, where he was employed. "One of the nurses came over and started to wake me up. She said, 'Pearl Harbor has just been bombed.' I said, 'Go away. Let me finish my nap.' She came back and woke me up again. I chased her back to the office."

He finally turned on a radio and got confirmation of the attack. "At first, I thought it was another Orson Welles hoax.* Then I realized it was true. I lived in Brooklyn and I immediately went home and got my uniform out and had it cleaned and pressed because I thought I'd get called up the next day." He was a few weeks off; on 22 January, the Army gave him six days to report for active duty.[37]

One member of the division was a celebrity of sorts, having actually fired at Japanese planes during the attack on Pearl Harbor. William T. Dillon, a second lieutenant with A Company, 16th Infantry, noted that in October 1940, with no job, no money, and no prospects, he had enlisted in the Army and, as a private first class, was eventually assigned to the 25th Infantry Division at Schofield Barracks, Hawaii. He related that, on that day of infamy, a Corporal Hicks and he "were up and about at 7:30 a.m. when the Japs flew over. I was a machine gunner and Hicks was the loader. We ran three or four boxes [of ammunition] through the gun on the first strike. The three battleships that I remember were the *Arizona, Oklahoma*, and *West Virginia*. They were in direct view across the water about a quarter mile away. The *Oklahoma* turned turtle, the *West Virginia* was smashed up, and the *Arizona* stayed up, burning and exploding for several hours. . . . The next day I saw a small boat with several men climb onto the *Oklahoma* with stethoscopes and hammers and pound on the hull, then listen with the stethoscopes. A barge with a cutting torch came out and cut a hole in the ship's belly, which was up, and out came thirty or thirty-two sailors, all alive."[38]

However, not everyone in the Big Red One was a willing volunteer, eager for combat. A mortarman from Cleveland, Private First Class Ralph A. Berry Sr., M

---

*Actor Welles and his Mercury Radio Theater troupe had panicked much of the nation on Halloween eve, 1938, with a startlingly realistic-sounding radio drama about an invasion of Earth by Martians.

Company, 16th Infantry, who had been drafted at age twenty-seven, had plenty of gripes for anyone who would listen. "It was not fair. I had a year-old son and [I was] paying on our new home."*[39]

During the waiting period, some men found themselves inadvertently getting into trouble. Private First Class Simon S. Hurwit of New York City, a member of K Company, 16th Infantry, remembered, "I was told to get a jeep at the motor pool and drive a warrant officer to see his girlfriend. After he left, I was arrested and court-martialed for having a girl in the jeep. It was [regimental commander] Colonel Taylor's jeep I had used."[40]

Captain Everett L. Booth, commanding officer of K Company, 16th Infantry, recalled that "two of my men were caught by the MPs urinating in the doorway of the Weymouth Electric Shop late one night. I was relieved of my command because I didn't control my men. My replacement was killed on the beach. He was replaced by one of the stand-bys from the States who turned out to be a yo-yo. I had my company back shortly thereafter."[41]

Eventually, as they always must in war, the slack times ended. In late April, with joint Army-Navy maneuvers concluded, the entire southern coast of England, including the ports and camps that were now bulging with troops primed for the invasion, was placed off-limits to all but essential visitors on official business. John Bistrica, a member of C Company, 16th Infantry, from Youngstown, Ohio, recalled that when his unit was moved from their billets at Lyme Regis to the marshaling area, "the people of Lyme Regis turned out to cheer the soldiers as they left early in the morning."[42]

All troops were "sealed" into camouflaged marshaling areas known as "sausages," so named because of the elongated shapes of the encampments drawn on maps. No one could come or go; soon, outgoing mail was cut off. (There was, of course, no such thing then as the Internet or, for the ordinary GI, a trans-Atlantic phone call.) Two thousand CIC (Counter-Intelligence Corps) troops guarded the invasion-bound soldiers as closely as if they were armed and

---

* Berry's gripes notwithstanding, he went on to distinguish himself during the war; he was awarded the Bronze Star with four Oak Leaf Clusters. In other words, Berry performed five acts of heroism worthy of the Bronze Star.

Technical Sergeant Allen Towne, B Company, 1st Medical Battalion. Photo taken 27 August 1944 near Melun, France. (Courtesy Allen Towne)

dangerous Nazi prisoners. There would be no more pub visits; no more meeting girls; no more trips to London for theater; no more tastes of civilian life; no more mock amphibious assaults. The next landing would be the real thing.

Medic Allen Towne remembered that orders directing his unit to move from its encampment at Cattistock to the secure "sausages" near Broadmayne came on 25 April. He did not especially like his new home: "We were behind barbed-wire enclosures. We could not leave the area because of security. We were not supposed to talk with anyone about our activities because there could be German spies in the area." The camp evidently was near a P-38 fighter-bomber base, for Towne could hear the twin-boom warplanes warming up their engines and then taking to the sky. "There must have been a target range nearby because I could hear planes bombing. I believe they were practicing coming in from the ocean and bombing the beaches."[43]

Captain Fred Hall, Operations Officer for the 2nd Battalion, 16th Infantry, recalled, "We moved into our marshaling areas where we were quarantined until the invasion. We were in a stand of trees surrounded by a barbed-wire fence. Security was tight. We were housed in tents, with foxholes nearby. There was a fair amount of air activity—strafing, bombing, and anti-aircraft fire—but none hit our area. We now broke out our unit invasion orders, maps, and photographs and briefed our battalion officers and non-coms with the help of a sand table [scale model of the invasion area]. Soon the other members of the battalion were briefed."[44]

Sergeant Ted Aufort, Headquarters, 1st Battalion, 16th Infantry, said that his unit's bivouac area was heavily forested and packed with hardware. "Tanks, half tracks, heavy artillery—every conceivable type of armament was placed under those trees. Tents were up and all over the place. Every nook and cranny was utilized in some way. We were strictly confined to the area; no one was allowed in or out. Rumors followed like crazy. But everyone knew this was *it*. 'When' and 'where' was anybody's guess."[45]

Sergeant John B. Ellery remembered that, in the sausages, "We lived in pyramidal tents. The weather was good, and so was the food. Many hours were spent studying a model of our invasion area. . . . It was impressive and exciting. The briefing officers were bright, articulate, and thoroughly confident. I was convinced that we would take the beach, but that we would leave a lot of casualties in our wake, and I was right about that."[46]

Private First Class Louis Newman, Cannon Company, 18th Infantry, said, "Once we were secluded, we started to get information. We didn't know exactly where we were going, but they started to get out maps and they showed us plans for Normandy and they showed us landmarks that we should recognize where we were going to land. This was my third landing, so I had sort of gotten adjusted to it. I was looking forward to getting it all over with. The thought didn't bother me as much as the first invasion we had going in against the French in North Africa. I was an old hand at it, but it didn't turn out to be exactly like the first or second one; this one turned out to be horrible."[47]

Second Lieutenant William T. Dillon, A Company, 16th Infantry, recalled being impressed by promises that enemy positions at Omaha Beach would be obliterated before the infantry even reached the shore. "The air general said we'd have 144 fighters over us at all times. As many as a thousand bombers would do their work beforehand. Everything would be blasted to smithereens—a push over! The Navy admiral said that four battleships with sixteen-inch guns would blow everything off the map—pillboxes, artillery, mortars, and the barbed wire entanglements. The combat engineer colonel said they'd be in a couple of hours ahead of us and take out the Teller mine ramps so the LCVPs could take us right up on the beach. The amphibious-tanks colonel said thirty-two tanks would make the landing with us. The *Sam Chase* captain knew we'd had to wade ashore in Africa and Sicily but this time he promised that we wouldn't even get our shoe soles wet."[48]

The 6th Beach Battalion's Jerome Alberts remembered feeling that all would be under control by the time his unit hit the beach, sometime in early afternoon.

"Well, for gosh sakes, there won't be any action," he worried. "We will probably walk in. . . . the crack 1st Division should have the Krauts battling for Paris by the time we get in!"[49]

On the other hand, Captain Robert E. Murphy, from Maine, commanding H Company, 18th Infantry, had a more realistic assessment of what to expect. "I don't think there was any question in our minds but that it was going to be a really tough proposition, because rumors had been going for quite some time that [the Germans] were fortifying the coast. But I don't think there was any doubt in anybody's mind that we would prevail. I knew that it would be as good a show as we could put on." Much of Murphy's confidence stemmed from the quality of troops who would be going ashore. "When I was a platoon leader of D Company, my platoon sergeant had been in the 1st Division in World War *One*! A number of the NCOs had had a lot of training. We had a lot of professional soldiers. . . . And that first draft in the fall of '40, they were all sharp kids. I think we were about as ready for war as anyone could be."[50]

Locked up behind barbed-wire enclosures, and watched over by stern-faced military policemen, the only thing left for the soldiers to do was physical conditioning, cleaning and re-cleaning their weapons, inspecting and re-inspecting their equipment, and studying and re-studying a huge, scale model of the Normandy coast that had been constructed and kept under armed guard in a locked building. Ray Klawiter recalled, "They had a room set up with a big model of the Normandy area—it took up the whole room. It had everything on it—the cliffs, the pillboxes, roads—everything."[51] While the men were not told exactly which part of the French coast the model represented, they were required to memorize every beach, cliff, field, road, enemy position, and town depicted on it, as if their lives—and the success of the mission itself—depended on it.

"A relief model had been made," said Lieutenant Harold Monica, "showing the beaches, the embankments, fields, villages, small streams, and even single houses to approximately six miles inland. Low-level aircraft pictures of beach obstacles were supplied to us daily. At first, we had a rigid schedule to be sure each platoon had time to see the model. Soon, squad leaders, platoon sergeants with small groups of men could come and go as desired. [Battalion commander] Colonel [Bob] York and staff were there most of the time to answer questions and deal with concerns any of the men had. Some good ideas surfaced and were incorporated into the battalion attack plan. We were soon advised of our D-Day objective, approximately four miles inland. Orders to every man and

Low-level aerial photograph showing German beach defenses in Normandy. This is a view of Utah Beach; the defenses at Omaha Beach were similar. Photo taken 6 May 1944, exactly one month before D-Day. (Courtesy Colonel Robert R. McCormick Research Center of the 1st Infantry Division Museum at Cantigny)

small units were, 'Should you become separated from your squad, platoon, or company, you are to proceed to your objective regardless.' The same order was issued to the 16th Infantry, 26th Infantry, and balance of the 18th Infantry. It became obvious to us that the object was to get a beachhead at any cost."[52] Every effort was made to prevent German spies or reconnaissance flights from noticing the buildup, which would tip off the enemy that the invasion was about to take place. Vast supply dumps and vehicle parks were sited beneath groves of trees or covered by acres of camouflage netting. Where the Allies wanted the Germans to think Patton's fictitious army was gathering for the invasion across

Vast stocks of anti-aircraft guns fill an English field prior to the invasion. Scenes like this were common all over England and Wales. (Courtesy U.S. Army Military History Institute)

from the Pas de Calais, just the opposite was done; vehicles were parked in the open, or driven back and forth to simulate increased traffic. Not all the vehicles were real, either; propmakers from English movie studios fabricated dummy inflatable tanks, trucks, and landing craft that looked, from a distance, astonishingly like the real thing. But would the Germans be fooled?[53]

As D-Day drew nearer, visible evidence that the invasion was imminent was stacked, piled, and lined up in neat rows throughout southern England. "Equipment, ammunition, artillery shells, and gasoline in five-gallon jerry cans were piled everywhere," recalled Harold Monica. "Trucks, half-tracks, howitzers, jeeps, and tanks were lined up in the fields, and artillery and mortar shells in stacks of 100–150 lined both sides of roads at fifty-yard intervals—convenient for future truck loading but dispersed in case of enemy attack. Word got out, if the Americans didn't leave soon, the island of England was going to sink from the load."[54]

While the men readied their weapons, vehicles, too, needed to be prepared for the mission ahead. Although military trucks, half-tracks, and jeeps are normally capable of operating in relatively deep water, some extra preparation was required. The main modification needed was the addition of exhaust extensions that would enable the vehicles to travel almost entirely submerged while their engines' exhaust was vented above the water. The tanks, too, required a large exhaust housing to be constructed on the back deck, behind the turret. A tankman from Calumet City, Illinois, Technician Ed Ireland of B Company, 745th Tank Battalion, recalled the process of waterproofing a tank. "There was a real heavy clay, like putty, and all the cracks and crevices and anything that would let water in, we went at."[55] Despite their best efforts, most of the crewmen of the amphibious tanks would soon discover that their efforts were for naught.

Time was growing short. The moment of truth was drawing near. The men were ready to go, ready to invade France, ready to get the war over with. General Omar Bradley observed, "By May 31, more than a quarter-million ground troops were waiting in their sausages—primed, briefed, and ready for The Day."[56]

Everything possible had been done to prepare the men of the 1st Infantry Division and the attached 29th Division regiments for the all-important, top-secret mission. As the very tip of the spearhead, they had been sharpened to a fine point. On their shoulders lay the success or failure of the entire invasion—and perhaps the future of the free world—but they would not be alone in their efforts. They would be supported by hundreds of thousands more soldiers, sailors, and airmen. They had the finest food, equipment, medical care, and clothing that money could buy. They had the best tactical and scientific brains that the Army, Navy, and Air Corps could assemble: men who had thought through every possibility, every contingency, and who had come up with a solid, workable plan, as close to foolproof as possible. They had at their disposal an entire fleet of warships, thousands of aircraft, and a tremendous arsenal of virtually every type of modern weapon. They had the hopes and prayers of their families and the entire free world behind them.

But nothing—not even their seven months of grueling training in England, two previous amphibious assault landings, and months of combat experience—could truly prepare the men of the Big Red One for the ordeal that lay ahead.

CHAPTER FOUR

"Rommel Had Thoroughly Muddled Our Plans"

A STRONG breeze was coming in off the English Channel, as it does at almost every day of the year. The April day was bright but chilly—cold enough to require *Generalfeldmarschall* Erwin Rommel and the covey of staff officers that fluttered around him to don their field-gray suede gloves and greatcoats that hung almost to their ankles. As he stood on the bluff overlooking the five-mile stretch of beach the Allies had named "Omaha," Rommel's sharp eye took in the sweating work parties on the beach below him, missing nothing.

The sounds of digging were everywhere. Thousands of German soldiers, Eastern "volunteers," and conscripted French laborers were working feverishly to complete the defensive system before the Allies launched their long-awaited invasion of Europe. Some of the men were busy improving the fighting trenches that snaked through the dunes just beyond the beachhead and connected one position to another. Other men, wearing heavy leather gauntlets, were gingerly uncoiling great hoops of barbed wire and attaching it to metal stakes driven into the sandy soil. Near the base of the bluff where Rommel and his entourage were standing, soldiers with axes and machetes worked to clear brush that might be used to conceal invaders. Here and there, details of troops were planting minefields by the score. Rommel knew that soldiers feared mines more than they feared artillery or machine guns, and he wanted mines planted in great profusion.

Still other troops—many bare-chested and perspiring from their labors despite the chilly day—were manhandling logs and emplacing them at acute

Field Marshal Erwin Rommel (right) inspects concrete obstacles being constructed in Normandy, April 1944. (Courtesy U.S. Army Military History Institute)

angles at the water's edge as a way of blocking the passage of Allied landing craft. Farther from shore, Rommel could see teams of draft horses dragging huge, gatelike structures across the wet sand and setting them in neat rows. To his right and left, giant cement mixers ground noisily away as members of *Organization Todt,* Nazi Germany's construction arm, poured yard after yard of liquid concrete into wooden molds that had been nailed together in the shape of bunkers and casemates and pillboxes. On already-completed bunkers, soldiers were draping camouflage netting over concrete that had been painted in broad stripes of earth tones.

Among the swarming herd of workers, more than one sweating soldier undoubtedly glanced up briefly at the tiny cluster of officers atop the bluff and muttered a quiet epithet at the man who was never satisfied at the millions of man-hours that had already been expended to turn this once-peaceful stretch of French coastline into one of the most heavily fortified patches of real estate on the planet.

As Hitler's "favorite general," Rommel had been given the task of preventing the Allies from invading France. He had built his reputation on the boldness of his attacks; the swiftness of his mobile forces; and the surprise of his tactics. Now he was being asked to become a master of static, defensive warfare, an assignment that went against the very grain of his aggressive nature. But, like the dutiful soldier he was, he threw himself wholeheartedly into this assignment, for he knew the fate of Germany hinged on how well he and his men performed.

Rommel became obsessed with stopping any invasion at the water's edge, to create such chaos and carnage that the only enemy troops to actually reach French soil would be dead ones, washed ashore by the tides and waves. To accomplish this, he planned to construct a "defense in depth" unlike anything the world had ever seen.

His plan called for a line of virtually impenetrable obstacles to keep landing craft away from the shore. Farthest from the beach—some 800 feet out from the high-water mark—were particularly nasty devices known as "Element C" or "Belgian Gates." Hundreds of these steel barricades—ten feet high and ten feet wide—were designed to impale landing craft on three vertical masts, causing death and destruction when the boat contacted the anti-tank mines strapped atop the vertical beams. At high tide, these obstacles would be just under water—and invisible to approaching craft.

The next row of obstacles consisted of heavy logs (*hemmbalken*) sunk into the sand, topped with mines, and angled at thirty to forty degrees to lift landing craft bodily out of the water. Even if the mine did not explode, Rommel had jagged steel plates attached to the logs to slice open the bottom of any LCVP unlucky enough to ride over them. Complementing these mined poles were other obstacles, made of steel and shaped like an inverted "V" and designed to rip open the hull of any landing craft like a can opener removing the end of a tin of beans. As with the Belgian Gates, these obstacles were all but invisible at high tide.

Nearest the shore were tens of thousands of obstacles known as "Czech hedgehogs" or "horned scullies"—three steel bars welded together and topped with mines. These originally had been made by the French and used as road blocks—road blocks that had failed to stop German tanks as they rolled into France in 1940. Rommel had stripped the French-German border of these hedgehogs and had them hauled to Normandy, where he hoped they would do a better job of stopping American and British boats than they had his panzers.

Interlacing all of the obstacles were strands of barbed wire designed to snag soldiers wading ashore and hold them up long enough for German machine gunners and riflemen to pick them off like ducks in a shooting gallery. If, by some miracle, a few struggling soldiers actually made it to the beach, they would find no safe havens, for the beaches were carpeted with hundreds of thousands of land mines and fenced off with miles of concertina wire. There was a fiendish array of explosive devices planted in the sands of Omaha Beach—Teller mines, box mines, "S" mines (also known as "Bouncing Betties," which would spring into the air when tripped and explode at groin height), French "buttercup" mines, pencil mines, mustard pots, butterflies, rock fougasses, T-mines, *tschechenagel* (literally, "Czech nails"—iron spikes sunk into concrete blocks), *beton teträder* (mined tetrahedrons fitted into concrete obstacles), and wooden and glass mines impossible to find with conventional mine detectors.

Even all that was not enough for Rommel, for behind the minefields and barbed wire were interconnected trenches; one-man concrete foxholes; machine-gun nests; stout pillboxes with embrasures for machine guns and small artillery pieces; and huge, well-camouflaged gun emplacements designed to hold Germany's most formidable artillery pieces. While many of the gunports faced out to sea, others were sited parallel to the water's edge, so that any invader who reached the shore alive would be caught in a murderous, enfilading crossfire. The few roads that led from the beach to the high ground above were blocked by anti-tank obstacles, all covered by preregistered artillery, mortars, and machine guns. For his *coup de grace*, Rommel also planned to have automatic flamethrowers installed that would roast any attackers who made it beyond the shoreline.[1]

Allied planners worried that the Nazis were also scheming to unleash a number of other unpleasant surprises on the invaders, including V–1 rockets, poison gas, and oil on the water that would be ignited to incinerate the landing force. The British and Americans were also reasonably sure that the Germans would attempt to disrupt the landings with whatever air and naval power they could muster. Perhaps even the rumored Nazi atomic bomb would be unleashed—no one could be certain. But one thing *was* certain: No invading army in history ever faced a more daunting challenge.

Erwin Johannes Eugen Rommel had no dearth of personal bravery, for he was a commander who always preferred to lead from the front rather than issuing directives from the safety of the rear. Born on 15 November 1891, in Heidenheim, near Ulm, Rommel became an officer in 1912 despite the stigma of

A German beach obstacle known as "Element C" or a "Belgian Gate," reinforced with logs. (Courtesy Colonel Robert R. McCormick Research Center of the 1st Infantry Division Museum at Cantigny)

being born to a humble schoolteacher rather than to a career officer of the aristocratic Prussian *Junker* class. As a lieutenant in World War I, Rommel earned Germany's highest decoration, the *Pour le Merit,* during the combat in the Alps. After Hitler came to power in 1933, Rommel was detailed to head his personal bodyguard, the *Leibstandarte Adolf Hitler,* where he became devoted to the dictator because of Hitler's boldness in rebuilding the German military machines in the face of international prohibitions. In turn, Rommel became Hitler's favorite general, partly because he was not one of the Prussian aristocrats around whom the ex-corporal felt insecure and uncomfortable.

Rommel was promoted to major general in August 1939. A week later, war with Poland broke out and Hitler gave Rommel his choice of combat commands; Rommel chose the 7th Panzer Division. The division suited him perfectly, and he whipped the unit into fighting shape in a matter of three months. On 10 May 1940, Rommel led his men—the so-called "Ghost Division," for its seeming ability to materialize out of thin air where least expected—as part of the spearhead of the invasion. In fewer than ten days, 7th Panzer helped drive a wedge between the French and the British Expeditionary Force, thus forcing the British to head for Dunkerque—and retreat to England. With the British *hors de combat,* Rommel turned his division westward and rushed toward Cherbourg, traveling more than 200 miles in two days; the city surrendered to him on 19 June and France capitulated on 22 June. During the six-week campaign, Rommel's division captured nearly 100,000 prisoners.[2]

Meanwhile, Italian dictator Benito Mussolini, while attempting to restore the martial glory of the ancient Roman Empire, had made a hash of things when he tried to oust a small British garrison from Egypt. In December 1940, a quarter million Italians attacked 30,000 British—and were promptly routed, with 130,000 of their number taken prisoner. It was a humiliating defeat for Italy and Fascism. In response, in early 1941, Hitler sent Rommel, just promoted to lieutenant general, and the newly formed *Afrika Korps* to reinforce or, rather, take over from the Italians who had lost their nerve and confidence.

No sooner had he arrived in Libya than Rommel proved himself a wily adversary and earned the respectful nickname, "the Desert Fox," from his British foes. In twelve days, the Germans pushed the British back to Tobruk and laid siege to the fortress city. The British stubbornly resisted, then mounted their own counteroffense.

Always outnumbered and short on supplies and matériel, the resourceful Rommel gave as good as he got—and sometimes better. Had it not been for Hitler's greatest blunder—the invasion of the Soviet Union in June 1941—the Germans might actually have won World War II. The slaughterhouse that the Eastern Front became would eventually impact Germany's ability to wage war on the other fronts. Rommel was convinced that, had not Hitler invaded Russia, his forces in Africa could have been sufficiently reinforced and defeated the British, thus opening the way for Germany to conquer the resource-rich lands of the Middle East. Rommel wrote, "Our demands for additional formations were refused on the grounds that with the huge demand for transport which the Eastern Front was making on Germany's limited production capacity, the creation of further motorized units for Africa was out of the question."[3] The inevitable result was that German and Italian forces in Africa were doomed.

By December 1941, the British were regaining lost territory and inflicting serious casualties on the *Afrika Korps*, but Rommel was far from defeated; in January 1942, the *Afrika Korps* became part of *Panzerarmee Afrika* and Rommel launched a counterattack that stymied the British offensive.

The war of attrition eventually swung in favor of the British, and supply problems became Rommel's Achilles's heel. With British strength increasing and his own supplies dwindling, Rommel called off a planned offensive and went over to the defense. Confronting Hitler with the dire situation faced by *Panzerarmee Afrika*, Rommel boldly informed his Führer that, without major assistance, North Africa was as good as lost. Hitler did not like bad news so, on 22 September 1942, an ill and exhausted Rommel was relieved of command.

While he recuperated in Germany and impatiently awaited a new assignment, Rommel couldn't help but ponder the potential consequences of Japan's attack on Pearl Harbor nine months earlier and Hitler's subsequent declaration of war on the United States. Just as America's entry into World War I had tipped the balance in favor of the Allies, Rommel feared that history was about to repeat itself.[4]

After his successor, *General* Georg Stumme, died of a heart attack on the battlefield in October 1942, Rommel was sent back to resume command of *Panzerarmee Afrika*. But the situation had deteriorated to the point that neither the Germans nor the Italians were capable of mounting or sustaining an offensive. Upon the arrival of American forces with Operation *Torch* in November, the death knell for the Axis in North Africa was sounded. Rommel returned to Germany to impress upon Hitler the importance of evacuating what was left of his army, but he was unable to convince the Führer of the seriousness of the situation, and so returned to Africa with Hitler's hollow promises for more support still ringing in his ears.[5]

Although he managed to score some victories against the Allies, the Desert Fox was unable to overcome the tremendous odds; in March 1943, a weakened, worn-out, and debilitated Rommel once again flew to Germany to paint for Hitler a picture of the situation in Africa. But so depressed was Hitler about the disaster that had taken place at Stalingrad,* he barely heard the pleas of his field marshal. Before the dejected Rommel prepared to return to Africa, Hitler ordered him to a clinic in Germany for treatment of rheumatism, heart troubles, and a nervous condition. During his absence, the Americans and British crushed the remaining defenders in Tunisia. Upon hearing the news, a disconsolate

---

* The German Sixth Army had been caught in a deadly trap in this industrial city on the Volga River, some 600 miles southeast of Moscow, from which there was no escape. The six-month-long battle was one of the major turning points of the war. German casualties were appalling; of the 284,000 Germans stranded in Stalingrad, it is estimated that 160,000 died. Another 90,000 men, including twenty-four generals and Sixth Army commander Friedrich von Paulus, were taken prisoner and marched off to captivity in Siberia; only about 5,000 ever returned home. (Shirer, p. 1,218)

Rommel wrote, "The front collapsed, there were no more arms and no ammunition, and it was all over. The Army surrendered."[6]

On 6 November 1943, Hitler named Rommel "Commander, Army Group for Special Employment," and directed him to prepare a report on the condition of the French coastal defenses. On 15 January 1944, because Hitler believed that Rommel grasped the situation and could still perform miracles, he was made head of Army Group B, whose area of responsibility included the northern coast of France; he was also given command of the Seventh and Fifteenth Armies. Despite this lofty title, he was not the "Supreme German Commander" with the broad, sweeping powers of Eisenhower. He was instead hampered by severe limitations on his authority and operational capabilities. For example, the nine panzer divisions in his area were not under his control. Instead they "belonged" to *General* Leo Freiherr Geyr von Schweppenburg, head of *Panzergruppe West,* and no fan of Rommel.

Rommel had other headaches, including the defender's age-old dilemma: When will the enemy come and where will he land? Hitler and many of his sycophants believed steadfastly that the invasion would come at the Pas de Calais but Rommel, as commander of Army Group B, could not afford to put all his defensive eggs in the one Pas de Calais basket; he had over 300 miles of coastline along the English Channel—from Cherbourg to Calais—to worry about. To fortify the coast, he wanted millions of mines planted; hundreds of reinforced concrete pillboxes, bunkers, and tank traps constructed; thousands of anti-landing-craft obstacles erected; and uncountable kilometers of barbed wired uncoiled.

He wanted thousands of machine guns, mortars, flamethrowers, and artillery pieces emplaced and preregistered to cover every square foot of coastline. He wanted hundreds of thousands of skilled, fanatical soldiers to man the weapons and guard every conceivable landing spot. He wanted vast, mobile reserves of panzers standing by near the coast, ready to repel the invasion at a moment's notice. He wanted the *Luftwaffe*'s planes on alert, and the *Kriegsmarine*'s ships and sailors at battle stations. He wanted the moon.*

---

*Neither Rommel nor *Generalfeldmarschall* Gerd von Rundstedt, Commander in Chief, West, had any control over the *Luftwaffe* (Air Force), *Kriegsmarine* (Navy), or SS units. Control of SS troops in the area was retained by *Reichsführer-SS* Heinrich Himmler, and the *Luftwaffe* and *Kriegsmarine* were also under separate commands and were off-limits to Rommel and von Rundstedt.

What he got was far less than what he wanted, and surely far less than what he needed.

The German high command responsible for the defense of France was hopelessly at odds with itself. While all believed that in German armor lay the hope for throwing back any Allied invasion, none could agree on how the panzers should be best utilized. *General* Heinz Guderian, Inspector General of Panzers and the architect of Germany's armored-force doctrine, got into the act and further muddied the waters; he did not want the armored formations concentrated to defend any particular expected landing area, for if that area turned out not to be the target, the tanks would be unable to respond quickly to the real invasion site. To Guderian, the panzers should be held well back from the coast until the enemy's main thrust became obvious.

Rommel fervently believed that any invasion must be stopped at the water's edge; to accomplish this, he said, he must be given command of the nine armored divisions in *Panzergruppe West*, a suggestion to which its commander, von Schweppenburg, strenuously objected. Nor did von Rundstedt agree with Rommel. OKW (*Oberkommando der Wehrmacht*, the German high command in the West) also disapproved of Rommel's ideas.

Hitler, as supreme arbiter and all-around meddler in military matters, came up with a compromise that, in effect, encumbered even further Rommel's ability to act. He placed three of the nine panzer divisions under Rommel's command; the remaining six, while under von Rundstedt's nominal authority, could not be released for battle without the Führer's personal approval.

Convinced that the Allies would attempt a cross-Channel invasion in the spring of 1944, Hitler ordered his army's efforts be devoted to strengthening the likely invasion sites—primarily the Pas de Calais. Furthermore, he decreed that, should the Allies land, they must be thrown back into the sea with powerful counterattacks. To *Generalfeldmarschall* von Rundstedt, Rommel's immediate superior, this meant Hitler was authorizing the formation of a strategic mobile reserve and placing less importance on stopping the invaders at the water's edge.

To Rommel, it meant the exact opposite. He needed tanks immediately available to destroy any beachhead penetration. By the time distant reserves could reach the front, it could well be too late to halt the invasion. But Rommel lost the argument. As one historian wrote, "The actual plan adopted was predominantly Rommel's, but lacked one crucial feature, a tactical reserve of armored divisions stationed not more than five miles from the coast. It was Geyr von

Schweppenburg who defeated this use of his armor, pointing out that experience at Gela in Sicily and at Salerno had proved tanks to be no match for naval artillery. He persuaded *Generaloberst* [Alfred] Jodl, chief of the operational staff of the high command [of the *Wehrmacht*], not only to keep his armored divisions outside Rommel's command, but to post them in the hinterland."[7]

Rommel faced another hurdle even more formidable than all the others—he had lost faith in Hitler and National Socialism. As early as the summer of 1943, it was clear to him that Nazi Germany's days were numbered. The recent defeat at Kursk on the Eastern Front (July 1943) had, for all intents and purposes, sealed the Third Reich's fate. Rommel's legendary fighting spirit—the drive and élan that had carried his armies to victory even when hopelessly outnumbered—seemed on the wane. He confided to *Generalleutant* Fritz Bayerlein, his friend and former chief of staff in the German *Afrika Korps,* and now commander of the Panzer Lehr Division, that a German victory was out of the question.[8]

Rommel's new-found pessimism must have come as quite a shock to those closest to him, for he had, from the very beginning of the war, exuded an air of confidence that had heartened his superiors and inspired his subordinates, even when the battlefield situation seemed at its bleakest. But now that confidence was gone. Convinced that Hitler was incompetent, if not insane, and was leading Germany into a catastrophe, Rommel tacitly lent his support to a group of officers who were secretly plotting to assassinate the Führer.

Although he tried to hide it, the once indefatigable Rommel was war-weary. He had been leading men into battle almost without a break since May 1940. He had seen so much battle since then, so much death and destruction, victory and defeat, triumph and disaster. Now, in April 1944, standing above Omaha Beach, Rommel knew that he must muster his last reserves of strength if he were to perform his mission. He squinted silently at the work details below as a subordinate with a clipboard ticked off the progress that had been made since the field marshal's last visit—so many mines emplaced, so many thousands of meters of barbed wire strung, so many gun positions built or improved, so many cubic meters of concrete poured, and on and on. It was good, very good, Rommel no doubt thought to himself, but it wasn't good enough. And he was quickly running out of time. He knew that the invasion had to come any day now, before the European winter approached to make such a thing impossible. His old soldier's bones could somehow *feel* the hundreds of thousands of men even now straining at their leashes across the gray expanse of water beyond the horizon, waiting for the moment when they would leap to the attack.

To try to stay one step ahead of the invaders, Rommel worked his men to exhaustion, constructing more underwater and beach obstacles, stringing more barbed wire, setting up more and more pillboxes, bunkers, and fighting positions, and emplacing mines, mines, and more mines; he demanded no less than 200 million mines to guard the Atlantic Wall. By 20 May 1944, however, "only" 4,193,167 mines were in place from Cherbourg to Calais.[9]

In his 22 April 1944 report to higher and subordinate headquarters, he wrote:

> My inspection tour of the Coastal Section during the past weeks gives me reason for the following comments and instructions. . . . Here and there I noticed units that do not seem to have recognized the graveness of the hour and who do not even follow instructions. There are also reports of cases in which my orders have not been followed, for instance that all minefields on the beach should be alive at all times. . . . In other cases, my orders have been postponed to later dates or even changed whereby minefields were to be alive only at night. . . . I do not intend to issue unnecessary orders every day. I give orders only when and if necessary. I expect, however, that my orders will be executed at once and to the letter, and that no unit under my command make changes, or even give orders to the contrary, or delay execution through unnecessary red tape. On the contrary, I expect that all my orders will be followed immediately and precisely, and that the carrying out of orders will be supervised [by the subordinate commanders]. . . .
>
> I have come to the following conclusions:
>
> *Beach defenses*: Again I have to emphasize the purpose of these defenses. The enemy most likely will try to land at night and by fog after a tremendous shelling by artillery and bombers. They will employ hundreds of boats and ships unloading amphibious vehicles, waterproofed and submergible tanks. We must stop him at the water, not only delaying him but destroying all enemy equipment while still afloat. Some units do not seem to have realized the value of this type of defense. . . . A lot has to be done until the defenses are complete. Right now, most battalion sectors show only a few mines, do not have any depth, poles are much too weak, and cannot even stop small boats. . . .

He went on to detail the shortcomings of other types of defensive obstacles and armaments, then gave detailed instructions in the construction of defensive measures to be taken against airborne and glider troops who might land behind the immediate area of the beachhead. "It is up to us to prepare the probable landing area in such a manner that the enemy planes and cargo gliders crash while landing, so as to cause heavy losses in men and matériel to the enemy," he wrote.

He concluded his report with what he hoped was an optimistic tone: "The enemy must be annihilated before he reaches our main battle field. In our army on this front, there are a lot of young, inspired National Socialists among our experienced soldiers. These boys do not have any battle experience, but they have proved on other fronts that they will live up to our expectations. From day to day, week to week, the Atlantic Wall will be stronger, and the equipment of our troops will be better. Considering the strength of our defenses, and the courage, ability, and the willingness to fight of all soldiers, we can look forward with utmost confidence to the day when the enemy will attack the Atlantic Wall.* It will and must lead to the destruction of the attackers, and that will be our contribution to the revenge we owe the English and Americans for their unhuman warfare they are waging against our homeland."[10]

While Rommel's words sounded confident, to Bayerlein he expressed his darkest expectations and deepest fears. He predicted that the invasion would follow a heavy air and naval bombardment and that parachute drops and glider landings would precede the amphibious assault. He even foresaw that the Allies would use swimming tanks.

He predicted, "The enemy will probably succeed in creating bridgeheads at several different points and in achieving a major penetration of our coastal defenses," and he expressed his fears that the operational reserves would be unable to react in time. Well aware that superior Allied air power would dominate the battlefield and impair the movement of his forces, he told Bayerlein, "[German] victory in a major battle on the continent seems to me a matter of grave doubt."[11]

The forces under Rommel were formidable, at least on paper. He had operational command of two armies; thirty-nine infantry divisions; and three armored divisions. The 21st Panzer Division, near Caen, in support of the Seventh Army,

*By the time Operation *Overlord* was launched, the Germans at Omaha Beach had eight major concrete bunkers with guns of 75mm or larger; four artillery batteries; thirty-five rocket-launching sites; thirty-five pillboxes equipped with machine guns or small artillery pieces; eighteen anti-tank guns; six mortar pits; and at least eighty-five machine-gun nests, not to mention hundreds of thousands of mines. (Ryan, p. 199n) was the only one near Normandy (but so obsolete were its weapons and tanks that it was considered by the Germans as unfit for duty on the Eastern Front); the other two—the 116th and 2nd—were stationed near Paris and Amiens, respectively, and were detailed to support the Fifteenth Army guarding the Pas de Calais. One month before the invasion, a worried Rommel again requested additional panzer divisions be moved nearer the coast, but von Rundstedt once more disagreed with this request, and OKW turned it down.[12]

Despite the impressive array of mines, barbed wire, casemated gun positions, interlocking fields of fire, fighting trenches, Belgian gates, and tetrahedrons, Rommel saw that his defenses were woefully inadequate in one key respect: the quality of troops manning those defenses. The sixty-mile crescent of shoreline that included Omaha Beach was held by the understrength German 716th Coastal Defense Division, under *Generalleutnant* Wilhelm Richter.

It was a stretch to even call the 716th a "German" division, for at least half of it was comprised of non-Germans—Poles, Slavs, and Russians who had been captured on the Eastern Front and who volunteered to serve in Hitler's army rather than be interred in a POW camp. There were even a number of Mongolians from Siberia in Nazi uniform. This low-grade fighting force, with only two regiments, was also immobile, for it lacked motor transport; the movement of troops, supplies, weapons, and ammunition was performed by horse-drawn wagons. Formed in Brittany in 1941, the 716th had been in Normandy since 1942, performing mostly coast-watching and construction duties. It had never seen combat or fired its weapons in anger.[13]

In early 1944, intelligence reports supplied to SHAEF by the French underground indicated that the 716th had only about 800 to 1,000 troops with which to man the defenses in the Omaha sector. It was further estimated that the 716th Division had only three battalions in reserve, and that it would take these reserves, without vehicles, a minimum of two to three hours to come to the aid of their comrades.

Since he was denied the use of two-thirds of the armored divisions in northern France, Rommel cast about for anything that could bolster the 716th. He found it miles back from the coast, in the Saint-Lô-Caumont area. This was the 352nd Motorized Infantry Division, commanded by fifty-five-year-old *Generalleutnant* Dietrich Kraiss.* The 352nd was an amalgamation of two other

---

* An experienced commander, Kraiss had led the 169th Infantry Division during the 1941 invasion of the Soviet Union.

Major General Dietrich Kraiss, commanding officer of the 352nd Division—the unexpected foe at Omaha Beach. (Courtesy Bundesarchiv, photo number 146-1984-058-20A)

infantry divisions—the 268th and 321st—both of which had seen considerable action on the Eastern Front and had been badly mauled before being transferred to Normandy in 1943 for rest, refitting, and redesignation as the 352nd. Since the 352nd was not a panzer division, Rommel did not need Hitler's permission to reposition it, and so, in March, he ordered the division moved closer to the coast. By May 1944, the division was fully reorganized, with three infantry regiments and three artillery battalions.[14]

Through low-level reconnaissance flights flown constantly all along the coast of northern France, and from agents behind enemy lines, SHAEF learned a great deal about the welcome the Germans were preparing. They knew where the bunkers and barbed-wire entanglements were. They knew where the minefields had been laid. They knew about the *Rommelspargel* ("Rommel asparagus"—

poles the Germans had implanted in likely glider landing zones). They knew the quantity and caliber of the guns facing them. They knew how many ships and planes the enemy could unleash against them. They knew what units were stationed in which areas, and what their level of readiness was. But, for some reason, they failed to discover the presence of Kraiss's battle-toughened 352nd.

Some information indicates that certain officers at SHAEF knew of the 352nd's existence, and that it might even have been conducting anti-invasion drills on the beach on 5 June. But everyone seems to have missed the fact that the 352nd had been moved closer to the coast, with two of its regiments in place behind Omaha Beach and the third at Gold Beach. Also backing up the two 352nd regiments at Omaha were elements of two grenadier regiments, the 914th and 916th.[15] In the official history of the cross-Channel attack, Gordon Harrison wrote, "Brigadier E. T. Williams, G-2 [Intelligence] of 21st Army Group, has said since the war that just before the invasion, he did find out about the 352nd's presence on the coast but was unable to inform the troops."[16]

The Allies' last opportunity to learn about the 352nd and the repositioning of other units came just a couple of days before the invasion was launched. This vital information was denied them because of one particularly skilled bird hunter.

On the warm, hazy day of Saturday, 3 June, a German sergeant by the name of Günter Witte was bird hunting in the eastern dunes of the Cotentin Peninsula. After scanning the skies with binoculars for several minutes, he swiftly raised his double-barreled shotgun and expertly brought down a pigeon. The bird was not a delicacy to grace that evening's mess table; rather, the pigeon was a military courier. It had strapped to its leg a tiny capsule that contained a small piece of rice paper with a strange code written on it by a secret agent in France. The note was destined for British intelligence.

Squads of sharpshooting Germans were stationed all along the Norman coast specifically for the purpose of bringing down these feathered messengers. The bird killed by Witte had special significance, for the message it lost its life trying to convey was that German reinforcements were moving into the Omaha Beach area.[17]

So, on D-Day, the 1st Infantry Division thought it would be landing on a stretch of beach manned only by one overextended, second-rate regiment, rather than by elements of a veteran division. (After the invasion, Lieutenant Colonel William Gara, commanding the 1st Engineer Combat Battalion, commented, "There were ten thousand more German troops there than we had anticipated.")[18] It was just one more thing gone wrong, one more miscalculation that would lead to a near disaster at Omaha Beach.[19]

North of the Channel, the Allies were putting the finishing touches on the opening moves of what Eisenhower would call "The Great Crusade." Never before had such an impressive invasion force been assembled. Three airborne divisions (two American, one British) would drop behind enemy lines shortly after midnight to sow confusion in the German ranks while simultaneously knocking out gun emplacements, capturing key highway intersections, or denying to the enemy the vital bridges and roadways that would be needed to counterattack the invaders. Six infantry divisions—including the American 1st, 4th, and 29th—assisted by special Engineer and Navy personnel, would land on five beaches during the first few hours of the morning and break through the prickly defensive crust along the shoreline.

The assault forces going into Normandy would have the use and support of 229 LSTs; 245 LCIs; 911 LCTs; 480 LCMs; 1,089 LCVPs; and sixty eighty-three-foot Coast Guard cutters converted into rescue vessels. And to provide what was termed "drenching" fire against enemy positions, there were six battleships, twenty-three cruisers, two monitors, seventy-three destroyers, and two gunboats.[20]

The planned air cover was equally impressive. To blast the German defenders to oblivion, the American and Royal Air Forces had at their disposal 3,467 heavy bombers, 1,645 medium bombers, and 5,409 fighter aircraft standing by on airfields across southern England.[21]

The average GI in the invasion force could be excused for thinking that all of this was being done strictly for his benefit, because it was. A hopeful Ray Klawiter, D Company, 18th Infantry, breathed a sigh of relief. "When they told us about the number of planes bombing and warships shelling, you figured the landings wouldn't be too bad."[22]

The Germans and Allies were playing a gigantic game of chess, with Normandy as the unwitting chessboard. Each time the Germans made a move to fortify the beachhead, the Allies would attempt to find a way to counter it—but not always successfully. Edward Ellsberg, who took part in the Allies' invasion planning, worried, "With his obstacles, Rommel had thoroughly muddled our plans. Attacking at high tide as we had intended, we'd never get enough troops in over those obstacles even to put up a decent battle on the beaches beyond. It would be a fiasco worse than Dieppe. There, though with no obstacles on the [Dieppe] beaches to hash up the British landings, it had taken the Nazis, with only such forces and beach defenses as they had already on the spot, not more than nine hours to wash up the invaders and force those few not already dead or captured to flee back to Britain."

In order to study the obstacles and find a way to overcome them, a full-size replica of the Normandy beaches, complete with faithful copies of the same types of obstacles, had been constructed along a beach in Florida. Bombers dropped ordnance on them, destroyers fired torpedoes at them, and LSTs with specially reinforced bows rammed them. Nothing worked. The results of the failed experiments were conveyed to SHAEF's planning staff and gave an already overburdened Eisenhower one more thing to worry about.[23]

After much thought, discussion, and head-scratching, the *Overlord* planners decided to launch the invasion shortly *before* high tide, while the obstacles were still visible—and vulnerable. The infantry debarking from the boats in the first wave would be exposed to enemy fire for about an eighth of a mile longer than at high tide, but at least they would be able to see and, it was hoped, avoid the death traps. To assist in this, demolition experts would go in just prior to the first wave to blow up the Belgian Gates, snip the barbed wire, detonate the mines, and emplace buoys to mark safe passages between the obstacles for later landing craft. As the day wore on and the tide rose, the coxswains in the second and third waves would be able to see the routes to the beaches and deposit their troops closer to shore.[24]

To aid in the amphibious and airborne landings, a new air arm, the Ninth Tactical Air Force, had been organized for the purpose of keeping the *Luftwaffe* away and providing close air support for the amphibious troops. According to the plan, shortly before H-Hour, hundreds of B-24 heavy bombers would plaster German positions on the Omaha beachhead with 13,000 bombs, turning concrete bunkers into smashed, smoldering ruins and giving the attackers bomb craters on the beach in which to take cover. Should any bunkers survive this aerial onslaught, small spotter planes would fly slowly over the invasion area and point out targets for the battleships *Texas* and *Arkansas* and cruisers and destroyers lying offshore.

Furthermore, nine LCT(R)s, armed with a thousand rockets each, would saturate enemy defenses, and seagoing trucks known as DUKWs* would carry several batteries of 105mm cannon that the gunners would use to support the infantry already ashore.[25]

The result of all this bombing, shelling, rocketing, and cannonading would leave the German defenders (those who lived through it, anyway) in a dazed and demoralized condition; they would barely have the strength or presence of mind to lift their arms in a gesture of surrender.

Or so went the theory.

The reality would be quite another thing.

* The designers of the DUKW, or "duck," as everyone called it, took the chassis of the standard two-and-a-half-ton truck, known as a CCKW, replaced the body with empty sealed tanks that gave it buoyancy, and added a pair of propellers. The Army's coded nomenclature translates as follows: D=1942; U=amphibian; K=all-wheel drive; and W=dual rear axles. (Ambrose, p. 44)

CHAPTER FIVE

"We Must Give the Order"

As THE MEN of the 1st Infantry Division in England prepared themselves mentally and physically for the invasion they would spearhead, life back in the U.S.A. during that first weekend in June was going on pretty much as before.

In New York City, the trees in Central Park had leafed out and lovers, many of them in uniform, strolled hand-in-hand. A group of Greater New York high school students was planning a patriotic "Monster War Bond Rally" for Tuesday, 6 June. And, despite the fact that many of America's most famous ballplayers—such as future Hall-of-Famers Joe DiMaggio, Bob Feller, Hank Greenberg, Gil Hodges, and Ted Williams—had traded their major league flannel uniforms for Uncle Sam's khaki, the baseball season was in full swing, with both St. Louis teams, the Cardinals and the Browns, leading the National and American Leagues, respectively. The New York Giants were in fourth place in the eight-team National League, nine games back, while the Brooklyn Dodgers were entrenched in sixth. On Sunday, 4 June, the Dodgers split a doubleheader with the Chicago Cubs at Ebbets Field while the Yankees, who were in second place, did likewise against the Cleveland Indians.

Although blackout regulations were still in effect in cities along the East Coast once the sun went down, dance bands in crowded nightclubs wailed into the night as though the war had never happened. Trumpeter Harry James and his Orchestra were helping bobby-soxers cut up the rugs at New York's Hotel Astor, while, on Broadway, the musical *Carmen Jones* was playing to full houses.[1]

In the nation's capital, armed sentries stood guard in front of important buildings and monuments, while government workers, in their free time, attended air-raid drills and classes in the proper use of gas masks. In Chicago, far from coastal waters that might hide a lurking enemy submarine, the lights burned brightly on Michigan Avenue and along the midway at Riverview Amusement Park; crowds still bet on the ponies at Arlington Park Race Track.

On the West Coast, civil defense officials were prepared to switch on the air-raid sirens at the first sign of a Japanese aircraft. On Hollywood sound stages, the movie industry was churning out training films for the boys in uniform, as well as diversions to help ordinary Americans—those with desk jobs, or assembly line work, or essential wartime occupations—escape the grinding reality of war news that blared incessantly from radios and leaped from newspaper headlines. To stop worrying, at least for a couple of hours, about the safety and welfare of a son or daughter or husband or father in uniform and "over there," people headed nightly to their neighborhood motion-picture theaters. The gung-ho, patriotic, inspiring films of the early years of the war—with such titles as *Bataan!* and *Wake Island* and *Flying Tigers*—had been, by June 1944, replaced by a more diverse choice of themes. Gary Cooper starred in Cecil B. DeMille's epic, *The Story of Dr. Wassell*, while Bing Crosby, playing a priest, tugged at hearts in *Going My Way*. Walt Disney captivated young and old alike with his animated *Snow White and the Seven Dwarfs.*

In short, the folks back home were doing their best to forget, momentarily, that there was a war on. But the visible reminders were everywhere. Cars sat on blocks, victims of the wartime shortage of rubber tires and gasoline. Ubiquitous billboards, movie trailers, and even Bugs Bunny cartoons exhorted people to buy war bonds; posters reminded everyone to conserve everything from tires to shoe leather. War-themed advertisements dominated every issue of *Time, Life, Colliers, McCall's*, and *Saturday Evening Post.* In fact, fully half the ads in nearly every magazine had some sort of patriotic or war-related theme. A Timken Bearings ad in May 1944, like so many others, told the nation of its contribution to the war effort: "Timken Bearings—Vital to Victory." Cadillac, along with all the other car companies that had stopped making civilian vehicles to devote 100 percent of its effort to war production, ran an ad featuring an illustration of an amphibious landing with the headline, "In the Vanguard of Invasion." Other companies ran ads that apologized for their inability to supply civilians with goods ranging from automobiles to razor blades to carbon paper to meat of all sorts to ladies' silk and nylon stockings. Yet, almost incredibly, nearly every ad also spoke optimistically of the future, of a post-war world where all the riches of the American civilization would be available once again, where the dark days of the Great Depression would be nothing but a dim memory, and where peace and harmony would reign. The essential prelude to this utopian new world was, of course, the successful invasion of the Continent.

A month before the invasion, the *United States News*, precursor of *U.S. News and World Report,* sought to calm America's fears about the difficulty of cracking the German coastal defenses: "Fortress Europa . . . differs greatly from the vision that is conjured by German propaganda. The vision is of a continuous and impregnable wall. In fact, there is no such wall. Neither forts nor men are available for it. Defenses must be concentrated around the best landing places. Troops must be distributed to man those defenses. Hitler probably would not have as many as 800 soldiers to the mile if his whole western force were spread evenly along 1,000 miles of western coastline. In fact, long stretches of coast that are thought to be unfavorable for invasion are only very thinly defended. . . ."[2]

Poignant reminders of the pervasive nature of the war could be found hanging in the windows of millions of homes and apartment buildings across America: small, red-bordered "service flags." A blue star (or two or more) on the pennant indicated that a family member was serving in the armed forces; a gold star indicated that that family member had been lost. While many Americans felt certain that the invasion of Europe must be launched very soon, except for the men at the very highest levels of government and the military—and the troops sweating it out in England—no one knew for certain that the invasion was imminent, or that more gold stars would soon be hanging in the windows of more homes across America.

The young men in England, packed tightly into their pre-invasion sausages, could only dream about life back home; long for their wives or girlfriends; distantly root for their favorite baseball teams; listen to Harry James's records; play cards or craps on a grimy Quonset-hut floor; or view a copy of a movie they had already seen a dozen times before—a Wild West shoot-'em-up or a fluffy comedy or a brainless musical. Despite the often lighthearted attitudes many of the soldiers strove to affect, there was a strain, a tension, in the air that was almost palpable. There *was* a war on, damn it, and the young men of the Big Red One wanted to get on with it and get it over, even if it meant that some of them would not return alive or whole to enjoy the peace.

GIs line up for chow at a typical American camp in England. The rounded buildings are "Quonset huts." (Courtesy National Archives)

On 23 May, the chain-smoking Eisenhower, after huddling with his staff, set the date for D-Day based upon the right combination of moon and tides. For the airborne troops, a late-rising moon was desirable while, for the seaborne troops, the tides had to allow the Engineers and Navy demolition personnel to see and destroy the obstacles before the sea covered them. The date deemed to meet all the criteria was Monday, 5 June.[3]

Now the opening notes of The Great Crusade could at last be played. At the end of May, the 1st Infantry Division, bulging with over 34,000 men thanks to the addition of the two attached regiments from the 29th Infantry Division, was herded into waiting vehicles and moved to Portland, where it began the precise process of boarding its assigned ships. At the docks, the men were checked off and assigned to a particular ship and to a certain hold or section within that ship.[4]

1st Infantry Division chaplain Edward R. Waters conducts a dockside worship service for troops destined to land at Omaha Beach. (Courtesy Ray Klawiter)

Impromptu worship services were conducted by chaplains on the docks and ships as men of all faiths—or none at all—prepared to board the vessels that would carry them into battle and, perhaps, oblivion. The services were full to overflowing. "The chaplains had boys all around them," recalled Lieutenant William Dillon, A Company, 16th Infantry. "Some were scared and crying, saying they didn't want to kill anyone. The chaplains' reply was always, 'If you must kill to protect your country, you will be forgiven. God works in mysterious ways.'"[5]

Louis Newman, Cannon Company, 18th Infantry, remembered a brief moment that touched him. "While we were waiting to get aboard an LST, I was sitting on the side of the halftrack and a chaplain came over to me and he said to me, 'God bless you, my son.'"[6]

In case the invasion troops weren't already suitably impressed with the importance of their mission, the soldiers of the Big Red One—and everyone else involved in the operation—were handed a small, printed leaflet with the flaming sword emblem of SHAEF at its top. It read:

Soldiers, Sailors, and Airmen of the Allied Expeditionary Force:

You are about to embark upon The Great Crusade, toward which we have striven these many months. The eyes of the world are upon you. The hope and prayers of liberty-loving people everywhere march with you. In company with our brave Allies and brothers-in-arms on other Fronts, you will bring about the destruction of the German war machine, the elimination of Nazi tyranny over the oppressed peoples of Europe, and security for ourselves in a free world.

Your task will not be an easy one. Your enemy is well-trained, well-equipped, and battle-hardened. He will fight savagely.

But this is the year 1944! Much has happened since the Nazi triumphs of 1940–41. The United Nations have inflicted upon the Germans great defeats, in open battle, man-to-man. Our air offensive has seriously reduced their strength in the air and their capacity to wage war on the ground. Our Home Fronts have given us an overwhelming superiority in weapons and munitions of war, and placed at our disposal great reserves of trained fighting men. The tide has turned! The free men of the world are marching together to Victory!

I have full confidence in your courage, devotion to duty and skill in battle. We will accept nothing less than full victory!

Good luck! And let us all beseech the blessing of Almighty God on this great and noble undertaking.

General Dwight D. Eisenhower[7]

Ray Klawiter appreciated the Supreme Commander's lofty, reassuring words: "It sort of picked you up a little bit."[8]

Not everything went smoothly at the outset, though. In his diary on 1 June, Medic Allen Towne chronicled the tension leading up to the debarkation that pushed at least one man to the breaking point: "Our company was as well-prepared as possible. . . . We had just been briefed on our specific job in the landing. Everyone now knew that the 18th Infantry Combat Team would land in Normandy on the second wave on June 5 about 10 a.m. We would land on a beach code-named Omaha Easy Red. . . . The new man in my platoon came over to me and started talking. At first, he was just rambling on about his family. Then he went on to say, 'I have seen the light. Everything is all right. We have nothing to worry about. God is with us.' He began talking incoherently and

Vehicles destined for Omaha Beach are backed into transports in a southern England port. (Courtesy National Archives)

every so often would say, 'I have seen the light.' After a short time, he was shouting and had to be restrained. We quickly got him out of the area and sent him to a hospital. He was our first casualty in the Normandy invasion!"[9]

The men of the Big Red One all knew they had drawn a tough assignment, but many, such as veteran Staff Sergeant Christopher J. Cornazzani, Headquarters, 1st Battalion, 18th Infantry, reflected on the confidence they felt: "Those of us who had survived this length of time were well-prepared to accomplish the job ahead of us. Our assault battalion was commanded by one of the best, Lieutenant Colonel Robert H. York, who successfully led us through all of the previous campaigns. We boarded the LCI and waited for the weather to clear."[10]

Allen Towne was surprised to see one of the world's most famous authors on his transport, the *Dorothea M. Dix*. "We found we had a celebrity on board. Ernest Hemingway was going over to France on our vessel. I am not sure he planned to land on D-Day, but he probably could get a good story about the landing from the Navy people.* Perhaps he could even interview some of the wounded when they returned to the ship. He held a lengthy bull session on the main deck. He was sharp-looking and stood out from the rest of us with his black beard and khaki safari jacket. He really looked like a war correspondent. He liked the attention he was getting from all the soldiers, and he did most of the talking. It was good to have a diversion because, for a while, we could forget what would happen tomorrow."[11]

The officers and men used their last few hours aboard the transports to check and recheck their weapons and equipment, and to write last letters home. Aboard his transport, Captain John F. Dulligan, executive officer of 2nd Battalion, 26th Infantry, penned a letter to his wife, Rita:

> My darling,
>
> I am aboard an invasion craft somewhere in the English Channel, ready for the "Big Show" and awaiting the signal that will start us off. It may be tonight, tomorrow, or a week from now. We don't know. . . .
>
> I love these men. They sleep all over the ship, on the decks, in, on top, and underneath the vehicles. They smoke, play cards, wrestle around and indulge in general horseplay. They gather around in groups and talk mostly about girls, home and experiences (with and without the girls). . . . They are good soldiers, the best in the world. . . . Before the invasion of North Africa, I was nervous and a little scared. During the Sicilian invasion I was so busy that the fear passed while I was working. . . . This time we will hit a beach in France and from there on only God knows the answer. I want you to know that I love you with all my heart. . . . I pray that God will see fit to spare me to you and Ann and Pat.[12]

As the hour of reckoning drew near, Captain Joe Dawson, commander of G Company, 16th Infantry, was still concerned that he had not completely won the trust of his men. "The night before D-Day, I went around to all of my men and spoke to them individually on board ship and told them that I wished them all

---

* The world-famous novelist-turned-war-correspondent Hemingway approached the shore in an LCVP under fire. He later landed in Normany and hooked up with the 4th Infantry Division. His exploits were detailed in the 22 July 1944 issue of *Collier's*. (Morris, p. 76)

Famed novelist and war correspondent Ernest Hemingway chats with troops prior to the D-day landings. Hemingway observed the invasion from an LCVP close to shore. (Courtesy National Archives)

the best and I expected the best out of them. And I think I had a mixed reaction from them. I think I was still an outsider and, frankly . . . I didn't know when we landed whether I was going to get shot from the back or the front."[13]

Everything was as ready as military efficiency could make it. The troops in the invasion force were loaded down with grenades, extra ammunition, cigarettes, and every other conceivable piece of hardware and equipment they could squeeze into their overloaded packs or strap to their bodies. Aboard more than 5,000 ships, boats, LSTs, LCIs, LCTs, and other craft in ports that stretched the length of southern England were packed some 175,000 American, British, Canadian, and French soldiers and sailors. Following them over the next few months would be 2 million more. Those taking part in the operation could not help being awed by the spectacle. "Never had I seen so many boats with their anti-aircraft balloons flying above them," commented Thomas McCann, Intelligence and Reconnaissance Platoon, 18th Infantry. "An airman told me it seemed like a person could walk on the balloons from England to France without getting his feet wet."[14]

The scenes at the ports were only part of the total equation. At airfields within flying distance of France sat thousands of heavy bombers, medium bombers, fighters, and artillery spotter planes, along with transport planes and gliders full of British and American airborne infantrymen, the wings and fuselages of each aircraft marked with special Allied D-Day identification stripes—three white and two black. Off the coast of France, minesweepers and submarines were already on station, marking lanes to the invasion beaches and preparing to fight off any enemy ships that might appear in the Channel.[15] Even the vehicles had been distinctly marked for the occasion. Prior to D-Day, the white stars painted on each American tank, truck, and jeep had been unadorned; each vehicle scheduled to go into France now sported a white circle around the star. Some circles were even painted with a special paint that would change color if exposed to the poison gas that the Allies thought the Germans might unleash against them. Virtually every possibility that could have been thought about had already been analyzed, discussed, debated, re-worked, and practiced. There were only two things over which the Allies had no control: the German response and the weather.

On 29 May, Royal Air Force Group Captain J. M. Stagg, SHAEF's senior meteorologist, had informed Eisenhower and the other commanders that it appeared the weather would be favorable for a landing on 5 June, and Ike cabled General Marshall that the date for the invasion was set. "Only a marked deterioration . . . would discourage our plans," he wrote. Shortly thereafter, weather conditions began to do just that. Stagg had the unenviable task of informing the assembled brass that a major storm was heading for the Channel; the group decided to postpone the invasion for seven hours but, because ships sailing from Bristol on the Irish Sea had the longest distance to go, they were allowed to set sail, subject to recall.[16]

Captain Fred Hall noted that it was the night of 3 June when his unit boarded the USS *Henrico* in Weymouth Harbor. "The morning of June fourth dawned misty and cool with heavy rain all day. There wasn't much to do aboard ship once everyone was accounted for. There was a poker game going on most of the time, day and night, in the officers' quarters, and crap games down below. There was tenseness and expectation in the air. We had been trained for our mission and were ready to go. We received word the invasion was delayed. There was nothing to do but wait."[17]

Lieutenant Harold Monica recalled that his unit, D Company, 18th Infantry, was also loaded into an LCI in Weymouth Harbor under cover of darkness on 3 June. "The daylight hours were spent checking weapons, and every man's equipment, especially canteens, had to be full, as we didn't expect water to be available for 36, maybe 48, hours in Normandy. By keeping busy in this manner, we had little time to think and dwell on the danger that we all faced. . . . It was now sit and wait. After daylight and breakfast, a couple of card games got organized—much better than to loll around and wonder. Some managed to nap for a couple of hours, but you could just feel the tension in the air. We were still tied up to the dock and many of the troops were walking the dock, while others were gossiping on the various LCIs."[18]

Early on Sunday, 4 June, the predicted storm was rattling the windows of Southwick House, Eisenhower's headquarters high on a bluff overlooking Portsmouth Harbor, with gale-force winds and heavy rains. It seemed impossible that the invasion could proceed, especially since the weather precluded launching the all-important air cover. After much consultation and consideration, Ike made the decision to send out the code word—"Bowsprit"—a code word that postponed the operation for twenty-four hours; a signal was then sent to recall the convoys that had already departed for France.*

Major Chet Hansen, Bradley's aide-de-camp, noted in his diary on Sunday, 4 June: "This morning, we were awakened at eight o'clock aboard the *Augusta*.** General Bradley was up with [Major] General [William B.] Kean, [U.S. First Army Chief of Staff], and the room in which our staff had been sleeping was

---

*Having failed to receive the recall signal, one group of minesweepers had almost reached France; it took speedy destroyers to intercept them and turn them back. A convoy of LCTs and LCMs heading for Utah Beach had also missed the signal; only a Royal Navy seaplane was able to reach them in time and return them to port. (Ellsberg, p. 180; and Morison, p. 80)

** The heavy cruiser USS *Augusta* had an illustrious career both before and after serving as flagship for the Normany Invasion. One of its first commanders was Captain (later Admiral) Chester Nimitz, and it saw service in the Pacific. In 1941, it was the flagship of the U.S. Atlantic Fleet and site of the Atlantic Conference talks between Roosevelt and Churchill; the Atlantic Charter, outlining the post-war goals of the United States and Great Britain, was signed on board. In November 1942, the *Augusta* was the flagship for Operation *Torch*, the invasion of North Africa. In August 1944, the ship served as the flagship for Operation *Dragoon*, the invasion of southern France. The *Augusta* also carried President Harry S. Truman to Europe in 1945 for the post-war Potsdam Conference. (www.mwci.org)

being stripped of beds for breakfast. Space was extremely tight aboard the vessel and it was necessary that each room do double duty. There was still no notice of postponement of the invasion. According to the first early morning weather report, there was an overcast in the early morning with a cloud base of between 500 and 1,000 feet, becoming clear or fair inland with only partial clearances. At sea, the cloud covering was lessening . . . the visibility was moderate with a risk of fog in all the sea areas on Sunday. We anticipated a change in the visibility after a change in the wind. At sea, there was still a five-foot wave in the open water, two to three foot waves on the lee coast of France. It was likewise a swell—a three-foot westerly swell—in the western channel.

"At seven o'clock this morning, Kean notified [U.S. First Army Assistant Chief of Staff Colonel Truman C. "Tubby"] Thorson that there would be a change or postponement of 24 hours for D-Day. We received our advice from the Navy and senior headquarters. Presumably the decision had been made by General Eisenhower in his headquarters near South Hampden [sic]. Thorson immediately sent the following message: 'Operation Neptune postponed 24 hours. Carry out procedure for notification of our units as outlined in our letter dated 25 May 1944. . . .'"[19]

Lieutenant Harold Monica's LCI had already started for France when it received the recall signal. While many of the men on the ships that were turned around breathed a sigh of relief at the one-day reprieve, Monica, full of pent-up emotion and determination, was not at all happy when his ship returned to Portsmouth: "Before daylight, we were tied up to the dock again. What a letdown. I was as ready as I ever would be to get on with it, and now this. Seemed like a good time to just say the h— with it and stay in England."[20]

Artillery communications specialist Al Alvarez noted that his LCT craft had also left port. "We were briefed by a naval officer that, 'we were the leading assault element for that coming morning.' Next came the inevitable '24-hour delay,' but for us, just another example of 'hurry up and wait.' The 24-hour delay was no great impact or significance for me, but for the 'old sweats' from North Africa and Sicily, it was an opportunity to regale us with stories of how tough it would be, saying, 'As always, we were the First—the first in and last out!' Since I was always the curious one, I asked some probably naïve and stupid questions, but Sergeant Alex Kowalski* of Greenfield, Massachusetts, our chief of detail,

*Alvarez related that Kowalski was later captured and died in a German prisoner-of-war camp.

said, 'Listen, you just get up that beachhead bluff and make sure the goddam radio goes with you!'"[21]

In his diary, Chet Hansen noted that church services were held aboard the *Augusta*. "The congregation stood and sang, 'Eternal Father, Strong to Save, For Those in Peril on the Sea.' It was a good song and it moved us there in the enlisted men's ward room where a low ceiling tended to amplify the husky chant of the sailor voices. . . . There was a communion service afterwards and practically the entire congregation took communion. Most of the congregation consisted of sailors aboard the ship; there was not much of an Army representation. There were heavy noises overhead throughout the service and a stretcher hung from the ceiling while we wondered what it predicted."

Hansen also noted that naval Task Force O commander Admiral Kirk "has a message indicating that Eisenhower will meet with Admiral Ramsay this evening in Southhampden [sic] to make a final decision on when or how long the assault is to be postponed. Bradley feels that a postponement of the invasion day to the 8th or 9th of June is preferable to a two-week delay. If we are forced to wait for two weeks, this would mean that many of the men must stay aboard their ships for almost two weeks—eleven more days. It is perfectly apparent that in the crowded quarters to which they have been assigned, many of them are already uncomfortable and stiff. These craft were built for short hauls and offer little comfort or conveniences. This is particularly true of the LCTs where the messing facilities are limited. When Bradley spoke of the possibility of changing D-Day to the 8th or 9th, Kirk replied, 'I'd prefer more daylight to see what I was shooting at. It would also permit us more accurate bombing of the artillery objectives.'"

Hansen was also furious when he learned that a test message declaring that the invasion had begun was prematurely released and broadcast in the United States. "Charlie Wertenbaker was striding impatiently up and down the deck of the *Achener* this morning. He spoke of the flap on the AP [Associated Press] story that broke this morning indicating that the Allies had landed on the coast of France. I had a long discussion with Jack Jarrell earlier this morning and Jack felt that if a correspondent had violated security to the extent of sending a prearranged code signal, he should be banished—perhaps shot. The operation is entirely too vast, too important to have its security menaced by a news-beat. All of us of course wondered how much security had been violated in the premature announcement. This would depend largely on the enemy's previous knowledge of our operations."[22]

At 2130 hours on that rain-lashed Sunday night, 4 June, Eisenhower and other members of the Supreme Command gathered in the library of Southwick House to hear Stagg's latest weather report. This forecast was much more optimistic. Stagg indicated that the weather over the invasion area would probably clear long enough on Tuesday, 6 June, to permit the invasion to take place—but just barely. Admiral Ramsay pointed out to the assembled officers that only a half hour remained in which to make the decision to launch *Overlord* in order to make a landing at dawn on 6 June; the moon and tidal conditions would not be favorable again for another two weeks. At a quarter to midnight, after receiving each officer's opinion—several of which were pessimistic—Eisenhower turned to General Montgomery and asked, "Do you see any reason for not going Tuesday?"

Monty spoke up. "I would say—*go*."

Ike, thinking of all the men cooped up in the ships, of all the bomber and fighter pilots and airborne and glider troops waiting anxiously by their aircraft, and of the entire Free World anticipating the greatest air and sea invasion in history, announced, "I'm quite positive we must give the order. I don't like it, but there it is. I don't see how we can possibly do anything else."[23]

As the clock neared midnight, the ships and planes were given the go-ahead. Even at this late date, however, there were still deep misgivings, especially among some British officers. Field Marshal Sir Alan Brooke, the anti-American chief of the British Imperial General Staff, confided to a colleague, "I am very uneasy about the whole operation. At the best, [the invasion] will fall so very short of the expectation of the bulk of the people, namely all those who know nothing about the difficulties. At the worst, it may well be the most ghastly slaughter of the whole war."[24]

Misgivings or not, the invasion was packaged and sealed, awaiting delivery. Even if the weather were not perfect, the Allies had committed themselves; there would be no more delays, no more turning back. The men detailed to carry out the mission were resigned to their fate; most just wanted to get it over with. Thoroughly trained, they knew no one else could be expected to do what they were about to do.

Don Whitehead, one of several war correspondents who would accompany the 1st Infantry Division ashore, caught the collective mood while aboard the USS *Samuel Chase*: "There was a strange lack of excitement among the men aboard the ship. In fact, they seemed relieved the long wait was over, and that within the next few hours or days a decision would be reached in battle. Reality is so much easier to face than the subtle fear of the unknown and the waiting . . . waiting . . . waiting. . . . In the ship's hold, company commanders, platoon and section leaders studied a giant sponge rubber map of the Normandy coast. Every house, out-building, ridge, tree and hedgerow was faithfully reproduced on the model designed from photographs of the beaches where the 16th was to land. The men were memorizing every detail of the landscape which would help them in battle, figuring how best to reach their objectives while giving their men as much protection as possible from enemy fire."[25]

The storm was not only pounding the southern coast of England; it was also battering Normandy. With the wind and rain raging and the forecast for it to continue for a week,* Rommel decided that now was as good a time as any for a quick trip to Germany. His wife's birthday was at hand and he wanted to spend some time with her at their home in Herrlingen, near Ulm, before traveling on to see Hitler in Berchtesgaden to, as he wrote in his diary, "win the Führer over by personal conversation." Still, leaving his headquarters at La Roche-Guyon on 5 June, Rommel worried about how much was still left to do in order to stop the invasion at the water's edge, whenever it might come.[26]

Rommel was not the only high-ranking German officer to be absent from his post on the critical night of 5/6 June. A map exercise—a war game simulating, of all things, an Allied parachute landing—was scheduled to take place on 6 June at Rennes, some ninety miles southwest of the Norman coast, under the supervision of *Generaloberst* Friedrich Dollmann, commander of the Seventh Army. Many of the major commanders in the Normandy area were either en route to Rennes, were preparing to go, or were otherwise absent. *Generalleutnant* Karl von Schlieben, commanding the 709th Division, was on the road to Rennes, as was the 243rd Division's commander, *Generalleutnant* Heinz Hellmich. *Generalmajor* Wilhelm Falley, head of the 91st *Luftlande* Division, was preparing to depart, while von Rundstedt's intelligence officer, *Oberst* Wilhelm Meyer-Detring,

* Unlike the Allies, the Germans had lost their ability to accurately forecast the weather in the North Atlantic, as they had abandoned their Schatzgräber meteorological station in Greenland a few days before Operation *Overlord* was launched. (Morison, p. 49)

was away on leave. The 21st Panzer Division's commander, *Generalleutnant* Edgar Feuchtinger, was in Paris with his French mistress. Sepp Dietrich, commander of the 1 SS Panzer Corps, was off in Brussels. Admiral Theodor Krancke, commanding the German navy in the west, was en route to Bordeaux, while *Oberst* Hans Georg von Tempelhof, Army Group B's operations officer, was on leave in Germany. Further complicating matters was the fact that most of the *Luftwaffe*'s front-line fighter aircraft had just been moved back from the coast and, with the storm in the Channel, most of the German E-boats were tied up in their ports. It was almost as though Providence had taken a hand and was stacking the deck in the Allies' favor.[27]

Correspondent Whitehead recorded, "Later that night, Jack Thompson [another civilian journalist, from the *Chicago Tribune*] and I went to the cabin of Colonel [George A.] Taylor [commanding officer of the 16th Infantry Regiment] and he unfolded the plan of the invasion for us. Not until we were underway did we know our destination and how the Allies planned to smash into Europe. The 16th Regimental Combat Team—supported by the 116th Regiment of the 29th Infantry Division—was spearheading the center of the invasion on the beach. . . . The British were on our left and the American 4th Infantry Division was on our right. Our initial assault force—known as 'Force O'—numbered 34,000 men and 3,300 vehicles. This was the spearhead, a reinforced unit stronger than two ordinary divisions, packing a terrific wallop. In addition to his own veteran 16th and 18th Regimental Combat Teams, Huebner was commanding the 116th Regimental Combat Team and the 115th Infantry, attached from the 29th Division, a provisional Ranger force of two battalions, and attached units of artillery, armor, engineers and service units.

"Following behind us was the 29th Division built up to a strength of 25,000 men and 4,400 vehicles. And the assault forces had to be clear of the beach in the afternoon or else the follow-up waves would pour in on them. As the Colonel explained the plan, I stared at the contour lines of the maps and saw the section of beach where our assault boat would land north of the little town of Colleville-sur-Mer was called 'Easy Red.' I wondered how easy it would be and how red the sands before another sundown. I wondered how many thousands of those battle-tough, homesick youths bobbing around us in assault craft would get beyond the beach known as Easy Red. . . .

"Then Colonel Taylor's voice broke into my thoughts. 'The first six hours will be the toughest,' he said. 'That is the period during which we will be the weakest.

But we've got to open the door. Somebody has to lead the way—and if we fail . . . well . . . then the troops behind us will do the job. They'll just keep throwing stuff onto the beaches until something breaks. That is the plan.'"[28]

The night of 5/6 June was a rough one. Some 175,000 young men peered into the darkness in the direction of France and were filled with a mixture of private yet commonly shared feelings—fear of the unknown; worry about being killed or maimed; uncertainty as to whether or not they would chicken out under fire; pride at being selected to take part in this momentous adventure; and relief that the months of waiting and training were behind them. Some even expected the Germans to surrender as soon as the Yanks and Tommies set foot on French soil.

Many of the veterans who survived the invasion recalled that they had never eaten as well in the Army as they did the night before *Overlord* was launched. It was as if the military were throwing one giant farewell party in their honor. Sergeant Ted Aufort, Headquarters, 1st Battalion, 16th Infantry, aboard the *Samuel Chase,* couldn't forget the royal treatment he and the other soldiers received. "The Navy personnel were excellent. They treated us like kings. At the evening meal, we were given three types of meat, which we hadn't had in years: steak, pork chops, and chicken. Or all three, if you wanted them. We drank Cokes, ate ice cream, etc. I momentarily thought to myself—a last request, just like in prison. You know, being executed." Gradually, however, worry and fear pressed down on each man scheduled to hit the beach the following morning. "None of us could sleep that night," Aufort said. "Most of us stood on deck, looking out. During the evening, we could hear the bombers going overhead. And then, finally, the ship stopped moving."[29]

Things had not been so quiet on all the other ships. Second Lieutenant Lawrence Johnson Jr., a forward observer with the 7th Field Artillery Battalion, recalled that his ship was home to "the loud and rambunctious behavior of the young infantry officers far into the night. Those young men understandably were feeling the strain of anticipation for the most important and dangerous day of their lives. No one in our hold got much sleep on that trip."[30]

Some soldiers enjoyed slightly better conditions than others. During the practice amphibious landings, Corporal William H. Lynn, a scout and observer with 3rd Battalion, 16th Infantry, had made friends with the captain of the LCT that would take him and the battalion to Normandy. "I liked to draw and I sketched a few of the guys. The captain asked me to make a sketch of his wife from a photo and I did. He invited me to lunch. . . . I found the Navy food was far better than our 'K' rations. So foxy me finished my food and took my mess plate to be washed and grabbed the captain's plate and washed it, too. This, plus the drawings, made a good friend, and I eventually ate in the Navy mess for the whole trip."[31]

Not all men were treated to sumptuous repasts, however. The troops aboard the USS *Henrico* were awakened at 0115 hours on 6 June and served a breakfast "consisting of bologna and luncheon meat sandwiches and coffee."[32]

To Ralph Puhalovich, a member of the 26th Regiment's Anti-Tank Companies, scheduled to be in the third wave, breakfast aboard a pitching ship held no pleasure. "We were on a British LCT. For breakfast, we had Heinz 57 celery soup that was in our ration packet. It was a self-heating unit. I ate it for five days. To this day, I can't stand celery soup."[33]

The time for waiting was over; the invasion of France was at hand. Like a child dreading a visit to the dentist, the inevitable could no longer be put off. A signal was sent to the ships in all the ports and the vast armada began to move. Private First Class Roger L. Brugger, K Company, 16th Infantry, recalled, "On the night of June 5, around ten p.m., our ship pulled out of the harbor to join the other ships for the invasion. We had a late meal on the ship from midnight to about two in the morning. Since this was a British ship, we were again served corned beef. After we had eaten, a buddy and I went up on deck for some fresh air. We left our assault jackets, steel helmets, rifles, and other gear on our bunks. When we came back to our bunks, someone had stolen my helmet. I reported my loss to the platoon sergeant and he jovially remarked that I wouldn't be able to make the invasion. We started to load into the [landing craft] around 4:30 on the sixth, and as we went up on deck, we passed through the ship's crew's quarters. The sergeant grabbed a British helmet that was hanging on the bulkhead and gave it to me, saying, 'Now you have a helmet.'"[34]

Everywhere across the great southern England ports, heavy hatches clanked shut; diesel engines revved to a throbbing crescendo; chains lifting anchors rattled; whistles screamed; and metallic voices from loudspeakers boomed orders in the darkness: "Now hear this, now hear this. . . ." The ships began to move in a way that can only be described as orderly chaos, each one maneuvering around other boats and ships and buoys at precisely scheduled times, moving off into the black night toward some previously appointed meeting place in the middle of the English Channel. The 1st Infantry Division, along with the rest of the seaborne invasion force, was heading for the German-held Norman shores.

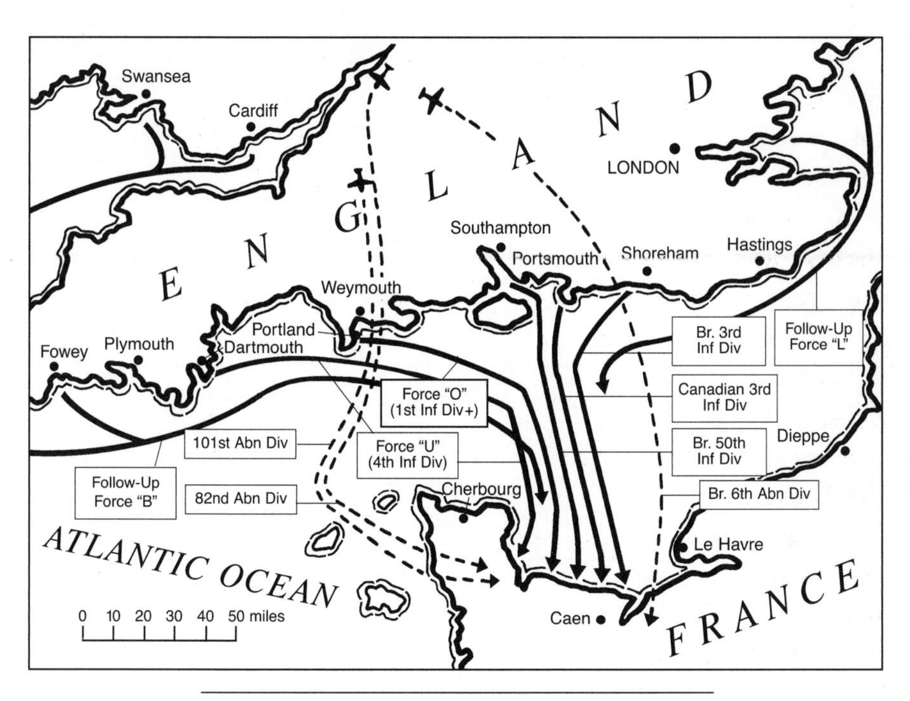

Ship assembly areas and routes to the invasion areas.

Almost in a single rush, as though plucked away by some giant, unseen hand, the assault troops were gone. The English roads, once clogged with bumper-to-bumper lines of olive-drab vehicles, were now empty. The green fields, so recently populated by hundreds of thousands of young warriors living under canvas and in curved, metal Quonset huts, were vacant. The coastal ports that had, just minutes before, held countless gray-painted warships now seemed denuded. The skies that had throbbed with the sounds of heavy engines were miraculously quiet enough for the English people to hear the birds singing once again.

A young John Keegan, who would one day become an eminent military historian, recalled D-Day eve at his parents home near the south coast of England: "the sky over our house began to fill with the sound of aircraft, which swelled until it overflowed the darkness from edge to edge. Its first tremors had taken my parents into the garden, and as the roar grew, I followed and stood between them to gaze awestruck at the constellation of red, green and yellow lights which rode across the heavens and streamed southward towards the sea. . . . The element of noise in which they swam became solid, blocking our ears, entering our lungs and beating the ground beneath our feet with the relentless surge of an ocean swell. . . . The Americans had gone. The camps they had built had emptied overnight. The roads were deserted."[35]

From ports and harbors all along England's southern coast, an armada of warships and troopships was heading out to do battle, to end the Nazi domination of Europe, to finish the war Hitler had started. Unlike the graceful, tall-masted, full-sailed warships of Sir Francis Drake's and Lord Horatio Nelson's day, these ships were squat and ugly and steel and gray. Instead of stout masts and billowing canvas sails, radio antennas pointed thinly skyward and radar disks spun silently. Instead of the sounds of ropes stretching and timbers creaking, these modern ships thrummed mechanically along, leaving clouds of oily exhaust in their wakes. And, instead of being manned by sailors and soldiers in colorful uniforms bedecked with regimental trim, these ships bulged with nervous, heavily laden, helmeted men in foul-smelling, mustard-colored wool battle garments.

Despite the many differences, these modern warriors had one thing in common with Drake's and Nelson's intrepid men: They were going in harm's way and they knew it. Many of them had but a few hours left to live, and those remaining hours would be filled with intense misery.

CHAPTER SIX

"What I Saw Was Terrifying"

NAMED FOR THE Norsemen who conquered the area in the ninth century, Normandy has been, throughout recorded history, a harsh land populated by a strong race. Located along the southern shore of the English Channel, Normandy has always been a chilly and somewhat forbidding place, given to leaden skies and much rain. The heavy, brooding Norman architecture matches the climate perfectly: cold, gray, Gothic stone buttressed against the prevailing northwest wind. The warm, sunny Mediterranean coast of France, and even the temperate climate of Paris, are as different from this part of the nation as Florida is from Maine.

For nearly a thousand years, Normandy has been a breeding place for warriors and a launching pad for invasions. Centuries before Operation *Overlord*, in 1066, William the Conquerer assembled his own, amphibious army of 5,000 men—the largest seaborne assault force since Xerxes invaded Greece in 480 B.C.—loaded them into hundreds of vessels, and sailed from France to England, where he gave King Harold's Anglo-Saxon troops a royal thrashing at the Battle of Hastings,* then marched into London where he had himself crowned King of England. Over time, the Norman and Anglo-Saxon cultures intermixed and produced great architecture, literature, and even the English language.

Normandy ceased being a place from which invasions were launched and took up a gentler occupation—that of a bucolic pastureland famous for producing thick creams, pungent cheeses, and a fiery apple brandy known as calvados.

* A 230-foot-long tapestry stitched together shortly after the historic battle commemorates the event and today hangs in a museum in Bayeux.

So famous is the drink that the entire Normandy coast is called the "Calvados Coast." Although occupied during the Franco-Prussian War of 1870–1871, Normandy was spared the bloody battles that turned the Somme region into a charnel house and cratered wasteland during World War I. After the Great War, Normandy remained a Gothic version of paradise—until July 1940, when the German jackboot was heard echoing through the cobblestone streets of the region's villages. As with their fellow countrymen throughout occupied and Vichy-controlled France, many Normans resigned themselves to life under the swastika and attempted to remain as neutral as possible. Others actively (albeit secretly) resisted the Germans, while still others collaborated with their conquerers.

Unlike in America, where farmhouses are often spaced miles apart from their neighbors, the farmers in the part of Normandy nearest Omaha Beach have always grouped their farmhouses closely together, forming small villages or hamlets, and sturdy stone walls line the lanes and roads. Since this part of Normandy is virtually flat, man-made features would become important resistance points following the invasion. Villages unfortunate enough to have been built at crossroads were destined to become battlegrounds, and the tallest structures around—church steeples—would be used by artillery observers and would themselves become targets. Many civilians who failed to flee would become casualties.[1]

Perhaps the most distinctive terrain features in this part of France are the hedgerows—a patchwork quilt of hundreds of irregularly shaped fields bordered by thick hedges. The Norman hedgerows take the place of fences and consist mainly of substantial banks of earth, the tops of which are crowned with densely packed walls of trees and bushes—an ideal place for a machine-gun or anti-tank team to hide and ambush an incautious enemy force blundering through. The size of the fields contained by the hedgerows varies from ten acres to a hundred or more, and the narrow lanes between fields are often sunken, allowing little room for maneuver. Allied planners greatly underestimated the barrier these hedgerows would be—as difficult for advancing troops as built-up urban areas. The invasion force, while it trained extensively in the art of coming ashore from landing craft, spent little or no time learning how to fight in hedgerow country. They would, however, soon learn.[2]

For the infantrymen crowded into their vessels, the time for the liberation of France was at hand. The last letters home had been written, the final handshakes with buddies and brothers exchanged, the final benedictions administered, the

1st Division troops descend a scramble net from their transport into waiting LCVPs during an exercise. (Courtesy Colonel Robert R. McCormick Research Center of the 1st Infantry Division Museum at Cantigny)

penultimate prayers uttered. For the men destined to be in the first wave, it was time to ride into the fire.

Four attack transports—the USS *Samuel Chase,* USS *Henrico*, USS *Dorothea M. Dix*, and HMS *Empire Anvil*—were carrying the 1st Infantry Division to a rendezvous point, dubbed "Piccadilly Circus," in the middle of the English Channel. From there the assault troops would transfer to smaller landing craft for the eight-to-ten-mile run into shore. Companies E and F of the 16th Regiment's 2nd Battalion were scheduled to hit Easy Red Beach a minute after the swimming Shermans from A Company, 741st Tank Battalion, reached shore at H-Hour—0630 hours. At the same moment, on Fox Green Beach, Companies I and L would swarm ashore. The troops on Easy Red would be reinforced a half hour later by the arrival of Companies G and H, while Fox Green would be backed up by Companies K and M. After nearly an hour on the beach, Lieutenant Colonel Herbert C. Hicks Jr.'s 2nd Battalion would be joined by the four companies of Lieutenant Colonel Edmund F. Driscoll's 1st Battalion, followed by Lieutenant Colonel George W. Gibbs's 7th Field Artillery Battalion; Colonel George A. Smith Jr.'s 18th Infantry Regiment; and, in the early afternoon, by Colonel John F. R. Seitz's 26th Infantry Regiment.[3] Many assumed that all the 18th and 26th Regiments would need to do would be to mop up after the 16th.

In the predawn darkness aboard the attack transport HMS *Empire Anvil*, Private Steve Kellman, L Company, 16th Infantry, felt the crushing weight of the moment: "In the hours before the invasion, while we were below decks, a buddy of mine, Bill Lanaghan—he was as young as I was—said to me, 'Steve, I'm scared.' And I said, 'I'm scared, too.'"

Then, at about three or three-thirty that morning, an officer gave the order and Kellman and Lanaghan and the nearly 200 men in L Company began to crawl awkwardly over the gunwales of their British transport and descend the unsteady scramble nets, just as they had done in training so many times before. "We went down the landing nets," said Kellman. "The nets were flapping against the side of the vessel, and the little landing craft were bouncing up and down. It was critical that you tried to get into the landing craft when it was on the rise because there was a gap—the nets didn't quite reach and you had to jump down. That was something we hadn't practiced before. We had practiced going down the nets, but the sea was calm. This was a whole new experience."[4]

Scheduled to hit the beach in the first wave with a movie camera instead of a rifle was a young Signal Corps cinematographer, Corporal Walter T. Halloran, destined to capture some of the most unforgettable images ever taken in combat. In addition to his Bell and Howell movie camera loaded with one hundred feet of film (he carried a total of ten rolls of movie film), he also had a 35mm camera, as well as two carrier pigeons in a cage strapped to his back. Once he exposed his roll of 35mm film, he was to slip it into a small pack on the bird's back and send it on its way to London. "We had our cameras strapped to our wrists," he said, "and wrapped in plastic. Our instructions were not to expose any film until we got on shore. Shooting footage on board ship was the responsibility of Navy cameramen."[5]

Officers and NCOs were giving last-minute instructions to their men. In *The Longest Day*, author Cornelius Ryan recounted the experience of Michael Kurtz, a corporal in the 16th Infantry. Gathering his squad around him before rail-loading into the landing craft, he said, "I want all of you Joes to keep your heads down. As soon as we're spotted, we'll catch enemy fire. If you make it, O.K. If you don't, it's a hell of a good place to die. Now let's go." As Kurtz and his men were loading into their boat, the davits holding another boat nearby gave way and dumped the thirty men in it into the sea. "Kurtz's boat was lowered away without trouble," wrote Ryan. "Then they all saw the men swimming near the side of the transport. As Kurtz's boat moved off, one of the soldiers floating in the water yelled, 'So long, suckers!' Kurtz looked at the men in his boat. On each face he saw the same waxy, expressionless look."[6]

The anonymous author of G Company, 16th Infantry's, invasion report noted, "At 0345 hours, the Company was called by boat teams to their respective debarkation stations and began loading into the LCVPs. A very heavy sea was running, which created considerable difficulty in loading the personnel from the *Henrico* into the assault craft. Loading was effected by means of loading all heavy equipment and ten men into the assault craft before lowering away these boats. The remainder of the boat team personnel was then loaded over the side of the *Henrico* by scramble nets. This was extremely difficult, due to the weight of the equipment carried by each man in his assault jacket and the slippery footing created [on] the scramble nets. All assault craft teams were loaded by 0415 hours, and the boat wave was formed approximately 500 yards off the starboard side of the *Henrico*. The boat wave rendezvoused in this position until 0445 hours, and then proceeded in line toward the beach. All craft were heavily loaded, and the very rough sea encountered caused the personnel and equipment to become thoroughly drenched before leaving the rendezvous area; all boats shipped more water than could be pumped out, causing them to be constantly in danger of foundering."[7]

An officer in a later wave recalled that the ride into shore was so rough, "it was like being inside a washing machine."[8] Another described it as "like being trapped on a never-ending roller-coaster ride."[9]

Private First Class Simon S. Hurwit, Headquarters, 3rd Battalion, 16th Infantry, had an impossible assignment. As a member of the Intelligence and Reconnaissance Platoon, he was part of a small patrol whose job it was to penetrate several miles behind the German beach defenses, set up an observation post, and by radio transmit information back to headquarters regarding German troop movements. Despite the darkness of the early hour, the sight of the assembled armada heading toward France helped Hurwit momentarily forget the enormousness of his task: "The ships stretched across the English Channel as far as the eye could see. It was inspiring to be part of such an effort." Yet, he couldn't help but worry and wonder about his own fate. "The war seemed interminable. I expected to die, that my luck would run out."[10]

Seaman First Class Robert A. Giguere, a member of the Navy's 6th Beach Battalion heading toward Normandy aboard LCI 85, recalled that he was lying in his bunk and unable to sleep, "so I put on all my gear, took my rifle which was an old Springfield 30-06, and went top-side. I really can't tell you what time it was. I was hungry and seasick as hell. A friend, Clare Mason, came top-side awhile later and we talked about what was going to happen. As we stood there talking and getting wet from the spray of the bow, the battleships started firing. You could see the flash of the guns and see the projectiles going through the air and . . . explode on the shore. As it was getting light, I could still see we were following one LCI after another. As we stood there, there was a loud explosion in the forward compartment. We had come out of that compartment where most of the Platoon C-9 were quartered. Smoke came pouring out the compartment door along with a lot of my buddies who had been hurt real bad. We had medical men from the 16th Infantry with us; they started helping with the casualties. The Coast Guard started putting the fire out. I know at least three that were killed in the compartment and twelve to fifteen wounded. We were told we had hit a mine."[11]

Staff Sergeant Harley A. Reynolds was aboard the USS *Samuel Chase* with the rest of B Company, 16th Infantry, "When it came time to load into assault boats," he noted, "we had to climb down cargo nets and drop into the boat. The water was rough from the storm; some men were injured when they dropped in. . . . We left the *Chase* for the last time and went in single file to our rendezvous area, following the little light on the stern of the craft ahead of us. The light would disappear, then reappear as we rose and fell with the waves. I thought several times we would crash into the craft ahead as we came up on them and would have to back off. I could see the trail of phosphorus the craft was leaving behind and I thought that the Germans must be able to see it, too, and pinpoint us."[12]

Ernest Hemingway, writing for *Collier's* magazine, was in an LCVP that had been launched from the *Dorothea M. Dix*. He wrote, "As the boat rose to a sea, the green water turned white and came slamming in over the men, the guns, and the cases of explosives . . . As the LCVP rose to the crest of a wave, you saw the line of low, silhouetted cruisers and the two big battlewagons [the battleships *Texas* and *Arkansas*] lying broadside to the shore. You saw the heat-bright flashes of their guns and the brown smoke that pushed out against the wind and then blew away."[13]

Even at this tense, drama-laden moment, there was time for levity. The sailors on one ship spotted another craft emblazoned with the letters "LCK," for "Landing Craft, Kitchen," heading for France. The crew of the first ship blinkered to the LCK in code: "Double malted and ham-on-rye—forget the mustard." The unamused crew on the LCK blinkered back an obscenity.[14]

The previous evening's rich meal, and the anxiety and fear gnawing in each soldier's gut, along with the endless rocking of the ships and boats, conspired to turn even the toughest GIs into seasick weaklings. "We had been issued a puke bag for seasickness but, as it turned out, one wasn't enough," remembered Private First Class Roger Brugger, K Company, 16th Infantry. "After the LCVPs were lowered, we kept going around in circles, rendezvousing. By this time, everyone in the boat had used their bag and were throwing up on the deck of the boat."[15]

First Lieutenant James Watts, the executive officer of A Company, 81st Chemical Mortar Battalion, admitted, "I was fighting desperately to avoid being seasick in front of the men. Somebody said we were eight or ten miles out. That's a long, long way to go."[16]

Steve Kellman said, "We circled in our landing craft for what seemed like an eternity. Then the battleships opened up and the bombers were going over. Every once in a while, I looked over the side and I could see the smoke and the fire and I thought to myself, 'we're pounding the hell out of them and there isn't going to be much opposition.' As we got in closer, we passed some yellow life rafts and I had the impression that they must have been from a plane that went down, or maybe they were from the amphibious tanks that might have sunk—I don't know. These guys were floating in these rafts and, as we went by, they gave us the 'thumbs up' sign. We thought, '*they* don't seem very worried—what the hell do *we* have to be worried about?' But, as we got in closer, we could hear the machine-gun bullets hitting the sides of the vessel and the ramp in front."[17]

Corporal Jess E. Weiss, a squad leader in the 2nd Battalion, 16th Infantry, did not believe he had much chance of surviving the invasion. "On the early morning of June 6, 1944, I found myself in the middle of the English Channel in five- to ten-foot waves, in a small amphibious landing craft that was launched from the troopship USS *Samuel Chase*. As we neared shore, 155mm howitzer shells began to rain on us from above. I could hear crossing bands of intense and accurate machine-gun and mortar fire hitting the water and the heavy metal hull of the LCT, from stern to bow. All of the GIs in the LCT, already weighted down with full field packs, gas masks, rifles, bazookas, ammunition, and bulky life preservers, were jammed together on both sides of the jeeps that were lined up in the center of the craft. When the shelling commenced, my battle-scarred combat buddies and I crouched down and hugged the bottom of the LCT, seeking whatever protection its metal hull could provide."

Weiss's previous experience as a squad leader in the North African and Sicilian campaigns had taught him how to best protect himself from incoming artillery shells, and he had even developed, as so many soldiers do if they want to stay alive, a sixth sense of when and where an incoming shell will land. "But many on our LCT were new recruits who had not yet experienced combat," Weiss said. "To these recruits, the shelling sounded like the Fourth of July. Several of them even stood up on the jeeps to get a better view of what was happening. Without a thought, I screamed to them, 'Hit the deck!' But it was too late. German artillery decapitated two of them, and several others were severely wounded."[18]

For many men in the rocking, bouncing boats, seasickness overrode their fear of death or injury. Walter Halloran recalled, "I don't think that fear was a recognizable element. We were so seasick, our only thought was, 'We've got to get off this boat.'"[19]

Corporal William H. Lynn, 3rd Battalion, 16th RCT, the artist who had sketched a portrait of the Navy captain's wife, recalled, "We now approached Omaha Beach and the captain went up to the poop deck to observe what was ahead. I started to follow him and was told by a sailor, 'No one is allowed on the poop deck but the captain!' I replied, '*I'm* making the landing—you're not. You're just my chauffeur.' With that, I grabbed his field glasses to see what was ahead. At this point, I could see nothing but ships, vehicles, and troops along the shoreline, and not one was able to advance." Perhaps sensing Lynn's anxiety, the captain of the LCT said to him, "'I'm the captain of this ship and anyone, and I mean *anyone*—even a general—is now under my command, and what I say is *law*. I can command you to stay on this ship and put you in my crew and you wouldn't have to make the landing.'"

Almost without stopping to think about it, Lynn brashly replied, "'Captain, I've made every battle in this war up to now, with the invasions in Africa and Sicily. I've fought every battle up front and I know every man on my right and

TIME	EASY RED BEACH	FOX GREEN BEACH
H-5	16 DD Tanks—B Co., 741st Tank Bn	16 DD Tanks—C Co., 741st Tank Bn
H-Hour	A Co.—741st Tank Bn w/ dozers	A Co.—741st Tank Bn w/ dozers
H + 1″	Co. E & F, 16th IR	Co. I & L, 16th IR
H + 3″	Special Engineer Task Force	Special Engineer Task Force
H + 30″	G Co., 16th IR, and Prov. AAA Btry	Co. K & I, 16th IR, and Prov. AAA Btry
H + 40″	H Co., 16th IR	M Co., 16th IR
H + 50″	16th IR Adv. CP, A Co. & 81st CW Bn	C Co., 16th IR & 81st CW Bn
H + 60″	Bulldozers, Halftracks, Misc. units	Bulldozers, Halftracks, Misc. units
H + 65″	B Co., 16th IR, Det. V Corps & 37th Engr Bn	A Co., 16th IR, 5th ESB, & 37th Engr Bn
H + 70″	Remainder A Co. & C Co., 16th IR	—
H + 80″	HQ, 1st Bn, B Co., 16th IR, & 1st Engr Combat Bn	—
H + 90″	D Co., 16th IR & Misc Units	62nd FA Bn
H + 105″	Btrys A, B & C, 7th FA Bn	HQ, 3rd Bn, 16th IR

16th Infantry Regiment—Scheduled Landing Times

my left. I know their every move and, if you don't mind, I'd like to stick with them.' The captain replied, 'Okay, I understand—and good luck!'"[20]

"While in training, we were told of all the things that would be done in order," said Harley Reynolds, B Company, 16th Infantry. "But to see it all come together was mind-boggling. The size of it all was stunning. We were trained to keep our heads down until time to unload but, . . . I felt it better to know what was going on around us. I looked over and ahead many times and what I saw was terrifying."[21]

Captain Fred Hall, operations officer for the 2nd Battalion, 16th Infantry, noted, "We reached our rendezvous area before daylight, 15,000–20,000 meters

Senior commanders of the 16th Infantry RCT (left to right): Colonel George A.Taylor, 16th Regiment commander; Lieutenant Colonel George Gibbs, 7th Field Artillery Battalion commander; Lieutenant Colonel Herbert Hicks, 2nd Battalion Commander; Lieutenant Colonel Charles Horner, 3rd Battalion commander; Lieutenant Colonel Edmond Driscoll, 1st Battalion commander. (Courtesy U.S. Army Military History Institute)

off the beach. The weather was low overcast and the sea was rough. We . . . rendezvoused in a circle near our ship before heading toward shore. My LCVP, carrying the Battalion Advance CP, had thirty-seven persons aboard. . . . The sea was choppy and we had poor visibility. Some in the boat were sick. We could see the battleships and cruisers stretched out parallel to the beach as they fired their guns. Closer in, I saw, for the first time, rocket craft releasing their rockets. We could hear aircraft overhead but the clouds were too low to see them."[22]

The planners at SHAEF, or so it had seemed to the invading troops, had thought of everything—everything to give the seaborne attackers every advantage. To start with, the planners had arranged for two American airborne divisions to drop behind enemy lines west of Utah Beach to create panic and seal off the beachhead from enemy intrusion. They had laid on squads of demolition experts to go in at H-Hour-plus-three-minutes to blow up and render harmless

Rommel's fiendishly arrayed underwater and beach obstacles. They had scheduled a heavy bombardment by the Navy's big guns, directed by slow-moving spotter planes flying over the beachhead. They had arranged for the sky to be filled with hundreds of bombers dropping thousands of tons of bombs that would create craters in the sand to provide safe shelter while also cracking open the enemy's concrete casemates like eggs; shredding the barbed-wire entanglements; and detonating the underground minefields. SHAEF had placed artillery in amphibious DUKWs to lend fire support to the infantry the moment they hit the beach. They had converted a number of landing craft into rocket-launching platforms that would saturate the beachhead with their lethal missiles. And they had taught tanks how to swim; the entire assault at Omaha Beach was to be led by sixty-four duplex drive tanks that would add their 75mm guns to the demoralization of the enemy and lead to his swift surrender.

The only problem was—none of these carefully planned and rehearsed activities even came close to working as planned and rehearsed. Not one. The infantry in the tiny boats, who had expected to walk ashore with little more to do than round up cowering prisoners, were in for a rude—and deadly—shock.

The operation had already begun to unravel around midnight, when the paratroopers of the 82nd and 101st Airborne Divisions, their Dakota C-47 transports rocked by blazing anti-aircraft fire, became widely scattered; almost no unit arrived intact at its intended drop-zone, and many troopers drowned when they landed in areas behind the coast that the Germans had flooded—in some places to a depth of over six feet.

No problem—the Navy's guns would send the enemy fleeing. But, shortly before dawn, virtually every round fired by the Navy overshot the target. The reason was simple: the spotter planes—the low-flying, slow-moving Piper Cubs from the Royal Navy's Fleet Air Arm—were knocked out of the sky by friendly fire! These planes carried the spotters who were supposed to radio targets to the big ships lying offshore. Without the spotters, the Navy was firing blind. Even though, in the days preceding D-Day, all personnel had been told over and over again that every plane in the sky would be Allied, nervous gunners on the landing craft nevertheless opened fire and the fragile aircraft plunged into the sea. As one historian wrote, "We had shot down all our own spotters! Now when the GIs most desperately needed naval gunfire . . . our warships had all been blinded. And the landing craft, that momentary burst of firing over, kept on for the beach, unaware even of what they had just done."[23]

Not to worry; if the Navy couldn't hit the target, then the Army Air Corps' precision bombers would do the job. At first light came waves of bombers—big, lumbering, four-engine B-24 "Liberators"—329 of them, their bellies pregnant with 13,000 bombs. But the bombardiers could not see through the cloud cover and the bombs completely missed their targets, landing far inland. Not a single German fortification, gun position, or soldier on Omaha Beach was put out of action. As one German soldier put it, "Not a scratch on the guns; the whole load missed."[24] Plump Norman cows, grazing in fields behind the defenses, and French civilians, were the only casualties.

But the Americans had another ace up their sleeve—swimming tanks! These mighty armored beasts would crawl onto the beach from the sea, sending the defenders fleeing in panic. Some two to three miles from shore, the bow doors of the LCTs opened and began disgorging their steel inhabitants, like creatures from another age. The first batch of thirty-two Shermans came swimming out, their inflated skirts all but hiding the fact that these were tanks, not tall, rubber rafts. At first, the tanks looked as if they might make it. Their tiny propellers whirled away and the monsters headed resolutely toward shore. But soon, the inflated skirts—the only thing keeping these thirty-three-ton machines afloat—were battered by the relentless waves and, one by one, the tanks began to sink. While twenty-eight Shermans emerged from the sea to support the infantry in the 116th Infantry's half of Omaha Beach, twenty-six of the thirty-two tanks detailed to support the 16th Infantry's landings at Easy Red and Fox Green went to the bottom of the Channel, some turning into tombs for their five-man crews trapped inside.[25]

What machines couldn't accomplish, perhaps men could. The specially trained Engineers and the Navy's underwater demolition teams jumped into neck-deep water being boiled by German bullets and did their best to clear sea lanes of mines and obstacles. Organized into sixteen teams of seven sailors and five soldiers each, the men faced an impossible situation—a rapidly rising tide and undiminished enemy fire. Initially scattered upon landing, and missing most of their specialized equipment, the men set about to fulfill their mission as best they could. With the tide rising a foot every eight minutes, the men managed somehow to blow five large channels and three smaller ones through the obstacles. But their work was all for naught as the buoys they had brought with them to mark the cleared lanes were lost during the chaos of the landing, and the tide was beginning to cover the deadly obstacles that still remained.

Now there was the barest inkling of concern. Perhaps the rocket-firing landing craft would save the day! These specially outfitted LCTs moved near to shore and unleashed their munitions with a fearsome, screaming, whooshing, skin-crawling roar. Again, they overshot—or undershot—the target.

It was looking a bit more serious. But wait!—there were still the DUKWs, those grand, improbable, ocean-going amphibious trucks from General Motors! Heavily and awkwardly laden with 105mm artillery pieces, the stalwart DUKWs drew close to the beach. But it was no good; within minutes, the two artillery battalions (the 7th in support of the 16th Infantry and the 111th in support of the 116th) lost eighteen of their twenty-four guns to enemy counterfire and rough surf.*[26]

Now, with no German gun position knocked out, no enemy soldiers dead, virtually no obstacles destroyed or mines detonated, and no craters on the beach in which they could take shelter, the men of the 16th and 116th Regimental Combat Teams discovered that they were naked in front of an awakened, determined enemy. Despite all the hard work and diligent planning of SHAEF's officers, despite all the minutely detailed rehearsals that had taken place for over half a year, and despite the millions of dollars that had been expended to create the mightiest combined amphibious-airborne operation the world had ever seen, everything had failed. The Atlantic Wall at Omaha Beach did not have a single dent in it.

Lieutenant Colonel William Gara, commanding the 1st Engineer Combat Battalion, recalled, "During that two-and-a-half-hour boat trip to shore, there was a great deal of apprehension. We heard a lot of firing. We wondered if the boats were going to get to their proposed landing sites. It wasn't until about three hundred yards from shore that we could see that things weren't going well. We could see that the paths and gaps between the underwater obstacles had not been opened, and so we recognized that we were very likely going to get blown up. We knew what those three rows of underwater obstacles were like. We thought that, perhaps by now, the firing from our battleships and the cruisers and the rocket ships and the air force had done the job—we discovered it wasn't so.

"The heavy fire from the battleships all went beyond the shore area. It was overcast; they couldn't get a good reading on where they were firing. The air

---

* The 7th Artillery was able to form a seven-gun battery but was unable to fire its first rounds from the shore until approximately 1600 hours that afternoon.

Private First Class Al Alvarez, 7th Artillery Battalion. (Courtesy Al Alvarez)

bombardment went inland. There was not a single shell hole created [on the beach] for the troops to jump into. The beach area of Omaha Beach was almost unscarred. We did not have a single one of those gun emplacements or pillboxes knocked out. Not a good situation."[27]

Private First Class Al Alvarez, 7th Field Artillery, aboard an LCT with the rest of his 105mm artillery battery observer party, recalled that "Sunrise came around 0600 hours that day, but I remember it as a still, dark, dismal, dank morning on the tossing English Channel. But we could have been in the middle of the Atlantic Ocean somewhere. Sopping wet and cold from our exposure on deck, we devoured a hot, frothy cream of celery soup from our British field rations. This ingenious self-heating can included a wick to an enclosed heating unit within the oversized soup can. Loading this mixture with ration crackers produced a hot mush that literally stuck to one's ribs and, for me, stayed on my stomach. The motion of the ungainly craft had proven too turbulent to attempt to make any morning coffee on our Coleman stoves."[28]

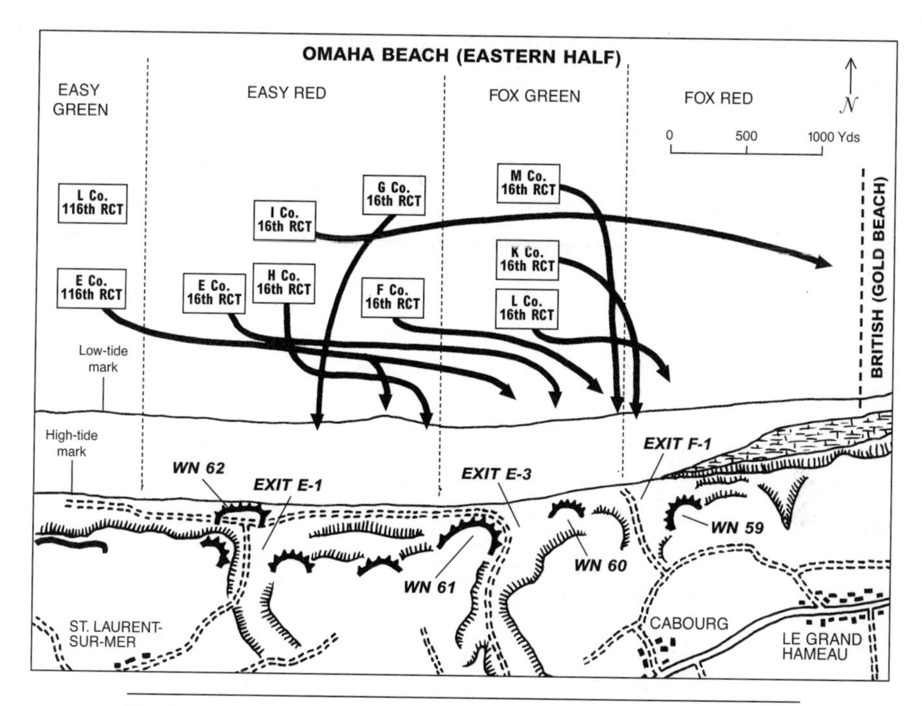

The first wave (2nd and 3rd Battalions, 16th RCT) at Easy Red and Fox Green beaches, at 0630 hours, 6 June 1944. (Positions approximate)

Aboard LST 375 was a young 1st Division military policeman, Allen Henderson, who noted, "We arrived off the French coast before dawn and watched the bombers set targets on shore ablaze. We saw a plane blink its lights, catch fire, and go down into the Channel."[29]

The wind and currents were playing havoc with the carefully laid landing plans. Moving from west to east in the unprotected waters of the Bay of the Seine, the strong current and five-foot swells prevented even the strongest Navy and Coast Guard coxswains from steering their boats in the direction they wanted them to go. The landmarks on shore that the sailors were using as their visual references seemed to drift off toward the west, and there was little or nothing the boat drivers could do about it. The most important thing now became—just land these boats anywhere!

One of those heading for Fox Green but far from his assigned landing place was Steve Kellman, Company L, 16th Infantry. His boat at last scraped Norman sand some distance to the east of Easy Red beach, the ramp went down, and the men scrambled toward shore amidst a hail of intense fire. "One of my jobs was a rifle-grenade man," Kellman said, "and I also had an aluminum ladder that was in two six- or seven-foot sections. We had been provided with photos of the beach we were to hit, and there was a tank trap; this ladder was to be used to get across the tank trap. Of course, with the weather being what it was, and the tides, we didn't land on the right beach; the first thing I did was get rid of the ladder."[30]

As his landing craft neared the untouched shore, Corporal Dan Curatola, 3rd Battalion, 16th Infantry, saw the beach untouched. He recalled with succinct understatement, "The air and naval gunfire did not appear very effective—."[31]

The slow-moving landing craft became choice targets for the German gunners. LCI 85, carrying the 6th Beach Battalion and much of the 16th Infantry's medical staff, impaled itself on a Belgian Gate and became immobilized; she was heavily shelled and set afire. The skipper, a Coast Guard reservist, managed to transfer his wounded to another craft before LCI-85 sank.[32]

Now those landing craft lucky enough to avoid the mines and the obstacles began grounding themselves on the sand, and the front ramps dropped, allowing enemy machine guns to play on the troops as they exited. It was a slaughter. Twenty-one-year-old German Lance-Corporal Hein Severloh, a farmer in civilian life but now a machine gunner cloistered behind the reinforced concrete of *Wiederstandnest* (resistance nest) 62, guarding the approaches to Exit E-3, squeezed the trigger of his big MG-42, a devastating automatic weapon. "I knew if I did not kill them, they would kill me.[33] The first burst streaked from the muzzle," he recalled. "The bullets smacked into the water. They caught the first wave of Americans. They sprayed them from end to end. . . . The mortars began to woof away. Screaming, the shells of the 1st Battery at Houtteville came sailing over, laying down a barrage of gunfire on the beach."* [34]

With beach obstacles providing only scant protection, and no shell holes in which to hide, the lone patch of semisafe ground on the entire stretch of beach seemed to be a line of small, rounded rocks known as "shingle." These rocks,

---

*A veteran of the Russian Front, Severloh was later captured and spent the rest of the war in an American POW camp.

worn smooth by rolling for eons along the bottom of the English Channel, had washed up along the high-tide mark of the beach. Several feet deep, the shingle extended ten to twenty feet toward the water and was protected only by a short lip of sand, beach grass, and, in some places, a short, man-made seawall. The shingle quickly became the sole refuge for GIs who managed to make it to shore; soon, the entire line of stones was covered with hundreds of wet, scared, hurt, crying, sand-encrusted soldiers over whose heads continually cracked tens of thousands of bullets. Writing about the Marine Corps' amphibious assault of Tarawa, author William Manchester observed, "Seawalls are to beachheads what sunken roads—as at Waterloo and Antietam—are to great land battles. They provide inexpressible relief to assault troops who can crouch in their shadows, shielded for the moment from flat-trajectory fire, and they are exasperating to the troops' commanders because they bring the momentum of an attack to a shattering halt."[35] So it happened at Omaha Beach. The slightest bit of defilade along the seawall acted as a human magnet.

Those soldiers who dared to try firing back found their weapons inoperable, clogged with sand and rusting as they watched. With no other options, the prone men began field-stripping and cleaning their weapons while under fire.

One of the first to reach the beach was Signal Corps cinematographer Walter Halloran. Dodging bullets and shrapnel all the way to the shingle, he flopped down, rolled over onto his back, and began recording scenes of Americans storming the coast of France. In one particularly startling shot, a soldier, struggling beneath a large pack, is seen leaving the surf with the steel hedgehogs all around him. As he runs to reach the safety of the shingle, a bullet hits him and he falls, heavily. This brief scene of instantaneous death remains one of the most indelible of all combat images.[36]

Only minutes old, the carefully crafted invasion of Omaha Beach was already unraveling, already turning into a bloody shambles. Every German gun within range of the beach—and there were thousands—was firing at the ragged line of oncoming landing craft. Exiting their boats, officers and NCOs were cut down in droves, leaving the soldiers wet, cold, frightened, and leaderless. Radios were full of seawater and useless; special equipment was missing; men with special skills and training were dead, wounded, lost.

Captain Ed Wozenski, of Terryville, Connecticut, commanding E Company, 16th Infantry, painted a chilling picture of the chaos and confusion experienced by those in the first wave: "About a mile off shore, we began to pass a few, and then more and more men tossing about in the water in life belts and small rubber rafts. At first, we thought that these men were shot-down airmen but soon realized that they must be tankmen from tanks that had sunk. . . . Nearing the shore, to a point where it was possible to easily recognize landmarks, it became obvious that [my] company was being landed approximately 2000 yards left of the scheduled landing point. How anyone briefed could have made such an error, I will never know, for the lone house which so prominently marked Exit E-3 was in flames and clearly showed its distinctive outline. Small-arms and AT [anti-tank] fire opened up on us as we were still 500–600 yards off shore. When told to fire back from our LCVP with the MGs [machine guns] mounted astern, the naval man on one gun fired a burst straight up into the air as he hid his head below the deck—a disgusting performance if I ever saw one. No one would man the second gun.

"MG fire was rattling against the ramp as the boat grounded. For some reason, the ramp was not latched during any part of our trip, but the ramp would not go down. Four or five men battered at the ramp until it fell, and the men with it. The boats were hurriedly emptied—the men jumping into water shoulder deep, under intense MG and AT fire. No sooner was the last man out than the boat received two direct hits from an AT gun, and was believed to have burned and blown up.

"Now all the men in the company could be seen wading ashore into the field of intense fire from the MGs, rifles, AT guns, and mortars. Due to the heavy sea, the strong cross current, and the loads that the men were carrying, no one could run. It was just a slow, methodical march with absolutely no cover up to the enemy's commanding positions. Many fell left and right, and the water reddened with their blood. A few men hit underwater mines of some sort and were blown out of the sea. The others staggered on to the obstacle-covered, yet completely exposed beach. Here men, in sheer exhaustion, hit the beach only to rise and move forward through a tide runlet that threatened to sweep them off their feet. Men were falling on all sides, but the survivors still moved forward and eventually worked up to a pile of shale at the high-water mark. This offered momentary protection against the murderous fire of the close-in enemy guns, but his mortars were still raising hell."[37]

Landing alongside E Company was F Company, commanded by Captain John Finke. His after-action report mirrored Wozenski's: "Company F landed on beach vicinity of Colleville-sur-Mer at 0640 hours. Smoke laid down by navy

An LCVP on fire races toward Omaha Beach. (Courtesy National Archives)

and artillery had already been lifted, which therefore enabled the enemy to observe the landing of the company. Enemy machine guns, rifles, and mortars were fired at assault teams as they ran out of the LCVPs. The water was about four and a half feet deep. The assault teams had to wade across thirty yards of water under fire and cross the beach of approximately one hundred and thirty yards under the same fire. The cost in casualties was six officers and about eighty percent of the company."[38]

One of Finke's men, Sergeant Fred Dolfi, was wounded shortly after making it to the beach. "I drove my jeep off the LCVP and it got hit by a wave and sank," Dolfi said. "I couldn't swim, but fortunately I had two lifebelts, one already inflated and the other as a reserve." Once he reached the beach, Dolfi "was hit pretty hard. I took two pieces of shrapnel, one in my spine, and I was knocked completely out. I couldn't raise up."[39]

One boat section each of Companies E and F of the 16th Infantry, along with two boat sections of E Company, 116th Infantry, landed on top of each other in an intermingled mess on the eastern half of Easy Red beach; men from the 16th Infantry found themselves suddenly in the midst of strangers from the 116th, and vice versa. Having been pulled far from their assigned beaches, the men in the defenseless craft jumped into the surf, unable to spot any of the landmarks their weeks of training told them would be there. There was no place to run and no place to hide.

Captain Joe Dawson's G Company, 16th Infantry, approached Easy Red at about 0700 hours. "When we landed, it was total chaos, because the first wave from . . . E Company and F Company had been virtually decimated. That was due to circumstances over which they had no control. In the first place, they were badly disorganized when thcy landed, whereas I was privileged to land intact with all of my men and my LCVP in the very point that I was supposed to land in. . . . I was the first man off my boat, or off of *all* our boats, followed by my communications sergeant and my company clerk. Unfortunately, my boat was hit with a direct hit, so the rest of my headquarters company was wiped out, as well as the [fire] control officer from the Navy, which was our communication, to give us support fire that was supposed to [neutralize] the village of Colleville, which was the objective that I was given. . . . I was fortunate enough to realize that there wasn't any point in me standing there and, frankly, I felt the only way I could move was forward and to go up and see if I could get off the beach."[40]

On Fox Green beach, things were as bad as on Easy Red. Five boat sections of F Company, 16th Infantry, were scattered across a thousand yards of sand. Two sections of the company did manage to land close together in front of enemy positions guarding the E-3 draw but were decimated by machine guns and mortars as they departed from their LCVPs. Six officers and half of the company became casualties in a matter of minutes. The remaining boat section of E Company, 16th, reached the shore where the water and sand were spouting in an endless flurry of artillery and mortar explosions. Four more boat sections of E Company, 116th, also arrived, only to face the same terrible greeting. Men discarded their equipment in the water and scrambled for the safety of the shore, but it was no better than the sea. Minefields and machine guns were in front of the invaders and a steadily encroaching tide was behind them. From the trenches in the high ground above them came a rain of "potato mashers"—German stick grenades. All around was death, destruction, carnage, and chaos. Among the survivors who had made it to the beach, there was a very real sense that no one was going to come out of this debacle alive.[41] As one historian noted, "The best planned, the best rehearsed, and the best supported invasion assault in history was falling on its face, mostly because of bad weather, partly because of the undetected placement by the Nazis of their 352nd Division. The generals were out of it now. If any of those GIs on the beach were to survive even the next hour, it was up to them alone. Every shield provided for their protection had been destroyed."[42]

To the Germans on and overlooking Omaha Beach, the packed GIs made for unbelievably choice targets. The enemy soldiers were doing all within their power to obey Rommel's command to stop the invasion at the water's edge and drive the Americans back into the sea. It appeared as if they would succeed. In any battle, not all bullets or shells fired hit their intended targets. A great quantity of munitions landed harmlessly in the water, sending great geysers shooting upward, but, with the sheer volume of weapons being fired, many were bound to find their mark. More than one landing craft took a direct hit, flinging the bodies of soldiers and sailors into the air like rag dolls. Some LCVPs were punctured by shrapnel, forcing their occupants to bail furiously with their helmets in a futile effort to keep the boats from sinking. Others rammed obstacles and sliced open their hulls in the process, then set off mines that finished off the survivors. Still other landing craft managed somehow to squeeze between the obstacles, scrape bottom, and drop their ramps, only to have the men scythed down by machine-gun fire the moment they attempted to debark into the surf. Men who were able to leave their craft safely found themselves snagged on underwater strands of rusty barbed wire, where they made easy targets for German gunners. Wounded men slipped beneath the waves, gulped salt water tainted with diesel oil and blood, and drowned. Medics going to the aid of wounded comrades were themselves picked off by the indiscriminate enemy. Everywhere one looked, Colonel Taylor's 16th Infantry Regiment was being torn to shreds. As Ike's naval aide, Captain Butcher, had feared, Easy Red beach was turning red.

While the boats in the initial waves had drifted several hundred yards off course, the boats carrying I and L Companies, which were supposed to land on Fox Green at the same time E and F Companies were hitting Easy Red, were pulled more than a mile off course, almost landing on Gold Beach, in the British sector. By the time the error could be corrected, Captain John R. Armellino's L Company was more than a half hour late and had lost a boat that capsized two miles off shore.* Originally scheduled to land in front of the E-3 draw, L Company's boats beached beyond the extreme eastern boundary of Fox Green, near the shelter of low cliffs that came down nearly to the water's edge. It would take an hour more for Captain Kimball Richmond's I Company to reach land.

---

* Many of these men managed to reach shore, but exhausted and without their weapons.

Cold, wet, scared, and wounded members of L Company, 16th Infantry Regiment, who have survived the harrowing run to the beach, take a moment to compose themselves under the protection of a cliff at the far eastern end of Fox Green beach before moving out to assault enemy fortifications. (Courtesy National Archives)

One of those in Armellino's company was Steve Kellman: "We were trained, when you hit the beach, to never run in a straight line—you were supposed to zig-zag. When the ramp went down, some of the fellows just went straight as an arrow, and a lot of them were cut down that way. The coxswain on our boat got us right up on the beach—I don't think the water was as high as our knees. We had a tremendous advantage—we didn't have to wade; we could run. We just ran like hell to get up against a little sea wall. Once we got there, we were exhausted. Some of the guys in the boats behind us, where the coxswains didn't get them close enough, they had to hide behind those obstacles that were in the water, thinking that they were going to provide them with some cover, but that was deadly."[43]

Organizing L Company in the relative safety of the cliffs, Captain Armellino saw that his unit, although it had already lost nearly half its strength, was basically intact—the only one of eight companies in this initial wave able to operate

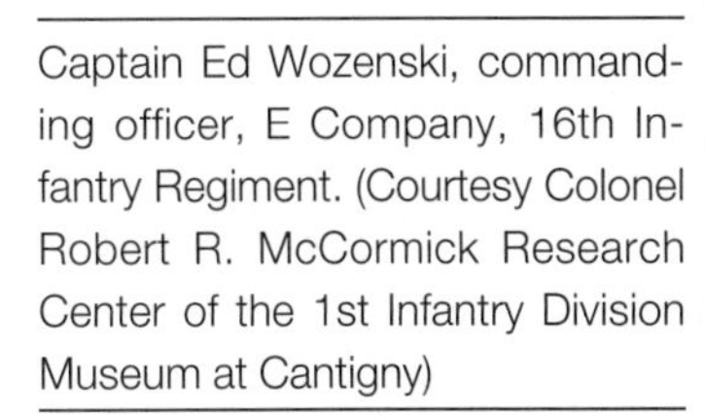

Captain Ed Wozenski, commanding officer, E Company, 16th Infantry Regiment. (Courtesy Colonel Robert R. McCormick Research Center of the 1st Infantry Division Museum at Cantigny)

as a unit. He decided to push inland toward the village of Le Grand Hameau. The only way up to the heights was a draw or ravine labeled on maps as "F-1," and it was sure to be well-guarded. Before the company was ready to move out, however, Armellino was severely wounded.[44]

"On the beach, it was like all hell had broken loose," said Kellman. "There was noise and smoke and dead bodies all over the place. We found we were not on the right beach where we were supposed to be; there was supposed to be a draw that we would go up. As we were working our way to the right beach, an artillery or mortar round must have landed fifteen feet away and the fellow that was in front of me and I both got flipped over backwards by the concussion. Then I started to crawl and I got against the sea wall. I knew we had to move and I used my rifle like a crutch to stand up. I got to a standing position and then fell down. I didn't know what was wrong—I didn't feel any pain; it was like a numbness. I tried standing again and I fell down again. I pulled up my trouser leg and I could see blood. I was so scared. I took off my leggings and sprinkled sulfa powder on the wound and wrapped a bandage around it.

"As the succeeding waves came in, I gave my rifle to one fellow and gave my grenades to another, so I was without anything. Then our company executive officer, Lieutenant [Robert] Cutler, came along and said, 'Come on—we're moving out.' I said, 'I can't.' He looked at me and said, 'Kellman, I didn't think I was going to have any trouble with you.' I said, 'I can't walk, sir.' He said, 'What's the matter?' I showed him my leg and he said, 'Oh, okay. I'll have an aid man come by.' I was there for hours. The guy who had been flipped over in front of me by the shell had also been hit in the leg, and we laid there and talked while we waited for the medic. The shells kept coming in. After the concussion of one of them, I kind of sat up and asked him, 'How're you doing?' But he had been hit again and was dead."[45]

Aiding in the devastation of the Americans were two squat, gray, ugly, concrete casemates that, like the mythological, three-headed dog Cerberus that guarded the entrance to Hades, guarded the approaches to Exit F-1, one of the routes off the beachhead. These casemates, known as *Wiederstandnests* 59 and 60, were anything but mythological. They were real, and the machine-gun bullets that poured from them in fiery torrents were real, and the deaths and awful injuries they caused were very real. Unless these two strongpoints were knocked out, the Yanks would never get up the pathway to the top. Unless these two strongpoints were knocked out, the bodies of young Americans would continue to pile up on the sand.

The slightly built, moustachioed Lieutenant Cutler took command of the company after Captain Armellino was hit. To silence *Wiederstandnest* 59, which was preventing the company's advance up E-1 draw, Cutler sent red-headed Second Lieutenant Jimmie Monteith and his platoon to take out the position, while First Lieutenant Kenneth J. Klenk was ordered to take his twelve remaining men and assault *Wiederstandnest* 60, a grenade's throw to the west.[46]

As confusion reigned, the boats that had carried I Company, 16th Infantry, miles to the east were returning and attempting to make a landing on the hot beach. The C.O., Captain Kimball Richmond, a rugged Vermonter, found himself in extreme difficulty; besides the company's being an hour late after drifting off course, the LCVP in which Richmond had been riding had taken a hit and was sinking. Crawling overboard, he swam to shore with the survivors of the craft. Miraculously avoiding being hit once on the beach, he organized the remnants of his company into a fighting force and set off on his mission, picking up cold and scared stragglers from other units along the way. The ad hoc company soon ran into an enemy emplacement that had been inflicting heavy casualties on troops on the beach; Richmond and his men assaulted the position and wiped it out. It was one of the first successes on a morning of nothing but failures.[47]

Near L Company, Captain Everett L. Booth, commanding M Company, was slightly wounded while wading in. "I had jumped off the landing craft in water over my waist, then I was hit by a machine-gun bullet in the upper left arm."[48] Booth also witnessed the fate of one of I Company's boats: "When we had landed, the tide was low and the mines were no problem because they were above water. But when I Company came in, the mines were submerged and one of the company's landing craft hit a mine. The mine exploded and many of the men were terribly burned all over their bodies. It was a terrible sight."[49]

Captain Fred Hall, S-3 (operations officer) of the 2nd Battalion, 16th Infantry, recalled that, on the way to the beach, his LCVP passed several rubber rafts filled with men in lifejackets. "At first I thought they were flight crews. Then it dawned on me that these were DD tank crews, which meant we would not have their support on the beach. The shoreline and bluff did not become visible until we were fairly close in because of the mist. . . . As we approached the shore, we came under some small-arms and artillery or mortar fire. . . . Our landing craft finally dropped its ramp and we unloaded into shallow water. . . . It was every man for himself crossing the open beach where we were under intense fire. . . . Captain [James R.] Dowd [7th Artillery Battalion] was killed about the time we reached the first line of obstacles. Out of twenty-eight men aboard my landing craft, fourteen reached the rip rap [shingle] including Hicks, Chandler, and myself. Staff Sergeant Al Cimperman, my operations sergeant, made it behind me carrying our map case wrapped in canvas, which contained our assault maps showing unit boundaries, phase lines, and objectives. I remember it seemed a bit incongruous under the circumstances.

"The beach was in a state of confusion. We had landed at a point east of our designated landing area. We were under heavy small-arms and artillery and mortar fire. It was apparent the naval and air bombardment preceding the landing had had little effect. Once ashore, it was a matter of survival, but I was so busy trying to round up unit commanders to organize their men to move along and eventually off the beach, there wasn't much time to think except to do what had to be done. The medics were helping the wounded. Some soldiers' weapons had been jammed in the sand and they were trying to clean them. There wasn't time to worry about the dead. Somebody reported that Lieutenant Colonel John

Mathews, our regimental executive officer, who had previously been my battalion commander, had been killed by a sniper. . . .

"There was no movement off the beach. Some of the boats were taking direct hits. I watched one LCI coming in with troops unloading on ramps down each side. The ramps were raked with small-arms fire as the soldiers came down. There were many casualties; it was pretty bad. . . . And the noise—always the noise—naval gun fire, small arms, artillery and mortar fire, aircraft overhead, engine noises, the shouting and cries of the wounded. No wonder some people couldn't handle it."[50]

One of those unable to handle it was a young soldier named Eldon Wiehe, with Headquarters, 1st Division Artillery. He had been separated from the rest of his unit and barely survived a near-miss from a German shell. "When that shell burst," he recalled, "I guess I panicked. I started crying. There was a ship to our right that had [run aground], and my buddies got me behind that ship, where I cried for what seemed like hours. I cried until tears would no longer come. Suddenly, I felt something. I can't explain it, but a feeling went through my body and I stopped crying and came to my senses." Wiehe picked up his rifle and got back in the war.[51]

Now it was the turn of Captain Anthony Prucnal's K Company to arrive at Fox Green beach. Originally intended to be the 2nd Battalion's reserve company at Fox Green, the company's members were thrust into an assault role after I Company had drifted too far east. A soldier in K Company, Private First Class Roger Brugger, recalled, "As we approached the beach about six-thirty a.m., the shells were dropping in the water and machine-gun bullets were whizzing over our heads. Sergeant Robey [the squad leader] told the coxswain to run our boat right up on the beach and not let us off in four or five feet of water. He did, and we got off on dry land. We ran straight for a shale [shingle] wall. I remember thinking as I ran from the boat and seeing the bullets tearing up the sand on either side of me, 'This is like a war movie.' After we got to the shale wall, I looked back at the boat we had just left when an 88mm artillery shell hit it in the engine compartment and it blew up. I watched another boat come in and, as the guys came running to the wall, one guy got a direct hit with a mortar shell and all I could see of him were three hunks of his body flying through the air. We were all sick and scared from the pounding and the ride. When we tried to throw up, there wasn't anything left. The tide was coming in and the beach was getting smaller. We could see the bodies of the dead. The Germans were using wooden bullets and they made a very nasty wound."[52]

One of Brugger's comrades in K Company, Private First Class Isadore R. Berkowitz, a Philadelphian, also noted the unreal, Hollywood quality of the scene. "It was like watching a movie—only the shells were killing people and blowing boats out of the water."[53]

Approaching the shore at about 0705 hours, K Company's six boats came under heavy enemy fire, and two were blown up by mines. The officer corps was decimated in the next few minutes. As Prucnal and his executive officer, Lieutenant Frederick L. Brandt, were attempting to organize the scattered, shaken remnants of the company, a shell screamed in and mortally wounded Brandt. Coming to his aid, Prucnal was killed by another shell. A platoon commander, Lieutenant James L. Robinson, attempted to rally the company, only to fall dead at the hands of a sniper. Another lieutenant, Alexander H. Zbylut, was badly wounded while struggling ashore. Taking command of the rapidly dwindling unit, Lieutenant Leo A. Stumbaugh organized a patrol of what was left of the first and second assault sections, dashed through a blaze of enemy fire, and forced Germans holding a defensive position to withdraw. But one patrol, one platoon, one company, or even one battalion could not hope to make a serious penetration in the Atlantic Wall.[54]

It seems almost incredible that anyone managed to live through the tremendous fusillade the Germans were laying down, yet some came through without a scratch while many others were wounded but lived to tell about it. During his first few minutes on Omaha Beach, Staff Sergeant William D. Behlmer, Anti-Tank Company, 16th Infantry, who had survived North Africa and Sicily, was hit and severely wounded. "Artery blown out of right leg," he recorded. "I lay on the beach on D-Day in shock and bled for about three or four hours without medical attention. Gangrene, amputation resulted. No fault of the medics, as they got hit on the way in."[55]

Those who dared to peek above the shelter of the seawall saw that to their immediate front was a virtual forest of concertina wire. Beyond that, as they knew from their many briefings, lay deep and deadly minefields. Unless they could brave the bullets, break through that wire, and pass through the mines, there was no hope of getting at the enemy soldiers inside their concrete fortifications. The naval fire, which had been totally worthless to begin with, now ceased completely, for the officers aboard the ships were worried about dropping shells on their fellow countrymen huddled on the beach. There also was no way for the infantry on shore to contact the ships and direct supporting fires, for most of their infantry radios were inoperable.

Captain Karl E. Wolf, Headquarters, 3rd Battalion, 16th Infantry Regiment. (Courtesy Karl Wolf)

One of those whose job it was to contact the ships was Murray Hackenburg, a sergeant from Pennsylvania assigned to a Joint Assault Signal Company, or JASCO. His mission was to go ashore in a small group at Omaha Beach and establish radio contact with the battleship *Texas*. "There were twelve men in my group, and we lost all of our equipment. Didn't even make contact with the ship because we didn't have anything to work with."[56]

More boats approached congested Omaha Beach. In one LCVP was First Lieutenant Karl E. Wolf, a West Point graduate from Wethersfield, Connecticut, and a member of Headquarters Company, 3rd Battalion, 16th Infantry. "Because of the storm, the water was very rough and our [LCVP] was tossed around in waves that were six to ten feet high. I remember getting very seasick and tossing up in a plastic bag someone gave me. Someone also gave me some Dramamine tablets and said they were good to help prevent seasickness. Not having been told any dosage, I took three of them. As we approached the beach, we could hear the German machine guns and artillery firing from the emplacements and fortifications. Of course, we saw small craft that had been hit, as well as rubber landing craft strewn around."

Instead of landing too far east, as did most of the LCVPs, Wolf's boat landed about 3,400 yards too far to the west, in the 116th's sector. "We hit the beach," Wolf recalled, "and our front ramp dropped down so we could run off into a few feet of water among the hedgehogs. . . . The first few people off the craft were cut down by German machine-gun fire. Captain Al Moorehouse, the battalion adjutant, was killed coming off the same landing craft and was just in back of me. . . . I could see machine-gun fire rippling the water all around and an occasional artillery or mortar burst. I scooted off the right diagonal as I went toward the shore. Ahead of me there was a row of tetrahedron hedgehogs in about two or three feet of water.

"Beyond that, the water became a little deeper. I stopped at one tetrahedron because machine-gun fire was heavy about five to ten yards ahead in the deeper water. On the right side of the tetrahedron were two soldiers—a sergeant and a private. After about five minutes of waiting for the machine-gun fire to lift, I looked to the high ground to my right diagonal to find the source of the machine-gun fire. I noticed a ripple of water in a straight line from the right diagonal come up to where we were and then the two men on my right floated away with the tide; they had been hit and killed by that machine-gun burst." Deciding that that spot was too dangerous, Wolf again made a dash inland. "While going into the beach, I did not recognize any of the fortifications or high ground that I had memorized from the maps and photos of where we were to land. The reason soon became clear when I looked at the division patches on the men laying around me on the beach. The Navy had landed us on the wrong beach. We were thousands of yards to the right of where we should have landed. It was in the adjacent [116th RCT] area.

"For a while, we had to dig in or lay on the beach because of enemy fire. The beach was fairly steep for about 20 to 30 yards, and at the top there was a little berm that afforded us a little protection." Although somewhat sheltered, Wolf found that he had crawled into a nightmare. "While laying there, I noticed the soldier near me was lying on his back and his whole leg was split open to the bone. He was in shock, but there was nothing I could do except keep pulling him up as the water rose. Nearby was half a body, the lower half having been blown away."

After lying on the beach for what seemed to him to be an hour, Wolf noticed an LCI (Landing Craft, Infantry) heading toward the shore near him. "The LCI was a fairly good-sized landing craft that drops anchor and goes up to the shore dropping a landing ladder on either side of the bow to let the infantrymen

An LCI (Landing Craft, Infantry) heads toward the French coast on 6 June. (Courtesy National Archives)

down. It could not get in far enough, unfortunately, and the first seven or ten men off on either side went into water over their heads. Many drowned because the assault landing jackets had been put on under their assault life tube, and they couldn't release the jacket buckles to drop the forty- to fifty-pound loads. We tried to throw a rope to some, but I am certain at least ten drowned. Finally, the skipper saw what was happening and pulled up the ramps and backed out.

"With Captain Moorehouse having been killed, I was the only officer left from my landing craft. Slowly, I assembled all the men from my landing craft who made it to the wrong beach. After locating all we thought had survived, probably about ten or twelve, I told them to follow me. We started down the beach to our left to get back to where we should have landed and rejoin our battalion. . . . Every once in a while, enemy fire would make us stop and lie in the sand. One time, after stopping, I felt someone shaking my leg. The Dramamine had finally kicked in and I had fallen asleep on the beach with enemy machine-gun fire going over my head! I finally woke up when a soldier shook my leg. I suspect the men behind me who didn't know anything about my having taken three Dramamine pills thought I was a pretty cool customer under enemy fire if I could nap under those conditions!

"Before we started down the beach, I remember an anti-aircraft halftrack coming in. The captain in charge was pointing out an emplacement for them to fire on. They got off a few rounds and suddenly part of the halftrack disappeared in an explosion and fire. A German shell had hit it broadside and destroyed it, killing all inside, plus the captain.

"While going down the beach leading these men, we came across everything imaginable in the way of dead and wounded, plus blown-up tanks, halftracks, and equipment." Wolf would not reach his assigned landing spot until after noon.[57]

The situation was no better on the 116th Infantry's portion of Omaha Beach. In fact, it was even worse. Men coming off LCVPs were torn to bits by machine-gun and artillery fire; others, leaping over the gunwales of their landing craft, were pulled under water by the weight of their packs and equipment and drowned. One LCA took four direct hits and blew apart. On Dog Green beach, A Company of the 116th Infantry was being systematically slaughtered even before it reached shore; every officer in A Company, and most of the NCOs, became casualties. A small, sixty-four-man company of Rangers, following A Company, was similarly decimated. They lost half their men; A Company lost two-thirds. And they had yet to fire a shot. Farther west, more Rangers were attempting to climb the sheer cliffs to get at the casemated battery of 155mm guns at Pointe du Hoc and taking heavy casualties in the process; the Rangers would soon discover that the guns had been removed and posed no danger to the fleet.[58]

At Easy Red and Fox Green, the leading companies of the 16th Infantry Regiment remained trapped on the beach. The only way to break out of the trap was for one man, or several, to risk their lives by crawling forward with little more than wire-cutters or Bangalore torpedoes—twenty-pound tubes packed with explosives—and exposing themselves to enemy fire while they attempted to break through the tangle of barbed wire. Several brave men tried it; all were cut down. Despite witnessing the suicidal nature of the mission, another soldier—Sergeant Phillip Streczyk, a New Yorker in Wozenski's E Company—attempted the impossible. With practically every German weapon within range zeroing in on him, Streczyk made a mad dash for the wire, snipped it, then waved for the rest of the troops to follow him. For his actions, Streczyk was later awarded the Distinguished Service Cross.[59]

Although E Company had taken a tremendous pounding, one of its surviving platoon commanders, Lieutenant John N. Spalding, a Kentuckian, gathered what few men he could find, and—faced with furious rifle, machine-gun, mortar, and artillery fire, and confronted by profuse minefields—set off through the slim gap made by Sergeant Streczyk in an attempt to crack the enemy positions to the east of Exit E-1. It was a pitiful, foolhardy attempt—a handful of sick, soggy, and scared soldiers throwing themselves at one of the most heavily defended places on earth. There was no way it could succeed. But somehow, incredibly, it did.

With Joe Dawson's G Company providing covering fire, Spalding and his men crept forward, leaving a path of death and destruction in their wake. As the regimental report said, "Of the 183 men [in E Company] that landed, 100 were dead, wounded, or missing." But the survivors being led by Spalding knocked out the strongpoint, consisting of an anti-aircraft gun, four concrete shelters, two pillboxes, and five machine guns, that guarded the east side of Exit E–1. "Extremely stubborn resistance was encountered in this strongpoint with its maze of underground shelter trenches and dugouts. A close exchange of hand grenades ensued and small-arms fire until the 1st Platoon cornered approximately twenty Germans and an officer who, overpowered, surrendered." Spalding would earn the Distinguished Service Cross for his courageous leadership.[60]

Captain Joe Dawson realized that he and his company would have to go it alone. After he had flopped onto the shingle, Dawson saw that there was a minefield right in front of his position. "But I detected a little, narrow path," he said. "There was a dead soldier who had penetrated into this path and, unhappily, had stepped on a mine. However, that clued us in as to where the damn thing was. . . . I saw what was ahead. From the beach flat to the top of the bluffs was a little over two hundred fifty feet, and it was almost sheer. But, just before you reach the crest of the ridge, there was a little opening and this path led right up to it. This was seemingly the only path down to the beach in that particular locality." Dawson had been lucky so far; would luck accompany him up the path?[61]

Dawson gathered his courage. "I felt the obligation to lead my men off, because the only way they were going to get off was to follow me; they wouldn't get off by themselves. . . . We dropped over [the shingle] and got into this minefield. . . . Sergeant Cleff and myself, and [Pfc. Frank] Baldridge, another man in my company, started up the hill. . . . There was a path and it seemed to generally go in the right direction toward the crest of the hill, so I started up that way. And about halfway there, I encountered Lieutenant Spalding with a remnant of his platoon. I think he had two squads and a person in a third squad, and they were the only survivors that I knew of at that time in E Company. He joined us . . . and became part of us; my men were still back on the beach.

"I told Baldridge to go back and bring the men up. I said, 'They've got to get off the beach. Tell them to come up here with me.' Well, they started up, but I had gone on ahead. Just before you reach the crest of the ridge, it becomes almost vertical for about a ten-foot drop. There was a log there and I got behind the log to see if I could see my men coming up. . . . I could see a single file beginning to develop off of the beach coming on up when I heard a great deal of noise just above me and, sure enough, there was a machine-gun nest up there and they were giving us a lot of trouble. I was able to get within a few yards of them. . . . I lobbed a couple of grenades in there and silenced them and, sure enough, that opened the beach up. It was a miracle. It doesn't mean anything on my part. It was just one of those wacky things that happen, that I was on the right spot."[62]

Although the 2nd and 3rd Battalions' assaults had fallen behind the precise timetable set for them, the next wave of troops—Driscoll's 1st Battalion—was right on time. At 0720, the LCVPs carrying Companies A, B, C, and D were roaring in to the beach, picking their way through the obstacles and bodies and derelict landing craft. Just one problem: There was no place to put them.

CHAPTER SEVEN

"This Time We Have Failed"

AT A CERTAIN point in virtually every battle, unit commanders lose their power to control their men and must relinquish their command to Luck, Fate, Error, and Chance. In a well-intentioned but ultimately futile attempt to preclude this from happening at Omaha Beach, the 1st and 29th Divisions both had scheduled their respective assistant division commanders, Brigadier Generals Wyman and Cota, to come ashore within the first few minutes of the landing to make sure that everything went according to plan.

The 1st Infantry Division had many outstanding officers, but none was better suited for the dangerous task at hand than Willard G. "Bill" Wyman. Possessing what the British call "command presence"—a lean, muscular frame, piercing blue eyes, square-cut jaw, no-nonsense voice, an imperturbable air—Wyman had an appearance and demeanor that immediately inspired confidence in subordinates. If General Wyman ordered you to take an objective, you took it, regardless of the dangers, difficulties, or consequences.

Correspondent Don Whitehead wrote, "We circled near the *Chase* for a few minutes and then headed for the beach. The senior officer in our boat was tall, lean, Brigadier General Wyman, who had been with [General Joseph] Stillwell in Burma. Wyman was to go ashore as quickly as possible, direct operations at close range, and organize 'Danger Forward,' the advance command post, so that General Huebner could transfer his headquarters from ship to shore. Until the command post was organized, the nerve center of the 1st Division would remain aboard a ship [the *Ancon*] in the Channel."[1] Part of Wyman's mission was also to link up with the 29th's Brigadier General Norman Cota (who had served as Terry Allen's chief of staff in North Africa) and coordinate actions on the beach.

Brigadier General Willard G. Wyman, assistant commander of the 1st Infantry Division. (Courtesy Colonel Robert R. McCormick Research Center of the 1st Infantry Division Museum at Cantigny)

The 16th Infantry Regiment's official report of 6 June painted a bleak picture in terse, unemotional language that barely hinted at the enormous difficulties faced by Wyman and Cota during the first hour of the landing: "No tanks, no bomb craters for cover. Three enemy strongpoints not knocked out. Men stripped and cleaned weapons. Radios not working, units scattered, equipment gone. Third, fourth, and fifth waves found first two waves trapped on beach, unable to advance."[2]

The 16th Infantry's Intelligence and Recon Platoon diary told the tale in more detail: "The ramp went down and out the men went into an inferno of machine-gun fire from the heights above the beach, cross-fired so that it seemed to cover every square foot, into mortar fire and artillery fire. Through the waist-deep water men by the hundreds waded beachward as the murderous fire cut them down. Those who reached shore found sanctuary behind a ledge that screened off the small-arms fire. As far as the eye could see, bodies were packed

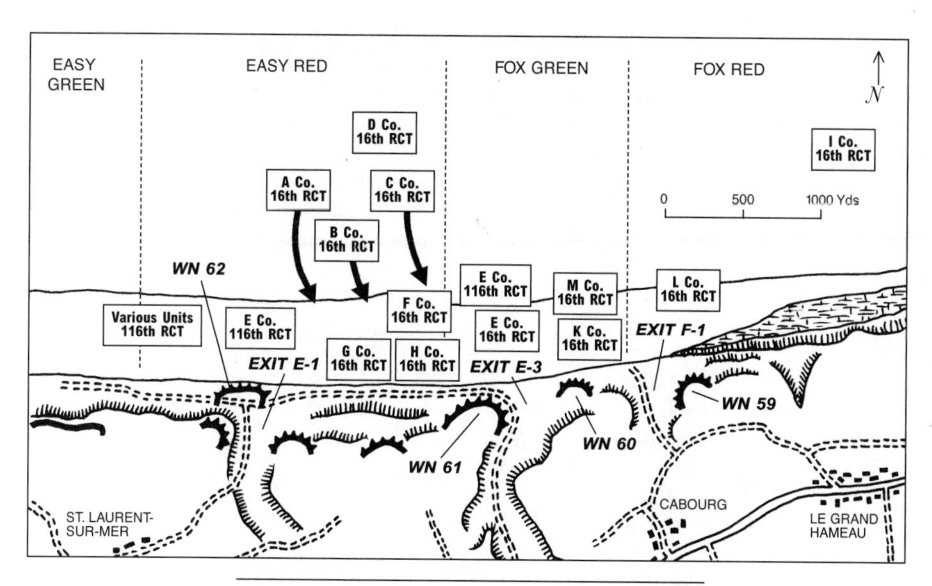

The 1st Battalion's landings at Easy Red and Fox Green at 0720 hours. (Positions approximate)

behind this ledge—men who were moaning with pain and those who would moan no more. The medics were everywhere, dressing wounds and rescuing men which the incoming tide stretched out its ever lengthening tentacles to impound. . . . It was impossible to move forward until there was at least one breach in the mine field. Behind the men, the tide crept relentlessly onward. Artillery and mortar fire grew heavier."[3]

While soldiers in battle normally are fervently grateful for the arrival of reinforcements, at Omaha Beach, the boats carrying Lieutenant Colonel Edmund F. Driscoll's 1st Battalion only added to the problems. With Hicks's 2nd and Horner's 3rd Battalions still hung up on the barest lip of sand, the German reception for 1st Battalion was as fearsome as that which greeted the 2nd and 3rd.

Harley Reynolds, B Company, 16th Infantry, in Boat Twenty-Two, remembered, "We circled for what seemed like hours in our rendezvous area. We were near enough to hear the action on the beach. There wasn't much conversation. We were listening to all that small-arms fire and swapping glances. We knew we were in for a hot reception. . . . I saw and heard the coxswain say to the other crewman, 'This is it. Here we go,' as he waved forward, like a cavalryman."

Sergeant Harley Reynolds, B Company, 16th Infantry Regiment. (Courtesy Harley Reynolds)

Reynolds noted, "I could see things were going wrong as we slowed down to go in. Some boats were coming back after unloading. Others were partly awash, but still struggling. Some were stuck, bottomed out, racing their motors and getting nowhere. . . . I was looking over the side often during these last minutes. We were moving slow because of the other craft and obstacles the coxswain had to avoid. I saw direct hits on craft still far away from land; I doubt those on board not wounded made it to shore. I saw craft sideways, being upturned, dumping troops into the water. I saw craft heavily damaged by shellfire being tossed around by the waves. I saw craft empty of troops and partly filled with water, as though abandoned, awash in the surf. Men were among them, struggling in the pitiful protection they gave."

Surprisingly, in the last few moments before the ramp dropped, Reynolds found himself becoming very calm and able to analyze the situation very clearly. "I was looking back at the men, that they were down and in their places, and ready. I remember how calm and intent the coxswain was, as he guided our craft in. I cannot give this man enough credit. I often think he must have calmed me some. It is surprising how few machine-gun bullets hit our craft. I kept listening for them to hit, because they certainly were flying overhead and hitting the water around us. . . . I felt things then that I would later recognize as *responsibility.* I felt that getting as many men off as possible, and into positions of safety on the beach in formation, was the greatest concern.

"On the last look over the side seconds before the ramp went down, I saw many motionless bodies at the water's edge. I saw wounded struggling with the rough surf. I saw men kneeling and lying in the water with only their heads exposed, for the protection it gave them. I believe these men were frozen with fear, unable to move closer to the beach with the incoming tide. They were of no use to us at that point, because they had no weapons; they just crowded the beach more, hindering movement."

Reynolds had already decided what to do when the ramp went down; he told the two squad leaders to fan out and go straight in. "There was a huge pillbox to our right front at beach level and at the base of the cliff. To our front was a draw that was designated as 'E-1' on our map. To our left front was a rounded hill with the pond [tank trap]at its base that we were told in training we would have to cross. The pillbox had large chunks of concrete blown out just above its left front aperture. Wisps of powder smoke were still visible. Direct fire from the Navy had just ended. I heard the shells whistle in and land close as we landed, and I believe they had hit the pillbox. . . .

"When the ramp went down, we were in kneeling positions. Private Tony Galenti, the radioman, and I rose to exit first. At about the second or third step, I started to fan right. At this second, Galenti was hit by what I believe was machine-gun fire. The radio was hit also, and fragments flew from it. Galenti went down on the boat ramp; I was maybe two feet ahead of him. . . . The burst hitting Galenti went between Steve [Cicon] and me. Arthur's story [Arthur Schintzel] almost ended here. When he came off, he went to the right, heading for a knocked-out tank, thinking it would give him cover. Wrong! A German rifleman had the tank covered. [Arthur] was hit and knocked down. He stayed down until he thought it would be safe to move. He got up and was knocked down again. This happened five or six times."

Reynolds dashed for the scant safety of one of the tetrahedrons. "It reminded me of the ball-and-jacks game we played as kids. . . . I knelt by the obstacle to look around. From the craft to this point, my constant thoughts were, 'What's keeping me up? I must be hit. What does it feel like when you get hit? Too many bullets flying *not* to be hit.' While crossing the beach, I felt tugs at my pants legs, several times. . . . Later, I found too many rips and tears to identify any as bullet holes. I think it's possible for bullets to pass close enough to tug at your clothing. Bullets coming so close make a hissing sound as they go by; those you hear are not the one that hits you. . . . I didn't stay at the obstacle long. Bullets were coming through and hitting the sand at my feet. . . . I could see bullets hitting the sand in bursts and ricocheting in front and to the sides of me. I believe the bullets were coming from a long distance, as they seemed to have lost some of their energy and I could hardly hear their hissing sounds. I spotted the 'shingle' . . . many men were lying behind it. Looking like the only cover, we headed for it, too. As soon as I reached the safety of the shingle, I called out to Sergeant Dean Rummell and Sergeant James Haughey. . . . I asked if they and the men were okay and they said yes. Once I got an answer from Donald Heap. He was our platoon comedian. His comment was serious, but laughable at any other time. He said, 'Sarge, how long do we have to put up with this shit?' As though *I* could do anything about it!"

Reynolds also recounted the experience of the badly wounded Arthur Schintzel: "He was unconscious some of the time until, after losing so much blood, he passed out until the afternoon. Somebody walked by and he groaned, getting their attention. It scared the man. Everyone had been walking by Art all day, thinking he was dead."[4]

The casualties began to pile up and form a grim greeting party for the new arrivals. Technician John E. Bistrica, a member of C Company, 16th Infantry, recalled, "I got to the beach and the first two men I seen, I stopped dead in my tracks and looked at them. They were both dead. They were combat engineers, and were there ahead of us." Taking cover at the shingle, Bistrica felt as if "the whole world was coming in on me. Then another GI hit the ground next to me. He said, 'I'm hit, I can't breathe.' But I don't think he was hit. His life preserver was too tight and was choking off his air. So I got out my knife and jabbed a hole in it. He was okay after that."[5]

An hour or more had passed, with little or no movement off the beach. The bullets and shells continued to rain in on the men lying prone on the shingle and, minute by minute, the number of living soldiers dwindled. A sense of impending doom hung over those miraculously still alive. Staff Sergeant Ervin Kemke, A Company, 16th Infantry, later told a *Yank* reporter: "I don't think any-

Technical Fifth Grade John E. Bistrica, C Company, 16th Infantry Regiment. (Courtesy John Bistrica)

one thought we'd stay on that beach that first morning. I think we all thought we'd be food for the fish, and a lot were. I kept thinking of everything I'd read about the Dieppe raid and I thought this was the same thing all over again."[6]

"I slowly peeked over the top [of the LCVP] and I could see the outline of the shore, which was about five miles away," recalled Sergeant Ted Aufort, on the boat carrying elements of Headquarters Company, 1st Battalion, 16th Infantry, toward land. "All hell was breaking loose on the beach. The engines were roaring. They had them wide open. The pilot of the boat was in a strong steel cage that was meant to withstand machine-gun and rifle fire. The front ramp went down with a thud into the water, and I wound up in about five feet of water. The further I went, the shallower it got, of course, and fellows were dropping all over the place. I kept thinking, 'God, let me make it to the beach, please!' I noticed a fellow to my right . . . he went face down in the water. . . . I turned him over and dragged him with his face out of the water up onto the beach."

Members of the 16th Infantry Regiment wade toward smoke-shrouded Omaha Beach during the early hours of 6 June 1944. (Courtesy National Archives)

Now that he had made it to the shore, Aufort's fervent prayer, undoubtedly shared by thousands of others that morning, became, "Dear Lord, get me off this God-damn beach!"[7]

Lying on the shingle, Harley Reynolds saw the beach behind him rapidly shrinking. He recalled, "Our area of the beach seemed relatively safe, but only if you stayed behind the shingle. . . . The tide was now almost lapping at our feet. Dead bodies are washing in and I'm thinking—'It's time to do something, but what?' Sticking your head up would draw fire."[8]

More boats came in. Aboard one was First Lieutenant William Dillon, of A Company, 16th RCT: "We were on the right flank of the 1st Division. Our orders were to punch a hole through; don't stop until you get to a hill one mile inland. We were to land on a high ebbing tide at 7:30 a.m. I looked over the ramp and could see the little valley which was to be on our right, but I could also see that the Engineers hadn't been there to blow the mined ramps about 600 yards from the beach. By now, we were getting all kinds of fire. There wasn't a footprint in the sand, nor a dead man on the beach—and we were supposed to be the second wave! Where was the first wave of troops?"[9]

First Lieutenant James Watts of the 81st Chemical Mortar Battalion recalled his thoughts as his landing craft neared shore: "It looked like we were running straight into hell. Lots of explosions, lots of fire on the beach. The explosions and the resulting smoke and debris laid a blackish pall over the beach. Survival that day was a matter of luck—you made it, the man next to you didn't." But fate was on his side. "When the ramp is dropped, you exit the craft on the diagonal to avoid the craft broaching and catching you in the back. I went off the left side of the ramp into waist-deep water. Even so, the ramp swung left, knocked me off my feet and under water. The sergeant coming off behind me said the water boiled with machine-gun fire just after I went under. I came up near the rear of the landing craft, untouched." Watts later heard that, on a nearby landing craft, "the coxswain put them in over their heads and he refused to go any farther [toward the shore]. He was persuaded to do so with a gun to his head.

"My platoon suffered eight casualties that day. My company commander was killed on the beach by a mortar round. He wouldn't have survived if an operating room had been five feet away. I also remember vividly the death of another one of my men. Each one of our mortar squads landed with two two-wheeled carts—one for the mortar, the other for ammunition. Each cart had a handle to the cart and two chains forward of the handle. Thus four men were pulling the cart as they hit the beach—quite an attractive target. Private [James W.] Bumgardner was behind one of the carts, pushing it. I could see his jacket puff from the impact of machine-gun rounds. Bumgardner went down, then struggled back up to his knees, trying to keep pushing, and then collapsed dead, an example of a brave man trying to do his duty with his very last breath."[10]

Although Lieutenant Colonel George W. Gibbs's 7th Field Artillery Battalion had lost many of its guns in the surf, it followed Driscoll's 1st Infantry Battalion onto the beach. Offshore, men continued to await their turn to brave the fire. Second Lieutenant Lawrence Johnson Jr., a forward observer with the 7th Field Artillery Battalion, recalled that his LCVP "circled off the beach for a seemingly interminable time, waiting for space on the beach. Finally, long after our scheduled landing time, we headed in, the ramp was lowered, and we all straggled off into about three feet of surf. Perhaps my most vivid memory is of the young seaman coxswain screaming from the stern cockpit, 'Get off! Get off! I want to get the hell out of here!' We can thank that young man for landing us in the correct place; many others were disembarked considerable distances from their intended destination on the beach. By some quirk of fate, we waded ashore and ran up the beach to the lee of the sea wall of loose rocks without a single casualty."[11]

Communications specialist Al Alvarez was part of an artillery recon party composed of two lieutenants, three enlisted men, and a driver in a waterproofed jeep. "The LCT was crowded with armor, tanks, and halftracks backed in first," he remembered, "and we (our jeep) backed in last, so I guess we would 'lead the charge' in exiting first. Consider our personal equipment: underwear 'long johns' impregnated with goo to preclude chemical gas contact, woolen ODs, gas flaps at the neck and wrists, field jacket and netted helmets, web equipment, two canteens, three first-aid pouches (one on helmet with morphine syrettes), haversack, grenades, extra ammo, while I carried a carbine enclosed in plastic with taped clips and one on my stock, assault jacket with many pockets, and a plastic-enclosed quarter-mile reel of commo wire, a telephone and 610 radio wrapped in a life preserver. It certainly was an understatement to say we were overloaded!

"I believe the LCT rammed some underwater obstacles because of the scraping noises and finally, amazingly and slowly, the ramp started to come down. At this time, all the vehicles were revving their engines, and the carbon monoxide and diesel fumes were overcoming us and we wanted out! The jeep went down and out. The ramp clanked and we jumped out both sides into five-feet, six-inches of surf. I'm five-feet, seven-inches, and had only my nose out of the water. I immediately exploded my life preserver and started to trudge in. I also inflated the radio's life preserver as I stepped into the surf and rode it in. Then I was out of the deep water and into waist-deep and then knee-deep. These changing depths were 'wave runnels' and what was fortunate for me was a death knell for others. Many 29th Infantry Division soldiers, inexperienced in beach landings, drowned when their inflated waist life preservers caused their heads to go under water. Their bodies with their blue-and-grey shoulder insignia sadly lined the beach tidemark the next day."

Alvarez recalled that his unit was slowly advancing toward the beach until "a rolling thunder, made by awesome explosions of the large-sized guns of the Navy's battle wagons, broke over us and seemed to push us forward." He was lugging one half of the big radio. "[My buddy] Eddie King and I got separated as we both hid behind large metal boat obstacles. However, both of us had identical portions of the radio, so when we got together, we had no commo; we needed George Rosner with the battery packs. After what seemed like hours, we finally left the comparative safety of these beach obstacles. Then, crawling and dragging, we emerged and hid behind a mounded row of pebbles, sort of a berm lined with hundreds of soldiers! Eddie King went back into the surf to pull in wounded, drowning soldiers, and then pointed to his head where blood trickled down his face. There in the center of his helmet was a bullet hole where a round had gone through his helmet, dead center! I had the task of sticking my hand in his helmet and feeling mush, but it was only his hair soaked in blood. It turned out to be only a crease. But then a medic was called over and sat down with his back to the enemy and bandaged Eddie, but was struck in the back. Both of us tried bandaging him and called other medics, but he died."[12]

First Lieutenant John B. Carroll, of Carlisle, Pennsylvania, came ashore in the LCVP carrying the 16th Regiment's executive officer, Lieutenant Colonel John H. Mathews. About a quarter mile from shore, a shell screamed in and destroyed the craft's navigational controls. With the boat foundering, Carroll and the other survivors bailed out over the sides. Carroll tersely noted, "Maintained carbine but lost bandolier of ammunition. Hid behind German underwater defenses and worked way to shore. Ran last 120 yards. Lost two good friends. Mathews shot through head."[13]

Reaching the beach, Corporal William H. Lynn, a scout for the S-2 section of Headquarters, 3rd Battalion, 16th Infantry, found himself scared and shaken at the horrors around him. "Men scrambled for shore. You had to practically push your way in to get cover amongst the pile of soldiers, sailors, and vehicles. No one was advancing. I threw myself alongside them and lay next to a soldier who had been decapitated at the shoulders and had no identification, for his dog tags were also gone. The next thing I did was take my [shelter half] and cover him."

With his name and serial number stenciled onto the shelter half, Lynn suddenly feared that he would be mistaken for the corpse and his family notified that he had been killed in action. "There was another soldier on my right, sitting next to his jeep, staring off into space. I asked him 'Where is 3rd Battalion Headquarters?' I then touched him to see if he understood me and he fell over; he had died from the concussion of a shell. I then found my officer in charge, Lieutenant [Paul N.] Demogenes. He called and said, 'Follow me.' We crept along the embankment. . . . We watched as troops tried to advance and saw some soldiers blown up by mines in a minefield ahead of us."[14]

To war correspondent Don Whitehead, trapped on the beach with the rest of the men from the 16th RCT, the invasion was a disaster: "Many officers were killed before they could reach shore. They died as shells smashed into their boats or as they waded toward the beach or as they stood on the few feet of French soil which they had helped to win. Boats landed far from their targets. Units were scrambled and left without leaders and without direction. And so the men dug in on that narrow strip of beach washed by waves and blood. They piled up by the thousands, shoulder to shoulder. Machine guns were set up a few feet from the water. . . . Mortar crews manned their weapons with the waves washing their boots. But nothing was moving off the beach. The invasion on Omaha Beach was a dead standstill! The battle was being fought at the water's edge! I lay on the beach wanting to burrow into the gravel. And I thought: 'This time we have failed! God, we have failed! Nothing has moved from this beach and soon, over that bluff, will come the Germans. They'll come swarming down on us.'"[15]

It seemed that every German gun within range of Omaha Beach was now firing as fast and as furiously as it could at the incoming landing craft; at the men struggling to get ashore; and at those who were pinned flat to the round rocks behind the low seawall. The ground shuddered and shook with each detonation, as though a volcano was about to erupt. Boats were torn apart by direct hits; men too badly wounded to extricate themselves from the surf were drowned by the rising tide; and those taking cover behind obstacles were slaughtered by the unceasing storm of artillery and mortar shells. The cries of the wounded rose above the awful din, and men who tried to assist the dying and injured were themselves killed or wounded. Some of the best-trained soldiers in the world became casualties before they could even get a glimpse of the enemy. As the German fire intensified to a thundering crescendo, like the last act of a Wagnerian opera, there seemed to be no possible hope for the 1st Infantry Division to establish a beachhead, let alone move inland and take its objectives. There seemed to be even less hope that anyone would survive the onslaught. The corpses strewn across five miles of beach provided mute testimony to what modern munitions can do to the human body. Men were cut in half, decapitated, disemboweled, torn apart, burned, punctured, shredded, emasculated, blown inside out. Some soldiers, on the other hand, bore nary a visible mark, killed by the violent force of concussion. Some lay on the sand totally nude except for their boots, their uniforms having been blasted from their bodies. Others were butchered beyond recognition. Some were reduced to parts—a head here, an arm there, a torso yon, while others were simply vaporized by the direct hit of a shell. Practically every way to die was found on Omaha Beach that cold June morning. Except old age. The 16th RCT, like the 116th to its right, had been halted dead in its tracks. Annihilation seemed to be the inevitable outcome.

At 0830 hours, a Navy beachmaster managed to signal the fleet that no more landing craft were to come ashore—there simply was no room for them, and no room for the men and vehicles they carried. At this time, there were some fifty LCTs and LCIs circling off shore, looking in vain for some place to deposit their cargo. Their skippers could see the landing craft from the previous waves foundering, sinking, burning, or hung up on obstacles, with the sea around them being ripped by tremendous explosions. There appeared to be no safe passages. Seeing the infantry pinned down and subjected to a murderous pounding, the Navy determined that its firepower, which thus far had been less than effective, must be brought to bear at close range against enemy targets, even if it meant risking ships and their crews. A flotilla of destroyers moved close to shore and began hammering German positions at nearly point-blank range. The USS *McCook* took under fire targets near the 116th RCT's Vierville exit, as did the *Carmick*. The destroyers *Frankford*, *Doyle*, *Harding*, *Thompson*, *Baldwin*, and *Emmons*, along with the battleship *Arkansas*, came to the aid of the 16th RCT in its struggle for Easy Red and Fox Green.[16]

The battered infantry was grateful for whatever support it could get. Major Kenneth P. Lord, a Vermonter and assistant G-3 for the division, remembered, "We had six destroyers that moved so close to the beach to give us direct fire support that their keels must have hit the bottom. It was the greatest help that we had the entire day. They were instrumental in breaking through the beach defenses."[17]

Lieutenant Colonel William Gara, commanding the 1st Engineer Combat Battalion, gave much credit to the U.S. Navy. "There were naval gunfire teams on shore; by radio they directed the ships to come closer to fire at the pillboxes. The destroyers had been about seven to eight miles offshore; they waved them in until these destroyers were about 700 yards from shore. They lowered their five-inch guns and began shooting at these pillboxes according to the directions of these naval gunfire teams. They were our only supply of artillery for the first four hours on Omaha Beach."[18]

The Big Red One's chief of staff, Colonel Stanhope Mason, would later write, "I am now firmly convinced that our supporting naval fire got us in; that without that gunfire we positively could not have crossed the beaches." And General

Huebner would echo those sentiments with a message to General Bradley once he had established his headquarters on shore: "Thank God for the United States Navy!"[19]

But those words were still hours in the future; the battle for the beachhead was still very much in doubt. Even British General Sir Bernard Montgomery commented that the Americans at Omaha Beach were "hanging on by their eyelids."[20]

Aboard his flagship, the *Augusta,* General Omar Bradley, out of touch with what was happening several miles away on shore, was understandably anxious. "As the morning lengthened," he wrote, "my worries deepened over the alarming and fragmentary reports we picked up on the Navy net. From these messages we could piece together only an incoherent account of sinkings, swampings, heavy enemy fire, and chaos on the beaches. By 8:30, the two assault regiments on Omaha had expected to break through the water's-edge defenses and force their way inland to where a road paralleled the coast line a mile behind the beaches. Yet, by 8:30, V Corps had not yet confirmed news of the landing. We fought off our fears, attributing the delay to a jam-up in communications. It was almost 10:00 before the first report came in from Gerow. Like the fragments we had already picked up, his message was laconic, neither conclusive nor reassuring. It did nothing more than confirm our worst fears on the DD tanks. 'Obstacles mined, progress, slow . . . DD tanks for Fox Green swamped.'

"Aboard the *Ancon*, Gerow and Huebner clung to their radios as helplessly as I. There was little else they could do. For at that moment they had no more control than I of the battle on the beaches. Though we could see it dimly through the haze and hear the echo of its guns, the battle belonged that morning to the thin, wet line of khaki that dragged itself ashore on the Channel coast of France. Alarmed over the congestion of craft offshore on Omaha Beach, Kirk ordered his gunnery officer in for a close-up view. I sent Hansen with him aboard a PT boat. They returned an hour later, soaked by the seas, with a discouraging report of conditions on the beach."[21]

Bradley's aide, Major Chet Hansen, recalled, "Admiral Kirk tells General Bradley that they are sending in the gunnery officer, Captain Wellings, to take a look at the beach. Kirk asks Bradley if he had anyone that he wanted to send in with Captain Wellings. General Bradley said no, but I prevailed on the General to see if I might go along. General Bradley nodded his head and said, 'Go ahead.' I transferred over the side of the *Augusta* down a rope ladder to PT boat #171, a rocking, battle-worthy craft commanded by a grayheaded Lieutenant [William

N.] Snelling, chewing a cigar, dressed in heavy oils, with a life preserver about him. In the PT boat as we move nearer inland, it is difficult to make sense from what is going on. A little scattered artillery is falling in the water. Suddenly, we see an LCT go up in a terrific explosion. Waves of troops are moving in toward the beach, and we wave to the doughboys who beckon back, crouching low in their craft. The water this morning is extremely cold and we are soaked to the skin in the booming, wild PT boat. . . . Off the coast of France there is an enormous concentration of craft where everyone looks. The heavy battleships are on the outside of the rim shelling the beach. Cruisers are nearer the shore, and the destroyers sail up against the shore, firing point-blank against the strong points. We followed the channels into the coast and were concerned about mines as we got there. Snelling has two men lying on the forward bow, keeping their eyes open for mines. . . . We did not go all the way into the beach, but lay several thousand yards off shore, took another look, and then returned to the *Augusta*, thoroughly wetted down."[22]

Although bruised and battered, and with their stocks of ammunition beginning to run low, the German defenders inside their concrete fortifications were holding up reasonably well. Communications between the artillery observers and the batteries were still intact, and accurate, deadly fire was still being directed onto the invaders. Soldiers manning the defensive positions were heartened by the large numbers of dead and dying GIs they could see piled in clumps about the beach and floating in the water; by the large numbers of landing craft that were burning, sinking, and disabled; and by the fact that the Yanks were, for the most part, stuck on the beach, unable to mount any type of strong attack or even raise their heads above the sea wall. To the Germans, the American assault at Omaha Beach seemed to be stopped. Now if only the reinforcements—especially the panzers—would arrive in time.

Correspondent Don Whitehead, who had earlier feared that the Germans would come pouring down upon the beachhead, now realized that, "as the minutes ticked by, no gray figures came off the bluffs. Our Navy was pouring a murderous fire into the enemy positions. From the beach too, disorganized as it was, there was a steady stream of small arms and machinegun fire. There was the heavy whack of the tank guns, too, and the thumping of mortars lobbing shells onto the bluff.

"'We've got to get these men off the beach,' [General] Wyman said. 'This is murder!'

"Wyman studied the situation for a few minutes—and then with absolute disregard for his own life and safety, he stood up to expose himself to the enemy's fire. Calmly, he began moving lost units to their proper positions, organizing leadership for leaderless troops. He began to bring order out of confusion and to give direction to this vast collection of inert manpower waiting only to be told what to do, where to go. . . .

"Up and down that bloody strip of beach he went from group to group, from soldier to soldier. Under Wyman's direction, messengers began moving between unit commanders. They stepped over the dead and wounded, flung themselves flat as shells whistled in to splatter them with mud and gravel, and then jumped up to carry out their orders. And gradually the fog of battle began to lift a little."[23]

On another part of the beach, the 16th's firebrand commander, Colonel George A. Taylor—almost a carbon copy of Wyman, strong shouldered, cut from granite, implacable under fire—had come ashore on LCM 26 at about 0720 hours and began doing the same as Wyman: inspiring and rallying the troops. Seeing the confusion and carnage all around him, and seeing men huddled where they could find the barest shred of safety, Taylor was filled with rage—both at the enemy and at his own cowering men. John Bistrica clearly remembered one of the most heralded moments of World War II, perhaps the single moment that turned the tide for the American assault on Omaha Beach: "Colonel Taylor . . . was roaming up and down along the beach. He yelled, 'There are two kinds of people who are staying on this beach—those who are dead and those who are going to die! Now let's get the hell out of here!'

"I says, 'Well, somebody finally got this thing organized. I guess we're going to move out now.' So we started up the draw."[24]

Don Whitehead wrote, "There were many heroes on Omaha Beach that bloody day, but none of greater stature than Wyman and Taylor. They formed the core of the steadying influence that slowly began to weld the 1st Division's broken spearhead into a fighting force under the muzzles of enemy guns. It's one thing to organize an attack while safely behind the lines—and quite another to do the same job under the direct fire of the enemy."[25]

To get through the barbed wire that was barring passage to the draws, however, took a great deal of courage—and more than a little luck. While a seemingly unending deluge of bullets and red-hot, jagged shell fragments continued to rip into the men lying exposed and helpless on the beach, in B Company,

16th RCT's sector, Sergeant Harley Reynolds, who had been hugging the shingle, glanced up. "I could see a narrow pond ahead with marsh grass. Between us and the pond was the wire strung on the roadbed and beyond that a three-strand wire fence with a trip wire only on the front of it. Beyond the pond was another fence without trip wires. There was a sign on the first fence that was in German, but two words I did understand: *Achtung—Minen*. The round hill to our front rose sharply from the far edge of the pond, almost ball shaped, rounding off to our right into a draw leading inland. On the right of the draw was a cliff-like high ground for as far as the eye could see, and got more cliff-like in the distance. It seemed at this time that I was able to stick my head up and down without drawing fire from our right, as we had been getting from atop the cliff and the entrenchments over the huge pillbox. The base of the hill to our front started looking safe and inviting. I felt it would be just a short dash across the pond, through a little flanking fire from our right, to put us beyond the pillbox's side vision. It worked textbook style, but with some unexpected help, and being in the wrong place at the right time. The unexpected help came from a man, small in size, pushing a twelve-foot-long Bangalore torpedo* under the wire on the roadbed. I don't know where he came from. The torpedo was in two sections; he exposed himself to put the first section under the wire. I then realized what was happening and I screamed to Rummell and Haughey and they answered. I yelled, 'We're going through!' They must have understood to respond so fast."

As Reynolds watched, the soldier with the Bangalore torpedo attached a second tube, then carefully inserted the fuse lighter and retreated a few yards from where the blast would take place. But the fuse was defective and the device failed to detonate. "After a few seconds, the man calmly crawled forward, exposing himself again. He removed the bad lighter, replaced it with another, and started to repeat his moves. He turned his head in my direction, looked back, pulled the string and made only one or two movements backward when he flinched, looked in my direction, and closed his eyes, looking into mine. Death was so fast for him. His eyes seemed to have a question or pleading look in them."

An instant later, the torpedo exploded with a sharp crack and Reynolds and his two comrades almost instinctively dashed toward the gap torn in the wire.

---

* The Bangalore torpedo was a hollow, three-foot-long, pipe-like device filled with explosives that could be assembled in sections.

"My men were behind me better than we had ever done in practice. I went through the trip wire, high-stepping just as we did on obstacle courses. I was running so fast, I hadn't made up my mind what to do about the next wire fence until I faced it. I literally dove through in a sideways dive. Hard to believe, but I completely cleared those strands. Not one rip or tear in my clothes or skin. I was into the pond in under ten seconds, with all my men except Schintzel and Galenti following. . . . The pond was deeper than I thought, but we had been instructed not to throw away our life preservers. . . . I was the first across the pond and as I paused to take off the life preserver, I looked back to see how the men were doing. I heard my name called and looked to see Dale Heap, about halfway across the pond. Dale was gunner on one of the machine guns. He had been shot through his upper arm—a good flesh wound. He was holding his one arm above his head and pointing his gun tripod at it, saying, 'See, I didn't drop the tripod.' Always the comedian, he was actually laughing. He kept yelling, 'Stateside! Stateside!' He handed the tripod to his assistant gunner, the first ammo carrier took the gun, and we had a battlefield promotion right there in the middle of the pond. Dale waved goodbye and headed back to the beach. Dale made it stateside and that was the last we heard from him."[26]

From their places of safety, men who had been paralyzed with fear slowly began to emerge. Many of them, to be sure, were killed or wounded the moment they showed themselves to the enemy above. But a handful of courageous captains and lieutenants and sergeants and corporals turned to the scared, soggy men next to them and issued a brief, no-nonsense order: "Follow me." And the men followed.

Incidents of individual bravery began to proliferate all over the beachhead. On Easy Red, an unnamed lieutenant of Engineers and a wounded sergeant unexpectedly stood up and walked calmly over to inspect the barbed-wire entanglement. Returning to the mass of men huddled on the shingle, the lieutenant looked down at them and, with hands on hips, asked, "Are you going to lay there and get killed or get up and do something about it?" When no one was persuaded by this question to assist him, the lieutenant and sergeant picked up a Bangalore torpedo and blew a gap in the wire.[27]

Sergeant Murray Hackenburg, the communications specialist with the JASCO group, was still on the beach, seeking shelter from the bullets and shrapnel. "You could hear the bullets zinging over our heads, and fellows on both sides of me were wounded, and many of them were killed. But finally, one of the officers, one of the brave ones, said, 'Everybody up and out!' And we went up over where one path had been partially cleared, and we followed that path up over the hills. As we were going, the Germans kept shooting at us all the time. I was one of the lucky ones that didn't get hit. Some of the fellows, instead of staying on the path, started off running through those fields and hit these mines and blew them up. That was because of fear—they were anxious to get up where there was more protection. . . . Of course, on top were the Germans with their pillboxes and machine guns and everything."[28]

John B. Ellery, a platoon sergeant in the 16th Infantry, noted, "I [saw] a captain and two lieutenants who demonstrated courage beyond belief as they struggled to bring order to the chaos around them; they managed to get some of the men organized and moving forward up the hill. One of the lieutenants was hit and seemed to have a broken arm . . . but he led a small group of six or seven to the top. It looked as though he got hit again on the way. Another lieutenant carried one of his wounded men about thirty meters before getting hit himself. When you talk about combat leadership at Normandy, I don't see how the credit can go to anyone other than the company-grade officers and senior NCOs who led the way. We sometimes forget that you can manufacture weapons and you can purchase ammunition, but you can't buy valor and you can't pull heroes off an assembly line."[29]

Three members of the 1st Infantry Division would be cited for extraordinary heroism on 6 June and receive the Medal of Honor. One of those was Technician Fifth Grade John J. Pinder Jr., from McKees Rocks, Pennsylvania—a radioman assigned to Headquarters Company, 16th Regiment. According to the citation, Pinder "landed on the coast 100 yards off shore under devastating enemy machine-gun and artillery fire which caused severe casualties among the boatload. Carrying a vitally important radio, he struggled towards shore in waist-deep water. Only a few yards from his craft, he was hit by enemy fire and was gravely wounded. Technician Fifth Grade Pinder never stopped. He made shore and delivered the radio. Refusing to take cover afforded, or to accept medical attention for his wounds, Technician Fifth Grade Pinder, though terribly weakened by loss of blood and in fierce pain, on three occasions went into the fire-swept surf to salvage communication equipment. He recovered many vital parts and equipment, including another workable radio. On the third trip, he was again hit, suffering machine-gun wounds in the legs. Still this valiant soldier would not stop for rest or medical attention. Remaining exposed to heavy

Technical Sergeant John J. Pinder, Headquarters Company, 16th Infantry Regiment, posthumous recipient of the Medal of Honor. (Courtesy Colonel Robert R. McCormick Research Center of the 1st Infantry Division Museum at Cantigny)

enemy fire, growing steadily weaker, he aided in establishing the vital radio communication on the beach. While so engaged, this dauntless soldier was hit for the third time and killed. The indomitable courage and personal bravery of Technician Fifth Grade Pinder was a magnificent inspiration to the men with whom he served."[30]

Not only did individual human courage begin to slowly turn the tide of battle, but American tanks—that precious armor that was supposed to have preceded the first wave of infantry—began to appear in greater numbers on Omaha Beach. A few LCTs drew close to shore to let the tanks crawl out. The commander of the 741st Tank Battalion clanked ashore and tried to organize what few tanks he still commanded into some sort of organized assault off the beach. For the infantrymen, the tanks became a sort of reprieve, for the Germans diverted their fire from the huddled masses of troops to the iron monsters.

From the shingle, Sergeant Ted Aufort watched in amazement as an LCT disgorged its cargo of Shermans. With explosions erupting all around, one tank made it through the beach obstacles and onto the shingle, where it bogged down on the small, smooth stones. "The treads acted like a shovel," Aufort noted, "and she sat with her belly on the rocks and couldn't move any more. But those guys that were inside that thing were letting everything they had go. They had two machine guns and they were firing over our heads at the bluffs. There were pillboxes up there that were shooting down at us, too."[31]

American tanks weren't the only tracked vehicles on Omaha; bulldozers, too, began to arrive although, of the sixteen 'dozers sent to the beach, only six made it. Of these, three were soon knocked out.[32] Correspondent Whitehead marveled at the sight of one in particular: "While the shells were flying thickest and bullets buzzed like hornets, Private Vincent Dove of Washington, D.C., calmly climbed into the seat of a bulldozer and began dozing a roadway off the beach—the first road over which tanks and trucks and guns could move. He sat up there on his 'dozer with only a sweat-soaked shirt to protect him from a slug of steel. He had driven a bulldozer for fifteen years before he entered the army. He wasn't going to let the Germans stop him now! And by some miracle he lived through the fire pouring from the bluff, his bulldozer snorting defiance."[33]

Another bulldozer—perhaps even the same one—caught Corporal William Lynn's eye as he was taking cover with his lieutenant. "We stopped here a moment and I saw a bulldozer landing on the beach. The driver raised the blade in order to protect himself from small-arms fire. In doing so, he couldn't see directly down in front of him. I noticed that he was headed for a wounded soldier. I said, 'Lieutenant Demogenes, that guy is headed right for that soldier! He'll squash him!'

"Lieutenant Demogenes said, 'You go for him and I'll have you court-martialed.' I said, 'Court-martial me when I get back!' and I left on a run, waving my arms to ward off the bulldozer. He saw me and turned away. I ran over to the [wounded] soldier and noticed his leg was shot off except for one muscle; I grabbed a rifle and strapped his leg to it like a splint. I put on a tourniquet and gave him a shot of morphine. We all had morphine packets tied to our shoulders. I then proceeded to carry him over my shoulders to the sea. A couple of men in a small craft like a rowboat came by and as I yelled to them, small-arms fire was landing all around them. They just turned the boat and yelled, 'The hell with you!' I carried the soldier into the sea and the water was up to my neck. However, by this time, an LCT came up to me and dropped the ramp. Lo and

Corporal William H. Lynn, Headquarters, 3rd Battalion, 16th Infantry Regiment. (Courtesy U.S. Army Military History Institute)

behold, it was the same ship I had landed with! They came to my aid and took the soldier from me and headed out to sea. I returned to Lieutenant Demogenes." Lynn was not court-martialed.[34]

Lieutenant Colonel William Gara, commanding the 1st Engineer Combat Battalion, recalled that one of his unit's jobs was to clear the minefields on the beachhead. "The infantry was terribly worried about anti-personnel mines. The Germans had developed a mine called a *schu*-mine that were made out of wood and were very difficult to detect with mine detectors, so they had to be literally blown up while they were still in the ground. Our job was to use Bangalore torpedoes to create gaps in the minefields so that our troops could make it through. That was done starting at about H plus two hours. It wasn't until about eight-

William Lynn's sketch of the incident when he prevented a wounded GI from being crushed by a bulldozer. (Courtesy U.S. Army Military History Institute)

thirty or nine o'clock that we were able to blow these gaps and mark them and get infantry troops ahead of us so we could get on with the job of clearing a fifteen-foot-deep anti-tank ditch, removing the obstacles, removing mines, and getting the road open, because now the beach was becoming cluttered with vehicles coming ashore. One of the 1st Engineer Combat Battalion's jobs was to open Exit E–1 on Omaha Beach so the vehicles could get up to the top of the bluffs and get on with the battle. Late that day, when we got to the top of the bluff, we couldn't believe it—there were signs up there, warning about mines. Without realizing it, we had gone through a minefield. We knew there were mines there, but we didn't think they were spread as far as they were. We were very fortunate."[35]

With the arrival of a handful of tanks and bulldozers at Easy Red and Fox Green, some of the soldiers began to think that they might, at last, have a fighting chance against the dug-in enemy. Certainly the arrival of the follow-up regiment—the 18th—would work to the invaders' advantage. Indeed, the line of landing craft—this time the larger LCIs and LCTs—could be seen through the smoke on the gray horizon, steaming toward shore.

But the problem of congestion along the shoreline and on the beach was bad, and was about to become immeasurably worse.

CHAPTER EIGHT

"The Feeling of Death in the Air"

EVEN THOUGH the survivors of the first wave were still pinned flat on rapidly shrinking Omaha Beach; even though advancement toward the enemy's positions could be measured in inches instead of yards; even though only a handful of fortified enemy positions had been knocked out; even though most of the gaps in the beach obstacles had yet to be cleared, and the vital exits to the top of the bluff had yet to be opened, Colonel George A. Smith Jr.'s 18th Regimental Combat Team was plunging toward Easy Red, hell-bent on making a landing. The 18th had originally been scheduled to hit the beach at 0930 hours, but the carnage and congestion on Easy Red had made meeting that timetable impossible.[1]

The troops crowded aboard the big, lumbering LCIs had no way of knowing that the beach was full; that there was no room for them; that the mines and underwater obstacles and machine guns and mortars and artillery pieces still awaited them; that the entire landing at Easy Red and Fox Green—as well as in the 116th's sector—was on the verge of disaster. So on came the ships, looking for the lanes that were supposed to have been created by the Engineers and UDT men who were now dead.

Certainly the scene ahead of them could not have been very encouraging: LCVPs and other landing craft wrecked, burning, submerged; corpses bobbing in the surf; exploding munitions turning the beach into a smoky, hellish landscape; artillery reaching out from enemy positions ashore and detonating uncomfortably close. Something terrible must have gone wrong, thought the men of the 18th Infantry, but what? What had happened to the air bombardment; the guns of the big ships; the rockets; the DD tanks; the DUKW-mounted artillery? What

A dead American soldier, his life belt still around him, lies on the sand of Omaha Beach, late on 6 June 1944. The fact that soldiers can stand around (background) indicates that the battle for the beachhead is essentially over. (Courtesy National Archives)

had happened to their comrades in the 16th Infantry Regiment? Were any of them even still alive?

War correspondent Don Whitehead recorded his impressions of the chaos still reigning on the beach: "The wounded lay at the water's edge with the glazed look of shock, waiting until someone could remove them. Dead men's bodies were sprawled in the gravel or rolled gently in the surf. A wounded man crawled out of the water to the edge of the protective embankment. A mortar shell hit him squarely between the shoulders."[2]

The 18th RCT's 2nd Battalion, commanded by Lieutenant Colonel John Williamson, was leading the charge onto shore just to the west of Exit E-1.[3] Aboard one of the assault ships was nineteen-year-old Ralph "Andy" Anderson, a private first class from Kansas City, Missouri, and an automatic rifleman assigned to E Company, 18th RCT. Before the invasion, several members of his company who had taken part in the North Africa and Sicily landings had attempted to buck up his spirits. Anderson said, "They kept telling me it [the landing] would be a piece of cake. They were just trying to encourage us poor souls that didn't know anything about it. My squad leader had been in the North Africa and Sicily campaigns and he told me, 'The first thing you do is take that bipod off the BAR* and drop it into the English Channel. They're gonna be looking for you the minute they see that automatic weapon.' So I did. It's still there, so far as I know."

Losing his weapon at the water's edge in his haste to reach safety, Anderson somehow managed to make it through the rain of artillery, mortar, and machine-gun fire and, teaming up with an assistant gunner from another squad named Lowery (whom Anderson vaguely knew and called "Buckeye" because he was from Ohio), took cover along the crowded shingle. Realizing he was weaponless, he dashed back into the surf to retrieve his BAR; he cleaned it three times before it would operate properly. Above Anderson and Lowery, a machine gun in a concrete fortification was spitting a stream of continuous fire. "We must have hit the beach almost perfect, but there weren't nobody else there that would go up the path, so I told Buckeye we've got to get off this beach or we're gonna get killed." Dodging bullets and shrapnel, the two of them began scrambling up the path past the still-active pillbox. "A destroyer pulled up broadside to the beach. Buckeye and I had already gone past that pillbox, maybe fifty or a hundred yards up the hill, when [the destroyer] started shooting at it. They put every round in that pillbox; none of the shells got close to us."[4]

Jack Bennett, a twenty-year-old private from Vernon, Texas, a member of E Company's mortar squad, recalled that his landing craft came in, was waved off, moved westward, and finally broached on a sand bar, where the troops debarked into deep water. "The water was up to my neck, and I'm six-two. I can't swim, but I *can* walk fast under water!" Lugging four 60mm mortar rounds in addition to the rest of his equipment, Bennett finally made it to shore where, he noted, "it seemed like there were jillions of people on the beach. The Germans were hitting everything—tanks and vehicles of all kinds. They had those all zeroed in. As a consequence, we tried to stay as far away from those things as we could. We

---

* Browning Automatic Rifle. Each rifle platoon had three two-man BAR teams.

had to move back to the left quite a long ways; it took us a long time to get to where we were supposed to be."[5]

Matters were soon complicated by the unexpected arrival of the 29th Division's 115th RCT, which was scheduled to hit Dog Red and Easy Green beaches but which had been unable to find its control vessel and thus had landed atop the still-disembarking 18th RCT. As a history of the invasion reads, "The result was further congestion and confusion off that sector, and considerable delays for both regiments, both in making shore and getting off the beach. Instead of getting in between 1030 and 1130, the 3rd and 1st Battalions of the 18th Infantry did not land until about 1300. Meanwhile, all the battalions of the 115th had come in together instead of at intervals, and the result was a partial scrambling of units on the beach."[6]

Captain Robert E. Murphy, the commander of H Company, 18th RCT, recalled that he and his company were loaded into five LCVPs and were heading abreast toward the exploding shoreline. "When we crossed the Line of Departure, which was an imaginary line staked by two patrol boats, we started in. It was mighty rough going; there wasn't anybody who wasn't seasick. On the way in, the Navy was firing, but most of their stuff was going over the bluffs. About twenty minutes later, we ran through a hell of a barrage fired on us by the Germans. As a matter of fact, you could hear the shrapnel beating on the sides of the boat. My right boat, number one, got really hit; several people were hurt."

Luckily, H Company landed intact only about 500 yards west of where they were supposed to be: at the entrance to Exit E–1. "We struck a sand bar, maybe twenty-five or thirty yards from shore, and had to wade in," Murphy related. "It was a botched-up affair. The 115th Infantry from the 29th Division landed at the same spot. When I hit the beach, I saw a man laying in the water. The tide was coming in, ebbing back and forth, rolling him around. I went over to him to see if he was one of my men. The thing I remember the most vividly is, he rolled over toward me and his face floated on top of the water; he rolled back over and [I saw] his head was gone."

Leaving the company under the temporary leadership of one of his platoon commanders, Murphy headed off to find the 2nd Battalion command group. After conferring with Lieutenant Colonel Williamson as to the plan of action, Murphy returned under fire to his company with plans on moving inland.[7]

Richard Borden, the eighteen-year-old Navy corpsman with the 6th Beach Battalion, recalled that he and about a hundred other members of his unit scrambled down the nets of their transport into an LCT that had pulled alongside. "Once aboard the LCT," he noted, "we settled down apprehensively as we slogged toward the concentration area offshore. It gradually dawned on us that we had been put on hold. Indeed, we were to spend a large portion of the day circling with others, with the battleship *Texas* booming its [fourteen]-inch guns to our left. We were just far enough off the beach to worry about our other members presumably ashore, the beach proper shrouded in smoke with occasional yellow plumes—enemy fire or our demolitions? Occasionally we would veer off to pick up a yellow-life-preservered tank crewman whose 'waterproof' tank had 'lead-sinkered' to the bottom. I especially remember a destroyer running so close ashore to surely go aground as it point-blank shelled what later I was to learn was a concrete German 88 gun position. It's hard to believe but we actually got bored waiting to land. Men were wandering around the LCT, packed as it was, scrounging canned biscuits, and we even found some new soup cans with fuses in the middle that lighted and heated the soup! At one point, I leaned at the stern watching the screws turn up beautiful lavender jellyfish!"

Borden wasn't bored for long. The LCT was finally ordered to make its run to the Easy Red beachhead. "All engines seemed to reply. In amongst the din, men scrambled in the well, snatching packs, guns, stretchers, radio back-packs, and all the assorted paraphernalia of a landing party. . . . Gone were the wisecracks, hands full of crackers and soup, and thoughts of lavender jellyfish. . . . As the huge landing craft sloshed in with engines wide open, no one was interested in taking a peek ahead. . . . We had sensed the confusion within the smoke from offshore. Now we began to smell the smoke of battle that hung along that long, confused shoreline with our own, adrenaline-spread nostrils. Packed as close as weighted humans can be, we waited. The jolt and rumble of the stern anchor paying out announced the nearness of the beach, and an even larger shudder midst more rattling as the forward ramp dropped. A never-to-be-forgotten initial view: the tide was out—not in, as practiced! The dust and smoke and smell almost overwhelming. Huge seaward-slanted posts topped with Teller mines facing us interspersed with huge steel girdered 'jack rocks' embedded in the wet sand of a five-hundred-yard beach—exposed! To the front, a couple of burned-out tanks, LCVPs and, to the right, an angled, dead LCI."

Borden and his mates stepped off into a swarm of machine-gun fire that kicked up the knee-deep water around him. The bullets were soon overshadowed by "the indescribable crack of the 88s at this point, with associated splashes. As I moved between the obstacles, laboring with the inordinate burdens upon my 118-lb. frame, the reality of stretcher cases abandoned on the wet flats of the beach became a paramount concern. Thus our (the corpsmens') first action was that of getting them either up to the protective dune line many feet ahead under fire and chaos, or jogging them seaward chaotically under fire and begging a stressed coxswain to wait before pulling off to accept our burden and get him off the beach."

Borden and the other corpsmen quickly found themselves pinned to the shingle by a torrent of enemy artillery fire. "Suddenly there was the ear-splitting, all-consuming jolt and both [my buddy] Rick and I dove [onto the shingle, which was] impossible to dig into—only a scoop with both hands to shield the face, the head shielded by helmet and the body and butt in the air! I remember the tingling of my entire body, the piercing pain in my ears, and reaching with my hand across my right ear and numb face. Then looking at my fingers for blood—nothing! I looked at Rick perhaps twelve feet away to my left and slightly forward. He, too, had pitched face down. 'Rick, let's move!' I yelled."

When his buddy did not respond, Borden tossed a small stone at him to get his attention. Still nothing. Only at this moment did it dawn on this tender eighteen-year-old that something was amiss. "I hunchingly scrambled over to my friend, rolled his dead-weight body over to be greeted by dust-glazed eyes and sandy face in that awesome fixed expression. . . . His helmet seemed intact, rolled upward and slightly aside, exposing a handful of gray-matter, surprisingly clean. In my shock or innocence, I almost panicked." Borden attempted to inject his buddy with serum albumen, but it was too late. "It was only then that I, in horror, accepted my first-ever encounter with death. Kneeling over the lifeless figure with an overwhelming sense of helplessness, I rewrapped the serum kit and replaced it in my first-aid pouch—all the while with the flashing memories of a nice kid—an assigned litter-mate on maneuvers in Wales and Devon—his young wife—his happiness at news from Chicago of a little daughter—a friend—a brother."

Breaking into tears mixed with a blind rage, Borden rose to his feet, "in full stance, an eighteen-year-old, battle-clad, red-cross-helmeted youth facing the smoky, dark green hillside, tears streaming, and [I] screamed at the unseen German forces: 'God-damn you, everyone!' . . . Here I stood, a less-than-average American youth in an alien land, yet part of a great crusade. Facing the enemy and my God, begging, 'Why don't you hear me? What is life about that you should do this to my friend?'"

Nearby frantic cries of "Medic!" and "Corpsman!" quickly brought Borden back to his senses and his mission on the beach—that of saving lives.[8]

On another part of the beach, Jerome Alberts, a sailor with Platoon A-3 of the 6th Beach Battalion, was flat on the beach and trying to get flatter. "While lying prostrate on the sand, I glanced behind," he recalled. "I noticed a buddy running [then] a shell exploded nearby, then he threw his hands in the air and dropped flat on his face! Holy hell, this is *war*!! Guys are getting it! A shrill scream sent me diving for earth! I lyed [sic] there until the second one went off, just about 20 yards away! They're coming too close! . . . I kept moving in toward the dune line, several yards behind our platoon leader, Lt. Woods. Then I witnessed something that shall linger in my mind as long as life itself. It was the commonest thing on any battlefield, an American soldier, lying on his back in a pool of water, his rigid, white hand suspended in air. . . .

"I viewed the beach—burning trucks, flaming tanks, other vehicles bogged down, and still more that could not move because of the heavy fire—members of the first assault waves still lying about, some dead, some wounded, and others pinned down and unable to go up the hill. . . . God, I was scared! I heard the whistle—it was very close. Would it hit me? Oh, Lord, spare me! Boom!!! A few yards off! There was Bill, and Ray; Sam was a few yards off. There's Eddie Burke and the Rebel. So far it looks like A-3 Communications [Platoon] is intact. No, no, where is 'Vermin?' Oh, hell, he is too smart—nothing could happen to Myrick. Get down you dope!! When the hell will we knock out those pillboxes? . . . Glancing back, a figure straggled forward towards me through a haze of smoke. I recognized him. 'Barney, Barney, come here!' It was Barnett, a radioman of Platoon A-2. In ten steps he was to me, and I yanked him in my shallow (so-far protecting) hole. He was wounded in the neck, but had already been rendered medical attention. He was shaken up and blood was caked over his mouth and hands. I tried to comfort his nerves. 'Do you want a smoke, Barney?' He nodded. . . .

"'Let's move to the left,' cried Lt. Woods. We dashed madly about 150 yards and dug in again. In two minutes, our area just vacated had suffered definitely at least six direct hits which surely would have sent us to Kingdom Come. So the living lay with the dead and wounded, waiting until the guns could be silenced."[9]

While the living lay with the dead, actions were being taken that would lead to the redemption of the men on the beach. It began when the destroyer *Frankford* moved to within a thousand yards of the shore and began blasting the pillbox that was preventing movement off the beach at Exit E-1. Then, at around 1100 hours, F Company, 18th RCT, under Captain Orin W. Rosenberg, had, along with a lone Sherman tank, flushed twenty dazed and dust-covered defenders from the structure. Captain Robert Murphy recalled, "Two of the [*Frankford*'s] rounds hit that bunker and, as I watched, the Germans came out of it and surrendered to F Company."

While G Company (Captain Gordon Jeffrey, commanding) secured the entrance to E-1, Murphy's H Company advanced up the path without suffering a casualty. "That bunker was the last stronghold on the beach, so that opened the draw. I married up with the command group there, and we went up," Murphy related. "We encountered minefields on the way up. There was one young lad with his foot blown off laying there and, as I came along, he said, 'Watch out for the mines, sir.' We made it to the top without any problems."[10] F and G Companies, along with the 18th's headquarters, quickly followed. With the 2nd Battalion, 18th RCT, moving uphill, Brigadier General Wyman ordered it to take over the mission of the decimated 16th RCT and head for Colleville.

Engineers cleared mines from the sandy draw, and bulldozers from the Engineer Special Brigade Group were making another path just to the west for use by American armor and other vehicles. Exit E-1 quickly became the primary focus of all the units trying to leave the beach and climb to the heights. The situation was rapidly improving for the 1st Infantry Division.[11]

Still sitting offshore, an anxious General Omar Bradley knew nothing of this. At 1330 hours, seven hours after the assault had begun, frustrated by the lack of timely news from the beachhead, Bradley directed Major Chet Hansen to make another reconnaissance run to Omaha Beach. "This we did in Snelling's PT boat," noted Hansen, "closing in on the beach and then transferring at about 2,000 yards off shore to an LCVP. Cox[swain] was reluctant to take us farther inland because of the danger of breaking his hull on underwater obstacles. The LCVP took us in to four feet of water. We jumped off and waded ashore. There on Omaha Beach lay a heavy pile of rubble with the wrecked boats, their backs broken in the low water. There were innumerable tetrahedrons, hedgehogs with Teller mines fastened to the tops of the steel or iron obstacles. There were some small-arms fire to the beach on our right, but the troops in front were just be-

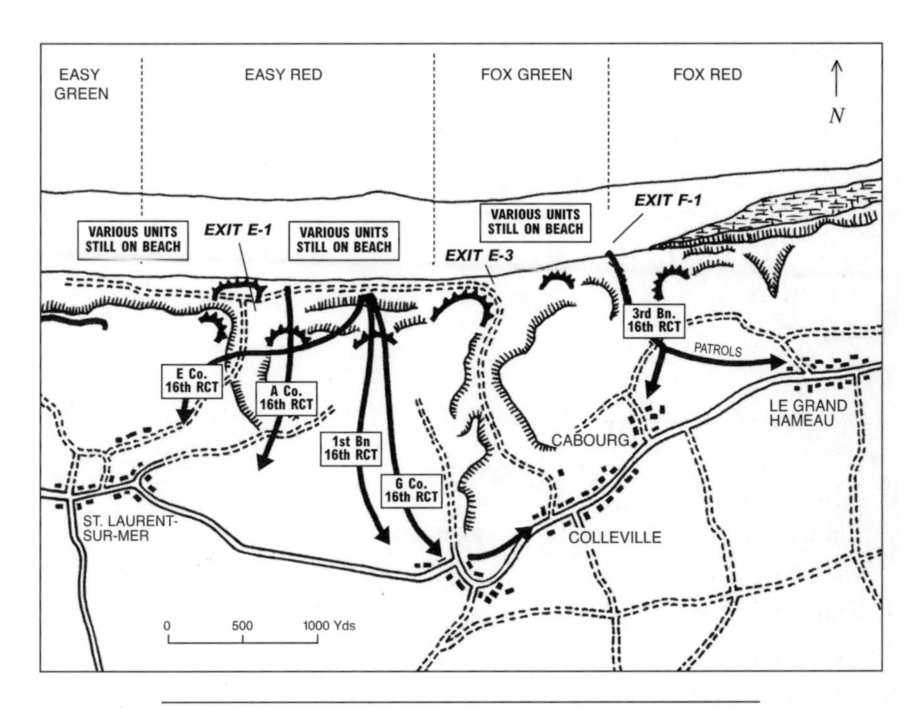

The progress of the 1st Infantry Division by noon, 6 June 1944.

ginning to get the exit from the beach in operating order. A single file of troops was passing up the hill to the left in a clear path through a minefield. The path had been indicated by white tape.

"There were a score of dead troops on the beach, sprawling and wet, lying where they had fallen. No one had as yet collected the dead. Off near the sea row, there were fifteen or twenty wounded receiving care from a battalion surgeon. All over the beach lay hundreds of gas masks and packs and all the equipment that men throw overboard quickly. Floating in the shallow water there lay rolls of film, thousands of discarded life belts, rations, smashed portions of landing craft. Floating nearby in the water we saw one body with a leg blown off. There was evidence that several boats had hit the mines that had been prepared for them atop the landing obstacles. . . . All the way in, trucks were lying up to their tops in water. Wreckage and disarray everywhere. . . ."

While conferring with a young captain who was acting as the beachmaster in that sector, Hansen noted that "an enemy artillery shell landed in a concentration of LCTs off to our left. Troops were scrambling ashore quickly in waist-deep

A German direct-fire artillery piece sits amid the rubble of its concrete gun pit overlooking Fox Green beach. (Courtesy Colonel Robert R. McCormick Research Center of the 1st Infantry Division Museum at Cantigny)

water. Wounded lay in shell holes near the bank on Omaha Beach. Rations were scattered about—K rations, their boxes wet and ripped open. Another shell landed nearby, hit a truck, and threw a soldier's body thirty feet into the air where it hung for a moment, turned over, and then fell lifelessly to the ground. We were told that another GI on a bulldozer had been similarly blown into the air, although not as high. He fell back to the beach, dusted off his seat, boarded another vehicle, and moved on."

Hansen returned to the *Augusta*, where he found Bradley and Admiral Kirk in the ward room, still receiving gloomy reports from the beachhead. "The division commanders had not yet gone ashore. Troops were milling up as the landing was slowed down by obstacles and by the severe resistance on Omaha Beach. The LSTs were unable to get close to shore. . . ."

Later that afternoon, Hansen and Bradley motored to the *Bayfield* to consult with the corps commanders. "We found the situation in Collins' VII Corps going very nicely with the 4th Division moving in on schedule," Hansen wrote. "V Corps presented us with a sticky situation, however; the 16th Infantry was ashore but calling for support. . . . the initial casualties were very heavy. . . . The beach commander, a Colonel Thompson, had been seriously wounded and knocked out of action right away, and that caused some confusion. We were told the beachmaster had been killed. Battalion commanders on the invasion were killed with a subsequent loss of control. The 116th Infantry Regiment [sic; it was the 115th] of the 29th Division had been landed on the wrong beach and was compelled to move laterally before striking inland towards its objectives. We still had no definite word from the Rangers, but the guns at Point de Hoe [sic] had not fired. Additional Rangers were sent up the coast after a smoke signal was received from the cliff indicating that the Rangers had scaled their objective. . . . The German is shelling the beach with his famous 88mm guns, shelling the boats after they have been beached, causing casualties and severe difficulties in unloading. Bradley shows no sign of worry. He told Collins, however, 'They are digging in on Omaha Beach with their fingernails. I hope they can push in and get some stuff ashore.' Kean shows great anxiety."[12]

In the early afternoon, following the landing of the 2nd Battalion, 18th RCT, Lieutenant Colonel Robert H. York's 1st Battalion came ashore. Lieutenant Harold Monica, D Company, 18th Infantry, remembered the scene: "We found ourselves kind of in the firing line of the big ships. I would guess we were 10,000–12,000 yards from Easy Red beach, our designated landing zone. The firing [by the Navy] picked up as we continued on our way. The sound was loud but not deafening, as the ocean is a big place and we were never closer than fifteen-hundred yards to any given warships. When they fired, the sound was heavy and more of a *rumph* than the sharp crack of rifle and machine-gun bullets. At this time, we were able to observe, with our field glasses, bomb bursts on the beach as our dive bombers went to work. Flights of medium bombers were passing over, headed for their targets further inland. Special LCTs that had been adapted to carry some five thousand five-inch rockets . . . were now being fired. They were closer to shore than we were at this moment, but their fire trail and smoke were clearly visible. Certainly this type of firepower must be having an effect. With this much force, the invasion *must* succeed. It really didn't occur to me that it wouldn't, as you just get caught up in the immensity of the operation that you are such a small part of. H-Hour was a couple of hours ago and we continued towards the beach to meet our landing time. No word of success or lack of same for the 16th was reaching us. Therefore, no way to know if we would have to assault the beach or land on a secured area. We were trained and prepared to continue the assault if the 16th Infantry had not been successful.

"I was at the top of the stairs of the LCI, and I reported to the platoon sergeant and the other people down below in the hold what I was seeing and telling them it didn't look that tough. It didn't quite turn out that way. We continued slowly toward the beach. The approach had been uneventful for us and for the 1st Battalion. LCIs were running abreast of each other 75 to 100 yards apart. At five hundred yards, the beach looked pretty hostile. We could see a couple of tanks and other vehicles that had been hit and were burning. However, there was no sound of rifle or machine-gun fire, but mortar and artillery fire was intense—smoke and dust everywhere."[13]

Eddie Steeg, one of Lieutenant Monica's men, recalled, "There was no guessing as to where we were headed this time. The going was rough and that old feeling of seasickness returned—this time coupled with a serious knot of fear, something we did not experience on the way to North Africa. This time we knew what the war could and would be like. I managed to keep everything down on the way across. . . . There is no way to describe the dreaded feeling of fear that persists—it has to be experienced. As I waited with the others, I was amazed at the number of vessels engaged in this operation. Although I feared what lay ahead, I was ready once again to put my feet on solid ground."[14]

Many men had barely set foot on solid ground when they were killed or wounded. As happened to virtually everyone who landed on 6 June, Private First Class Lewis C. Smith, I Company, 18th Infantry, found himself surrounded by gruesome scenes of gore and violent death. "When I hit the beach, the soldier on my right had his head blown off; the one on my left had a hole in his back about twelve inches wide."[15]

More landing craft continued to come in, picking their way through the flotsam of battle. Aboard different craft were two brothers from Kansas, Walter and Roland Ehlers. Twenty-three-year-old Walter was a staff sergeant with L Company, 18th Infantry, and Roland, also a sergeant, four years older, was assigned to K Company. "Brothers were not allowed to serve together in the same combat unit," Walter Ehlers said. He had enlisted in 1940, and had served with both the 7th and 3rd Infantry Divisions before being transferred to the 1st in North

Private Carlton W. Barrett, Headquarters Company, 18th Infantry Regiment, recipient of the Medal of Honor. (Courtesy Colonel Robert R. McCormick Research Center of the 1st Infantry Division Museum at Cantigny)

Africa. Ehlers's orders were to take an advance recon patrol into Trévières, about six miles inland. "We were all in pretty good spirits. Most of us had been in combat before and didn't seem to have too much anxiety. The only thing we knew was that the odds [of getting killed or seriously wounded] get higher as you go along."[16]

On a day of incredible heroism, Private Carlton W. Barrett, from Fulton, New York, a member of the Intelligence and Reconnaissance Platoon, Headquarters Company, 18th Infantry, would earn the Medal of Honor "for gallantry and intrepidity at the risk of his life above and beyond the call of duty."

Debarking from his LCVP, Barrett waded through neck-deep water with bullets and shrapnel flying all around him. "Disregarding the personal danger," the citation read, "he returned to the surf again and again to assist his floundering comrades and save them from drowning. Refusing to remain pinned down by the intense barrage of small arms and mortar fire poured at the landing points, Private Barrett, working with fierce determination, saved many lives by carrying casualties to an evacuation boat lying offshore. In addition to his assigned duties as a guide, he carried dispatches the length of the fire-swept beach; he assisted the wounded; he calmed the shocked; he arose as a leader in the stress of the occasion. His coolness and his dauntless, daring courage while constantly risking his life during a period of many hours had an inestimable effect on his comrades and is in keeping with the highest traditions of the Army of the United States."[17]

Private First Class Louis Newman, Cannon Company, 18th Infantry, recalled how he wound up on top of a mostly submerged Army truck just off the blazing shore. When it had come time for the vehicles of his unit to roll out of the LST they were on, he elected to ride out on a deuce-and-a-half cargo truck rather than on a half-track. "The truck was taller than the half-track, and I couldn't swim." There were seven or eight men in the half-track but he was the only one, except for the driver, a fellow named Stewart, on the truck. "The LST commander was afraid to get too close to shore," he remembered. "We went out about fifty feet and there were some soldiers who were stranded in the water, trying to get back to the LST, but they were being shoved back into the water by people on the LST."

The submerged engine of Newman's truck then died. "We couldn't move and I started looking around me. There were bodies floating in the water and there was shelling in the water and I was maybe three hundred yards from shore. The tide started to come up and I crawled up on top of the cab. The driver did the same. Halfway between our truck and the shore was a three-quarter-ton truck, and Stewart said, 'I'm going to try to swim out to that other truck.' He wanted me to go with him but I said, 'I'll go in later.' He made it. I sat on top of the cab of the two-and-a-half-ton truck and started looking around. To the right of me there was a small landing craft and I saw a sailor who had his head wedged in between the ramp and the side of the craft. Some distance away to the left of me was a landing craft shooting rockets toward the shore. Straight ahead, there were shells going off. And there were DUKWs going back and forth, but they wouldn't stop to pick up any of the wounded men in the water.

"I'm still on top of this truck and the water is rising and I say to myself, 'I'm going to drown if I stay here much longer,' so I decided to go for that three-quarter-ton truck where Stewart was. I took my bedding roll and wrapped it around my carbine and threw it as far as I could in front of me and held my breath and jumped after it. I don't know how, but I got to the three-quarter-ton truck. It was a good thing the current was going from east to west because that helped me get to the truck. There was a boom on the truck and Stewart stuck it out and I grabbed it and he pulled me in. We sat on the truck for awhile and then he said, 'I'm going for the shore.' I said, 'Okay, I'll stay here for awhile.' The beach was clogged. I sat on top of the cab and saw a soldier walking in the water in front of me, hollering, 'Mama, mama, mama,' and then he went down. There was still firing on the shore—artillery shells and everything. The small-arms firing started to die down a little, but there was still shelling and sniping. While I was on the truck, an American destroyer came up behind me and fired shells right into a strongpoint on the shore." Above the din, Newman yelled encouragement to the Navy gunners: "Give it to 'em! Give it to 'em! After about four rounds, they hit the mark. I found out later that twenty Germans who were in the strongpoint surrendered.

"Right to the side of me was a group of Royal Air Force men. This one guy was helping get his buddies in to the shore, and he passed me and said to me, 'Jump into the water!' I said, 'I can't swim.' He said, 'I'll watch out for you.' The water was about five feet deep. I started to take off but it was over my head. The next thing I know, I felt the bottom and I started walking in. I had no lifebelt or helmet. I finally made my way to shore and I saw a guy from the 29th Division; I didn't know any unit other than the 1st was supposed to be there. He was a mortarman and he was next to an 81mm mortar with no ammunition. When I saw his patch, I said, 'What are you doing here?' I didn't think anybody but the 1st Division would be here.

"There was a bunch of knocked-out vehicles to the right of me and these RAF men were hiding behind them, trying to get some cover. I says, 'I gotta get off this beach.' To the left of me was the shingle, and I noticed a lot of soldiers behind the shingle, not moving, and bodies and wounded all over. I said, 'Follow me,' but the RAF men had other ideas. I decided to go up against the cliffs to my right. On my way, I tried to help some guys, but it was too late; they were dead. I kept on moving because I had no protection. I picked up a helmet but it was full of brains, so I threw it away. To get to the cliffs, I had to go through a German minefield—the signs said '*minen*'—but it was a place that had no mines, just signs. I went through a marsh and passed an anti-tank ditch, went across that, and made my way to the side of the cliff. I was now about two hundred yards inland from the shore. It so happened that I found my first sergeant there; he was the only one of my company to make it there. About three or four o'clock in the afternoon, we started getting more fellows showing up along the cliff. Some of them were wounded. About 4 or 5 o'clock, a truck came around and started picking up the bodies. There were still a lot of German artillery shells going here and there, and then we had a lot of sniper fire."[18]

Ray Klawiter, D Company, 18th Infantry, recalled, "There was a lot of noise, a lot of shelling going on. It was a gray, nasty day—with the feeling of death in the air. We were taking some artillery and mortar and small-arms fire, but nothing like the first wave. There was wreckage and dead bodies lying all around. Some of the wounded had been taken back to the boats before we got in. We didn't stay on the beach too long. The engineers had cleared a path and marked it with toilet paper. If you stepped just a little off that path, you would get it. We lost one of the lieutenants from the mortar company. He just stepped back and got blown up."[19]

Eddie Steeg, carrying the bipod for an 81mm mortar, recalled, "Jerry was still shelling and we had to hit the dirt quite a number of times. I was really 'shitten-and-a-gitten.' There have been many descriptions of what the Normandy beach looked like at that time. All I can say is the beach was really messed up. We did not have much time to look around and sight-see. My concentration was focused on the person in front of me and the direction he was heading. We scuttled across the sand as quick as possible and started up a slope in a draw that had been cleared of mines by the Engineers. We were told to stay within the boundaries or limits that were outlined with toilet paper laying on the ground. A couple of lieutenants made the mistake of stepping out of bounds, which set off some mines, killing one instantly and blowing a leg off the other. I paused long enough to pick up a Tommy gun that an unfortunate someone would no longer be able to use. Not that I needed any more weight to carry but, for some reason, I just couldn't resist being the possessor of a real Tommy gun that I had so often seen being used in the movies. Maybe I could now copy Jimmy Cagney, and use the weapon to eliminate those 'dirty rats,' the Jerries."[20]

Seaman Jerome Alberts and his 6th Beach Battalion unit finally found the courage to get off their stomachs and begin moving toward the bluffs. "Every step I took, I learned that someone I knew was lost—Wade, Albertson, Collins,

Black, Higgins, Murphy—I can go on. Many others were wounded. Albertson's death was the greatest shock to me because we went to the same naval training school for four months. Morgan, Gil, and I were the only ones from that school and we stuck together in Scotland and England. At Lido Beach, in New York, he practically cried to me, telling me how much he wanted to be home for Christmas. He seemed so much younger than his actual age of nineteen. He was too young to die. . . . God bless his soul, for his mother will not see him again. I knew Franny Collins just as well. He was in that group under the small boat and he and quite a few others perished when it was the object of that German eighty-eight. Damn the 88's!! I played cards quite often with Franny, and his luck at poker was remarkable. He talked of his brother, the admiration he had for him, [and] of his girl. Franny was a regular church attendant, so I know that he was good, and that God accepted him. God bless his and their souls, and let them rest in peace."[21]

Staff Sergeant Christopher Cornazzani came ashore with the headquarters party of the 1st Battalion, 18th Infantry. "When we reached the beach, we gave the enemy new targets to occupy them. Many thoughts go through your mind in moments like this, but you learn not to dwell on them and to keep a clear mind. I just followed Lieutenant Colonel [Robert] York's footsteps. Everyone watched him; he never showed any fear and was like a rock. He made you feel that everything was what we expected, so everything was normal." Once ashore, the headquarters group moved up a gulley. "This gulley had a four-foot-thick concrete pillbox at the top. A Navy destroyer managed to place itself within a thousand yards and hit the fortification with about five rounds of their big guns and blew part of the roof off. There was no more enemy fire from it.

"There was still the job of walking up the gulley planted with anti-personnel mines from the bottom to the top. . . . Some were designed to blow your legs off; others, like the 'Bouncing Betty,' would propel itself out of the ground to a height of about five feet and explode in your face. The one feared most was the 'castrator.' These were little tubes with a bullet that had a soft percussion cap set on a pin; when you stepped on it, it would fire."[22]

Sergeant Theodore L. Dobol, K Company, 26th Infantry, who would come ashore later that day, also recalled these nasty devices: "We tried to avoid the thousands of mines. The mines called the 'Castrating Pencil' were especially on our minds. After stepping on this mine, lifting your foot would cause the spikes to explode, driving a sharp pencil into your groin and causing permanent damage to your vital organs. We were lucky, because our sector, we found out later, did not have many of these."[23]

A chaplain from Miami, Florida, Second Lieutenant John Burkhalter, found himself accompanying one of the waves ashore. "When my part of the division landed, there were impressions made on my mind that will never leave it. Just before landing, we could see heavy artillery shells bursting all up and down the beach at the water's edge under well-directed fire. As I stood in line waiting to get off the LCI to a smaller craft to go into shore, I was looking toward land and saw a large shell fall right on a landing craft full of men. I had been praying quite a bit through the night as we approached the French coast, but now I began praying more earnestly than ever. Danger was everywhere; death was not far off. I knew that God alone is the maker and preserver of life, who loves to hear and answer prayer. We finally landed and our assault craft was miraculously spared, for we landed with no shells hitting our boat."

Once he came ashore, Burkhalter observed, "The enemy was well dug in and had set up well-prepared positions for machine guns, and had well-chosen places for sniping. Everything was to their advantage and to our disadvantage, except for one thing: the righteous cause for which we are fighting—liberation and freedom. For the moment, our advantage was in the abstract and theirs was in the concrete. The beach was spotted with dead and wounded men. I passed one man whose foot had been blown completely off. Another soldier lying close by was suffering from several injuries; his foot was ripped and distorted until it didn't look much like a foot. Another I passed was lying very still, flat on his back, covered in blood. Bodies of injured men all around. Sad and horrible sights were plentiful."[24]

Naval Seaman First Class Robert Giguere was approaching the beach aboard an LCI when "all HELL broke loose. We were getting hit from everything. The machine-gun bullets hitting the side of the LCI sounded like hail hitting a tin roof. My friend Clare Mason was hit in the left arm; I put a tourniquet above the wound to stop the bleeding as the LCI hit bottom. The port ramp dropped, the Coast Guard linemen started for shore, and a lot of men started to follow. The starboard ramp would not drop all the way; it had been hit. I said goodbye to Clare Mason, took off my pack, blew up my life preserver, and ran down the ramp into the water. . . . As I was working my way towards shore, I felt like a bee sting on my left shoulder. I put my hand on it and felt blood, and kept on going until I found a steel obstacle I could hide behind to dress my wound. As I lay there dressing my wound, I could see machine-gun bullets kicking up the sand as they were spraying the beach. After they passed me, I ran as fast as I could to the high-water mark. . . . I did not know what beach I had landed on. I think it could have been Fox Green, as I found out later.

"After laying there awhile [and] getting my composure, I would run out to help some of the wounded to shore. I had never seen so many wounded, dying, and dead. I never saw such a mess—trucks, jeeps, tanks, halftracks burning everywhere. The first wave was still lying at the high-water mark."

Giguere eventually crawled through a blown gap in the barbed wire—and was handed two grenades by an Army officer who evidently thought he was a soldier. He crawled about a hundred feet toward the embrasure of a bunker from which machine-gun fire streamed ceaselessly. "I threw the two grenades I had with me in the opening. Guys from the other side of the anti-tank ditch would throw grenades over [to me] and I would pull the pin and throw them in. In all, I must have thrown six to eight grenades and got the hell out of there in a hurry because a destroyer was coming in to start shelling the gun emplacement. I was crawling back and there was an awful feeling of having those five-inch guns shooting over my head. As I crawled back towards where I started from, I picked up my equipment and an Army officer took my name and told me I had earned recognition for a decoration."[25]

It was mid-afternoon now, and there seemed to be no letup in the concentrated German fire against the troops on shore. Little by little, however, small groups of men who had grown weary of the pounding, of waiting to be hit, began to wriggle forward, through the barbed wire, into the minefields, looking for routes off the beach. "One of our platoons had cleared and marked the way off the beach," noted Sergeant Cornazzani. "I remember walking up this gulley cleared by human mine-sweepers. They were lying there dead, wounded, and missing limbs. That they were about to lay down two rolls of ribbons to make the safe path for us to follow had to be one of the most important efforts made by a small group of soldiers that day. . . . I can't help feeling that the men who went up this gully planted with anti-personnel mines were very special. . . . We owe these men our lives and the success of the operation that day."[26]

Thomas McCann, Intelligence and Recon Platoon, 18th Infantry, found himself and the others of his unit surrounded by sheer terror. "You would have had to be insane if you said you were not afraid, having to face the ordeal we saw on the beach. . . . I saw sights I had never seen before and hope to never see again.

Vehicles were stalled and burning on the shore; tanks were sunk; soldiers were lost from their units; medics were working on the wounded and evacuating them to the boats for a trip back to England; dead bodies were covered. It was chaos, looking like a grand wrecking yard. Many obstacles were handicapping the vessels bringing soldiers and supplies into the landing beach. Finally reaching our area, I tried to dig a foxhole. This was difficult because of the rock on the side of the embankment. We were soon on patrol trying to find out what had happened to our forward companies. Communications were very difficult. It was very frightening and awful hearing soldiers tell of their experiences and how few of their company had survived—three or four out of a company."[27]

Bob Hilbert, a radioman in K Company, 18th Infantry, was laboring under the weight of a big SCR-300 radio when he descended the ladder of his LCI. "I carried a thirty-eight-pound radio for communication with battalion and regiment, and one of my men—Sidney Lindenberg—came behind me with the microphone and earphones, and he was to hook me up when we got ashore. The company commander went off first, and then his 'dog-robber,'* and then I came. The company commander went to the bottom of the ladder and turned around and stood there helping all his men off; Captain [William E.] Russell was quite a guy. The water there was just about hip-deep; it wasn't too bad at all. About the time we came off the boat, the Germans started shelling with 88s, and Captain Russell got one scratch across the forehead—that was all. But some of the guys got hit as they were coming off the boat. We got a pretty good complement off the boat before we got too many casualties."

Hilbert made a dash for the shingle and took cover just as a shell exploded nearby. A chunk of jagged metal "went straight up and came straight down. I heard it singing—*dee-dee-dee-dee-dee.* I heard that and said, 'Oh God, I hope that doesn't hit me. Well, it hit me right square in the ass. It didn't draw blood, but it stung all day long."[28]

Medic Allen Towne related that the landing craft in which he was riding "grounded on a sandbar in about two feet of water. We ran down the ramp and waded to shore, picking our way through the obstacles. There did not seem to be any small arms fire on this part of the beach. The German artillery fire was not very heavy. The shells were landing up and down the beach in a somewhat

*An enlisted man detailed to serve as his commanding officer's orderly.

predictable manner, so we could gauge when to run and when to dive to the ground. We ran as fast as possible over the hard-packed sand and went inland for about 20 feet to an area of shingle. . . . The shingle led farther inland to the ravine, or draw [E-3], we were supposed to use in exiting Omaha Beach. . . . I went on until I came to where about 20–30 infantrymen were lying at the approach to the draw. I yelled to them to see why they were not moving out. There was no response, and none of them moved. I crawled over to the nearest man to see what the problem was. I found that he was dead, and so were all the others. There was a German machine gun nest at the mouth of the draw, and they had all been caught in the fire as they tried to leave the beach."

Towne also could not help but be dumbfounded at the detritus of war strewn everywhere: "There was wreckage all along the beach. There were tanks, trucks, and all kinds of gear. I went by one landing boat that had dropped its ramp right in front of another exit, and the Germans had opened fire as the soldiers left the boat. Many of them had been hit and killed as they tried to run down the ramp. All of the wounded had been removed, but the dead were still sprawled in front of the vessel. The landing craft was disabled and burning, half out of the water."[29]

Besides the bullets and flying shards of metal, Ted Aufort, Headquarters Company, 1st Battalion, 16th RCT, and the men around him were prevented from advancing by a forest of barbed wire. The only way to break through the wire was to use Bangalore torpedoes. Aufort said, "We were laying on our backs . . . and we started putting the Bangalore torpedoes together. We got enough fellows to push those heavy Bangalore torpedoes under the barbed wire and through the entire four or five rows. Somebody yelled 'Fire!' and they blew up the barbed wire. Immediately, the fellows got up and started running. . . . When we blew that wire, there were anti-personnel mines beyond the barbed wire and Sergeant Ford stepped on one. It blew the flesh off his legs and just the bones were exposed." Moments later, Aufort stumbled across a friend of his, a trumpeter in the regimental band, serving as a stretcher bearer. "As I turned to go up the bluff, I heard a voice call out to me, 'Ted, Ted!' I looked around and he was laying there with a tourniquet on his arm, where his left arm was blown off and just a bloody stump was sticking out."[30]

On the left flank of Fox Green beach, First Lieutenant Kenneth J. Klenk of L Company, 16th RCT, leading a small patrol, came across two assault sections from the 116th that had become stragglers. He integrated them into his force, then set up a base of fire to allow Captain Everitt Booth's heavy-weapons M

Company, along with the rest of L Company, to advance. A short while later, Klenk sent five men from the 116th to clear barbed wire and a minefield. This patrol soon came under fire from an enemy outpost but, with the assistance of five men from Captain Kimball Richmond's I Company, beat back the counterattack. With the help of a Sherman tank and a 60mm mortar, Klenk's patrol next captured fifteen Germans, wounded sixteen, and killed an undetermined number more.[31]

Almost imperceptibly, and despite the best efforts of the German gunners, the thickets of barbed wire, and the innumerable minefields, the surviving invaders were gradually beginning to chip small fissures in Hitler's Fortress Europa.

Now on the other side of the water-filled tank trap, Harley Reynolds and his squad found an unguarded pathway and began following it. "I was leading and had gone maybe fifty yards when a man I didn't know rushed by. He got maybe fifteen feet when he tripped a mine hanging about waist-high on a fence post. It blew him in half and splattered me. This slowed us down again. Everyone seemed glad to let me pick the way for a while. I then turned uphill. About two-thirds of the way up the hill, more men I recognized from our Company B started passing and fanning out to the left. Another man from Company B passed going in my direction. A short distance away, he stepped on a box mine, blowing his heel off. Medics had not gotten to him, and he was trying to get off what was left of his shoe. His name was William Boyd and, because of his size, we nick-named him Wee Boy. He was the platoon runner for the second platoon and, thinking his platoon leader was ahead, he was trying to catch up. He just didn't know there was no one ahead of us."

Another pause gave Reynolds the chance to look back at the beach. "Men were now pouring through the blown wire where we came through. By chance, I looked to our left when a second Bangalore torpedo blew wire about three to four hundred yards away from us. Men started streaming through there just as fast as we did. I believe they were the first men through the wire in that area." Reynolds and his men continued to follow the path which, fortunately, was not mined. "At the rim of the hill, the path led to trenches. Noticing fresh tracks in the bottom, I felt them safe and got in to see where they led. I was armed with a rifle with grenade launcher. I pushed the safety to 'off.' I knew if I ran into Germans, I might not have the time to push it off and pull the trigger. With the grenade pointed down the trenches, I hunched over and went all the way to the end without seeing any Germans. . . .

"While scouting the trenches, we noticed movement in the entrenchments across the draw in the 29th's sector, 400 to 500 yards away. Germans were carrying what appeared to be cases and satchels from a dug-out type of shelter on the edge of the cliff over the big pillbox. They were setting the things down at the end of the trench, picking up other things, and taking them back to the shelter. It appeared they were exchanging things—maybe empty ammo cases for full—I don't know. I directed one machine gun to set up and start firing on them. It was out of range for a rifle grenade, so I removed the one on my rifle and started firing also. It caught them completely by surprise; I saw several Germans go down, and the ones standing ran back into the shelter." A 29th Division soldier nearby then threw a hand grenade at the shelter. "After throwing the grenade, he motioned to other men that came into sight and they threw grenades, also. The Germans then started coming out with white flags and their hands up. . . . As I paused for a moment watching the scene below, the men were searching the shelter and trenches. Suddenly, Germans were sneaking at them from near where they were exchanging the cases. I started firing at them and they jumped up, raised their hands, and moved very fast towards the men clearing up the trenches."

Reynolds again glanced down at the still-confused scene on the beach. He could see GIs making their way up the hill in B Company's wake, while more landing craft continued to disgorge their human and vehicular cargo into the surf. In horror, Reynolds watched as a truck on the beach, loaded with cans full of gasoline, took a direct hit from a German shell. "There was a huge, fiery explosion. The largest pieces left were the frame, half-buried in the sand, and one single wheel that continued to roll down the beach as though nothing had happened."[32]

On another part of the beach, First Lieutenant William Dillon, A Company, 16th RCT, and a sergeant named Sheetenhelm were also attempting to blow the wire with a Bangalore torpedo. Dillon noted, "As we got to the top of the dune, there was a big concertina barbed-wire entanglement. Our one Bangalore torpedo wouldn't go through. Soon, some more men came up and we got two more torpedoes from them. We slid all three under the barbed wire and pulled the fuse and jumped behind the sand dune. It went off and made a hole big enough to drive a truck through. As we went through the gap, we came to bull rushes, waded through them, and came to a wide canal or tank ditch. I stepped into the water and went in over my head. That's when I found out what the CO_2 tubes in my Mae West were for. I pulled both triggers and up I popped! I paddled across and started up the hill. I looked at the ground and could see both types of foot mines: one looked like a horse chestnut and would blow your leg off; the other had three metal prongs sticking out of the ground and would pop up face high and go off.

"Off to my right, Lieutenant McElyea, Sergeant Pat Ford, Sergeant Benn, and Babcock the aid man, kept going a few steps at a time until Ford stepped on one of the horse chestnuts. It blew Ford's leg off, threw him into the air, and he came down on his shoulder on another one that tore up his arm and threw him onto a third mine. . . . Babcock gave him three morphines intermuscular. This is also where McElyea had some of his brains shot out*. . . . We couldn't go up that hill, and our orders were to punch through, so we couldn't go back. We slid left and stayed close to the ground. At this point, the captain's runner came crawling up and said Captain [James L.] Pence has been shot and he says you are to take over the company. I knew then why I'd been made first lieutenant in England. As I lay there, I realized that now I was responsible for 275 men, or what was left of them."

Like Harley Reynolds, Dillon was certain that the Germans had a path up the hill between the minefields—and he was determined to find it. "When I was younger, I'd been a good hunter and could trail a rabbit easily. I studied the ground and saw a faint path zig-zagging to the left of the hill, so I walked the path very carefully. Some mines blew up behind me." Dillon looked back to see a young soldier on the ground, one of his legs missing. "He had stepped on a 'horse chestnut' and it had blown off his foot up to his knee. After a bit, I went back and brought the company up the path. At the top, we saw the first and only Russian soldiers I have ever seen. They shot a mortar at [1st Battalion commander Lieutenant] Colonel [Edmund F.] Driscoll and the rest of us—fortunately, they missed!"[33]

Second Lieutenant Lawrence Johnson Jr., 7th Field Artillery, recalled that he and three enlisted men were still hugging the sand, seeking shelter from the fly-

* Dillon thought McElyea had died from his wounds but later learned that he had recovered and married a nurse from the hospital at Lyme Regis. After visiting him in North Carolina after the war, Dillon said that McElyea "couldn't remember anyone nor anything connected with D-Day."

ing lead. "We four lay on the beach for a long period; there was no place to go because to our direct front was a mass of barbed wire. Finally, some brave infantryman blew holes in this barbed wire with Bangalore torpedoes. As luck would have it, just as this hole in the wire was blown, Lieutenant Colonel George Gibbs, C.O., 7th Artillery, appeared behind us, standing as tall as if he was at West Point on parade. He asked us what we were doing lying on the beach, and ordered us up the hill. Obediently, I started through the wire and the marsh beyond, telling Corporal Harold Bechtel and the others to wait until I radioed them that it was safe to follow. I was no more than fifty yards on my way when I turned and saw the other three following me. 'I told you guys to wait,' I shouted. Bechtel shouted back, 'The colonel told us not to let you go alone.'"[34]

On the far eastern edge of Fox Green, the battle between the remnants of the 3rd Battalion, 16th RCT, and the Germans for Exit E-3 was raging furiously. In the absence of the 3rd Battalion staff, Captain Kimball Richmond, I Company commander, had his hands full attempting to reorganize the splintered battalion and to form it into some semblance of an effective fighting unit. Richmond sent another patrol toward Le Grande Hameau, followed by 104 men led by a lieutenant named Williams—all he could scrape together of the 3rd Battalion's original force of 871 men; the patrol would not reach the village before 1600 hours that afternoon.[35]

Private First Class Roger Brugger, K Company, 16th Infantry, still wearing the British helmet that his sergeant had "borrowed" for him from the transport ship, recalled, "After what seemed like an eternity, we started up the draw to the top of the cliff overlooking the beach. Out of the eight of us in the squad, only four rifles would fire, the others being clogged with sand from the beach. On the way up from the beach, a wounded man from L Company gave me his helmet and took the British one I had been wearing. A little farther up the road, I saw my first dead German. His helmet was off and I could see the name 'Schlitz' printed in his helmet."[36]

L Company, 16th RCT, or what remained of it, was still inching its way forward, attempting to knock out German positions that barred the path from the beach to the bluffs. First Lieutenant Jimmie W. Monteith Jr., after enlisting the support of two Sherman tanks that had miraculously made it to shore, led a small patrol upward, but quickly ran into strong resistance that temporarily halted their progress. Three soldiers—Sergeants Wells and Griffin, along with a private named Jones—slithered forward through two minefields and three

First Lieutenant Jimmie W. Monteith Jr., L Company, 16th Infantry Regiment, recipient of the Medal of Honor, posthumously. (Courtesy Colonel Robert R. McCormick Research Center of the 1st Infantry Division Museum at Cantigny)

bands of barbed wire and destroyed one of the enemy emplacements. Lieutenant Williams, in charge of the 3rd section, led his men through another minefield, marking a safe route for units he hoped would follow; Williams's men soon reached the high ground and, after joining with another section behind them, consolidated their gain, set up a perimeter defense, and dug in to await either reinforcements or the inevitable German counterattack.

The Yanks soon discovered that German resistance did not end at the top of the bluff. Williams sent a small patrol from the 3rd section to advance toward the German-held village of Le Grande Hameau, but it was forced back by a hot blizzard of small-arms fire as it approached the stone houses and barns. A two-man patrol was sent out to reconnoiter the route to the hamlet of Cabourg, west of Le Grande Hameau, but was overwhelmed by Germans in the village and taken prisoner. As so often happens in battle, the incredible took place. The two GIs, one of whom was wounded, convinced the Germans that *they* were the ones who should do the surrendering—which they promptly did!

But it was Lieutenant Monteith, a tall redhead from Low Moor, Virginia, who was perhaps most responsible for the breakout at Exit E-3. So courageous was he that morning that he was awarded the Medal of Honor, posthumously.[37] The citation for the medal reads, in part, "He moved over to where two tanks were buttoned up and blind under violent enemy artillery and machine-gun fire. Completely exposed to the intense fire, First Lieutenant Monteith led the tanks on foot through a minefield and into firing positions. Under his direction several enemy positions were destroyed. He then rejoined his company and under his leadership his men captured an advantageous position on the hill. Supervising the defense of his newly won position against repeated vicious counterattacks, he continued to ignore his own personal safety, repeatedly crossing the two or three hundred yards of open terrain under heavy fire to strengthen the links in his defensive chain. When the enemy succeeded in completely surrounding First Lieutenant Monteith and his unit, and while leading the fight out of the situation, First Lieutenant Monteith was killed by enemy fire. The courage, gallantry, and intrepid leadership displayed by First Lieutenant Monteith is worthy of emulation."[38]

During the course of World War II, sixteen men of the Big Red One would earn the Medal of Honor—five of them during the first four days of the Normandy Invasion.

CHAPTER NINE

"I Was King of the Hill"

BY MID-MORNING on the other Normandy Invasion beaches, things were going much better for the Allies than anyone had previously dared to hope. On Sword, the easternmost beach, the leading brigade of the British 3rd Infantry Division had punched through the thin crust of German defensive positions at about 0800 hours and was heading inland in the direction of Caen; most of the division's armor had gotten ashore without major difficulties. On Juno Beach, adjacent to Sword, the Canadian 3rd Infantry Division had met tougher resistance than at Sword but was, by 0930 hours, advancing against crumbling opposition; at noon, the Canadians would be four miles inland. At Gold Beach, between Juno and Omaha, the British 50th (Northumbrian) Infantry Division initially had met heavy enemy resistance, but by late morning had overwhelmed the defensive positions and were rolling toward Creully. British paratroopers had secured the two bridges over the Orne River and canal at Benouville, and British glider-borne troops had knocked out the casemated gun batteries farther east, at Merville.

To the west of Omaha Beach, the U.S. 4th Infantry Division, landing a few miles from its assigned target, had encountered halfhearted resistance, had suffered only light casualties, and was marching to link up with the 82nd and 101st Airborne Divisions, whose battalions were hopelessly scattered but holding their own in small pockets of resistance. Even the formidable, tenaciously defended heights of Pointe du Hoc had not prevented the Rangers from scaling the sheer cliffs and taking their objective.[1]

It was only at Omaha Beach that disaster and defeat still loomed as real possibilities. Aboard the *Augusta*, Omar Bradley was still gravely concerned about

Omaha. "Despite the setbacks we had suffered as the result of bad weather and ineffective bombing," he wrote, "I was shaken to find that we had gone against Omaha with so thin a margin of safety. At the time of sailing we had thought ourselves cushioned against such reversals as these. Not until noon did a radio [message] from Gerow offer a clue to the trouble we had run into on Omaha Beach. Instead of the rag-tag static troops we had expected to find there, the assault had run head-on into one of Rommel's tough field divisions [the 352nd]. . . . Had a less experienced division than the 1st Infantry stumbled into this crack resistance, it might easily have been thrown back into the Channel. Unjust though it was, my choice of the 1st to spearhead the invasion probably saved us Omaha Beach and a catastrophe on the landing. . . ." It was nearly 1330 hours before Gerow radioed Bradley with the day's first encouraging news: "Troops formerly pinned down on beaches Easy Red, Easy Green, Fox Red advancing up heights behind beaches."[2]

One of those advancing up the heights was Captain Fred Hall, operations officer for the 16th Infantry's 2nd Battalion. Getting units reassembled and reorganized now became the most urgent order of the day. Hall noted, "Colonel Hicks and I, with other members of the advance CP [command post], quickly moved over to where the path had been cleared through the mine field and climbed to the top of the bluff. The path was very narrow and had been marked with white Engineers' tape along each side. At one spot, a couple of soldiers were lying on each side to keep people out of the mine field. Anti-personnel mines were clearly visible and anyone who strayed might be wounded or killed. We did not come under direct fire as we reached the top of the bluff, and moved inland some distance to the edge of a field where there was a clump of trees and a hedgerow. Here we established our temporary CP. My job was to stay there, make contact with our units, find out who was who and who wasn't around, and keep track of the situation. E Company had heavy casualties and was pretty well disorganized. F Company on our left was engaged in a fire fight. G Company and H Company had moved ahead toward Colleville-sur-Mer. The battalion commander was out checking on their progress. During the early afternoon, we saw several German soldiers running toward the pillboxes commanding the beach area; I believe F Company took care of them."[3]

The commanding officer of F Company, 16th Infantry, had indeed taken care of them, but then Captain John Finke reached the bluff above Exit E-3. "I had about a hundred men with me," Finke reported. "I had only one officer who, at the time, hadn't been killed or wounded, and I went up the hill. Anyway, we got up the road and here was battalion headquarters." Finke and the battalion C.O., Hicks, got into an argument. Hicks wanted Finke's company to be posted as guards around battalion headquarters, while Finke wanted to move ahead and engage the enemy. During a brief shouting match, a German mortar round whistled in and settled the issue, wounding Finke in the leg. Before being evacuated, Finke put his first sergeant in command of the company with orders to take the unit on to Colleville.[4]

Lieutenant James Watts, A Company, 81st Chemical Mortar Battalion, and his unit "set up a mortar on the beach and tried to fire at areas of resistance at the top of the hill. It was a futile effort because the distance to the top of the hill was under our minimum range of 600 yards. At too short a range, the shell would not nose over so that it would detonate on impact. Our rounds landed tail first and did not explode, so we abandoned the effort. When the infantry had overcome resistance at the top of the hill, we were able to move our mortars part way up the hill where we set up firing positions. The Germans were still firing mortars and artillery at the beaches; unfortunately, we would be hit by the rounds that fell short of the beach. Several rounds hit in the area at almost the same time; I threw myself toward a shallow depression for protection from the fire. Only after I got up did I find what a close one that had been. There were entry and exit holes in my jacket, shirt, and underwear across my back. The straps to my musette bag were cut so that the bag flapped loose, and my carbine had several nicks in it and the magazine dented enough so that it was inoperative. I was very close to having my spine severed. All I got was a non-bleeding bruise across the middle of my back."[5]

Captain Robert Murphy and one of his lieutenants from H Company, 18th Infantry, had just reached the top of the bluff when they heard a German shell announcing its arrival. Murphy dove into a ditch and the lieutenant jumped into a shell hole. Murphy recalled, "The damn shell came into the shell hole with him." The lieutenant miraculously escaped with relatively minor wounds. "His first question to me was, 'How's the family jewels?'"[6]

First Lieutenant Nelson Park's C Company, 18th Infantry, was climbing "the cliff by going up a path that zig-zagged along the way. The Germans had placed mines in the path and we looked very carefully to locate them as we advanced up the path. The fact is that many of the mines (perhaps most) had already been detonated. We could observe where they were by looking at the bodies of American soldiers who had set them off." Finally, Park and C Company made it to the

Lieutenant Nelson Park, C Company, 18th Infantry Regiment. (Courtesy Nelson Park)

top. "We fired at some German soldiers until they all started to run farther inland." One of the other lieutenants in the company was Craig Ben Hannum, from Arizona. "Ben was inexperienced, like me, and he aggressively followed two or three of them. One of the Germans whirled around and fired one shot. It went into Ben's chest and out of his back. As he lay on the ground, I said, 'Don't worry, Ben, we'll get you out of here!' I will never forget telling him that. The truth of the matter was that Ben was probably already nearly dead. I couldn't do anything more because all hell broke loose, and we had to charge ahead and just leave him there."[7]

Staff Sergeant Walter Ehlers, L Company, 18th Infantry, made it to the summit with his small patrol. "We saw a GI with a satchel charge—a pole charge—going up to one of the pillboxes and was going to stick it in the breach, but he didn't make it; he was killed before he got up there. We got into one of the trenches that took us right around to the back of the pillbox and we captured the Germans that were manning it."[8]

Sergeant John B. Ellery, 16th Infantry, struggled up the sandy path to the top of the bluff, surrounded by more scenes of horror and heroism, of courage and carnage. "There was a man beside me who was dead. Another was on the ground about fifteen meters behind me. I ran back to him and started dragging him to some cover. A medic ran up and helped me, and he took over. From the looks of that wounded man, I doubt that he lived." Briefly pinned down by a German machine gun, Ellery threw all four of his fragmentation grenades. "When the last one went off, I made a dash for the top." Four or five other GIs dashed with him. "Those other kids were right behind me and we all made it."[9]

The tremendous intensity of fire from the German positions could not be sustained, and the enemy's stocks of ammunition of all caliber began to run low. Gunners of the 352nd Artillery Regiment, emplaced six kilometers south of Omaha Beach, were ordered not to waste rounds; two weeks earlier, half of the regiment's ammunition had been trucked to a safer area well back from the coast. Now there was no way to get those shells to the front; trucks that attempted the run were blasted into oblivion by Allied fighter-bombers. Fearsome saturation artillery barrages of the kind that had shredded GIs and boats in the first few hours of the landings were now verboten; only random shells were allowed to be fired. Machine-gun ammunition, too, was becoming exhausted.

German pillboxes and trenches were being swept away by the hot breath of the Navy's guns. The pinned-down American infantrymen were pinned down no longer. As German fire slackened, the Yanks crawled through the barbed wire and minefields, like an inexorable, olive-drab swarm of angry, heavily armed insects, bent on overcoming all obstacles in their path. The Germans manning the fortifications, their ears and noses bleeding from the concussions of the direct hits and near misses, and their throats choking from concrete dust and cordite, began scrambling out the steel rear doors in hopes of making it to the top of the bluffs and safety; many never made it.[10]

In England, at the SHAEF Advance CP near Portsmouth, Eisenhower and his staff were receiving sporadic radio reports from Bradley's and Montgomery's floating headquarters and were cautiously optimistic that the largest of all amphibious invasions just might succeed. In his post-war memoir, *Crusade in Europe*, the Supreme Commander wrote, "The first report [about the invasion]

came from the airborne units I had visited only a few hours earlier and was most encouraging in tone. As the morning wore on, it became apparent that the landing was going fairly well. Montgomery took off in a destroyer to visit the beaches and to find a place in which to set up his own advanced headquarters. I promised to visit him the following day. Operations in the Utah [Beach] area, which involved the co-ordination of the amphibious landing with the American airborne operation, proceeded satisfactorily, as did those on the extreme left flank. The day's reports, however, showed that extremely fierce fighting had developed in the Omaha sector. That was the spot, I decided, to which I would proceed the next morning."[11]

Ike's naval aide, Harry Butcher, also recorded his thoughts on this most momentous of days: "The landings have gone better than expected. Every outfit is ashore, but we have just had a report that Gee, Major General Gerow, with his V Corps, can't get off one of the beaches because of hostile mortar and artillery fire. This is Omaha Beach. They called the air for some bombing; air came back and said pin-point the places, and there the matter rests to the moment, Ike, however, wondering what the 21st Army Group is doing about it. That is really the only bad news of the day."[12]

Meanwhile, Captain Joe Dawson's G Company, 16th Infantry, had made it to the top of the bluff. Dawson said that once his unit reached the top and was heading toward Colleville-sur-Mer, "a very friendly French woman greeted us with open arms and said, 'Welcome to France.'" Dawson also recalled that he felt, at last, that his men were beginning to accept him as their leader, an acceptance forged in the heat of combat. "A mutual respect began to develop, and it was almost incredible. I felt it in every one of my men. We had casualties. We had lost men there on the beach. . . . We took our positions in the town, and we fought into it and I led my men in there. The little village was dominated by a church with a steeple. In that steeple had been one of the forward observers of the Germans, and they were directing artillery fire down on the beach. I went in the church with two of my men—a sergeant and a private—and we had a little encounter in there with the Germans and I lost the private. The sergeant and I . . . were able to survive and neutralize the situation. As I left the building and started across the street from the church . . . a sniper caught me with a bullet through my left knee. I was carrying a carbine—the only time that I had a weapon other than my .45. . . . The bullet had gone through the stock, and [one of] the fragments lodged in my knee and the other came through the fleshy part of my right leg, which somewhat incapacitated me, but I didn't think anything about it at the time. Then I debouched my men into a defensive position around the town."

At 1530 hours, with the town now under G Company control, Dawson and his men began to settle in for whatever new surprises the Germans might have up their sleeves. A half hour later, however, it wasn't the Germans who surprised them—it was the United States Navy. "At 4:00, we were devastated with an artillery barrage from the Navy. It leveled the town, absolutely leveled it, and in doing so we suffered the worst casualties we had the whole day. . . . I was angered by it, angered beyond all measure because I thought it was totally disgraceful. And I was quite bitter about it, and the General was very bitter about it. . . . We brought the matter to the attention of the authorities and, sure enough, the Navy's response was that the order called for the leveling of Colleville at H+60 minutes, or as soon thereafter as visibility would permit. Well, the pall of battle was over us. There was no vision and we had no communication because my [naval] fire control officer had been destroyed on the beach. . . . I was frantically throwing up smoke bombs to alert them to the fact that we were in the town, but it was too late to prevent the barrage from occurring. Their contention was that the pall of battle had obscured their vision until 4:00 that afternoon, which was H+8 hours or H+10 hours, and they said that was when visibility permitted it so, typical Navy, that's what they did."[13]

More tanks appeared on shore to bring direct 75mm fire against German positions still holding out. Tanker Ed Ireland, B Company, 745th Tank Battalion, recalled that while his tank was heading through the surf toward shore, he "had a little camera and I got nosy and wanted to take a picture of the beach, and I opened up the hatch. We ran into a shell hole and the water poured back into the tank and I got kind of soaked, but we made it. We kept right on going. We had problems with bodies laying around on shore. The infantry were moving some of the bodies so that we didn't run over them. The Engineers came in and they made a path for us. There was a lot of mortar fire and stuff coming in on the boys on the beach. . . . [We went up] the side of the hill where the Engineers made this road for us and we were able to make it up to the top and start inland. We had to watch for the giant shell holes that the big ships made inland. . . . A lot of them were filled with water already. . . . If you ran into one of those, forget it . . . you'd probably go to the bottom and drown."[14]

At 1335 hours on 6 June, *General* Kraiss's 352nd Division headquarters radioed a strangely optimistic message to Dollmann's Seventh Army headquarters, a message that said the landings at Omaha Beach were very nearly repulsed. Perhaps, by looking down at all the sinking boats, all the burning tanks, and all the dead and dying GIs, an excited officer in an observation post near the beach could have come to that conclusion. But it was surely the *wrong* conclusion, as the German high command would soon discover.

At 1700 hours, von Rundstedt's headquarters issued an order that was more hope than substance: The Allied bridgehead was to be wiped out immediately. What no one in the German high command yet understood was that the opportunity to wipe out the bridgehead had already come and gone. At 1800 hours, the 352nd sent another message—this one much more accurate—indicating that Allied forces, including tanks, had penetrated the coastal defenses and were now on the line Louvières-Colleville-Asnières.[15]

The Germans were in disarray, and the situation for Hitler's forces along the Normandy coast was quickly going from bad to worse. In Rommel's absence, *General der Artillerie* Erich Marcks, the LXXXIV Corps commander at Saint-Lô, was trying desperately to convince anyone he could reach by telephone—Seventh Army, Army Group B, even Hitler's headquarters in the Obersalzburg—that he needed help and he needed it *now*. But higher headquarters remained skeptical; the Normandy landings were merely a diversionary raid, they continued to tell him; the real invasion was still expected to come at Calais. They were convinced that Patton's fictitious army, which they believed was real and would spearhead the main assault, was still in England. Even if Marcks had succeeded in securing the panzer units for which he so urgently cried out, chances are good that they would never have reached the front. With clearing weather, hundreds of American and British warplanes were hunting for tanks, trucks, and trains—anything that might come to the aid of the embattled coastal defensive units. Because of complete Allied mastery of the skies, the roads below became sites of terrible slaughter for the Germans.[16]

Panic and confusion on D-Day weren't caused solely by Allied firepower. Confusion also reigned in the German ranks as commanders tried to assess the situation based on sketchy reports and then acted on the fragmentary, often-erroneous information. An order would be given, carried out, then countermanded by someone at a higher headquarters. For example, the 12th SS Panzer (*Hitlerjugend*) Division was ordered from its assembly area—thirty miles from the coast—to Lisieux, eighteen miles from Omaha Beach; a few hours later, it was ordered to change direction and head toward Caen. While on the road, the division, made up predominately of fanatical teenagers, was pounced upon by Allied fighter-bombers and torn apart.[17]

At 1540 hours—ten hours after Allied troops began wading ashore—Kurt Meyer's 12th SS Panzer Division and Fritz Bayerlein's Panzer Lehr Division, both in the vicinity of Aleçon, finally were released to Seventh Army control and ordered immediately to the front. Bayerlein's panzers, on the road at 0500 hours on 7 June, were swiftly turned into scrap metal as American and British aircraft swooped down like a swarm of hawks on a pack of field mice. So badly mauled was Panzer Lehr that it would take twenty-four hours for it to reconstitute itself as a fighting force. Bayerlein admitted that "By noon on the 7th, my men were already calling the main road from Vire to le Bény Bocage '*Jabo-Rennstrecke*' ['fighter-bomber racetrack']. . . . Every armored vehicle was covered by branches of trees and made to hug the edges of the hedges or woods so as to appear from the air to be a mere projection of the foliage . . . but by the end of the day, I had lost forty fuel wagons and ninety other trucks. Five of my tanks had been knocked out, as well as eighty-four halftracks, prime movers, and self-propelled guns. These losses were serious for a division not yet in action." Bayerlein himself would be injured, and his driver and adjutant killed, when their car was attacked and forced into a ditch by Allied fighter-bombers on 8 June.[18]

At 1700 hours on D-Day, with the 16th and 18th Infantry Regiments having suffered the brunt of the fighting on Easy Red and Fox Green up to now, it was the turn of Colonel John F. R. Seitz's 26th Infantry—known as the "Blue Spaders" from their distinctive, spade-shaped regimental emblem—to land on the beach, climb the bluff, pass through the 16th and 18th, and spearhead the drive inland. Lieutenant Colonel Frank J. Murdoch's orders were to march his 1st Battalion toward Etreham and Mt. Cauvin, while Lieutenant Colonel Derrill M. Daniel's 2nd Battalion, landing west of Colleville, was to head southeast, toward Mosles, on the Bayeux-Isigny highway. Lieutenant Colonel John T. Corley's 3rd Battalion would assault in the direction of Ste.-Anne, further east on the same road.[19]

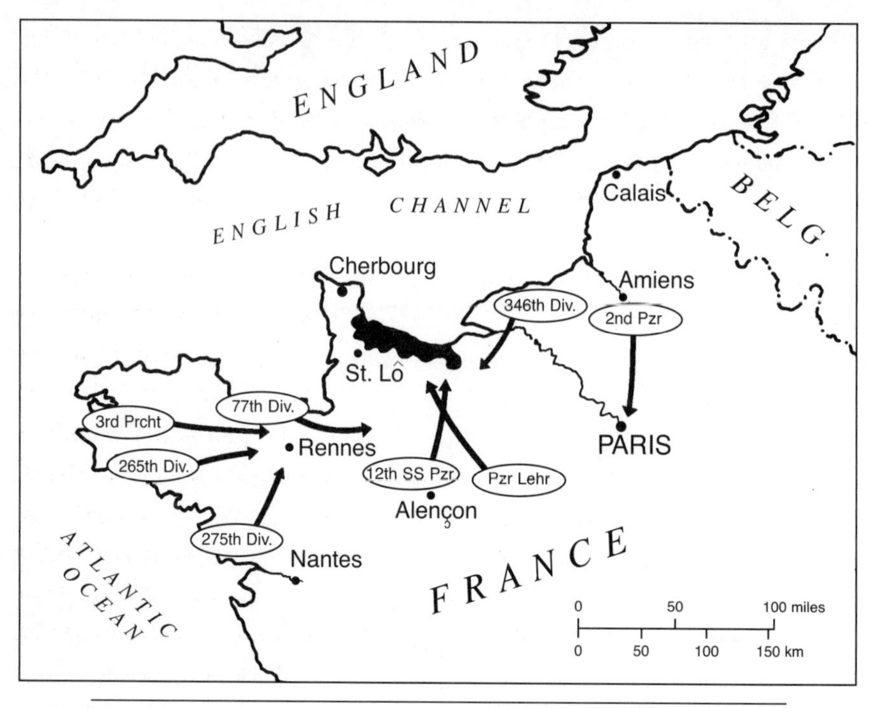

The Germans race to bring in reinforcements to seal off the invasion area.

The fulfillment of those assignments was still many hours away; the 26th still had to land on a beach that was very much "hot." Most, but not all, of the fortified positions had been knocked out, and snipers still picked off unwary soldiers; German artillery batteries, several miles inland, were still lobbing shells randomly onto the shore.

Aboard an LCT heading for the beach, Private Ralph Puhalovich, Anti-Tank Company, 26th RCT, inadvertently caused a bit of panic amongst the Navy. While looking over the side of his craft, his helmet fell off into the water and began floating back toward the *Augusta*, Bradley's flagship. "Here's my helmet bounding back in the water and there's a lookout on the prow of the cruiser and he sees the helmet and yells, 'Mine!' So they take evasive action and as far back as you can see, ships are taking evasive action. So I have no helmet, and they tell me just to take one off a casualty on the beach. When I got to the beach, there was a guy in a foxhole, all ashen color, and I thought about taking his helmet, but it had all this big Ranger insignia all over it and I said, 'Nah, I don't want that for a target.' I did find a helmet later on." Puhalovich related that his unit had three trucks that would each tow a 57mm anti-tank gun, along with a jeep with a trailer and radio equipment, and one more jeep from E Company, 26th Infantry. The LCT tried to approach the shore but found no open lanes; the LCT would remain at sea until the following day.[20]

Another 26th RCT soldier, Sidney Haszard, recalled, "Our landing craft didn't want to go where *we* wanted to go, so we forced them in and got a bit closer. But we were still dropped a long way from shore. When we got off, we took a few steps and then went down under water. Our first sergeant turned around, took a fifty-caliber machine gun and pointed it at the control officer and told him: 'Raise the ramps, back off, and try again.' I'll never forget [Major] Paul Skogsberg splashing around, saving guys from drowning. We had dead guys floating in the water. Four days later, when we came back down to the beach to get our vehicles, I saw their corpses. They had been put in trucks. It was awful—all those men killed by drowning, all purple, stacked like cordwood on trucks."[21]

Although the battle for the beachhead had died down considerably by the time the 26th Infantry reached shore, there were still plenty of opportunities for a man to get killed or wounded. Polish-born Theodore Dobol, a platoon sergeant with K Company, who would later become the division's command sergeant-major, recalled, "I had been assigned a new platoon leader, First Lieutenant [William L.] Emerson. I felt he would get adjusted after a few skirmishes. During our Channel crossing, he received a cable from the States, notifying him that his wife had given birth to a baby boy. He was very happy, in spite of the forthcoming landing." But Lieutenant Emerson would not live to see his son; he was killed on 6 June.[22]

Chaplain John Burkhalter attached himself to a group of infantrymen battling their way up the bluffs. "We crawled most of the way up," he remembered. "As we filed by those awful scenes going up the hill and moving inland, I prayed hard for those suffering men, scattered here and there and seemingly everywhere. We filed over the hill as shells were falling on the beach back of us, meaning death for others who were still coming in. . . . We crouched for a while close to the ground just below the top. While lying there, I did most of my praying. The shells were falling all around and I knew that God alone was able to keep them away from us. I shall never forget those moments. I am sure that during that time, I was drawn very close to God."[23]

Captain Raphael Uffner, commander of M Company, 26th Infantry, recalled that a group of the regiment's officers had chosen a house on the beach as a rallying point—a house that also served as a German artillery aiming point. Uffner tried to warn the men in the house to abandon it, but it was too late. A German barrage howled in and destroyed the building. Uffner recalled, "I reversed direction after the salvo and found my old D Company executive officer, Lieutenant Billy Hume, dead, and his D Company commander, Captain Bridges, among others, wounded; Captain John J. Kelly of H Company [sic; Kelly commanded F. Company] was on the beach, laid out like a side of beef. He was in the arms of his commander of the 2nd Battalion, Lieutenant Colonel Daniels." In addition to Kelly, a mortar round killed Captain John Simon, the battalion S-2 (intelligence officer).[24]

At 1900 hours on 6 June, General Huebner and the rest of the 1st Division command group came ashore and established their headquarters on Easy Red beach in one of the knocked-out German bunkers.* [25]

Nightfall brought a tense but merciful end to "the longest day." No one believed that the war, or even the battle for Normandy, was over, but it was a great relief to know that a foothold—no matter how tenuous—actually had been made on French soil. Much remained to be done, however, even in the darkness. Men emotionally and physically drained from their ordeal still needed to dig foxholes; officers needed to post sentries, establish fields of fire, send out patrols to ascertain the enemy's positions, and write reports of their unit's activities. Great spools of communication wire needed to be unrolled and hooked to field phones; ammunition had to be distributed to men whose weapons and ammo pouches were nearly empty; water and rations had to be humped from the beachhead to soldiers who had thrown up their breakfasts nearly twenty-four hours earlier and were dehydrated and desperately hungry; the wounded needed to be gathered, treated, and evacuated; the dead and missing catalogued. Mundane-but-necessary administrative duties needed to be performed by men almost too tired to keep their eyes open.

---

* The next day, V Corps commanding general Leonard Gerow would allow the 115th and 116th Infantry Regiments, which had been attached to the 1st, to revert to the command and control of Major General Charles Gerhardt, the 29th's commander; the two divisions would then go their separate ways. (*Omaha Beachhead*, p. 127)

A heavily damaged German bunker after its capture by the 1st Infantry Division. The large number of stretchers leaning against the concrete wall indicates it may have been used as a medical aid station. (Courtesy Colonel Robert R. McCormick Research Center of the 1st Infantry Division Museum at Cantigny)

At nearly midnight, Lieutenant Karl Wolf, Headquarters, 3rd Battalion, 16th Infantry, and another lieutenant, both dog-tired, were directed by their battalion commander, Lieutenant Colonel Charles T. Horner Jr., to reconnoiter the beach and find the unit's missing vehicles. "We walked quite a distance and could hear the wounded moaning," Wolf said. "One of the reasons there are so many killed in an invasion is that there is no way to treat and evacuate the wounded in the early hours of the invasion. It is impossible to get the injured off the beach and there aren't enough medics to go around to all of the wounded. When we got to regimental headquarters, we told them about the wounded so they could send out any available medics. We searched all over for the vehicles but were unsuccessful and finally returned to the command post."[26]

Private Steve Kellman, L Company, 16th Infantry Regiment, wounded at Omaha Beach. (Courtesy Steve Kellman)

One of the wounded who had remained on the beach for hours was Private Steve Kellman, L Company, 16th Infantry. After being hit early that morning on Fox Green, he was finally evacuated at about 1900 hours that night. A medic carried him piggyback toward an LCVP that was standing by to transport the wounded. "I could hear more shells coming in, and one hit and we went down, and I thought, 'The poor bastard trying to help me was hit,' but what he was doing was just getting flat. He eventually got me down to the water and they put me on a stretcher; the LCVP took me out to an LST loaded with tanks that had an operating room on board. We got alongside the ship, and they lowered four ropes to put on the four handles of the stretcher and the sailors up above were pulling to hoist me up. The problem was the fellows pulling on one side were pulling faster than the fellows on the other side, and they almost tipped me off into the water." After surgery, Kellman was taken below and given one of the sailors' bunks. "The young man whose bunk I was in came by and said, 'How would you like something to eat?' He brought me a bowl of cold peas—it was the only thing he could find. He also shaved me. I found out that in civilian life he worked for his uncle, who was an undertaker—and his job was to shave corpses!"[27]

Jack Bennett, a mortarman with E Company, 18th Infantry, spent most of D-Day trying to find his unit. "By the time we caught up with the rest of E Company, it was late afternoon or early evening. They were already near the village of Colleville. That's where we stayed for the night; it didn't take me long to dig a hole. This was just at the beginning of hedgerow country. We cut the road that runs along the top of the bluff."[28]

After trading shots with an enemy machine gunner in a trench below the crest of the bluffs, Private First Class Andy Anderson and "Buckeye" Lowery, E Company, 18th Infantry, reached the top and set up the Browning Automatic Rifle in a ditch beside the Caen-Cherbourg highway late on 6 June. They remained on guard all night, separated from the rest of their unit and nervously expecting a German counterattack at any moment.[29]

Louis Newman, Cannon Company, 18th Infantry, recalled, "We had lost all our 105mm guns. They all sank; we had nothing to fight with. About eleven at night, my first sergeant heard some voices coming from the cliff. He called me over and said, 'Listen.' We heard German voices so we threw some grenades and didn't hear anything more. About 4 or 5 o'clock in the morning [7 June], most of my company assembled there."[30]

Lieutenant Karl Wolf remembered that, while he was temporarily in command of a rifle company until a new C.O. was assigned, he did his part to disrupt the Germans' ability to communicate. "The maps we had, and the intelligence, were quite good. I remember looking at my map and seeing markings for what was supposed to be buried cable that the Germans used for communications from their fortified emplacements to their command bunkers located inland. I found the spot shown on the map, had a man dig there and, sure enough, we located the cable, which we then cut."[31]

John Bistrica, C Company, 16th Infantry, noticed that his platoon's BAR man was "up against a hedgerow and I came around his right side. I asked, 'Schur, where are the other C Company guys?' He didn't answer. Then I saw he was dead, with a bullet through his head. . . . That first night off the beach, we dug in as they taught us, because there might be a counterattack with tanks. I dug a hole about four feet deep. I was tired, wet, with nothing to eat but a D bar. That night, I was called to go on a patrol. The lieutenant told the sergeant, 'See where the Germans are.' We found nothing. The next morning, we got up and heard noises on the other side of the hedgerows. You guessed it! The Germans were just getting up, and we captured them."[32]

The first few days after the landings were a jumble, with lost infantrymen finding themselves in the midst of paratroopers who were themselves separated from their units. Add to this the fact that the enemy, too, was equally confused; some German units had attempted escape, only to be cut off and decimated, while other units were trying to reach the beachhead to reinforce those who were, or had been, there. A great many soldiers on both sides had no idea where they were, or where they were supposed to be.

Late on the night of 6/7 June, Sergeant Harley Reynolds, B Company, 16th Infantry, found himself separated from his unit and lost in hedgerow country. After marching a short distance, Reynolds came to an unpaved road and asked some soldiers where B Company or 1st Battalion was. "They pointed to a road going left. It wasn't far until I realized there wasn't anyone on this road. I turned right at the next road and the road was completely deserted. It's getting dark and suddenly, in the middle of the road, I walked up on a German Tiger tank. I froze. It took me a second to realize it was knocked out. I must have acted peculiar, because I heard a chuckle from the ditch alongside the road. It was an outpost of paratroopers, only five or six men on guard for the night; their main body was just down the road. They said some of their people had knocked out the tank and suggested I not go any further, as there were more of their troops on the road and they weren't using passwords; they were using the now-famous 'cricket' call.* I spent the night in the ditch with them. Several times during the night, I heard the cricket sound being exchanged as more troops joined them. It was surprising to me how close some of the calls were when they were challenged; they were the *quietest* troops I've ever heard. I later learned that I had spent the night within shouting distance of my company; I caught up with them just south of Colleville."[33]

---

*Prior to their combat jump, the paratroopers were issued metal toy crickets to use as a recognition device in place of the normal challenge-and-password system.

Ray Klawiter, a member of D Company, 18th Infantry, recalled, "Once we got to the top, we hooked up with another company. We went down a road and into the woods and we heard firing; we couldn't tell where it was coming from. We went a mile or so and set up a defense in a field. They gave us a stick of dynamite to start the hole, to get it dug in a hurry. The Germans counter-attacked our positions—not ours as much as others alongside of us. We had to wait in that position until the British moved up. The 2nd Infantry Division came in the next day and went in along one of our flanks. The 32nd Artillery that was supporting the 18th Regiment got counter-attacked and the Germans even got into their motor pool. They killed five Americans and the artillerymen killed five of theirs and captured most of the rest of the Germans."[34]

Eddie Steeg, another of Lieutenant Monica's men, described the laborious-but-necessary task of digging foxholes whenever a unit came to a prolonged halt: "It was important, in the interest of self-survival, that each GI protect himself as much as possible from enemy shell fragments, small-arms fire, and anything else coming our way. An essential element of that self-protection was the often-joked-about, bitched-about, 'hard-to-dig' foxhole. Whenever we reached a 'hold' position where our advance was delayed, we usually heard the command, 'dig in.'" Steeg recalled that, on the night of 6/7 June, his unit "had been issued small blocks of TNT to use as a helper in starting a foxhole. As darkness was closing in on us, you could hear the common loud cry repeated throughout the area, 'Fire in the hole,' quickly followed by a loud blast and a shower of loose earth flying through the air. As ordered, everybody was digging in. Unfortunately, the dynamite only started the hole; the rest of the digging was done by hand with our fold-away entrenching tool.

"Worried about a possible counter-attack, I stayed at the task through most of the night, digging and digging till I had fashioned what, to my memory, was the most elaborate foxhole I had ever dug. It wasn't just your plain, old hole in the ground. First, I dug down to a depth of about three feet, six inches. Then I dug horizontally the length of my body—a provision that would permit me to lay down in the hole without being cramped. It was in the shape of an 'L.' With my short stature, the depth of the hole allowed me to stand comfortably with my arms resting on the ground. Although this hole took me considerably longer to construct, usually my size came to the fore; I would usually be finished 'digging in' and I would be resting while the bigger guys were still throwing dirt. Without a doubt, foxholes were dug as a matter of self-protection.

"I really understood that principle but, for a person who can't stand being confined in small places, some funny thoughts ran through my head. Was digging an elaborate hole like this one an act of cowardice or an act of bravery? Could it be cowardice for trying to hide from the enemy (at the same time trying to be comfortable to a point), or could it be bravery for having the guts to stretch out at the bottom of your hole, knowing full well you could be buried under several feet of dirt if a nearby shellburst caused the hole to cave in? As it turned out, my elaborate foxhole was all for naught; there was no enemy counter-attack that night. By early morning of June 7th, we were on the move again."[35]

That evening, after his sergeants had reported the results of their roll calls, Lieutenant William Dillon, A Company, 16th Infantry, was stunned by his unit's thinned ranks, the result of the day's savage fighting. "I had eighteen men with me that night [6/7 June] and twelve more joined us [later], so I had thirty men in A Company instead of 280."[36]

Yet, others remained hopeful and in amazement of what they had done. Looking down from the top of the bluffs at the great armada spread out below him, Medic Allen Towne marveled, "It looked as if all the ships in the world were here. If Hitler had seen this, he would have sued for peace."[37]

Nightfall gave men the opportunity to reflect upon all that had been endured and accomplished by themselves and the division that day. Instead of feeling frightened or worried, Sergeant John B. Ellery, 16th Infantry, felt elated. He was spending his first night in France "in a ditch beside a hedgerow, wrapped in a damp shelter-half and thoroughly tired. It had been the greatest experience of my life. I was ten feet tall. I had made it to the beach and reached the high ground. I was king of the hill, at least in my own mind, for a moment. I had walked in the company of very brave men. Everyone realized that there was a long road and a lot of fighting ahead of us, but I don't think that anyone doubted that we were in France to stay."[38]

When the survivors finally reached the top of the bluff and dug in, they were not greeted by hordes of grateful French handing them flowers and wine. No bands played. No scoreboard displayed the result: U.S. 1, Germany 0. No telegrams came from the president, inviting them to lunch at the White House. In other words, there was no tangible evidence that they had won the first battle in the liberation of the northern European continent. They had simply accomplished their mission: They had established a foothold in France. It was up to the divisions that would arrive the next day and the next and the next to widen the breach in the fortress wall. Maybe now, some 1st Division soldiers thought, they'll let us go home.

If anyone had pulled out a map and checked, they would have seen that Berlin was still more than 700 miles away. They knew from bitter experience in North Africa and Sicily that the Germans never yielded ground easily. At any moment, even as they dug their holes, the exhausted Yanks expected to see phalanx after phalanx of gray-coated infantry, accompanied by deep ranks of rumbling panzers and a sky full of bomb-laden aircraft storming over the horizon and heading straight for them. But none came.

The first phase of the battle for Normandy may have gone to the Allies, but there was no way for them to see the difficult days that lay ahead. There was only time to take a deep breath and savor the fact that, for the moment at least, they were still alive.

Six June 1944, at Omaha Beach, had been an especially bloody affair. With the invaders packed into such a confined target area, the human cost of the operation was high, very high, although the exact number of casualties may never be known. What *is* known is that 291 landing craft had been lost off all the D-Day beaches, and numerous destroyers, LCTs, LCIs, and DUKWs had been sunk, cruisers hit, and aircraft downed. Dozens of swimming tanks had gone to the bottom of the Channel. Within the 1st Infantry Division, it is estimated that eighteen officers and 168 enlisted men had been killed or died of wounds on D-Day; a further seven officers and 351 men were missing; and forty-five officers and 575 men had been wounded in action. In addition, seventy-six officers and men were reported sick and hors d'combat.[39] The 115th and 116th Infantry Regiments of the 29th Infantry Division also had suffered heavily, with 328 men killed or died of wounds; 281 wounded; and 134 listed as missing in action.[40]

Despite the terrible toll, many thousands more had stormed ashore over the bodies of their fallen comrades; braved the intense fire; crawled through the minefields; lobbed grenades into pillbox embrasures; battled with defenders in their trenches; and reached the top of the bluffs by late morning and early afternoon.[41] Those who died on Normandy's chilly shore had not died in vain; Hitler's vaunted Atlantic Wall—a defensive fortification that had taken Germany

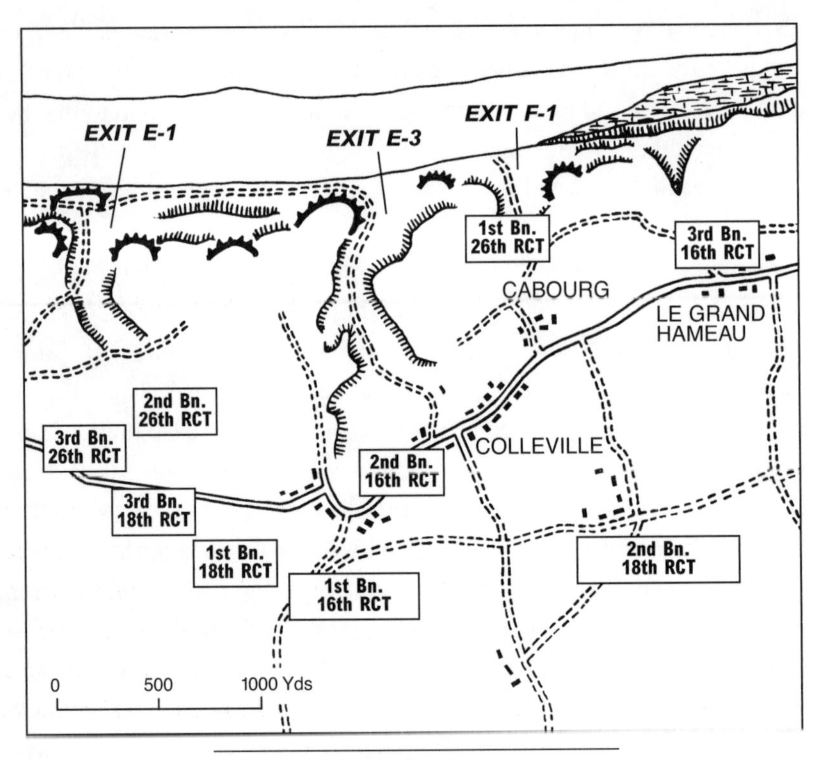

1st Infantry Division positions by evening, 6 June 1944. (Positions approximate)

many years and many billions of *Reichsmarks* to construct—had been cracked wide open by the invaders in the span of a morning. The Allies had at last gained a foothold on the continent of Europe; could the demise of the Nazi empire be far behind?

The ordeal on the beachhead was almost over.

The ordeal in the hedgerows was about to begin.

CHAPTER TEN

"Pastures of Green Grass, Full of Beautiful Cows"

EVEN AS the Allied armies were still battling their way onto the continent of Europe, the confirmation that the long-awaited invasion had begun was being telephoned to President Roosevelt by Army Chief of Staff General George C. Marshall at 0300 hours on 6 June, Eastern War Time. Eisenhower had just reported to Marshall (who had been the 1st Division's operations officer in France in World War I) that preliminary reports indicated the operation had gotten off to a satisfactory start.[1]

A little over a half hour later, the electrifying news began flashing across America—an America that had been holding its collective breath for months. Like the Germans, the Americans had no idea when or where the invasion would take place, but everyone on the Home Front knew it would come sooner rather than later. And Americans would remember for the rest of their lives how they learned of the invasion. In an era before television and instantaneous mass communication, radio was the medium that carried the news first. Networks and local stations interrupted their regular programming for the invasion bulletins, sketchy though they were. Suddenly, on that Tuesday morning, 6 June, church bells began pealing, factory whistles began to blow, and car horns began to honk.[2] Neighbor phoned neighbor or rushed excitedly across lawns with the breathless question: "Have you heard the news?" In countless downtowns, the bulletins blared out from speakers set up in front of stores, stopping passersby in their tracks. Work in factories and offices came to a halt as workers crowded around radio sets to gather what scraps of news there were.

Movies, plays, horse races, and ball games were called off. Boys stood on street corners and waved Old Glory. People with tears in their eyes stopped stateside servicemen on the street and shook their hands and thanked them profusely. An impromptu parade was held through New York City, and the mayor, Fiorello La Guardia, stood up on a makeshift platform and addressed a huge throng that had gathered in Madison Square. Many headed straight for the nearest blood bank to donate the life-giving fluid, for they knew the boys in Normandy would desperately need it. Motorists, overcome with emotion, pulled off the roads to take in the news as NBC, CBS, and Mutual broadcast and rebroadcast the too-brief, maddeningly vague "Communiqué Number One": "Under the command of General Eisenhower, allied naval forces, supported by strong air forces, began landing allied armies this morning on the northern coast of France. The communiqué will be repeated. . . ."[3]

The first newspapers that day provided only slightly more information. Under a screaming banner headline—"ALLIES INVADE FRANCE"—the 6 June 1944 edition of the *Chicago Tribune* was typical: ". . . It can now be disclosed that the allies have been conducting a series of feints in advance of the invasion. . . . Berlin first announced the landings in a series of flashes that began about 6:30 a.m. (11:30 last night, Chicago time). . . . The allied communique was read over a trans-Atlantic hookup direct from Gen. Eisenhower's headquarters at 2:32 a.m. Chicago time. . . . A second announcement by SHAEF said, 'It is announced that Gen. B. L. Montgomery is in command of the army group carrying out the assault. This army group includes British, Canadian, and United States forces.'"[4]

A week later, *Time* magazine reported, "Across the land, generally, the mood was solemn. There was no sudden fear, as on that September morning in 1939 when the Germans marched into Poland; no sudden hate, as on Pearl Harbor day. This time, moved by a common impulse, the casual churchgoers as well as the devout went to pray. The U.S. people had wondered for weeks how they would behave on D-Day. When it came, they went about their regular business. . . . The citizens stuck to their radios, read newspaper extras as they rolled off the presses, sat and thought, talked and drank, knelt and prayed. . . .

"Winston Churchill, appearing before a cheering House of Commons, tantalizingly devoted 650 words to the fall of Rome.* Then he added jubilantly: 'I have also to announce to the House that during the night and early hours of the

---

*On 4 June 1944, after nearly eight months of brutal fighting in Italy's rugged mountains, Lieutenant General Mark Clark's 5th Army finally entered Rome.

morning the first of a series of landings in force upon the European continent has taken place. So far, the commanders . . . report that everything is proceeding according to plan. And what a plan!' . . .

"In Moscow the people literally danced in the streets. There the populace, from Stalin down to the lowest party member, had waited for two and a half years for the Second Front. This was the happiest capital. . . . In the lobby of the Metropole Hotel, an ecstatic Muscovite threw her arms around an American correspondent, exclaimed: 'We love you, we love you, we love you. You are our real friends.' German civilians did not get the news for several hours after the invasion began. In Northern France, the long-waiting, long-suffering populace heard it in the drone of planes and the roar of guns."[5]

Hitler had slept through the early hours of the invasion, his staff fearful of waking him. When he finally received the invasion reports, he confidently crowed, "The news couldn't be better! As long as [the Allies] were in Britain, we couldn't get at them. Now we have them where we can destroy them."[6]

That evening, President Roosevelt went on the air with a special message to the nation:

> My fellow Americans—
>
> Last night, when I spoke with you about the fall of Rome, I knew at that moment that the troops of the United States and our allies were crossing the Channel in another—and greater—operation. It has come to pass with success thus far. And so, in this poignant hour, I ask you to join with me in prayer.
>
> "Almighty God, our sons, pride of our nation, this day have set upon a mighty endeavor, a struggle to preserve our republic, our religion, and our civilization, and to set free a suffering humanity. Lead them straight and true; give strength to their arms, stoutness to their hearts, steadfastness in their faith. They will need thy blessings. Their road will be long and hard, for the enemy is strong. He may hurl back our forces. Success may not come with rushing speed, but we shall return again and again; and we know that by thy grace, and by the righteousness of our cause, our sons will triumph. They will be sorely tried, by night and by day, without rest—until the victory is won. The darkness will be rent by noise and flame.
>
> "Men's souls will be shaken with the violence of war. For these men are lately drawn from the ways of peace. They fight not for the lust of conquest. They fight to *end* conquest. They fight to *liberate*. They fight to let justice arise, and tolerance and good will among all thy people. They yearn but for the end of battle, for their

return to the haven of home. Some will never return. Embrace these, Father, and receive them, thy heroic servants, into thy kingdom. And for us at home—fathers, mothers, children, wives, sisters, and brothers of brave men overseas—whose thoughts and prayers are ever with them, help us, Almighty God, to rededicate ourselves in renewed faith in Thee in this hour of great sacrifice. . . . With thy blessings, we shall prevail over the unholy forces of our enemy. Help us to conquer the apostles of greed and racial arrogance. Lead us to the saving of our country, and with our sister nations into a world unity that will spell a sure peace—a peace invulnerable to the scheming of unworthy men. And a peace that will let all men live in freedom, reaping the just rewards of their honest toil. Thy will be done, Almighty God. Amen."[7]

Everywhere across America, in small towns and large cities, people flocked to their churches and synagogues to follow the president's lead and give prayers of thanksgiving—and to pray for the safety of their loved ones, their fathers, sons, husbands, and brothers, many of whom were, even now, lying wounded or dead on the beaches and in the hedgerows of Normandy.

A short distance from the edge of the bluff above the Omaha beachhead begin the hedgerows, which extend southward for some fifty miles. Although the word "hedgerow" sounds bucolic and innocuous, in early June 1944, they were anything but. And, although the Americans had had plenty of practice in making amphibious landings, attacking through hedgerows was something new, unfamiliar, and deadly. While the storming of a beachhead must be done quickly and with great dash, advancing through hedgerows meant just the opposite for, to the average infantryman, the trees and brambles of the Norman hedgerows were as impenetrable to the human body as a stone castle.

War correspondent Ernie Pyle captured the difficulty of combat in this type of terrain: "I want to describe to you what the weird hedgerow fighting in northwestern France was like. This type of fighting was always in small groups, so let's take as an example one company of men. Let's say they were working forward on both sides of a country lane, and the company was responsible for clearing the two fields on either side of the road as it advanced. That meant there was only about one platoon to a field, and with the company's understrength from casualties, there might be no more than twenty-five or thirty men. The fields were usually not more than fifty yards across and a couple of hundred yards long. They might have grain in them, or apple trees, but mostly they were just pastures of green grass, full of beautiful cows.

"The fields were surrounded on all sides by the immense hedgerow—ancient earthen banks, waist high, all matted with roots, and out of which grew weeds, bushes, and trees up to twenty feet high. The Germans used these barriers well. They put snipers in the trees. They dug deep trenches behind the hedgerows and covered them with timber, so that it was almost impossible for artillery to get at them. Sometimes they propped up machine guns with strings attached [to the triggers] so they could fire over the hedge without getting out of their holes. They even cut out a section of the hedgerow and hid a big gun or tank in it, covering it with bush. . . .

"We had to dig them out. It was a slow and cautious business, and there was nothing dashing about it. Our men didn't go across the open fields in dramatic charges such as you see in the movies. They did at first, but they learned better. They went in tiny groups, a squad or less, moving yards apart and sticking close to the hedgerows on either end of the field. They crept a few yards, squatted, waited, then crept again. . . . The attacking squads sneaked up on the sides of the hedgerows while the rest of the platoon stayed back in their own hedgerow and kept the forward hedge saturated with bullets. They shot rifle grenades too, and a mortar squad a little farther back kept lobbing mortar shells over onto the Germans. The little advance groups worked their way up to the far ends of the hedgerows at the corners of the field. They first tried to knock out the machine guns at each corner. They did this with hand grenades, rifle grenades, and machine guns. . . .

"In a long drive, an infantry company often went for a couple of days without letting up. . . . The soldiers sometimes ate only one K ration a day. They sometimes ran out of water. Their strength was gradually whittled down by wounds, exhaustion cases, and straggling. Finally they would get an order to sit where they were and dig in. Then another company would pass through or around them, and go on with the fighting. The relieved company might get to rest as much as a day or two. But in a big push such as the one that broke us out of the beachhead, a few hours' respite was about all they could expect. . . .

"This hedgerow business was a series of little skirmishes like that clear across the front, thousands and thousands of little skirmishes. No single one of them

American infantrymen engage the enemy force in a thick Norman hedgerow, June 1944. (Courtesy U.S. Army Military History Institute)

was very big. Added up over the days and weeks, however, they made a man-sized war—with thousands on both sides getting killed. . . ."[8]

Everyone who fought in the hedgerows, it seems, has a story of his experiences. Second Lieutenant Lawrence Johnson Jr., 7th Artillery, remembered that he had been "surprised at the hedgerow and lane system that represented the bocage* country of Normandy. We had not trained how to operate in this rather unusual terrain, nor were we even warned of its existence. It was strictly on-the-job training, particularly for artillery forward observers who found it impossible to see more than a hundred yards from one hedgerow to the next."[9]

Lieutenant Harold Monica, D Company, 18th Infantry, was impressed—no, awed—by the sturdiness of the hedgerows. "They were of dirt and roots four to six feet high, with trees and shrubs growing out of them—tight enough to serve as fences that cattle and other farm animals could not get through. In fact, nei-

* A French word meaning a mixture of pasture and wooded land.

ther could we. . . . The farm roads were generally sunken between two hedgerows. At times, it seemed as if you were in a tunnel. At daylight, we found ourselves in a small field surrounded by these hedgerows, with cows and their droppings everywhere. Good thing the cows didn't move much or we probably would have gone to war with *them* during the night."[10]

First Lieutenant James Watts, A Company, 81st Chemical Mortar Battalion, recalled, "The Normandy countryside is beautiful. Its small fields, the hedgerows, the stone-walled lanes and villages make for a lovely pastoral countryside. It is a peaceful scene today but [was] a difficult place to fight in. All the advantage is with the defender. Each successive hedgerow is a ready-made fighting position. The relatively static fighting can be fierce and destructive. I remember one poignant scene that hurt us all who were there. A family came through our position carrying a door on which was the body of a young boy. How he was killed, we did not know. The pain on the faces of the innocent family affected each of us and made us feel for the people of the area and what they must be suffering."[11]

Many men had particularly close calls with death in the hedgerows. Twenty-four-year-old Jack Ellery, a platoon sergeant in the 16th Infantry, recalled such a moment: "I was about to climb through a break in the hedgerow and as I did so, an ID bracelet on my right wrist got hung up on a rather sturdy piece of brush. I slid back down and broke off the branch to get loose. Meanwhile, a fellow from another company who had joined my group decided to pass by me and go on over. As his head cleared the top of the hedgerow, he took a round right in the face and fell back on top of me, dead. That was about as close as I came to stopping a bullet during the invasion."[12]

Roger Brugger, K Company, 16th Infantry, remembered the tactics his platoon used to overcome German opposition in the hedgerows: "We had to crawl through the hedgerows to get from one field to another. As we crawled, we had to crawl over the dead and wounded. In the corner, there would be openings and the Germans had set up machine guns to fire into these openings. We'd give each other covering fire to make the machine-gun crew keep their heads down, then three or four of our men could dash through the openings."[13]

Lieutenant William Dillon, Company A, 16th RCT, said that his platoon "always had a front-line hedgerow—*always!* This is where the tanks were mounted with bulldozer blades on front and would run full blast and hit a hedgerow to make a new gate; all the old gates were mined."[14]

A "Rhino" tank with "hedgebuster" device welded to the front of the hull. (Courtesy Colonel Robert R. McCormick Research Center of the 1st Infantry Division Museum at Cantigny)

In order to break through the earthen berms and dense, tangled vegetation, one enterprising sergeant—Curtis G. Culin of the 2nd Division—came up with an ingenious solution. By welding steel blades to a tank's hull, the tank would be able to crash through the hedgerow, taking dirt, trees, and roots with it—and creating a neat hole through which vehicles and troops could follow. The steel for hundreds of such "hedge choppers" was readily available—on Omaha Beach. The same steel tetrahedrons that had once been used in a vain attempt to halt the German panzers from crossing the French border, and had been used by the Germans in an equally vain attempt to keep the Allies from storming Fortress Europe, would now be cut up and used to tear through the hedgerows. By working around the clock, welding crews jury-rigged the devices, which worked with remarkable efficiency—good old American know-how in action.[15]

For the most part, though, it was still the dogface with a rifle who had to make his own, less spectacular penetration through the thickets. In one part of the hedgerows, Bob Hilbert, the radioman with K Company, 18th RCT, who had already been hit in the buttocks with a chunk of shrapnel on the beach, discovered that the thorny bushes could also be a literal pain in the posterior: "We went inland the next day [7 June], maybe a mile or two, and we came upon some enemy fire in the hedgerows. The company commander went up real quick to two of the scouts to see what was going on. I was back in another hedgerow and the company commander sent word back that he wanted the radio so he could contact battalion. So I started out and ran across that open field between the two hedgerows, and the bullets were flying pretty good and that gets you scared just a little bit, but I was running like crazy. When I got close, I wanted to get in the shelter of that trench [at the base of the hedgerow] and just jumped up in the air and sat down real quick—right in a bunch of brambles. I finally got the radio to the company commander and he was very gracious and got me a Silver Star for it."[16]

Chaplain John Burkhalter reported that he and ten other soldiers were crossing a field "when we heard sniper bullets whiz by. We all fell to the ground. As we lay there hugging the earth . . . the birds were singing beautifully in the trees close by. As I lay there listening, I though of the awfulness of it all; the birds were singing and we human beings were trying to kill each other. We are the greatest of God's creation, made in the image of God, and here human blood was being spilt everywhere. About three minutes later, and only forty yards away, we filed by one of our own boys lying by the side of the hedge, crouched over with a hole in the back of his head. His eyes were open, but he was dead, hit by a sniper."[17]

For the Germans, all the years of preparation for just this moment—the command exercises, the war games, the reams of plans detailing how to react when the invasion finally came—went out the window. Key personnel were absent, communications between units was in tatters, and units that could have made a difference were in the wrong places, hundreds of miles from where they were badly needed. On the morning of 7 June, Seventh Army commander *Generaloberst* Friedrich Dollmann ordered XXV Corps, sitting inactive in Brittany, to alert the *kampfgruppen* (battle groups) of the 265th and 275th Infantry Divisions for deployment to Normandy. Dollmann also wanted the entire 77th Division and the *kampfgruppe* of the 266th as well, but Rommel, who had finally returned to his headquarters, was concerned about denuding Brittany; he had received intelligence indicating that more airborne units might drop into the province. Only when he learned that Kraiss's 352nd Division was on the brink of disaster did he allow Dollmann to alert the units; the delay would be costly.*

The 352nd was, indeed, on its last legs. The division had been severely pummeled during the afternoon of 6 June, suffering the loss of most of its coastal defense units and their equipment; in fact, the 352nd—spread out from Omaha Beach to Caen—had lost about 20 percent of its strength in one day. While he waited for reinforcements, General Kraiss scrambled to locate whatever reserves were available and throw them into the widening breach. All he could find was a lone engineer battalion near St. Martin-de-Blagny, which he attached to the 916th Regiment south of Omaha Beach.[18]

The Germans' situation all along the Normandy coast on the morning of 7 June was precarious, verging on desperate. Only two beat-up battalions of the 915th Regiment stood between Bayeux and the British 50th Division driving inland from Gold Beach; by noon, the British had cut the Caen-Saint-Lô highway and entered Bayeux, virtually destroying the 915th in the process. The German 30th Mobile Infantry Brigade was ordered to reinforce the 352nd Division but, mounted mostly on bicycles, the inexperienced troops of the brigade were no match for the Typhoons and Mustangs and Thunderbolts roaring low over the terrain. The hindrance of German troop movement was aided by French resistance fighters, who cut lines of communications and blew up bridges and railroad tracks, often at the cost of their own lives. Kraiss's pleas to *General* Marcks for more assistance were turned down. Marcks had already sent up every unit he could find; he simply had no more troops to spare.[19]

Rommel attempted to impose his will on the battle, but it was already too late. Trying to salvage the situation, he ordered the 3rd Fallschirm Division and 77th Infantry Division to head for Normandy. Plans to employ the units of the II Fallschirm Corps into reinforcing the Cotentin were drawn up, then changed; the II Fallschirm Corps would instead be brought up to the Saint-Lô area to assist the I SS Panzer Corps in attacking either the British at Bayeux or striking the

---

*It would take ten days for the German reinforcements to reach Normandy and, by then, the 352nd was all but destroyed; the reinforcements, too, would be mere shadows of their former selves, having been bombed and strafed all along the route of march by overwhelming Allied air power.

Allied bridgehead north of Carentan—no one could decide where the greater danger lay. Rommel also threw the 12th SS Panzer and 21st Panzer Divisions into a counterattack, a counterattack that never got itself organized; the two divisions contented themselves with digging in and frustrating Montgomery's attempt to take Caen. Other units found themselves cut off with no way to inform upper-echelon commanders of their plight. Mostly, confusion and communications problems reigned throughout the German high command.

Convinced that Cherbourg and not Normandy or Calais was the real target of the invasion, von Rundstedt got into the act and began rushing units toward the vital port city, basically ignoring the danger posed by the American landings at Omaha Beach.[20] The Norman wall of Hitler's Fortress Europe was not just cracked, but crumbling; besides the 352nd, other divisions were also on the verge of destruction. One historian noted, "On the German left flank, the U.S. 82nd Airborne Division linked up with the U.S. VII Corps, advancing inland from Utah Beach. The 795th Georgian Battalion collapsed and Turqueville fell. Lieutenant General [Karl Wilhelm] von Schlieben realized that the situation was deteriorating rapidly and that only a determined counterattack could restore it. His 709th Infantry Division, supported by three artillery battalions and the *Sturm* Battalion, attacked again. They pushed the paratroopers back to the outskirts of Ste.-Mère-Eglise, but at that moment the U.S. 4th Infantry Division arrived, along with about 60 Sherman tanks. They quickly overran the 1058th Grenadier Regiment, which broke up and ceased to exist as an organized combat force. The 709th Infantry Division was crippled."[21]

Infantrymen, who spend their time in combat being shelled, strafed, and shot at, walking gingerly through minefields, and sleeping in muddy holes in the ground, are always inordinately grateful for the small comforts that most civilians take for granted. For example, on 7 June, Roger Brugger and K Company, 16th Infantry, were making good time heading eastward toward Port-en-Bessin. Not only did they *not* have to hoof it (they were riding atop tanks provided by B Company, 745th Tank Battalion), but they joyfully linked up with the British 50th Division, which had some wonderful trading material. "This British unit had fresh eggs!" Brugger recalled. "We traded American cigarettes for some of them. First fresh eggs I had had since leaving the States on November 19, 1943."[22]

A line of troops from the 2nd Infantry Division arrives as reinforcements on Omaha Beach, 7 June 1944. (Courtesy National Archives)

As reinforcements from the follow-up force began to land on Omaha Beach on 7 June, Louis Newman returned to the beach to search for his lost equipment and, "sure enough, I found my bedding roll and my carbine. I had two or three blankets and socks and toothpaste. As I was picking it up, I watched the 2nd Infantry Division come in and then went back to my position and tried to clean my carbine. It was all rusty and full of sand."[23]

On that same day and on that same beach, Ernie Pyle wandered the most expensive beachfront property in the world and recorded his impressions:

> I took a walk along the historic coast of Normandy in the country of France. It was a lovely day for strolling along the seashore. Men were sleeping on the sand, some of them sleeping forever. Men were floating in the water, but they didn't know they were in the water, for they were dead.
>
> The water was full of squishy little jellyfish about the size of your hand. Millions of them. In the center each of them had a green design exactly like a four leaf clover. The good-luck emblem. Sure. Hell yes.

> I walked for a mile and a half along the water's edge of our many-miled invasion beach. You wanted to walk slowly, for the detail on that beach was infinite. The wreckage was vast and startling. The awful waste and destruction of war, even aside from the loss of human life, has always been one of its outstanding features to those who are in it. Anything and everything is expendable. And we did expend on our beachhead in Normandy during those first few hours. . . .
>
> There were LCTs turned completely upside down and lying on their backs, and how they got that way I don't know. . . . In this shore-line museum of carnage there were abandoned rolls of barbed wire and smashed bulldozers and big stacks of thrown-away life belts and piles of shells still waiting to be moved. . . . On the beach lay, expended, sufficient men and mechanism for a small war. They were gone forever now. And yet we could afford it. The strong, swirling tides of the Normandy coast line shifted the contours of the sandy beach as they moved in and out. They carried soldiers' bodies out to sea, and later they returned them. They covered the corpses of heroes with sand, and then in their whims they uncovered them.[24]

Above the beach, dug in along a hedgerow on 7 June, Staff Sergeant Walter David Ehlers, L Company, 18th RCT, was worried that he hadn't seen his older brother Roland, a sergeant in K Company, since before the landings. Suddenly, K Company came marching by and Ehlers asked the first sergeant if he knew where his brother was. The sergeant replied that Roland was missing in action. "I knew that he had to have been either killed or wounded in action—he wouldn't be missing," the younger Ehlers said. "But you can't go back down to the beach and look for him, you know. There was just an unbelievable amount of humanity and vehicles and obstacles on the beach—you couldn't have found anybody if you'd wanted to. It would have been like looking for a needle in a haystack. Roland and I had a pact that if one of us fell in combat, we would not stop to take care of the other one because we wouldn't be accomplishing our mission. We said we'd leave it up to the medics, and that's what we did."

It was later confirmed that Roland Ehlers had been killed on D-Day. He had been leading his mortar squad down the ramp of an LCI when a German shell screamed in, hit the ramp, and wiped out the squad.[25]

Meanwhile, the follow-up units were on the move, heading toward their objectives. Colonel Seitz's 26th RCT of the 1st Infantry Division was moving eastward, and it and the British 50th Division, driving westward from Gold Beach, had trapped the remnants of the German 30th Mobile Brigade and elements of the 726th Regiment in a narrow pocket along the Drôme River near Mt. Cauvin, southwest of Port-en-Bessin; the enemy units, caught in the squeeze, fought for their lives.[26]

Back at his headquarters at Southwick House near Portsmouth, and unable to sit idly by and simply receive reports of the invasion's progress, Eisenhower, on 7 June, boarded a fast mine-laying ship, the *Apollo*, and crossed the Channel, tying up next to the *Augusta* for a meeting with Bradley, Kirk, and Hall. Ike later wrote, "We . . . found that the 1st and 29th Divisions, assaulting on Omaha, had finally dislodged the enemy and were proceeding swiftly inland. Isolated centers of resistance still held out and some of them sustained a most annoying artillery fire against our beaches and landing ships. I had a chance to confer with General Bradley and found him, as always, stout-hearted and confident of the result. In point of fact, the resistance encountered on Omaha Beach was at about the level we had feared all along the line. The conviction of the Germans that we would not attack in the weather then prevailing was a definite factor in the degree of surprise we achieved and accounted to some extent for the low order of active opposition on most of the beaches. In the Omaha sector, an alert enemy division, the 352nd, which prisoners stated had been in the area on maneuvers and defense exercises, accounted for some of the intense fighting in that locality."[27]

Harry Butcher echoed Ike's observations: "On Omaha Beach, the 1st Division had encountered the ill-luck of running into the German 352nd Division, prisoners from which had disclosed that the division happened to be in that area on maneuvers. Landing had been slowed and landing craft sunk or holed by mortar and field artillery fire from well-concealed positions. The established gun emplacements had not caused trouble. . . . The obstacles were really effective. The Teller mines on the steel posts had been hit by some landing craft, the mine making a hole about a yard across, repairable when our salvage crews get to work. I asked Major C. B. Hansen, aide to Bradley, about casualties, and he said he had seen on the beach during the morning forty dead Americans, with many wounded lying in the bushes. . . . Now the [1st Infantry] division was two or three miles inland."[28]

After his meeting with Eisenhower, Bradley issued new orders to Gerow; the 29th Infantry Division was to concentrate on seizing Isigny while the 1st Infantry Division would push to the east to effect a link-up with British forces, and south to increase the depth of the bridgehead.[29] Already piling onto Omaha and Utah Beaches were the follow-up forces—the 2nd, 9th, and 30th Infantry Divisions. If any 1st Division soldiers thought, as they had after Sicily, that their job was done and that they might be patted on the back, then shipped home to receive a hero's welcome, they were sorely mistaken. The whole reason for invading the Continent was to strike at the heart of the Reich and bring this war to a close; the only problem was, Berlin was 700 miles from Normandy, and the Germans would never give up without a fight for every inch of ground along the way. The Big Red One's services would be required once more.

Gerow's staff drew up a plan that called for V Corps' three infantry divisions—the 1st, 2nd, and 29th—to push southward on 9 June and create a deep and wide penetration toward the high ground of Forêt de Cerisy, some five miles inland. The 1st was to advance upon the villages of Agy, la Commune, and Vaubadon, situated along the Saint-Lô-Bayeux highway, while the 29th, on the west flank, would advance in the direction of Saint-Lô; the 2nd Division was to head south toward Trévières, directly into the heart of what was left of the German 352nd Division. The Big Red One, on V Corps' left flank, would then continue toward Caumont l'Evente, where seven roads intersect. As it turned out, a ten-mile gap between German units existed, and Caumont was in the very center of that gap.[30]

Caumont, some twelve miles south-southwest of Bayeux, approximately halfway between Saint-Lô and Villers-Bocage, was a position the Germans needed to hold. And the Americans assumed they would do everything in their power to hold it. According to Allen Towne, a medic, Caumont was located at "a road junction of importance. Caumont lies on a hill mass more than 750 feet above sea level and is forward of the Cerisy Forest and would give our artillery control of the upper Drôme valley. Its capture would make the hold on the beachhead secure and serve as a base for further offensive action into the hilly country to the south. Possession of Caumont would threaten the enemy's lateral communications from Caen to the Saint-Lô-Vire-Avranches region."[31]

If the men of the 1st could take and hold Caumont, they would drive a wedge between enemy forces; it was conceivable that the entire invasion force could plunge through that gap, split the Germans, and race into the center of France. The collapse of Germany's Western Front was suddenly a very real possibility. Caumont would become the focus for the V Corps' offensive, scheduled for 9 June—and the 1st would again be playing a leading role.[32]

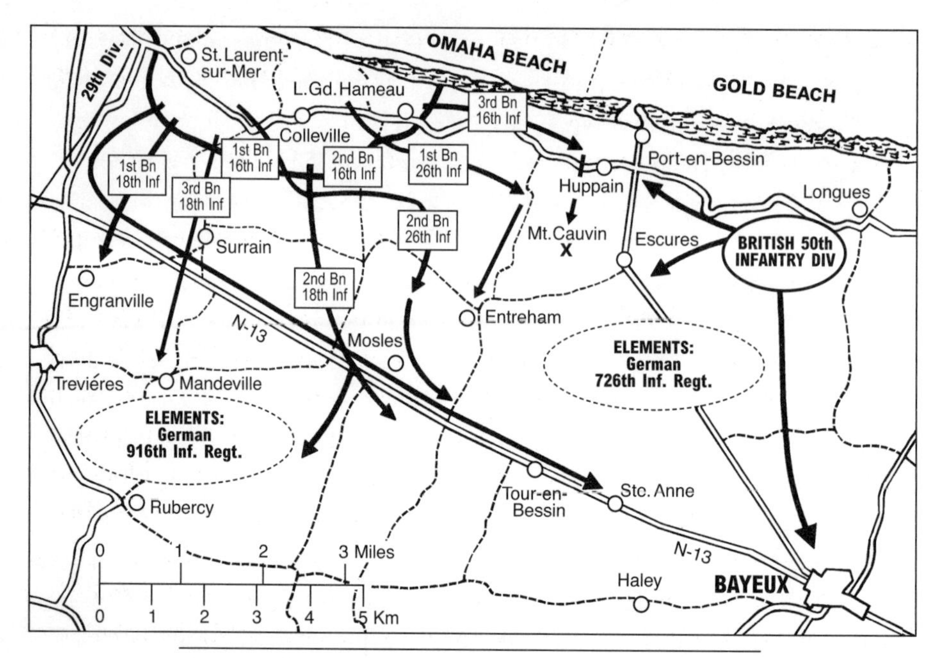

The 1st Division's progress by the evening of 7–8 June 1944.

On the evening of 7 June, Sergeant Walter Ehlers and his platoon from L Company, 18th RCT, were dug in in a hedgerow when, he recalled, "Our position was overrun by a German patrol. Our front line was kind of zig-zag, so when they overran our positions, and after they got into our lines, we couldn't fire on them because we'd be firing on our own troops."

Higher headquarters ordered Ehlers to find out where the Germans were. "I took four men and we went up and down this road. It was dark and we didn't know where the heck we were going. We could hear the Germans going, so we kept following them; we probably went out about a mile. Finally, we came upon a briefcase one of them had dropped. I told the squad, 'we're going back because we don't know where we're going and we can't see anything.' We went back and gave the briefcase to the company commander and he sent it up to 3rd Battalion headquarters. They found maps showing the second and third lines of defense of the German positions." The information would be vital for the coming offensive.[33]

Ralph "Andy" Anderson, a BAR-man with E Company, 18th Infantry, finally linked up with the rest of his company on the morning of 7 June and headed for Mosles. There, a sniper in a church steeple sent the GIs to ground. "Kenny, my squad leader, said, 'Just fire on that church and I'll take what I got here and we'll go in and clean it out.' So I started firing that BAR up in that church and pretty soon Kenny came down and said, 'Cease firing.' He said it was a woman sniper. Somebody took care of her—I don't know who." It was later determined that the woman was French and a German sympathizer.[34]

"On the afternoon of the second day," wrote Chaplain Burkhalter, "we were quite a way inland and two of my assistants and I were out trying to locate bodies of dead soldiers. We always take care of the American dead first and then the enemy dead. . . . Since we did not have any vehicles yet to send bodies back, all we could do on the move was to put the bodies in mattress covers and leave them in a marked place to be taken care of later by rear echelons. Our business was to keep fighting on inland and push the enemy back. On the roadside, my assistants and I saw a dead German officer. He was a tall fellow; must have been about six feet four. We turned him over and stretched him out the best we could. I looked at his face and was surprised to see how young he looked. No doubt he was in his twenties, but he had the face of a boy. I thought surely this fellow was too young to die. It almost seemed that he had asked for it. I became conscious of an awful evil force behind it all to cause a young fellow like this to seemingly hunger and delight to kill and be killed. We slid his body into a mattress cover and left him by the side of the road."[35]

Meanwhile, Frank Murdoch was leading his 1st Battalion, 26th Infantry, in an attack against German positions nearby. "As we moved along the road," Murdoch said, "we encountered small groups of enemy. Usually they pulled out when they saw what they were up against, but some would stay, shooting to the last, and then try to surrender. I came across a group of five young Germans sprawled dead on the road, and when I asked what had happened, a sergeant nearby remarked that they had been too slow in getting their hands up.

"Near Cabourg, we approached some woods, and beyond I could see a German artillery unit firing on the beach. I shouted for my naval gunfire officer—we had the destroyer *Harding* in direct support. . . . I showed him the German guns and he called for fire. The response was quick. When it came, it sounded like a fast freight passing close overhead, and the explosions nearly knocked us over. Because the target was an enemy artillery battery, the Navy had assigned it to the French cruiser *Montcalm*, and her big guns literally blew those Germans off the face of the earth. . . . As darkness was falling, we attacked into Etreham, and onto Mt. Cauvin. By daylight, we had established a defense forward of Etreham and

Chaplain John Burkhalter checks the identification of a dead German before his body is removed for burial, June 1944. (Courtesy U.S. Army Military History Institute)

on the south slopes of Mt. Cauvin. The next morning (8 June) Company C met a party of British commandos, so the Allies were linked up."[36]

By nightfall on 7 June, Colleville-sur-Mer and Le Grande Hameau were in 1st Infantry Division hands, as were Cabourg, Huppain, Surrain, Etreham, Formigny, Bellefontaine, Mosles, Tour-en-Bessin, and portions of the Bayeux-Isigny highway. Patrols sought out the enemy's front-line positions, and the ensuing firefights, although small in scope, were nevertheless violent, bloody affairs.[37]

During the night of 7/8 June, Lieutenant Colonel Derrill Daniel's 2nd Battalion, 26th RCT, moved from the vicinity of Etreham to secure its objective: the crossroads on the Isigny-Bayeux highway, between Mosles and Tour-en-Bessin. An air strike was called on stubborn German resistance the next morning, followed by what was supposed to have been an infantry assault supported by tanks and tank destroyers. But only one company from Murdoch's 1st Battalion had made it across the river by the evening of 8 June. With their infantry support lagging behind due to difficulties crossing the Aure River, the armor pulled up and waited.

The Army's official account of the day's action read, "The 3rd Battalion [Lieutenant Colonel John T. Corley] remained at Formigny during the morning [8 June] until it could be relieved by a battalion of the 115th Infantry. In the early afternoon it began a march down the Bayeux highway. At 1800 it attacked through the 2nd Battalion positions, and through Tour-en-Bessin to Ste.-Anne, which it reached shortly after midnight. During the night a violent and confused action took place at Ste.-Anne as the Germans, now in the process of withdrawing from the corridor, fought to keep the escape route open." The British, pressing from the east, were also beaten back, and the 726th Regiment was able to slip the bulk of its forces out of the Allied noose.[38]

The fighting proved to be fierce. Lieutenant Harold Monica noted, "Our orders were to continue the attack at daylight [8 June]. . . . Immediately on moving to the attack, our lead scouts drew rifle and machine-gun fire. The enemy was in small groups, but they didn't need many troops to cover one of the small fields. We found the going slow, as we had to build up a fire base. Even if we couldn't see them, we knew they were there. . . . We picked up some prisoners and made some advance, albeit damn slow. Around mid-morning, one of the Sherman tanks joined up for support. We figured this is what we needed, but we found out the tank couldn't get through the damn hedgerows, either. What a let-down."[39]

Tanker Ed Ireland, B Company, 745th Tank Battalion, agreed that the hedgerows were difficult, even for a thirty-three-ton Sherman. "The hedgerows was kind of steep for us. We'd have to hunt for an opening to get through, because some of our tanks that tried to make the hedgerows, they would turn over," Ireland said. "They would go up to the hedgerow and the walls were so high—they were probably six or eight feet high—and they would turn the tanks over, and also they would expose the tank to fire. . . . And then they started fitting us with one bulldozer with each company or tank outfit, and that did real good for us because it made openings where there wasn't any. . . . Our bulldozers would go over there and scoop the dirt in right on top of [the Germans] and bury them alive."[40]

Meanwhile, Harold Monica was overcome by frustration and disappointment. "Everything is against us and seems to be getting no better," he said. "Casualties, though light on D-Day, now started to mount. Lieutenant Hannum from C Company was shot; a platoon sergeant from B Company—his name slips me—was shot through the neck, but shot and killed the man who shot him before he died. . . . They were less than fifty yards apart.

"Due to the nature of the terrain, the advantage was with the defenders, in that we could not determine where they were until they opened fire. If you will, that gave the enemy the first shot. We would have to build up a fire base in order to cover our leading troops. The fire fight would continue until we could overrun that next hedgerow, taking prisoners, or their abandoned positions, whatever the case, and prepare to repeat the process at the next hedgerow the enemy decided to defend—a very slow and expensive process. All this time, from the battalion and regimental commanders: 'Get that resistance cleaned out and get moving—*now*.' Due to the number of these hedgerows, it just wasn't possible for the enemy to defend each field, but how to determine which ones were not concealing enemy troops? So we would have to have men in position to give covering fire before proceeding hedgerow to hedgerow. A time-consuming, slow process. In this fashion, we advanced some 3,000 yards on D+1 and were approaching our D-Day objectives in the Surrain-Formigny sector. During our 30–36 hours we had been ashore, our initial positions had been secured and we . . . were advancing inland.

"Lieutenant Bobbie Brown was having a field day. He enjoyed the war—the only man I knew who did, and it showed.* Ran into him in the afternoon [7 June] and he already had six notches on his rifle, which he showed me. One of them was a woman who was in uniform. I asked, 'How do you know, as I don't believe it.' He said, 'One of my men told me, "Lieutenant, you just shot a woman," so I checked the body and, sure enough, it was a female.' To Bobbie, male or female didn't make any difference if in the uniform of the enemy. This was just a continuation of his civilian life style in Phenix City, and in war he didn't have to be concerned with the authorities. Such is life, in war or peace; it takes all kinds to keep things going.

"After 300 or so yards, we were ordered to hold in present positions. We were finding men in small groups—two, three, five—that had been separated from

* According to Monica, Brown had grown up in the tough environment of Phenix City, Alabama, across the river from Fort Benning, Georgia, and truly loved war. Two years older than his battalion commander, Lieutenant Colonel Robert York, Bobbie Brown carried scars from innumerable knife and gun fights. He had joined the Army before the war and became a sergeant in Patton's 2nd Armored Division. Refusing a commission, Brown reportedly told Patton, "General, if I am going to take a commission, the only place I'll go is the Infantry." Brown transferred to the Infantry and was made a second lieutenant. Monica said, "To this man, war was an extension of his lifestyle, where he didn't have to worry about killing anyone who might want to do him harm." Brown went on to earn the Medal of Honor at Aachen in October 1944 but, after the war, committed suicide.

their units. From the pounding on the beach, their command structure did not exist. Therefore, some sort of order had to be restored and [we had to] determine the positions that the 16th held. . . . Communications were established by runners to the next higher unit, i.e., platoon to company to battalion headquarters. . . . As a result of this activity, Colonel York . . . was able to report [to regiment] the battalion's exact location, extent of casualties, and our readiness to execute any order from higher headquarters."

A day later, with his battalion catching enemy fire, Monica had a chance to see, firsthand, the tremendous power of the American air support. "The Air Force liaison officer, attached to the 1st Battalion, 18th Infantry Headquarters, had established good radio communications with our direct-support aircraft," Monica said. "His radio equipment was carried in a Sherman tank and operated properly. On D+1, the battalion received only minor mortar and artillery shelling. On D+2, this shelling increased as the enemy had been able to better determine our location and direction of attack. We quickly found use for the P47s the liaison officer could call down. Our leading men were equipped with twelve-inch-square fluorescent orange [panels] on their backs to aid recognition by the pilots. So when we were in position, the P47s were called and they would strafe the next hedgerow. They came in over us at 100–150 feet altitude with their eight fifty-caliber machine guns firing. What noise—their engines wide open and guns going! It seemed nice not to be on the receiving end. For this operation, we had twenty-four aircraft, airborne all day, that the battalion could call on. Pieces from the metal ammunition belts and the brass cartridges were landing all around us. None of the platoon were struck by any of these pieces—good thing, as these pieces were going some 350 miles per hour! Whether getting hit would have been lethal or not, who knows? But they certainly could have left some bruises."* [41]

---

*A German paratrooper, a member of *Fallschirmjäger* Regiment 6, encamped near Carentan, was on the receiving end of the terrific Allied bombings and artillery barrages—and lived to tell the tale. On 7 June, he wrote in his diary, "At first light, vast numbers of enemy bombers reappear, bringing death and fire into the French hinterland. Naturally, their targets are the railway junctions, strategic concentration points and channels of communication, as well as our advancing armored units. They know well enough that if they can eliminate our reinforcements, they should be able to achieve their objectives without massive casualties. As for our own pilots—they are nowhere to be seen." (Pöppel, p. 179)

The morning of 8 June found the Germans in further disarray; 352nd Division headquarters had temporarily lost contact with the 726th Regiment. That afternoon, however, communications were re-established and Kraiss ordered the 726th to make a stand against the advancing 26th RCT until dark, when it could continue its withdrawal and form a line of resistance farther to the south, between the villages of Blay and Haley, west of Bayeux. Shortly after issuing the order, Kraiss was visited by the corps commander, *General* Marcks. Knowing that Hitler's orders were to defend every inch of ground to the last man, Kraiss informed his commanding officer what he had done and explained that his directive was aimed at trying to stabilize the defensive line. Marcks, realizing that a strategic withdrawal would buy time for his corps and perhaps prevent an immediate Allied breakthrough to the south, did not countermand Kraiss's order.[42]

That same day, General Omar Bradley and his party went ashore to pay a special visit to 1st Infantry Division headquarters in the knocked-out bunker. Bradley's aide, Major Chet Hansen, noted in his diary: "Trip to the 1st Division was really a reunion. [Lieutenant Colonel Frederick W.] Gibbs [the G-3], Huebner, [Colonel Stanhope B.] Mason [Chief of Staff], and the others looked as they did the last time we saw them. . . . Brad wrapped his arm around Huebner, 'Hello, fellow, I'm glad to see you.' Huebner answered, 'Brad, we've got a bunch of goddamn *boche* here that won't stop fighting.' Brad answers, 'Well, it'll simply take time and ammunition.'"[43]

Bradley and Huebner studied a map and discussed the 1st Division's situation. The battered 16th Infantry was holding its positions atop the bluffs while the 18th and 26th Infantry Regiments had passed through to take up positions farther inland. Huebner explained that a battalion each from the 16th and 26th RCTs was moving eastward to link up with the British on their left, near Port-en-Bessin. Satisfactory progress was being made everywhere, although elements of the 352nd Division, almost completely surrounded by the 1st Division, continued to resist southeast of St. Laurent-sur-Mer.[44]

Outside the 1st Division CP after the meeting, Chet Hansen noticed the hard-won road that "twisted up the hill where 'ducks' were climbing slowly and troops wading ashore, waist-deep in the cold channel, struggled up the hill, bent under the equipment, their shoes caking in the dry French dust. . . . [Bradley] walked out to the road, thumbed a ride on a two-and-a-half-ton truck. Smiled at the driver, stepped on the running board, said, 'Mind giving me a ride to the top, corporal?' A soldier looked around, shouted, 'My God, it's General Bradley!' I jumped on the vehicle behind. . . . During a stop, a Pfc came up with the top of a ration box, apologized for his lack of decent paper, thrust a stubby pencil in front of the General and asked him for his signature. The General laughed, bent over, and scribbled out his name."[45]

German resistance to the American advance varied. While some German units fought to the last man, others were more than willing to give themselves up to live another day. Louis Newman, Cannon Company, 18th Infantry, recalled the time he captured fourteen Germans: "We were following the riflemen in front of us; I was on a two-and-a-half-ton truck, manning the machine gun that was mounted on top of the cab. We came to a small town where there were pockets of Germans that were cut off from their unit. I saw the Germans and let go a burst and they all gave up. Most of them were very young—maybe fourteen or fifteen years old. I searched them; I knew some German; I had been sent to division headquarters in Blandford for instructions on how to question prisoners. One of them was an old guy—he had some black bread in his pocket. Another guy was twenty or twenty-two and I took out a blue card from one of his pockets and he started laughing. He said, 'Don't you have that in the American army?' I said, 'No, what is it?' He said, 'It's for a whorehouse. They stamp it every time you go in.' He used to go to Bayeux, where they had a brothel. The sergeant in this group had fifteen years in the army. I spoke to them for a while and then I started to march them back. But we were moving out, and I had to get rid of them; I turned them over to a fellow from the anti-tank company."[46]

From Mt. Cauvin, John T. Corley's 3rd Battalion of the 26th RCT pushed into Ste.-Anne. No sooner had the battalion begun settling in when it was attacked by probing elements of a 600-man battalion from the German 30th Mobile Brigade, moving westward to escape British pressure near Sully. At 0230 hours on 9 June, platoon sergeant Theodore Dobol, K Company, 26th Infantry, and two privates were on a patrol to establish contact with the British to the east. Along the pitch-black road, the patrol ran into five of the enemy. "We came across a German squad moving into position," Dobol said. "My two men were to my rear. . . . [The Germans] moved toward me, thinking I was one of them. . . . I quickly started to fire point blank. The first to fall was the sergeant with the machine gun; others quickly followed after receiving this point-blank fire. I could hardly believe it; five men in just a few seconds and none of them able to discharge their personal weapons because two were carrying ammo and

Sergeant Theodore Dobol, 3rd Battalion, 26th Infantry (post-war photo). (Courtesy Colonel Robert R. McCormick Research Center of the 1st Infantry Division Museum at Cantigny)

the other the machine gun. . . . We started to run and I ran into another German. This one had his weapon at port arms with a fixed bayonet." Dobol managed to disarm the enemy soldier—a Pole—and take him prisoner. Because Dobol himself was Polish, he interrogated the man and learned that the enemy was moving toward Ste.-Anne.

As dawn approached, so did a convoy of German trucks. A German officer was standing on the running board of one of the trucks when Dobol "disposed of him." A flurry of hand grenades flew Dobol's way from the troops in the truck, blowing him into a ditch. "I was wounded on the left side of the face, hitting my eyes, and the pain was excruciating. When I came to, I was dazed and did not know where to go. It was daylight by this time and I could not pull myself together."

The wounded Dobol was found by his battalion commander, Lieutenant Colonel Corley, and evacuated to an aid station in the rear. For his actions,

Dobol was recommended for the Medal of Honor, one of the few medals he did not receive.[47]

One of the two privates with Dobol (the other had been killed) rushed back to the battalion CP with news of the approaching enemy column; the unsuspecting enemy was ambushed as soon as it entered the village and a full-scale battle broke out, the red lines of tracer bullets crisscrossing the sky. In the predawn darkness of 9 June, the Germans struck L Company just as it was being reinforced by American tanks. The fighting in the village was savage, and nearly hand-to-hand, with grenades being tossed back and forth from one house to another.

The battalion's journal hints at the ferocity of the combat: "At 0300, as tanks are moving up to L Company position, the enemy launch an attack at L Company. Enemy using concussion grenades and potato mashers. All except two platoons of L Company forced to withdraw. Second platoon of M Company overrun. Enemy forces come down main road in trucks! Leading truck full of ammo hit by tank fire and bursts into flame right in front of CP. Two other trucks, one of which tried to bypass the first, are also knocked out. Enemy on bicycles, motorcycles, and one on a horse, are thrown into utter confusion. Close fighting fast and furious. Heinies are utterly demoralized—screaming, crying, and yelling as they jump into ditches and into foxholes in K Company's positions. Situation very critical until dawn. Grenades being thrown into CP. . . . At daylight, naval gunfire helps break up enemy attack and routs them. We capture one officer and 94 enlisted men. They are scared to death, many of them under shock. Many dead 'Jerries' near L Company position and eight or ten in front of CP. . . . At 1300 hours, we move out towards final beach-head objective in vicinity of Agy."[48]

At dawn on 9 June, the V Corps offensive stepped off. The 1st Infantry Division spearheaded the push toward Caumont, but the road to Caumont proved to be anything but easy. Private Ralph Puhalovich, Anti-Tank Company, 26th Infantry, remembered the terrific poundings he and his unit suffered along the way—from both German and American fire. He said, "We were told to move out, and we moved out. We were making dust, naturally, and pretty soon we were taking shells. Our own tanks were firing at us because somebody screwed up—we weren't supposed to be up there; we were way out in front of everybody." His unit then was shelled by the other side. "We were bringing the rations and the mail up to the front. I don't know how the Germans spotted us, but they

Private Ralph Puhalovich, Anti-Tank Company, 26th Infantry Regiment. (Courtesy Ralph Puhalovich)

did. They started shelling us. My buddies jumped into foxholes but I didn't. The shells picked me up and turned me around about four times. Every time I tried to hit the ground, another would hit and lift me off the ground. The ration box and water can I was carrying were completely riddled with holes, and I took a tremendous head pounding. My nose and ears were bleeding, but I did not go to the aid station immediately—I was a young kid and wanted to show the veterans I was as tough as they were."[49]

Sergeant Walter Ehlers recalled that the 18th RCT attacked through 9 June and into the following day, when his determination earned for him the Medal of Honor. "We were hitting the German positions right on the nose. We had a platoon of men over on our left in a field beyond us and we were coming up through another field on their right. They got fired upon over there, so I told my men we've got to rush up to the hedgerow immediately, otherwise we'll get caught in the middle of the field and they'll just pick us off. So we did. When we rushed up there, I went down to where a machine gun was firing and I ran into the enemy patrol and knocked them out. They were about four or five feet from me; I shot all four of them and kept going. It didn't draw the attention of the machine gunner that his own men were getting shot by somebody in the hedgerow. I guess he thought his men were shot by guys coming across the field; he got his targets all mixed up. I got close to the machine gun and knocked it out and killed the three men who were on it with my rifle.

"There was another machine gun in the corner of the next field and I snuck up on it and knocked it out. I had my squad following me all the time. I went upon a mound and saw two mortar positions and about ten men in there. They saw me with my bayonet and got frightened and started running. I tried to halt them, but they wouldn't halt, so I shot them, because we didn't want to have to fight them again later. Of course, my squad helped me knock them all off. We went on further and got another machine gun that day.

"Next day, we were going along up the side of a hedgerow instead of out in the middle." The hedgerows were infested with enemy troops—Germans to Ehlers's left, to his right, and directly in front. "They started firing on us and the company commander ordered us to withdraw. I knew that if we turned and withdrew, we'd probably all get knocked off. So we started firing in a semi-circle; my automatic rifleman knew what his job was, so he came up to help me—he fired to the right and I fired straight ahead and around to the left. As soon as our squad got back to the hedgerow behind us, we started back. As I was coming down the hedgerow, I saw [the Germans] putting another machine gun in the corner with a three-man crew. So I sent three men down there and, about the time I sent the last one, I got hit in the back and it spun me around. I saw a German in the hedgerow and shot him. Then I noticed my automatic rifleman was laying out in the field and I went out and got him. I got his arm around my shoulder and picked him up and carried him over to the hedgerow behind us."

A medic came up and Ehlers asked him to check the BAR man's condition. He then asked the medic to look at the wound in his back and put a patch on it. "He turned me around and saw a hole in my trench shovel and he said, 'My God, you've been shot clean through. You should be dead!' The bullet had hit my rib and went into my pack and hit my mother's picture and a bar of soap, then turned and hit my shovel, so it looked like I had been shot clear through. But the word went out that I was dead. The next day, when I saw the guys, they said, 'We thought you were dead.'"

Newly promoted Second Lieutenant Walter D. Ehlers, L Company, 18th Infantry, is presented with the Medal of Honor by Lieutenant General John C. H. Lee, commander of ETO Services of Supply, in Paris, 14 December 1944. (Courtesy Colonel Robert R. McCormick Research Center of the 1st Infantry Division Museum at Cantigny)

Several months later, Ehlers learned while reading *The Stars and Stripes* that his actions in the hedgerows had earned him the country's highest decoration for valor; by then, he had already been wounded twice more.* [50]

On 10 June, near Vaubadon, Staff Sergeant Arthur F. DeFranzo, of K Company, 18th Infantry, who had already earned the Silver Star three days earlier, was advancing across an open field with an advance party of scouts when the line came under fire. One of DeFranzo's men was hit and the sergeant went to his aid, only to be wounded himself. Ignoring his injury, DeFranzo carried the man to safety, then turned and led the patrol across the field that was being swept by the fire from two machine guns. Without regard for his own life, DeFranzo fired back, silencing the enemy positions with his M-1 Garand rifle. Despite being wounded again, Sergeant DeFranzo continued on, waving for his men to follow him. Hit once more, the Saugus, Massachusetts, native "suddenly

*While most surviving Medal of Honor recipients were removed from combat and sent home for public-relations and war-bond fundraising drives, Ehlers requested—and was granted—permission to rejoin his company in combat. He remained with them until the end of the war.

Sergeant Arthur F. DeFranzo, K Company, 18th Infantry Regiment, posthumous recipient of the Medal of Honor. (Courtesy Colonel Robert R. McCormick Research Center of the 1st Infantry Division Museum at Cantigny)

raised himself and once more moved forward in the lead of his men until he was hit again by enemy fire. In a final gesture of indomitable courage, he threw several grenades at the enemy machine-gun position and completely destroyed the gun. In this action, S/Sgt. DeFranzo lost his life, but by bearing the brunt of the enemy fire in leading the attack, he prevented a delay in the assault which would have been of considerable benefit to the foe, and he made possible his company's advance with a minimum of casualties. The extraordinary heroism and magnificent devotion to duty displayed by S/Sgt. DeFranzo was a great inspiration to all about him." For his display of self-sacrifice, Arthur DeFranzo was awarded the Medal of Honor, posthumously.[51]

On the same day as DeFranzo's actions, with the 1st still on the march, the regiments received a message that they proudly passed along to their subordinate units: "Generals Montgomery, Bradley and Huebner wish to convey their pride in the 1st Division having continually been the first to reach their objective."[52]

With the generals' praise on their minds, the dogfaces of the Big Red One—dirty, dusty, smelly, and many with bandages covering wounds that would have hospitalized less battle-hardened men—walked a little taller down the roads and lanes of northern France. And even though they griped about it, they knew

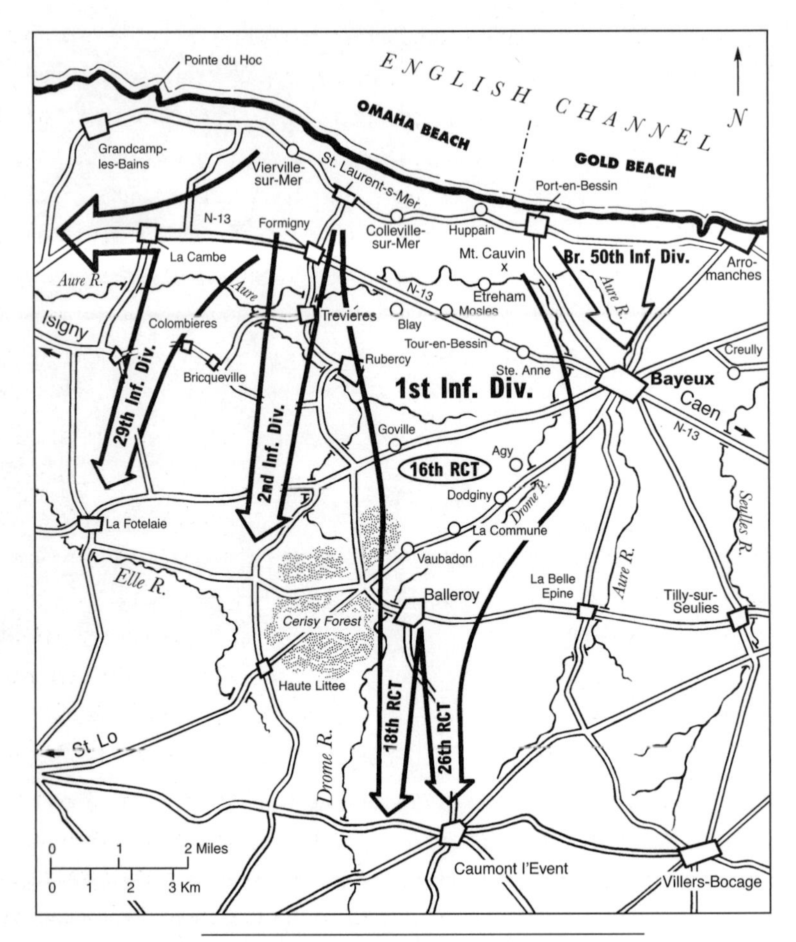

Breakout from the beachhead: V Corps Offensive, 9–13 June 1944 (positions approximate).

that when the going got tough, the top brass always depended on one outfit to get the job done: the 1st Infantry Division.

German reinforcements were at last reaching the area, although many were in no shape to fight, having been shredded by Allied fighter-bombers all along their routes of march. The 12th SS Panzer (*Hitlerjugend*) Division rolled into the gap between Caen (where the 21st Panzer Division was fighting off British attacks) and Bronay, a town halfway between Caen and Bayeux; to the 12th's south and left came the formidable Tiger tanks of the Panzer Lehr Division, its left flank seeking to make contact with what remained of the 352nd Division. The two armored divisions had been scheduled to launch an attack against Courseulles, on the coast between Arromanches and St. Aubin, but had been severely depleted by air attacks.

The phones between Rommel's and von Rundstedt's headquarters rang constantly as staff officers frantically tried to make sense of the crumbling front; the whereabouts of the decimated reserves; the continual Allied build-up on the beachhead; and the sudden V Corps offensive. It seemed as if the dike were bursting at several points and the Germans did not have enough fingers to plug all the holes. The Germans should have had a good idea of what the Allies were planning to do, for copies of both the VII Corps field order showing that Cherbourg and Saint-Lô were 1st Army objectives and the entire V Corps Order of Battle and maneuver plan had fallen into their hands; a boat with the VII Corps orders had drifted into the mouth of the Vire River, while the V Corps plans were found on the body of a dead American officer near Vierville.

But having knowledge of American intentions did not mean the Germans would be able to thwart those plans. Rommel worried that the British might break through the defenses around Caen and make a dash for Paris, so he was loathe to strip the Caen front of units and send them to Cherbourg. And who was to say that these plans weren't all part of some elaborate ruse, planted in a boat and on a corpse, to mislead the German high command? This smattering of knowledge of supposed American plans also served to further paralyze the Germans into inaction; some officers thought the plans made it clear that Normandy was indeed the main thrust and there would be no massive, Patton-led attack hitting the Pas de Calais, but Hitler and OKW continued to believe otherwise. The absence of any similarly discovered British plans left the Germans in the dark—and, for all intents and purposes, immobilized.[53]

The 1st Infantry Division was moving rapidly through the villages and hedgerows now, overcoming the spotty resistance that the disorganized Germans tried to throw in its path. Lieutenant Harold Monica noted, "For the next five days (D+4 through D+8), the 1st Battalion, 18th Infantry, including D Company, did not make contact with the enemy. In other words, we fired NO shots in anger. Even though each hedgerow was treated with caution, we were advancing rapidly. . . . The 26th Infantry on the left was having the same success, and the 1st Division was advancing on a six- or seven-thousand-yard front, approximately five- to six-thousand yards per day."[54]

There was an overall sense of movement, of a gathering momentum. The slogging through the hedgerows seemed about at an end. Except for isolated pockets of resistance, the Germans were on the run. On 11 June, a half mile south of Balleroy, Medic Allen Towne noted, "We moved eight miles from our last area by truck. We were now about twelve miles from Omaha Beach. We dug in and set up the aid station and continued to evacuate the wounded. We knew another attack was to start soon, and the combat team was waiting for other units to protect the flanks. The 1st Division was now farther inland than any other Allied unit. The British, who were supposed to be on our immediate left flank, had not been able to keep up, and there were no U.S. Army units on our right flank."

That morning, a French resistance fighter entered the aid station and handed Towne a letter written by three British servicemen who had been wounded and were being secretly sequestered by the Underground. Wary but wanting to help, Towne said, "I got one of the ambulances and, with Corporal Mike Katchur driving and the Frenchman on the running board, we left the aid station. We went off in a southwesterly direction. This was a different direction than the 18th Infantry's advance toward the next objective. . . . We were proceeding into unknown territory. We were traveling along a small, narrow road with tall hedgerows on each side. . . . We had no idea what was behind them and could not see if there were any German units in the area. This worried me, and I hoped we did not meet up with any German patrols or drive into an ambush."

The small group finally reached a barn where they found the wounded trio, placed them in the ambulance, and returned to American lines, where the casualties were treated. "We saw no one on the trip, which was about 3 1/2 miles each way, and there was no sign that any soldiers had ever been there. The Germans must have left, and none of the U.S. Army units had filled the gap. I believe the U.S. 2nd Infantry Division was supposed to be there. It is amazing that sometimes, in an important battle, you can drive for miles between the opposing forces and not see any soldiers."[55]

Nearby, and on the same day, Sergeant Harley Reynolds, B Company, 16th Infantry, came upon a gruesomely surrealistic scene: "I remember moving into a wooded area that I believe was near Balleroy. In the middle of the area my platoon was assigned, we found the bodies of a mature man and woman and a young woman in her late teens or early twenties. They were lying on their backs, feet almost touching, and heads pointed outward similar to a three-pointed star.

They were in formal dress, he in long tails, she in a black gown, and the girl in a white gown with pink embroidered flowers on the front. The mid-section of all three had been blown away. The local authorities from a town a short distance away were brought, and the only thing we got from them was that it was a suicide—they had simply stood embracing themselves about a German 'potato masher.' The handle to the grenade was lying amid them; they were suspected Nazi collaborators."[56]

Caumont was reached on the morning of 13 June with the 1st Battalion, 26th RCT, in the van. The expected stiff resistance did not materialize; only scattered firing was encountered, and the Americans soon routed the few defenders from the town. As the rest of the division quickly took up positions in and around Caumont, Bradley told Huebner to halt his advance; the 1st's swift and successful drive had created a salient and Bradley wanted to give the 2nd and 29th Divisions to the west, and the British units to the east, a chance to catch up and form a more-or-less straight front line.[57]

About this time, Al Alvarez, 7th Field Artillery, recalled the loss of the despotic, hard-drinking old soldier in his outfit whom he first encountered during training in England and whom he identified only as "The Corporal." "Sadly, the law of averages was against this corporal," Alvarez recalled. "He got his 'German marksmanship medal'—the Purple Heart—somewhere around Caumont. He left us on a warm afternoon on a stretcher, laughing uproariously at some joke. We didn't join in, as the medic nodded forebodingly. We remained, saddened at our family loss, unknowingly, still on our deadly conveyor belt to oblivion, curiously feeling that we had come too late to share this war with him. We had seen him as an ordinary loudmouth corporal, the unit's lowest-level non-commissioned officer, yet he had cared only about our welfare and subtly or brutally energized our potential. In the end, it was not what he *did* that made him unique, but what he eventually caused us to do. We never knew whether we liked him or disliked him, but we sure never could ignore him. He, as he avidly proclaimed, was our master or disaster. Somebody said he died that night in lonely obscurity in a medical tent back of the lines, still calling out obscenities on the doc and his medics, but I don't accept that. No sir, I believe he's ensconced on the right seat of that throne in Valhalla, greeting the newly arrived warrior angels, his raucous assertions still occasionally mixed with nettled harassments persisting!"[58]

A history of the 26th Infantry Regiment noted, "From mid-June until late July, Caumont remained the point of deepest penetration from the beach. As the linchpin between the British Second Army and the American First Army, it immediately drew German counterattacks from the 2nd Panzer, Panzer Lehr, and 3rd Parachute Divisions. One determined thrust at 1st Battalion [26th RCT] involved an infantry battalion supported by scout cars that succeeded in penetrating one company's position, only to be ejected by a tank-led counterattack. The 26th's position held firm. . . . There followed a period of position warfare, with the 1st Division dug in on favorable ground and the Germans lacking the strength to dislodge it."[59]

Whenever the American advance halted, unit scroungers did their work, seeking out minor comforts to ease the pain of the infantryman's existence. Captain Fred Hall, operations officer of the 2nd Battalion, 16th Infantry, remembered that some troops had "liberated" a cask of calvados, the fiery apple brandy of Normandy. "A bullet hole served as a spigot in the big casks found in farmers' cellars. The favorite drink was calvados with grapefruit juice. It was said that calvados was a good fluid in our cigarette lighters."[60]

Noting that GIs, during a lull in combat, have traditionally looked forward with eagerness to four events—mail call, hot showers, a sip of the local hootch, and an intimate encounter with local females—Eddie Steeg observed, "We got some mail and sent some out. Once again, I got some cookie crumbs, hard candy, chewing gum, face cloth, dainty napkins, more shoe whitening, and a pair of spats. No mom's apple pie or ice cream; I really yearned for a big plate of vanilla ice cream. They had hot showers set up and, not having time to clean up properly during our push inland, we were a bunch of dirty and smelly dogfaces. The showers were a real luxury, even though we had to run around naked at times to get to them. . . .

"I was introduced to a common French liqueur known as calvados—a clear, pure whiskey made from apples, much like our own moonshine made at home, I was told. I poured some of it in my canteen cup and watched as it sizzled and cleaned the coffee stains off the sides of the cup. . . . I am strictly a beer man, but I felt after the night I went through [full of German shelling], I was ready to have something to settle me down. After swallowing the first couple of swigs, I thought my stomach was on fire. This, of course, prompted the idea that I could use something to eat. *Voila!* I ignited the remains of the calvados in my canteen cup and proceeded to heat up a can of bacon and eggs for breakfast!"

As far as women went, however, Steeg said, "Contrary to the common perception that a lot of our military forces enjoyed fraternizing with the female

Members of a 1st Infantry Division platoon receive mail from home while "somewhere in France." A military censor has blocked out the Big Red One sleeve insignia for security purposes. (Courtesy U.S. Army Military History Institute)

populace in foreign lands . . . there were some notable exceptions to the premise. Take me, for example. I . . . was still a virgin, with no likely prospect of that situation changing."[61]

During the brief respite, Chaplain John Burkhalter reflected on what he and the rest of the men had experienced since 6 June: "Nobody can love God better than when he is looking death square in the face and talks to God and sees God come to the rescue. As I look back through hectic days just gone by to that hellish beach, I agree with Ernie Pyle that it was a pure miracle we even took the beach at all. Yes, there were a lot of miracles on the beach that day. God was on the beach [on] D-Day; I know He was, because I was talking with Him."[62]

According to Lieutenant Monica, "On D+8 [14 June], we were in the La Vacquerie sector and the 26th Infantry was in Caumont. During this advance, the small towns of Rubercy, Saonnet, Saon, Balleroy, Cormlain, and parts of the

Cerisy Forest that were in the 1st Division sector were secured. On a four- to five-mile-front, we were approximately twenty miles inland. We had moved ahead of the British on our left, as they had run into stiff street fighting in Bayeux. . . . The 2nd Division on our right was bogged down in the hedgerows, and we found ourselves with both flanks exposed—an undesirable position on the battlefield. There, it was necessary to order the 1st Division to halt its advance and wait for friendly forces to move up and be in position to protect our flanks. The 18th Infantry was ordered to defend and hold the La Vacquerie sector and the 26th Infantry was to do the same in the Caumont sector. The 16th Infantry was in reserve and this lull enabled them to replace personnel and lost equipment, reorganize, and secure the rear area."

To Monica, the sudden cessation of constant combat seemed odd; fighting, shelling, noise, and death had become the norm. "Dawn of D+9 was strange indeed, as we were not attacking as we had been since the landing. Our rear echelons were now well established [and] ammo, food, water, spare parts, and other items were reaching us via jeep, as required. Combat patrols were sent out one to two thousand yards and did not make contact with the enemy. In fact, for the day, not even a stray mortar or artillery shell came into the battalion area. I wondered a little: what is going on? Here we are, some twenty thousand troops twenty miles inland, and the enemy doesn't know we are here? This started to change on D+10 as enemy patrols became active and short fire fights took place. Their probing actions were to determine our positions. Our patrol activity contacted some enemy as well.

"At this time, the enemy did not know what our strength was—whether we were a recon force or a position of strength. There is only one way to find out, and the enemy organized an attack, estimated at perhaps one company. This attack took place mid-afternoon on D+11 [17 June], after a preliminary mortar barrage of some 200–300 shells. This shelling, of course, drove everyone into their foxholes; you can bet I was in mine very quickly. One shell came too damn close, close enough that I could reach out and touch the spot where it exploded. The attack was by German paratroops and they pressed the attack for two to three hours before pulling back. Machine gun and rifle fire was intense during this short battle. They found out we were in force and not a line of outposts. They left approximately twenty dead spread out in front of the battalion positions. One was a lieutenant who was wounded and, rather than be taken prisoner, decided to kill himself, which he did. This made me wonder a little just how fanatic a man could be to prefer dying to being taken prisoner, even after being wounded."[63]

On the night of 5 July, Lieutenant William Dillon, A Company, 16th Infantry, was holed up with some of his men at the gate leading into a hedged field near Caumont. He sent out two scouts to reconnoiter the area ahead. One of the scouts returned to report that he was sure there were at least two Germans on the other side of the hedgerow a short distance away. "I asked how he knew how many; he said he could hear one walking and one snoring. I said, 'Let's go get them,' so away we went crawling. Feeling our way in the dark, I soon found the leg of one of my scouts and at the same time someone grabbed me by the ankle. It was Lieutenant [Harry S.] Tripp. He said if his eyes weren't fooling him, our patrol is almost twice as big as it was when we left battalion. Quickly I got my scouts and Lieutenant Tripp and we moved back to the gate. That's when the shit hit the fan—machine guns and mortars started going off. The last thing I remembered at the gate was our bazookas going off. When I came to, there were Germans all around me. Lieutenant Tripp was dead and there were no live Americans in sight—just me."

Taken prisoner, Dillon was marched to a goat shed "surrounded by barbed wire, with straw on the floor. This shed was under the control of the Germans. Later that night, I heard Americans talking. I said, 'Who are you?' They said, 'Who the hell are you?' After we finished with the pleasantries, they told me they were two fighter pilots who had had a day off and had come to the front to pick up some souvenirs and had walked into the German front lines! I told them my story and they said, 'Good, you can get us out of here.'

"We were here about three or four days with no food or medicine when a column of American prisoners stopped for the day. About a dozen prisoners and two or three German guards had been shot by one of our aircraft so they were moving at night now. We joined them. There were about two or three hundred prisoners, with thirty or forty older guards. They had a buggy in back and bicycles in front, and walkers on the sides of our column. They also had no food or medicine. One prisoner who was walking had a shell splinter as big as your thumb in one of his eyes. The ones who couldn't walk were in the buggy. They dumped these in the first German hospital we came to. The first food we got was on the seventh night when the Germans brought a big, bony cow from a farmer. With two or three hundred prisoners and one cow, we all got a piece of beef about the size of my fist and a can of soup." Dillon remained a prisoner of war for a week until he escaped near Mortain while on a forced march with 535 other Americans. After being hidden by the Underground behind enemy lines for weeks, Dillon was found by men of Patton's Third Army on 13 August.[64]

Lieutenant William T. Dillon, A Company, 16th Infantry Regiment. (Courtesy Mrs. William Dillon)

With the once-mighty *Luftwaffe* strangely absent during the struggle for Normandy, the Allies maintained complete mastery of the skies. The bombers, however, were still vulnerable to anti-aircraft fire, as Captain Fred Hall remembered. "One evening while at Caumont, as the sun was setting, I suddenly saw a long stream of several hundred British bombers at heights of 1,500 to 5,000 feet flying out of the setting sun on a bombing run on the city of Caen. Enemy anti-aircraft fire was intense and I saw a couple of the planes explode in the air. Several others were shot down. It was a spectacular sight. . . . We stayed in the Caumont area until about 13 July, when we were relieved and went into a rest area [near Colombières] for showers, food, and some rest. At this time, we had been engaged five weeks in front-line activity."[65]

While the division was off the front lines, Ralph Puhalovich, Anti-Tank Company, 26th Infantry, found time to jot a note to his parents back in Oakland, California:

> Dear Mom:
>
> I know you know why I haven't written. It was impossible to write for a while but now I have become accustomed to it and I think I'll be able to write quite regularly. And don't worry about me, Mom, as I'm taking every precaution that I can and I think I'll be home for Christmas. . . .
>
> I can't tell you exactly where I am, but you can get a good idea by looking for the name of my outfit in the papers. . . . There are a bunch

> of fellows sitting here and someone just asked what the date was; so far we have six different dates. We all agree the month is June; about the rest we're undecided. We finally agreed it was the sixteenth or thereabouts anyway. You ought to see me now; I'm growing a moustache and I have a goatee, my hair is short on top and hanging over my ears on the sides. The dirt was an inch thick all over my neck and ears but I washed today and I feel a whole lot better, also cleaner. . . .
>
> How does Johnnie [his brother] like the Navy? By now, I guess he thinks it's pretty nice. A lot of times I wish that I had joined the Navy, and this is one of the times. . . .[66]

Gradually, the world learned that it was the 1st Infantry Division that had spearheaded the assault at Omaha Beach, and that it was Clarence Huebner who had, for the past eight months, trained the men of the Big Red One and prepared them for Operation *Overlord*. Many, however, gave the credit to the division's previous commander, Terry Allen. Unaware that Allen was no longer at the helm of the division, war correspondent and radio commentator Quentin Reynolds, a few days after D-Day, detailed to his audience much of the 1st's combat record on Sicily, recounting a moving incident that occurred just before the battle for Troina:

> Dusk was beginning to settle a soft blanket of darkness over the Sicilian hills. Terry Allen, in the midst of giving orders, asked to be excused. He walked away in the thin, gray dusk, and his officers waited. After a while, two correspondents followed Terry Allen. They found him about a hundred yards away, kneeling in prayer. The correspondents asked General Allen if he was praying for the success of the operation. 'No,' Terry Allen said, 'I'm praying that tonight there will be no unnecessary casualties; I'm praying that tonight no man's life will be wasted.'

"Do you wonder," Reynolds asked his listeners "that the men of the Fighting First—the rough, tough, wise-cracking, hell-raising sons of guns who belong to that division—worship Terry Allen? Well, I worship him, too, and if I had ten sons, I'd be proud and happy to know that they were serving in the Fighting First under this wiry, little, smiling-eyed man. I don't know whether Terry Allen led the First in the assault on the French coast. This hasn't been revealed yet. But, believe me, no matter who led them, it was Terry Allen who trained them; it was Terry Allen whose name was on their lips when they landed; it was Terry Allen who made the First Division the 'Fighting First.'"[67]

Once Reynolds learned that Allen had been relieved of command well before the Normandy invasion and was back in the States, training the 104th Infantry Division, he wrote a personal letter to Allen's wife, Mary Fran, in El Paso, Texas: "Never in my life have I seen a man so worshipped as Terry was and is—not only by his men in the First, but by every war correspondent who has ever come in contact with him. As far as I am concerned, Terry Allen is the greatest leader of men and the greatest tactical general in our Army. . . . It looks, I guess, as if you and I are in love with the same fellow."[68]

As daunting as the amphibious assault landing at Omaha Beach and the slugging match in the hedgerows had been, the 1st Infantry Division, now enjoying a much-deserved rest, was about to be faced with an even greater challenge.

To the south of the beachhead lay nothing but German-occupied France. Now that it must be obvious to the Germans that Normandy was the main—and only—thrust and not a diversionary feint, was it not logical that Hitler would throw everything he had at the Allies in a last-ditch attempt to forestall an invasion of the Reich from the west? The 1st's veterans knew from bitter experience that, whenever attacked, the Germans always—as regular as clockwork—launched a devastating counterattack, and every GI in Normandy expected that counterattack to come at any moment. Indeed, Hitler was finally convinced that the invasion of Normandy, diversion or not, represented a serious threat that could not be ignored. He would do whatever necessary to destroy the invaders.

CHAPTER ELEVEN

"The Men Are Worn Out"

ON 2 JULY 1944, the Allies' Supreme Commander arranged for a simple ceremony to take place at the 1st Infantry Division command post near Balleroy, south of the Cerisy Forest. On this day, he would pin medals on the uniforms of men of the 16th Infantry Regiment and personally honor them for their gallantry.

A correspondent present for the ceremony reported, "Heroes of the fighting 1st Division who led the American assault on France and lived to cross that hellish strip of beach where so many fell, stood in the shade of the tall Normandy elms today and received an accolade from General Dwight D. Eisenhower. They had tried to clean the stains of battle from their clothing for the occasion, but still their uniforms showed that they had just returned from the front, not far away. No one cared about spit and polish with these men, least of all General 'Ike,' who pinned the Distinguished Service Crosses on the chests of twenty-two men and gave the Legion of Merit award to two others. They stood at attention on the lawns of an old gray chateau when jeeps carrying General Eisenhower, Lieutenant General Omar N. Bradley, and Major General Leonard T. Gerow halted before their ranks.

"The three generals shook hands with Major General C. R. Huebner, commanding the 1st Division, and an officer began reading the names of men receiving awards. . . . As General Eisenhower moved down the double rank, he spoke a few words to each man, asking him his job and where he was from in the United States. After pinning on the medals, he called the group around him. 'I'm not going to make a speech,' he said, 'but this simple little ceremony gives me the opportunity to come over here and . . . say thanks. You are one of the

General Dwight D. Eisenhower, the Supreme Allied Commander, pins the Distinguished Service Cross on Captain Joe Dawson, commanding G Company, 16th Infantry Regiment. Photo taken 2 July 1944 near Balleroy, France. (Courtesy Colonel Robert R. McCormick Research Center of the 1st Infantry Division Museum at Cantigny)

finest regiments in our army. I know your record from the day you landed in North Africa and through Sicily. I am beginning to think that your regiment is a sort of Praetorian guard which goes along with me and gives me luck.

"'I know that you want to go home, but I demanded if I came up here [to England and Normandy] that you would have to come with me. You've got what it takes to finish the job. If you will do me a favor when you go back, you will spread the word through the regiment that I am terrifically proud and grateful to them. To all of you fellows, good luck, keep on top of them, and so long."[1]

On the front lines, the focus of the soldier is usually on the here and now; sometimes on the past; rarely on the future, for the future—for thousands of soldiers—never came. But now, with the beachhead consolidated and the build-up in France impossible for the Germans to throw back, the men of the 1st allowed themselves the luxury of thinking that they might actually live to see the end of the war, to see the end of *all* wars. Germany was defeated—it was just a matter of time before it toppled over; even a fatally wounded beast does not always collapse and die immediately. The *Luftwaffe* was decimated, the *Kriegsmarine* sunk, the *Wehrmacht* in full retreat. *General* Marcks, the commander of LXXXIV Corps, was dead, killed on 12 June. Geyr von Schweppenburg's chief of staff had died in a bombing raid. *Generals* Hellmich and Stegmann, commanders of the 243th and 77th Divisions, respectively, were both killed in action; *Generaloberst* Friederich Dollmann, commanding the Seventh Army, died in late June of a heart attack at age fifty-two. Rommel himself was gravely wounded on 17 July when a British fighter pounced upon his open staff car on the road between Livarot and Vimoutiers.* Of course, in those heady days following the Normandy landings, no one could foresee that nearly a year of heavy, bloody combat in Europe still lay ahead.[2]

The yard-by-yard slugging match could not go on indefinitely. A massive, violent breakout operation was needed to prevent a loss of momentum. By 20 July, the Allies had assembled enough troops, tanks, trucks, food, fuel, ammunition, and the other necessities of war on the beaches of Normandy to now begin that operation, known as *Cobra*. Heading the drive would be the 4th, 9th, and 30th Infantry Divisions, plus the 2nd and 3rd Armored Divisions. D-Day was set for 24 July.

For once, the 1st Infantry Division would not be required to spearhead an operation; the division was transferred from V Corps to Major General J. Lawton Collins's VII Corps, and placed in reserve. Once the German line had been cracked, plans called for the 1st to exploit the corps' gains and thrust westward toward Coutances. To accomplish this rapid movement, the Big Red One would be mounted in vehicles and supported by Combat Command B of the 3rd Armored Division. Preliminary to the ground assault would be a two-and-a-half-hour aerial bombardment of terrifying proportions by nearly 3,000 aircraft. Close coordination between the air and ground assaults was essential, as Bradley's plan called for the tanks and infantry to hit the stunned Germans while they were still trying to recover from the bombardment. The medium and

---

* Implicated in the 20 July plot on Hitler's life at Rastenburg, Rommel would be forced to commit suicide on 14 October 1944. The field marshal was rewarded with a state hero's funeral.

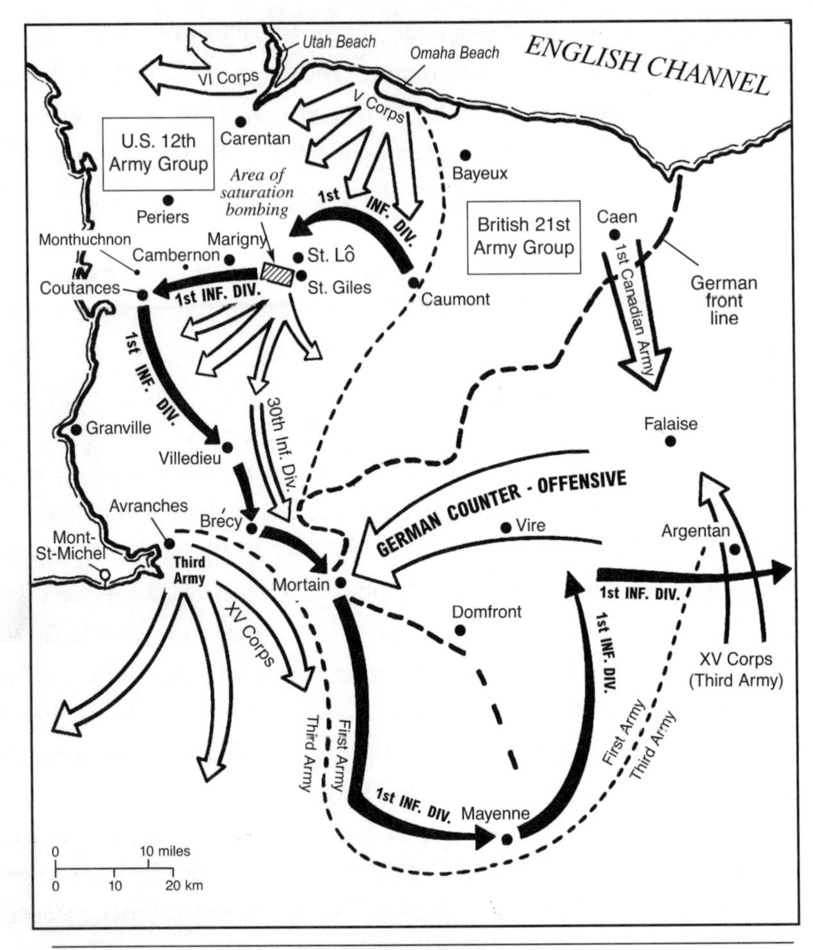

Operation *Cobra*—12th Army Group's massive breakout from the hedgerows and exploitation of the enemy—4 July–13 August 1944. (Positions approximate)

heavy bombers of the Eighth and Ninth U.S. Air Force were to drop their ordnance no closer than 1,450 yards to the American lines. The timing was crucial. Once the German forces occupying the Marigny-St. Gilles gap—units from *Generalleutnant* Dietrich von Choltitz's LXXXIV Corps of *General* Paul Hausser's Seventh Army—were neutralized, the bulk of the American Army could plunge through and begin a long sweep south and then east through central France.[3]

As usual, all did not go according to plan. Overcast skies obscured the target area on 24 July, forcing Air Chief Marshall Leigh-Mallory to recall the bombers.

But many aircraft did not get the message and dropped their bombs anyway—with tragic results. In meetings with Air Force representatives on 19 July, General Bradley had insisted that the aircraft must fly parallel to the American front lines, but the Air Force disregarded Bradley's concerns and bombed on a perpendicular line of attack. Twenty-five men of the 30th Division were killed and 131 were wounded in the "short bombing." In addition, an American ammunition dump was destroyed and several American aircraft on the ground were damaged. Some observers had likened the ferocity of the bombardment to "the end of the world."

Despite the disastrous bombing error, the ground assault began that afternoon, but the expected sudden breakthrough failed to materialize. As at Omaha Beach, the bombing only served to alert the Germans that a major assault was coming, and the enemy was ready. American casualties were high and progress was slow; for example, it took an entire battalion of the 9th Infantry Division all day to gain a single hedgerow. With little to show for a day of heavy combat, Bradley re-launched *Cobra* the next day. As it turned out, Fritz Bayerlein, whose Panzer Lehr Division was holding the target area, thought the abortive assault of 24 July had been a diversionary attack that had been turned back by his forces and thus did not believe his sector was in much danger. He would soon discover the error of his thinking.

On the 25th, tragedy struck again. This time, the 4th and 9th Divisions, as well as several artillery and engineer units, bore the brunt of erroneous short bombing by the "friendlies." Nearly 500 men were wounded and 111 were killed, including Lieutenant General Leslie McNair, commander of Army Ground Forces and pro tem commander of U.S. First Army Group. The ground troops were dispirited and furious at their own air force, and Eisenhower vowed never again to use heavy bombers in support of a ground operation.[4]

Lieutenant Harold Monica, D Company, 18th Infantry, had a ringside seat for the bombing. "Our assembly area was five to six thousand yards away. . . . The fighter-bombers were to mark the area, which they did, and the big bombers took over. Their orders were to bomb on the dust line created by the first bombs. The initial waves of B-17s and B-24s were pretty much on target and created a lot of dust and smoke. Each succeeding wave of bombs just added to this. Somehow, no one had thought what would happen to the dust line that was the aiming point for the following bombers. Whatever the cause—a breeze or heat from the bombs—the dust line drifted toward our lines and bombs began to fall short

GIs move through a blasted hedgerow during Operation *Cobra*, 25 July 1944. (Courtesy National Archives)

on [9th Division] troops. . . . Enemy ack-ack began to fire and we could see the black shell bursts in the stream of bombers. Seven were shot down. There was no glide down; they fell straight down like rocks. . . . Anyway, the bombers completed their part of the plan and now it was the infantry's turn. The 9th Division was to attack through the bombed area and roll up the shoulders, and the 1st Division was to pass through and continue the advance."[5]

American troops weren't the only ones feeling the devastating effects of the bombing. Bayerlein had moved some of his units into the precise sector that was hit by the Allied air forces. It was estimated that at least a thousand German soldiers were killed by the bombing, along with scores of panzers destroyed. Three battalion command posts were obliterated, yet many more positions had been untouched. At 1100 hours, American foot soldiers, unsteady and unsure if the bombing had also affected the Germans, moved forward in the attack, followed by the armor. The Germans emerged from their concealed positions in the hedgerows and blasted the advancing Yanks, stopping the advance short of its objectives. But Collins was willing to gamble that the outer line of German defenses had been penetrated—even if only slightly. It was time for the armor—and the 1st Infantry Division—to push through and head for Marigny.[6]

When the Big Red One followed the 9th, Monica was aghast at the scope of the destruction: "Having seen . . . dead soldiers in North Africa, Sicily, and D-Day had not prepared me for things I was to see and experience now. We were advancing and closing on the action area of the 9th Division. Sporadic small-arms fire to our front. Bomb craters, approximately ten feet wide and four feet deep, were everywhere; how anyone living through this would still want and be able to fight is hard to believe. But survivors were there and resisting. I first saw the squad leader, a staff sergeant, dead in a bomb crater in a hedge-row. Through this opening in the hedge-row, I could see a small field, perhaps eighty yards wide by 150 yards long. Spread out in this field were seven dead soldiers all with their rifles pointed in the direction of the source of the deadly machine-gun fire. I went over to what had been the enemy position and it was obvious from their field of fire why no one in that field survived. . . . This was the largest loss of life that I saw in such a small area."[7]

The following day, the 4th, 9th, and 30th Divisions continued moving against German units that refused to yield. The 83rd Infantry Division was also thrown into battle, while the 9th was withdrawn for a rest on 28 July. Supported by tanks from 3rd Armored, the Big Red One moved slowly but steadily forward, overcoming pockets of opposition. Outside of Marigny, the 1st Division ran into heavier resistance in the form of the 353rd Division and two companies of the 2nd SS Panzer Grenadier Division. Sherman tanks dueled with the enemy and a tactical air strike late in the day pounded enemy forces, but no progress was made; the decision was made to "button up" and resume the assault at dawn. That night, however, a battalion of the 18th Infantry Regiment, mistakenly thinking that Marigny had fallen, bypassed the town and took some high ground south of it. Not only was the battalion wrong about Marigny, but it also didn't know its exact location.

Mistakenly believing that Marigny was in American hands, Collins ordered Huebner to resume the night advance toward Coutances. But Huebner was unsure as to the location of his front-line units; whether or not Marigny had been captured; and where the enemy was. To stumble blindly about in the darkness would only invite disaster, so Huebner chose to stay put. On the eastern flank of the VII Corps drive, however, more progress was being reported; tanks of the 3rd Armored's Combat Command A were punching through German resistance all the way to St. Gilles.[8]

Still, the 1st Division and 3rd Armored's Combat Command B were held up at Marigny. On 27 July, Huebner sent CCB westward toward Coutances, while

A bulldozer of the 1st Engineer Combat Battalion shoves a wrecked German Pz Kpfw IV tank off the road near Marigny, late July 1944. (Courtesy U.S. Army Military History Institute)

he "leap-frogged" his three infantry regiments around to the rear of Marigny. Medic Allen Towne noted that the advance was slowed by huge numbers of destroyed German vehicles that littered the highways. "They had to be bulldozed off the roads," he noted.[9]

That afternoon, the 18th Infantry penetrated Marigny while Combat Command B reported that it had driven all the way to Coutances against light and sporadic opposition; the infantry, however, was only halfway to Coutances and pockets of resistance in Marigny still held out. Huebner then ordered elements of CCB to take Cambernon; the 16th RCT to take Monthuchon; the 18th to mop up in Marigny; and the 26th to relieve CCB at Cambernon so the armor could continue its drive to the coast. Meanwhile Major General Troy Middleton's VIII Corps had reached Monthuchon, so Huebner directed CCB to avoid that town and press on to Coutances. The 16th Infantry found itself in a major firefight near Monthuchon, and Huebner ordered CCB to turn around and assist the 16th. By this time, however, the bulk of the German LXXXIV Corps had slipped out of the VII Corps' noose in the lower Contentin.[10]

Although it had been relatively inactive since D-Day, the *Luftwaffe* was also still capable of inflicting casualties. Allen Towne remembered a frightening incident on 31 July. His unit was enjoying a beautiful summer night under a grove of trees when they heard the unmistakable sound of Junkers JU-88 bombers approaching. "I hadn't heard that sound for a long time," he noted, "and I started to shiver a little, and so did some of the other men. We remembered the many times the German JU-88s had bombed us in North Africa. The planes came closer until they were directly overhead. Then I heard the screams of anti-personnel bombs coming down. The bombs were exploding all around, and I could hear men yelling as they got hit by bomb fragments. I was lucky and did not get hit, but men all around me had been wounded, and one of our trucks was on fire." Even the nearby division command post suffered casualties. Towne's unit quickly set up an aid station to care for the wounded. "The next morning, I looked over our area in daylight and counted about 100 bomb holes in an area the size of an acre," Towne said. ". . . We were lucky."[11]

The air raid was quickly forgotten as the division pressed on. At the end of July, with *Cobra* at last a general success, Huebner's 1st and Major General Raymond O. Barton's 4th Infantry Divisions, supported by 3rd Armored, were ordered to lead a drive to the south. The 4th was to head for St. Pois, while the 1st's objective was Brécy—some eighteen miles northwest of Mortain. By the first week of August, the 1st Division had fought its way to Mayenne.[12]

At the end of July, Lieutenant General George S. Patton Jr., with his Third Army, came on the scene in the lower Cotentin. Patton's was a powerful force consisting of the VIII, XIII, XV, and XX Corps, and it gave the Germans a whole new set of problems with which to contend.[13]

The *Luftwaffe* wasn't quite finished with the 1st Division, however, and a new weapon was introduced to warfare. On 6 August, Allen Towne noted in his diary, "We were assembled in a field ready to move out, when we heard rockets screaming overhead. They exploded in front of us. Seconds later, we saw a large flight of German planes, traveling extremely fast, zoom over low. Then we heard the tremendous roar of engines. We did not know what they were until we were told they were a new type of warplane powered by jet engines. They were the first jet planes we had ever seen. They were faster than all the other planes. . . . I hoped that the Germans did not have many of them."[14]

With the Cotentin Peninsula and the west coast of Brittany now firmly in American hands, Hitler once again demonstrated his poor generalship by mounting an ill-conceived counterattack—this time westward to retake Avranches—a counterattack that would crash through Mortain. Bradley noted: "It was not until 1 a.m. on the morning of August 7 that the enemy collected sufficient strength to launch [its] fatal attack. He struck toward Mortain, just 20 miles east of the shallow Bay of Mont St. Michel. Five panzer and SS divisions formed the hammerhead of this attack, the Germans' first offensive in France, his last until the Bulge. To mount the attack, he had drawn his armor from Montgomery's front, reaching back to the Pas de Calais for infantry reinforcements. After two months, the enemy was chagrined to learn he had been hoaxed by a cover plan [Operation *Fortitude*] that had immobilized an entire Army during the most crucial hour of his struggle for France. Only the night before, the 30th Division of Major General Leland S. Hobbs had gone into position on the hinge to relieve the 1st [Division] while the latter leapfrogged around the German flank. Understrength and winded from the two weeks of combat that had followed the breakout, the 30th dropped wearily into positions vacated by the 1st. These positions had been sited by the 1st while it was still attacking and, as a result, they lacked sufficient depth for defense."[15]

The U.S. 30th Infantry Division became the focal point of the massive, ill-conceived German Seventh Army counterattack; luckily, the 1st skirted the fighting, heading for Mayenne and then northeastward toward Falaise and Argentan with VII Corps in an attempt to bag as many Germans as possible in what became known as the "Falaise Pocket." Once the Germans realized that their drive to Mortain had done little but create a long, narrow salient, they began a desperate attempt to escape to the east. But it was too late; already the First Canadian Army was driving southward from Falaise and XV Corps from Patton's Third Army was driving northward from Argentan to close off the neck of the bag that surrounded *Generalfeldmarschall* Günther von Kluge's Army Group B (Fifth Panzer Army and Seventh Army).

On 13 August, the First Army and VII Corps resumed their offensive from the vicinity of Mayenne, with the 1st, 4th, and 9th Infantry and 3rd Armored Divisions pushing in a northeasterly direction to support the southern shoulder of the American drive while Patton's Third Army dashed farther to the east. Once the German escape route was closed, every Allied weapon within range, including hundreds of sorties flown by British and American fighter-bombers, mercilessly pummeled the packed lines of Germans on the narrow lanes and roads of France.[16]

"There, in one of the costliest battles of western Europe," Bradley wrote, "the enemy lost his Seventh Army, and with it went his last hope of holding a line in France."[17] It was estimated that at least 10,000 Germans were killed in the pocket and another 50,000 were taken prisoner. In the two months since the D-Day landings, some 160,000 Germans in Army Group B had died. Von Kluge, overwhelmed with guilt for the disaster in the west, committed suicide.[18]

While *Overlord* and *Cobra* sent the Germans reeling in the west, two large-scale offenses in the east and south sealed the fate of the Nazi regime. The first occurred on 22 June, when nearly 2 million Russians taking part in Operation *Bagration* tore into German lines along the Eastern Front. On 15 August, Operation *Dragoon* was launched, with Alexander Patch's Seventh Army hitting the beaches of the French Riviera; German forces were forced to make a fighting retreat all the way to the Alsace-Lorraine region.

The 12th Army Group's race toward Paris was now in full gallop. Bradley wanted desperately to bypass the city, for he knew that its 4 million inhabitants were on the verge of starvation, and he worried that he would have to divert his already overburdened supply line to feed the populace. Although some believed that the 1st Division would be given the honor of liberating Paris, Free French troops of the French 2nd Armored Division, under Major General Jacques Leclerc, on 23 August, were the first Allied soldiers to roll into the city; shortly thereafter, Allied units marched triumphantly down the broad boulevards of Paris. While the men of the 1st Infantry Division certainly deserved to be cheered and kissed and fêted by the Parisians, the prospect of urban warfare in Paris was not a comforting thought. Instead, Huebner's men were ordered to stay hot on the heels of the retreating Germans. The honor of representing the United States and marching down the broad Champs Elysées went to the 28th Infantry Division (Pennsylvania National Guard, now under the command of Major General Norman D. Cota), which had landed in France on 22 July.*[19]

Harold Monica was not unhappy to bypass Paris. "We figured it would fall to us to enter Paris and get involved in city street fighting. Let me tell you, we were

---

* Perhaps the honor resulted from Bradley's having been the division's commander from June 1942 to January 1943. At any rate, although relatively unblooded, the 28th would see plenty of combat in the months ahead; the division would lose 5,000 men in the savage fighting in the Hürtgen Forest. (MacDonald, *A Time for Trumpets*, p. 83; and Stanton, pp. 103–108)

not enchanted with this possibility. On reaching our daily objective some ten miles from Paris, for some reason we were ordered to stop our advance. The next day we found out why. The French 2nd Armored Division would pass through the 1st Division and Paris was their objective."[20]

Denied a wonderful meal in Paris, Eddie Steeg's thoughts inevitably turned to food during the drive eastward. "To most of the combat soldiers pushing their way across France, exposed to enemy fire almost every day, living day to day under miserable conditions, huddling in foxholes, crawling through the mud, trying to stay warm and dry from the rain, and eating cold C or K rations, the chance to eat fresh fruit, vegetables, or meat was like a dream come true. . . . Sometimes during the heat of battle across France, an unfortunate cow would blunder into our gun sights and became a casualty of war. Whenever this occurred, it would be strung up and butchered by our knowledgeable cooks, and we had steak for dinner that night. . . . There were also dead German horses along the way and we would often see the local French people carving up their own [horse] steaks for dinner."

One evening, Steeg and his company encamped alongside a clear, fish-filled stream, where he had a sudden craving for a fresh fish dinner. "With no line, hooks, or bait available, fishing the old-fashioned way was out of the question. Watching the multitude of those silver suckers swim by finally got to me, and I determined that if I couldn't snare them in the usual way, then I would just have to shoot them. I unslung my old-faithful Tommy gun and aimed it at the stream. When the next batch of fish came swimming by, I let them have a blast. The gun recoiled in an upward sweep and I think I may have killed a couple of perching birds in a nearby tree; certainly no dead fish floated to the top of the water."

Steeg fired another burst, but still no dead fish. He then had a brilliant idea. "One of my TNT foxhole starter blocks would surely do the trick. Boom! The water and fish shot up in the air in all directions and I got wet as hell. To my chagrin, the largest dead fish floating on top of the water were not a helluva lot bigger than sardines."

Steeg soon forgot about his disappointment when his unit was back on the road and suddenly attacked by low-flying enemy planes. "As we were moving forward, we were strafed by the *Luftwaffe,* which sent everyone scurrying for cover. Back in my junior high school days, when I ran for the school track team, I was considered pretty fast. In this instance, however, as we ran to escape the strafing, I was passed so fast by a couple of Quartermaster dudes of the Red Ball Express* that it made me think I was standing still. Funny, ain't it, how pure, unadulterated fear will kinda tie a rocket to your ass.

"One of our jeep drivers who happened to be riding in the back seat of the jeep during this strafing decided to stay in the jeep, and began firing at the low-flying planes with the jeep's mounted .30-caliber machine gun. Either he was one helluva dead-eye or just plain lucky, 'cause he managed to hit one of the planes and shoot it down as we watched from the ditches we were in. The irony here is that he was in the back seat of the jeep to start with because the CO told him he was too drunk to drive. He was!"[21]

Harold Monica also recalled the raid, believing that approximately thirty Focke-Wolfe 190s fighter-bombers attacked D Company's sector. "As trained infantry, we dispersed and sought cover, thereby presenting no worthwhile target. However, some ten to fifteen 2-1/2–ton trucks were not as lucky and were set on fire. As for D Company, no casualties. During the attack, one plane came over low and close enough that the pilot was very clear and visible to me. Managed to react soon enough to get a couple of shots at him, with no effect as he was going some 300–400 miles per hour."[22]

The 1st Division, as part of the VII Corps' drive, swung south of Paris and then, on the east side of the City of Lights, the route of march took the division due north, through the Soissons battlefield, where General Huebner had fought with the 1st in World War I. Then it was on to Belgium.

After traveling nearly 300 miles in the backs of trucks from 24 August to the 27th, from its rest camp at La Ferte Mace to Maubeuge, France, on the Belgian border, the men of the Big Red One stretched their cramped limbs and prepared once more to go into combat. At the end of August, large numbers of German troops were fleeing France, trying to make it back to Germany via Belgium; in fact, the enemy and VII Corps were racing side by side in parallel flying columns. Their paths would converge at the France-Belgium border, near the city of Mons, where the 1st Infantry and 3rd Armored Divisions delivered a blow that ended in hundreds of Germans being killed or wounded and thousands being taken prisoner.[23]

---

*The Red Ball Express was the American supply lifeline, consisting of thousands of trucks that ran at full speed night and day from the ports to the front lines. Most of the truck drivers were African American.

Many of the fleeing German troops were too demoralized to offer much resistance. On 3 September alone, the 1st Division and 3rd Armored took an estimated 7,500 to 9,000 prisoners; in three days, the entire VII Corps bagged approximately 25,000 prisoners. For those unlucky enough not to be taken prisoner, death and destruction awaited them; the IX Tactical Air Command said that it destroyed fifty armored vehicles, 652 horse-drawn vehicles, 851 motor vehicles, and 485 soldiers.[24]

At around midnight on 4/5 September, near the Belgian village of Sars la Bruyere, near the city of Mons, Private Gino Merli and fourteen other men from H Company, 18th Infantry, were manning a roadblock at a crossroads. A force of at least one hundred enemy soldiers attacked the roadblock and knocked out one of the two machine-gun positions. Behind the other gun, Merli poured streams of fire into wave after wave of the attackers. His assistant was killed, and the rest of the men at the roadblock were either killed, captured, or retreated, but Merli remained at his Browning through the night. When his battalion counterattacked the next morning, they found Merli still at his post, still alive. Scattered all around him were the bodies of fifty-two dead Germans. As he later related, he was overrun two or three times, each time playing dead. The Germans prodded him with their bayonets but when he did not cry out, they left him alone—until he resumed his fire against them. During his ordeal, he suffered only one slight wound to a finger and four bayonet wounds. For his courageous night of heroism, the native of Scranton, Pennsylvania, was awarded the Medal of Honor.[25]

Captain Fred Hall, S-3, 2nd Battalion, 16th Infantry, recalled, "As we approached Maubeuge, about 5 September, I could see P-47 fighter planes bombing and strafing along a line across our line of march. Large numbers of Germans were reported retreating from west to east ahead of us. The elements of the 2nd Battalion I was with were now deployed west of our line of march into a little village. Suddenly, flags appeared in the windows and several armed members of the Resistance appeared. We began patrolling toward the west to pick up German prisoners. I set the CP up in a house on the outskirts of the village. Shortly, a firefight broke out which lasted most of the night. We had reports of German tanks and troops heading in our direction. The flags and members of the Resistance disappeared and windows were shuttered again. . . . Early the next morning, German soldiers began to surrender in droves, casting their weapons on the ground. We didn't have the manpower or a secure place to guard them. We simply rounded them up in a field behind a barbed-wire barrier. The battalion medics attended their many wounded."

After remaining in this location for three days, the division was ordered to resume the march toward Liége. Although he had seen much carnage since Oran, Hall was stunned by horrors piled up in grotesque mounds along the highway. "We came across the remains of a German column that had been napalmed and strafed by the P–47s we had seen earlier. It was pure desolation. Trucks, armored vehicles, horses, men—bodies all over the place. It was a stinking mess. I can still see the charred body of a motorcyclist sitting astride his upright motorcycle with his hands gripping the handlebars. We had virtually no enemy resistance as we moved through Liége."[26]

There was, however, a different type of obstacle in Liége. Lieutenant Harold Monica recalled that the city was filled with civilians overjoyed at the sight of the liberating American Army. "With no enemy to contend with, the major hindrance to our convoy was the *people,*" Monica said. "They were packed solid, wall to wall—flags waving—arm waving, happy, exuberant people. Many who had fought the Germans in 1940 had donned their old uniforms and were in the celebration. Nearly every house was displaying Belgian flags and the Stars and Stripes. . . . What a sight—so many joyous, appreciative, and thankful people. No more worries of 'knocks on the door' at night, and no more executions in the city and town squares. What a relief it must have been after some four years of brutal occupation by the enemy."[27]

The entire American and British juggernaut was closing in on Germany; on 11 September, the Big Red One, still with First Army and VII Corps, stood astride the Liège-Aachen highway, ten miles from Aachen, on a line with Louis Craig's 9th Infantry and Maurice Rose's 3rd Armored Divisions. Ahead of them lay the pillboxes and minefields and anti-tank obstacles (known as "dragons' teeth") of the *Westwall,* or Siegfried Line—a line of heavily fortified positions guarding the German border that rivaled those of France's Maginot Line.

Eddie Steeg noted, "World War II in the ETO [European Theater of Operations] had come to a screeching halt for us fast-paced American cowboys of the wonderful, enjoyable race across France during the 'Champagne Campaigns.' Thuddingly, we had encountered these broken, grey teeth of the vaunted Siegfried Line, with its defense in depth. Our previously unstoppable advance was now being checked by fanatical German troops fighting to protect their holy Fatherland."[28]

Private Gino Merli, H Company, 18th Infantry Regiment, recipient of the Medal of Honor. (Courtesy Colonel Robert R. McCormick Research Center of the 1st Infantry Division Museum at Cantigny)

By this time, the 1st Division troops were exceedingly weary—and wary, for they knew that once they set foot on German soil, they would run into resistance unlike anything they had thus far experienced. They would also be facing the ravages of the oncoming European winter.[29] A host of logistical problems also plagued them. As the history of the 26th Regiment states, "After more than ninety days of battle, the men . . . were tired, their vehicles and guns were worn and battered, maintenance was lagging, resupply was faltering. Allied forces had dealt the Germans severe blows, but they were at the end of their logistical tethers."[30]

Fuel shortages were especially critical. "Had sufficient forces and the necessary supplies been available at this time," wrote the 16th Regiment's historian, "it is possible that the war might have ended months earlier. Gasoline for vehicles was at a premium. Every move had to be planned with the fuel limitations in mind. This handicap was becoming so great that the probability of continu-

A 1st Division machine-gun crew keeps German troops pinned down with fire along a rubble-strewn street in Aachen, 15 October 1944. (Courtesy U.S. Army Military History Institute)

ing much farther on the present drive didn't seem good." Despite the problems, Collins's VII Corps stepped off at 0800 hours on the morning of 12 September to probe the Siegfried Line with a "reconnaissance in force" near Aachen.[31]

With the prospect of more hard fighting ahead, Lieutenant Harold Monica, D Company, 18th Infantry, reflected upon everything the division had been through up to this point. "In the three and a half months since the D-Day landings, we had gone through the hedge-row fighting, the holding of the LaVacquerie-Caumont area, heavy fighting for the break-out, open warfare of movement through France and Belgium; we are now in position to cross the border into enemy territory. What beholds us in the way of fanatical resistance in protection of the 'Fatherland'? We will find out tomorrow."[32]

Aachen, a city of 165,000 people lying on a flat plane to the north-northwest of the dense Hürtgen Forest, was not of great military significance. It was not a major transportation hub. It had coal mines and resorts, but little vital industry to speak of. Its healing waters did not make it a prime target. It controlled no major river crossing. The significance of Aachen lay in its psychological importance to the Third Reich. It was the closest major German city to the border with Belgium and Holland, and its rich and storied past had elevated the city to almost mythic proportions. It was here in A.D. 742, amidst the ruins of Roman temples and thermal baths and arenas, that one of Europe's greatest rulers, Charlemagne, was born. As the seat of the Holy Roman Empire under Charlemagne, Aachen became a place of great monetary and intellectual wealth; a place where civilization in the untamed wilderness of the barbaric Teutonic warriors first took root; a place forever associated with what would be called the First Reich. Over the centuries, thirty-two German kings and emperors were crowned here. If for no other reason, the symbolic value of Aachen to the Germans made it worth defending to the death, even though seventy-five Allied air raids since the start of the war had fairly well pulverized it. Under the command of *Generalleutnant* Gerhard Graf von Schwerin, head of the depleted 116th Panzer Division, an estimated 12,000 enemy soldiers in and around Aachen were prepared to make their last stand. A personal order from Hitler that the 7,000 civilians remaining in the city should be evacuated had sent the residents into panic.

But von Schwerin, thinking that it would be better to surrender the city rather than preside over its further destruction, halted the evacuation and wrote a letter that was to be held by a postal official and delivered to whichever American commander might be the first to approach the city: "I stopped the absurd evacuation of this town; therefore, I am responsible for the fate of its inhabitants and I ask you, in the case of an occupation by your troops, to take care of the unfortunate population in a humane way."

Instead of the letter reaching the Americans, however, it fell into the hands of Nazi officials, who demanded that von Schwerin resign his command and appear before a "People's Court." Von Schwerin refused and hid out with his troops. Once it appeared that the Americans were going to bypass Aachen, he turned himself in to German Seventh Army headquarters to accept his punishment.* The defense of

---

* Instead of being court-martialed, von Schwerin was temporarily demoted but later received command of another division and a corps in Italy. (MacDonald, *Siegfried Line Campaign*, p. 82)

the city, therefore, was left to rag-tag elements of the 9th and 116th Panzer Divisions, and the 353rd Infantry Division, all under German LXXXI Corps commander *Generalleutnant* Friedrich Schack, in whose sector Aachen lay. Hope that promised reinforcements would soon arrive bouyed German confidence.[33]

The belief that Aachen would be bypassed soon faded. VII Corps' drive toward the Rhein was stalled by bad weather, the supply shortage, and growing enemy resistance during the last two weeks of September. Aachen became a salient stabbing into the American line of advance, and First Army saw the need to reduce the salient with a pincers movement. The 1st Infantry Division was to encircle Aachen from the south and link up on the east side of the city with Major General Leland S. Hobbs's 30th Infantry Division, a part of Major General Charles H. Corlett's XIX Corps, driving down from the north. Rose's 3rd Armored was to head south of the city and secure the high ground at Stolberg, about five miles east of Aachen. The 9th Infantry Division was to capture the towns of Hürtgen and Kleinhau to block any German counterattack from that direction.[34]

Surprisingly, the assaulting forces initially faced little resistance as they approached the thick lines of concrete bunkers and obstacles to the west of Aachen. Although the anti-tank obstacles themselves presented some difficulties, many of the guns in the fortifications had been removed years earlier to guard the coast of France, and the low-grade troops manning the defensive positions were too thinly spread to offer much resistance. Lieutenant Karl Wolf, now the executive officer of K Company, 16th Regiment, recalled, "We penetrated this German defensive position that was supposed to be impenetrable. The Germans had been routed in Belgium and had not had time to set up their defenses in the Siegfried Line. In fact, some of the pillboxes were not even manned."[35]

Sergeant Harley Reynolds, B Company, 16th Infantry, noted, "Our company was in the lead as we crossed the border. My section set up machine guns to cover the rest of Company B as they crossed the 'dragons' teeth.' Company B went on into Germany, and into a park where they spent the night. We were withdrawn the next day for what, I think, was to reorganize. Then, on the 14th, we crossed the border again. We did not go into Aachen; the 26th Regiment was given this job. We were diverted east at this point to take [the suburb of] Stolberg."[36]

Eddie Steeg remembered that, as his unit approached the Siegfried Line, "It was time to be alert, more cautious, and worry once again. . . . The reception we were accorded by the Krauts was far from friendly. It felt more like a good, swift, kick in the ass."[37]

Steeg's unit had found some concrete fortifications full of defenders willing to put up a fight. After knocking out several of these positions with tanks, they encountered another in a wooded area on the outskirts of Aachen. Harold Monica recalled, "We approached from the rear until we could see the entrance and the general outline. Question: how to get a tank in here and blast the door?" Then Monica saw the small sheet-metal vent protruding from the concrete roof and his platoon sergeant got an idea—they would stuff a quarter-pound TNT block into the vent and detonate it. It worked. From his position, Monica noted that the explosion "was very muffled and didn't seem too loud. Inside was an entirely different set of circumstances—can't even imagine!!! Immediately a white flag appeared from the aperature in the door and out come nine Jerries. All were covered with dust, rubbing their eyes, ears, and stumbling up the stairs. Sergeant Aiello and I were pleased, and we only needed one charge."[38]

It was only after the American tanks and infantry broke through the outer ring that they began to run into more determined opposition at Aachen. Mortars, artillery, machine-gun, and 88mm fire began to take their toll on the attackers, but the advancing Yanks pressed forward until, by nightfall on 13 September, they were well inside the Siegfried Line's outer defenses.[39]

The battle for Aachen and its many suburbs inexorably turned into a meat grinder as the defenders—mostly members of the recently arrived 12th Infantry, 183rd *Volksgrenadier*, and Colonel Gerhard Wilck's 246th *Volksgrenadier* Divisions—fighting their first battle on their home ground and following Hitler's order to hold the city to the last man, refused to yield a single pillbox, house, barn, or road crossing without a desperate, to-the-death fight.[40] First Lieutenant Karl Wolf, K Company, 16th Infantry, recalled, "Our 1st Battalion had taken Münsterbusch and then had been ordered to advance on Stolberg. The battalion had lost 300 men in five days at that point. In Stolberg, which had pretty well been destroyed, the fighting was house to house."[41]

Harley Reynolds felt that the battle for the suburb of Stolberg did not receive the attention it should have, given the ferocity of the fighting. "Aachen was a bigger name and the first German town and made the better story," he said, "but Stolberg was a very important objective. It was high ground but, better yet, it was the location of the valves for the main water line to Aachen. We took this to cut off the water to Aachen, and held this objective until Aachen surrendered. I had two light machine guns set up here, guarding the valves. This is where the ammo shortage first hit us; we could only fire if we had a target to fire at. This included mortars, as well. No firing for dispersal. If the Germans could have sustained their counter-attacks, they could have run us out of ammo! We repulsed counter-attack after counter-attack by the Germans for this prize. This was one of the few times the Germans used their air force to try and dislodge us. They were able to dive bomb us every night for the whole time we were there."[42]

Soldiers who had for months and years survived combat now had their luck run out. On 19 September, Private First Class John Bistrica, C Company, 16th Infantry, who had survived the Normandy fighting, became a casualty. Listed for two days as "Missing in Action," he turned up wounded on the 21st but without any recollection of what had happened to him, or where he had been.[43]

The bitter fighting at Stolberg earned another 1st Infantry Division soldier the Medal of Honor. On 24 September, Staff Sergeant Joseph E. Schaefer, I Company, 18th Infantry, was part of a platoon that was defending a crossroads when two companies of German infantry assaulted his position. The enemy captured one of the squads and forced another to abondon its position, leaving Schaefer's squad alone to fend off the attack. Under tremendous fire, he moved his men to a nearby house for safety, but soon enemy artillery fire began to fall on the building. Expecting a ground assault on his position, Schaefer stationed his men at windows while he covered the door. The attack materialized and Schaefer gunned down with his M-1 a number of German troops who attempted to storm the house. The enemy attacked again, this time with grenades and a flamethrower, but again Schaefer held them off. The Germans regrouped for a third attack, this time hitting the house from two sides. Once more, Schaefer and his men beat back the attackers, and the sergeant even left the protection of the building to engage both groups of enemy. Fighting furiously, and firing with unerring accuracy, he accounted for eleven of the German dead and forced the attackers to withdraw. But Schaefer was not finished. Leaving the house again, he took ten Germans prisoner and even freed the American squad that had been captured earlier. His citation reads: "In all, single-handed and armed only with his rifle, he killed between 15 and 20 Germans, wounded at least as many more, and took 10 prisoners. S/Sgt. Schaefer's indomitable courage and his determination to hold his position at all costs were responsible for stopping an enemy break-through."[44]

While the Allies' gasoline shortage was critical, the ammunition shortfall was worse. After all, the advance could be held up if there were insufficient stocks of

Sergeant First Class Joseph E. Schaefer, I Company, 18th Infantry, receives the Medal of Honor from Major General Walter M. Robertson, commanding general of XV Corps. (Courtesy Colonel Robert R. McCormick Research Center of the 1st Infantry Division Museum at Cantigny)

petroleum, but troops could not defend their positions if they had no bullets, shells, or grenades. Even General Bradley was worried. On 2 October, the Army reinstituted ammunition rationing. But even at this reduced rate of fire, the Yanks would be out of ammo by the first week of November. Fortunately, under prodding by SHAEF, Com Z, the supply arm of the Allied drive, was able to increase ammunition shipments and avert disaster.[45]

While the battle for Aachen was heating up, there was still plenty of resistance to the east, near Verlautenheide and Stolberg. One German counterattack after another hit 1st Division positions and were repulsed only after considerable heavy fighting and much bloodletting. The battle went on for days, then weeks. Some GIs were convinced it would never end. This report on the fighting in the 16th's sector was typical: "Following the shelling came an assault by enemy engineers and infantry carrying flame-throwers, blinders, and demolitions [at dawn on 4 October]. Supporting them were four assault guns, two of which were carrying part of the assault force. As these self-propelled guns reached a crossroads in front of K [Company], one was disabled by mines which the company had laid a few nights before. . . . The attack persisted for three hours, penetrating part of

K Company's line before it was repulsed with the help of fourteen battalions of artillery and fiercely counterattacking American infantrymen."[46]

Karl Wolf noted, "We came under fire directed from the German observation post on Crucifix Hill and the Verlautenheide Ridge. . . . Just before midnight on October 3, the Germans launched the heaviest artillery barrage I was in during the war. Fortunately, we were in [an abandoned German] pillbox and no direct hits occurred. I saw one report where Regiment estimated between 3,000 and 4,000 artillery rounds were fired on our K Company position within a half hour."[47]

Stories of courage were repeated a hundredfold in and around Aachen as small bands of Americans overcame uncountable pockets of resistance or threw back innumerable, frenzied counterattacks. The battle for Aachen lingers on in the nightmares of 1st Infantry Division veterans as one of their worst battle experiences. Illustrating again the difficulty of the task that faced the 1st Division to the northeast of Aachen, a history of the Siegfried Line campaign reads, "In terms of distance, the 18th Infantry's attack [against Verlautenheide] was no mammoth undertaking—only two and a half miles. On the other hand, terrain, pillboxes, and German determination to hold supply routes into Aachen posed a thorny problem. The first objective of Verlautenheide in the second band of the *Westwall* was on the forward slope of a sharp ridge, denied by a maze of pillboxes provided with excellent fields of fire across open ground. Crucifix Hill* (Hill 239), a thousand yards northwest of Verlautenheide, was the next objective, another exposed crest similarly bristling with pillboxes. The third and final objective was equally exposed and fortified: Ravels Hill (the Ravelsberg, Hill 231)."[48]

The assignment to take—and hold—these terrain features east of Aachen fell primarily to the 18th Regiment, although much of the 1st Division soon would be sucked into the battle's maw. A salient sticking into German lines, these three features—Crucifix Hill, the Verlautenheide Ridge, and Ravels Hill—attracted much enemy attention. Holding the territory were elements of Wilck's 246th Division, plus an understrength battalion from the 275th Division, a battalion of *Luftwaffe* ground troops, a machine-gun fortress battalion, and a *Landesschützen* battalion.

---

*The hill, so named because it was surmounted by a large cross, commanded a view of Stolberg and was the perfect spot for German artillery observers who could call accurate fire down upon the attackers.

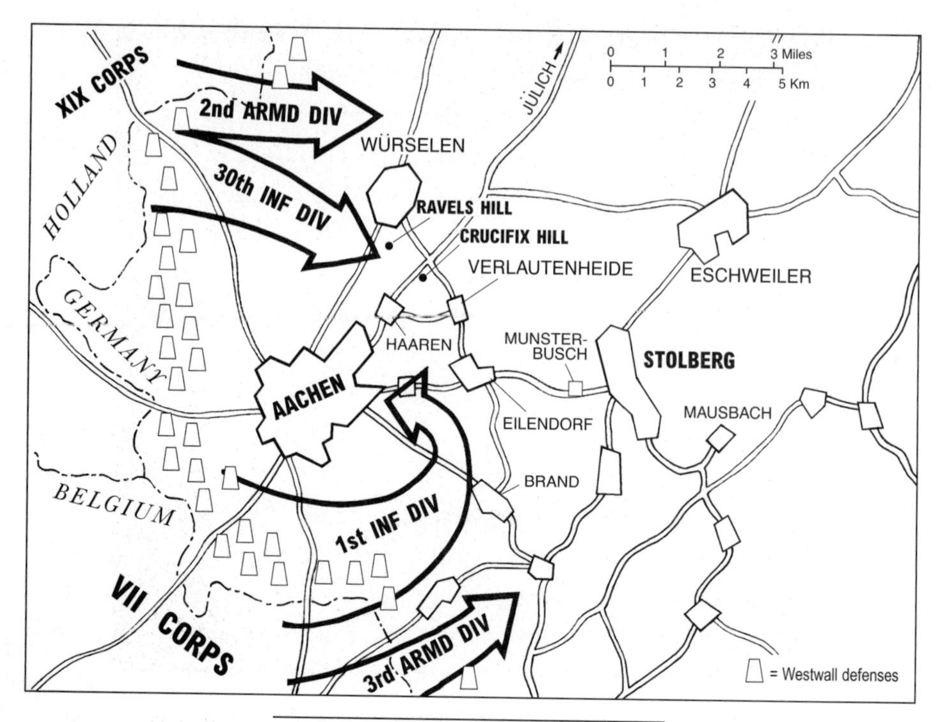

The assault on Aachen, September 1944

The 18th RCT was already preparing to crack the fixed fortifications using flamethrowers, Bangalore torpedoes, satchel and pole charges, heavy artillery, tank destroyers, aircraft, and the knowledge gained previously on Omaha Beach and at the outer line of *Westwall* defenses. An hour-long saturation bombardment by eleven battalions of artillery and a company of 4.2-inch chemical mortars lit up the predawn darkness of 8 October 1944. The dazed defenders at Verlautenheide put up little resistance to Lieutenant Colonel John Williamson's 2nd Battalion.

The 1st Battalion, under Lieutenant Colonel Henry G. Learnard Jr., met similar success at Crucifix Hill, but it did not come easily. Captain Bobbie Brown, commanding C Company, 18th Infantry, spearheaded the attack and capture of Crucifix Hill, earning the Medal of Honor in the process. On 8 October, he led his company up the slopes of the hill into a firestorm of enemy bullets and artillery shells. Obtaining a pole charge, Brown thrust it into the gun aperature of one of innumerable pillboxes that studded the hill and blew it up. He then

President Harry S. Truman attaches the Medal of Honor around the neck of Captain Bobbie Brown, C Company, 18th Infantry, at a White House ceremony. (Courtesy Colonel Robert R. McCormick Research Center of the 1st Infantry Division Museum at Cantigny)

crawled to another fortification and demolished it, too. Another nearby pillbox had his men pinned down, and the captain once again crawled through intense fire to the enemy position with another pole charge. As his citation reads, "With heroic bravery, he disregarded opposing fire and worked ahead in the face of bullets streaming from the pillbox. Finally reaching his objective, he stood up and inserted his explosive, silencing the enemy. He was wounded by a mortar shell but refused medical attention and, despite heavy hostile fire, moved swiftly among his troops, exhorting and instructing them in subduing powerful opposition."

Later that day, Brown reconnoitered enemy positions and was wounded twice more, but his scouting mission paid off; "He succeeded in securing information which led to the destruction of several enemy guns and enabled his company to throw back two powerful counterattacks with heavy losses. Only when Company C's position was completely secure did he permit treatment of his three wounds."[49]

In the darkness of the following night, American infiltrators slipped into German positions atop Ravels Hill and took the objective without firing a shot. Unaware that the Yanks were in control of the high ground, German supply teams were captured while bringing hot food for their comrades—hot food that went directly into the stomachs of the weary GIs. The victory seemed almost too easy.

And it was.

The German counterattacks began almost immediately. The German 12th Division hit the Americans, and German artillery began to pummel the 1st's positions with an intensity that had no rival. Poor weather conditions kept Allied planes grounded, and Sherman tanks and M-10 tank destroyers, attempting to come to the aid of the pinned-down infantrymen, were knocked out. Even counter-battery fire was ineffective due to the low clouds and poor observation. The 1st Division soldier had no choice but to dig his foxhole a little deeper, grit his teeth, say his prayers, and take the pounding. Despite the shelling, two rifle companies of the 18th Regiment managed to crawl from their holes, organize an attack, and seize the town of Haaren, on the road between Aachen and Jülich, one of the Germans' major supply lifelines.

But the Germans would not give up. Advance elements of two German divisions arrived east of Aachen, and they were spoiling for a fight. Dug in, the thinly stretched 18th Infantry was beginning to feel the first pinpricks of 3rd Panzer Grenadier Division probes. Captain Robert Murphy was now the S–3 of 2nd Battalion, 18th Regiment, and was in a building, talking to G Company on a field phone when "a shell hit the roof right over my head and I caught some of it in the arm." Hospitalized for two months, Murphy would rejoin the outfit on 16 December—just in time for the start of the Battle of the Bulge.[50]

The same day that Murphy was hit, General Huebner issued an ultimatum to Colonel Wilck, still stubbornly holding out inside besieged Aachen: either cease fighting and surrender all forces or the city will be leveled by American bombers and assaulted by infantry. When the ultimatum went unanswered, a two-day bombardment of Aachen commenced, with nearly 10,000 artillery shells and 160 tons of aerial bombs plastering the already heavily damaged city.[51]

To the north of Aachen, the 30th Infantry Division was still attempting to drive southward to link up with the 1st, but was encountering stiff resistance.

Deciding not to wait any longer for Hobbs, General Huebner gave Colonel John F. R. Seitz's depleted 26th RCT the thankless task of laying seige to Aachen. With only two of his three battalions available, Seitz and his staff laid out a careful plan to overcome the 3,500 to 5,000 German soldiers who were estimated to be holed up inside the ruins of the city. While the enemy was wrongly deemed to be of fairly low fighting ability, the Yanks knew it did not take much training to squeeze a trigger or throw a grenade or fire a *panzerfaust*. The 26th would execute a wide "end run" and penetrate Aachen from the east and northeast. The 3rd Battalion, under Lieutenant Colonel John T. Corley, was assigned to capture and hold the high ground to the northeast while Lieutenant Colonel Derrill M. Daniel's 2nd Battalion would strike directly from the east. Each of Daniel's three companies was reinforced with either three M-4 Shermans or three M-10 tank destroyers; additional machine guns; flamethrowers; and bazookas. A huge, self-propelled 155mm howitzer was also added to the attackers' arsenal. For two days, seventy-four artillery batteries and scores of fighter-bombers pounded the defenders—all to little effect. As the Allies had discovered during the battle of Cassino in Italy the previous year, all the heavy firepower did was to turn buildings into thousands of ready-made bunkers and clog the streets with debris, making them virtually impassable to vehicles.

The 2nd Battalion, unaware that few of the defenders had been touched by the bombardment, stepped off its line of departure at 0930 hours on 13 October, clambering over a high railroad embankment to enter the city. Quickly confronted by a maze of streets filled with rubble, the GIs adopted a strategy they called, "Knock 'em all down." If a building—or walls of a building—stood in their path, the Americans quickly used their firepower to knock down any standing structures, chasing the enemy soldiers into basements and finishing them off with grenades, flamethrowers, and automatic weapons.

As walking down a street was too dangerous, Daniel's men also developed a simple expedient for moving from one building to another. The 155mm gun was brought up, aimed point-blank at a block of buildings, and then fired. The projectile blew holes through all the adjoining walls, allowing the infantry to pass from one building to the next without ever stepping outside. Although fighting was fierce in some quarters, the Blue Spaders, working almost microscopically to clear out every resistance nest, eventually won out; it took Daniel's men nine days to secure the city center, during which time the 155mm gun performed good duty, knocking out enemy guns, tanks, and bunkers.[52]

"We had a front row seat watching the 26th take Aachen," Harley Reynolds, B Company, 16th Regiment, remembered. "You can't believe the empty shells dropping on us from all the planes of ours doing their strafing and diving runs on Aachen."[53]

In combat, a soldier never knows when his "number is up." Jack Bennett, a mortarman with E Company, 18th Regiment, had his war come to an end on 13 October. During the battle of Verlautenheide, a shell exploded near him and nearly blew off one of his legs. "When I fell, my leg went back up underneath me. I looked down and part of my little finger was also cut off. Then I looked at my leg and couldn't see it; the femur had been shattered." He would spend nineteen months in Army hospitals. Fortunately, his leg was saved. Even more fortunately, he would miss the next seven months of combat.[54]

At dawn on 15 October, the 18th and 16th Regiments (the latter of which was holding the ground between Stolberg and Verlautenheide) could see another large German counterattack, this one by the 3rd Panzer Grenadier Division, taking shape across open ground to the east. An aerial assault by American fighter-bombers at 0900 hours failed to break up the concentration and, an hour later, the enemy commenced the battle. The attack, although supported by armor, was conducted in piecemeal fashion and failed to penetrate the 1st Division's lines. Captain Joe Dawson, still in command of G Company, 16th Infantry, and Captain Kimball Richmond, I Company, were holding the high ground along a 2,000-yard front between Verlautenheide and Eilendorf, with Dawson's left flank touching the 18th Regiment's right. One veteran described Verlautenheide Ridge: "This ridge is 838 feet high and 400 yards long in its highest part, and runs southeast of Verlautenheide toward Stolberg, which are two places that the guys who fought and died here never heard of before. This ridge had been divided into pasture lots and farming ground, but the sides are torn now and the three brick houses are shattered and broken, their power lines dangling to the ground."[55]

Dawson noted, "We were given the mission of maintaining a spot on the ridge overlooking . . . Verlautenheide. It's really nothing but a farm. It was a very vital thing that we maintain it because it gave us an observation to interdict [the Germans] with artillery fire as well as to defend it against any flanking action that the Germans might employ against our approaches. . . . And they threw everyhing they had at us. On the second day . . . they launched a major attack against us." Pouring out of the woods, German tanks and infantry came in a swarm across an open meadow, slashing into American positions and creating panic and casualties. Dawson's and Richmond's companies on the battalion's left flank were unable to repel the assault and were partially overrun; the right-flank company of the 18th was similarly overrun before help rained down from the sky. "It was a fierce battle that only was saved by the fact that we had not only our own division artillery, we had the corps artillery," said Dawson. "Believe you me, we relied on them, and they were deadly accurate. I had to call for the artillery right on us, only ten yards in front of us, and they saved our lives because [the Germans] were literally overwhelming us in numbers."[56]

American artillery continued to burst among the enemy force, and fighter-bombers began to appear, unleashing their ordnance wherever targets of opportunity presented themselves. But still the enemy came on. At one point, Dawson reported to headquarters that he didn't know "if he can hold another attack through here. The men are worn out."

No one can adequately explain the courage of desperate men for, despite their exhaustion, they held. Slowly, the field-gray tide began to subside, was beaten back, and melted into the woods from which it had come, leaving mangled bodies and burning panzers strewn about the landscape. By 1500 hours on 15 October, the crisis had passed and, somehow, Dawson's and Richmond's companies—or what was left of them—began to retake lost ground.[57]

After the smoke had cleared, Joe Dawson felt he had finally won the trust of the men under his command. "The highest honor and privilege that I had was to command the finest group of men God ever put on the earth. I've enjoyed their respect and love as a result of my experience as their commander, and we all share in one respect an accolade that was given us up there on the ridge where it was changed officially . . . to Dawson's Ridge, which is in the record."[58]

Meanwhile, Corley's 3rd Battalion, 26th Infantry, had been busy clearing the enemy from the factories near the hilly northeast corner of the city. On 14 October, the battalion ran into an SS battalion that had fought its way through the 30th Infantry Division to come to Wilck's aid. The next day, Corley's troops linked up with Daniel's men, and the 3rd Battalion headed for the luxurious Hotel Quellenhof, recently abandoned as Wilck's headquarters. A counterattack by the SS force threw the 3rd Battalion back into a defensive position, which it held for two days. On 18 October, Corley's men resumed the offensive and engaged in room-by-room fighting with the enemy holed up in the opulent hotel. Finally, the 3rd Battalion forced the enemy into the basement, where they were finished off with grenades and automatic weapons fire.[59]

On 18 October, near the town of Haaren, between Aachen and Verlautenheide, the name of Sergeant Max Thompson, K Company, 18th Infantry, became enshrined in the 1st Division's registry of heroes. Thompson's company was holding a hill when it was subjected to an hour-long artillery barrage, then attacked by tanks and a battalion of infantry. His Medal of Honor citation stated, "While engaged in moving wounded men to cover, Sgt. Thompson observed that the enemy had overrun the positions of the 3rd Platoon. He immediately attempted to stem the enemy's advance singlehandedly. He manned an abandoned machinegun and fired on the enemy until a direct hit from a hostile tank destroyed the gun. Shaken and dazed, Sgt. Thompson picked up an automatic rifle and although alone against the enemy force which was pouring into the gap in our lines, he fired burst after burst, halting the leading elements of the attack and dispersing those following. Throwing aside his automatic rifle, which had jammed, he took up a rocket gun [bazooka], fired on a light tank, setting it on fire."

That evening, with the Germans in control of part of the hill, including three pillboxes, Thompson's squad was given the mission of evicting the enemy from the pillboxes. Since night had fallen and American fire proved to be ineffective, Thompson crawled to within twenty yards of one of the pillboxes and fired rifle grenades through the embrasure. The enemy fought back, wounding Thompson, but he kept up his one-man assault, eventually forcing the Germans to abandon their position. As his citation concluded, "Sgt. Thompson's courageous leadership inspired his men and materially contributed to the clearing of the enemy from his last remaining hold on this important hill position." [60]

The battle for Crucifix Hill, the Verlautenheide Ridge, and Ravels Hill was, for all intents and purposes, over, but the battle for Aachen went on. All the horrors and difficulties of urban fighting were visited upon the attackers during their attempts to root out the last of the enemy holdouts from a rabbit warren of streets, cellars, sewers, and church steeples. On 19 October, Captain Thomas F. O'Brien, C.O. of Cannon Company, 16th Infantry, reported a strange and disturbing incident to battalion Intelligence: "We just got four children. The oldest one isn't over seven years old. They were firing at one of my gun sections. One was using an M-1, used the wrong ammunition and blew off the end of the gun. These kids probably have been influenced by the talk of the folks at home. Something has to be done about this sort of thing."[61]

At last, German resistance withered away and, on 21 October, after ordering his men to fight to the last bullet, Wilck surrendered to Corley. The operation netted 5,600 prisoners and an uncounted number of dead Germans; 498 men of the 2nd Battalion alone had been either killed or wounded in the seige of Aachen.[62]

Sergeant First Class Max Thompson, K Company, 18th Infantry, recipient of the Medal of Honor. (Courtesy Colonel Robert R. McCormick Research Center of the 1st Infantry Division Museum at Cantigny)

At the conclusion of the battle, war correspondent Drew Middleton observed: "Battles are not great because of the numbers engaged or their duration but because of their effect on the contestants. The best history of the war would be a record of what went on in the minds of the opposing commanders. If such a history were written of World War II, I am sure we would find the capture of Aachen by the 1st Division ranked high among the defeats which convinced the high command of the German Army that it had lost the war. The battle was unique in two other respects: it was fought and won almost entirely by the 1st Division and at that time the Division had been in action almost continuously since June 6 and was very tired. Despite this, it fought with more precision, skill, and more surely, I think, than ever before."[63]

As they rested after their hard-won victory, many of the GIs wondered if they would be forced to repeat this same type of combat at every village, town, and city between Aachen and Berlin. If so, there would be damned few of them left by the time it was over. Medic Allen Towne reflected on the fact that his aid station was seeing more cases of "battle fatigue." "We were having quite a few men come in with anxiety state (a complete breakdown). . . . This happened to some of the men who had been wounded before and had returned. These men with anxiety state were never considered as battle casualties but rather as sick men. I

1st Division troops look on as Colonel Gerhard Wilck (head bowed, foreground), commander of the 246th Division and the German garrison that held out at Aachen, and his staff in the back seat, are taken into custody following the city's fall on 21 October 1944. (Courtesy U.S. Army Military History Institute)

often wondered if this was fair because somehow anxiety state leaves a stigma. Some of these men had been in tough combat for years and finally the continual stress broke them."[64]

Shortly after the battle of Aachen, Eisenhower and his staff paid a visit to 1st Infantry Division headquarters. Ike's naval aide, Captain Harry Butcher, recalled, "I asked [Huebner] how he had managed to gain the confidence of his division after his relief of the popular Terry Allen in Sicily. He said it had been simple. He required all of them to practice shooting, and ample ammunition was furnished. He said there wasn't a man in the division who hadn't improved his shooting. There's nothing the GIs like better than to shoot, particularly if they are not supervised too closely. He said he had the 'shootinest' division in the Army."

Army Chief of Staff George C. Marshall had once expressed to Eisenhower his desire that the U.S. Army Band should play a concert in the first major German city captured by the Americans. Butcher noted, "He said he wished this could be done [in Aachen], but the concert would have to be on an occasion such as a ceremony to include General Hodges [First Army commander]. He felt it unwise to permit the band to play within 3,000 yards of the front line. If the Germans heard the music, there would be a refrain of artillery, and not only members of the band, but General Hodges might be killed. Consequently, he had disapproved the idea."[65]

With Aachen in American hands, General Bradley ordered the 12th Army Group to continue its drive toward Germany's heavily industrialized Rhein River region to the northeast, a drive that Lieutenant Harold Monica dreaded. "The high command had their plans for crossing the Rhein," he said, "but to those of us who would have to do it, that river was an immense obstacle. All kinds of thoughts running through our minds. Would we have to pay for our good fortune and luck during the D-Day landings by some sort of disaster waiting for us at the Rhein?"[66]

But before the Americans could even think about the Rhein, they would first have to penetrate the thickly wooded Hürtgen Forest, some ten miles to the southeast of Aachen—an area of fifty square miles that Eddie Steeg and other members of the division would rename "the Hurtin' Forest." Here the Big Red One was reunited with an old, dear friend, its former commander, Terry Allen. His recently arrived 104th Infantry Division (the "Timberwolves") had slipped into the front line beside the 1st Division and would soon give Huebner's men a rest. Correspondent Drew Middleton recorded his impression of the reunion: "The Division turned itself inside out to do him honor, and spectators said the sight of hairy-eared veterans trying to show their affection for Terry through barriers of discipline and rank was incredibly moving."[67]

Without bitterness or jealousy, Clarence Huebner recalled the warm greetings and observed, "The men respected me, but they loved Terry Allen."[68]

On 16 November, the 1st, along with the 104th and 3rd Armored Division, pushed into the woods east of Stolberg near the village of Hamich—and immediately ran into a German buzz saw. Deep mud and a lack of paved roads hampered movement, and the dense forest drastically reduced visibility and fields of fire. Progress was measured in feet instead of miles. The battle went on for weeks as ferocious fighting became commonplace in this green hell, over which

Men of F Company, 16th Infantry Regiment, march along a narrow lane past the towering pines of the Hürtgen Forest near Hamich, 18 November 1944. Many 1st Division veterans felt the fighting in the Hürtgen Forest was worse than what they experienced at Omaha Beach. (Courtesy U.S. Army Military History Institute)

snow and sub-freezing temperatures descended; men suffered from frostbite and could be evacuated only when a lull in the battle permitted. Day after day, the Germans counterattacked with everything they had, and they still had plenty. Tank fought tank, artillery and mortar rounds crashed through trees, and American dive bombers joined the fray.[69]

Technical Sergeant Jake W. Lindsey of C Company, 16th Infantry, typified the courage it took to succeed in this wintry battlescape. At Hamich, he was dug into the frozen landscape about ten yards in front of the rest of his platoon when the enemy struck his unit's position. "By his unerringly accurate fire, [he] destroyed two enemy machinegun nests, forced the withdrawal of two tanks, and effectively halted enemy flanking patrols. Later, although painfully wounded, he engaged eight Germans, who were reestablishing machinegun positions, in hand-to-hand combat, killing three, capturing three, and causing the other two to flee. By his gallantry, T/Sgt. Lindsey secured his unit's positions, and reflected great credit upon himself and the U.S. Army." So reads his citation for the Medal of Honor.[70]

Technical Sergeant Jake W. Lindsey, C Company, 16th Infantry, recipient of the Medal of Honor. (Courtesy Colonel Robert R. McCormick Research Center of the 1st Infantry Division Museum at Cantigny)

Three days after Lindsey's heroic stand, a private first class by the name of Francis Xavier McGraw, a machine gunner with H Company, 26th Regiment, immortalized himself. As wave after wave of German troops attempted to infiltrate through the thick, snowy woods near Schevenhutte, McGraw held them at bay with his .30-caliber machine gun until he was out of ammunition. Dashing to the rear for more, he rushed back to his gun and continued to spray the relentless enemy. An artillery round exploded nearby, bringing down a tree that blocked his fields of fire. Nonplussed, he lifted the gun off its tripod, braced it atop the log, and continued to fire. Another shell crashed down, exploded, and tore the gun from his hands; he retrieved it and kept up his steady stream of fire until his supply of ammunition was again exhausted. Nearly surrounded, McGraw realized he had no chance of going back for more ammo and resumed the fight with a carbine. It was too late; one man with a puny carbine could not continue to hold back the overwhelming strength of the enemy; McGraw died at his post trying to prevent a German breakthrough. For his valor, he was awarded the Medal of Honor, posthumously.[71]

The casualties among both officers and enlisted men continued to mount. Technician 3rd Grade Bert Damsky of Birmingham, Alabama, and E Company, 18th Infantry, recalled the loss of his best friend. "My squad leader took me as his foxhole partner. He always taught me and explained things to me; he was a

Private First Class Francis X. McGraw, H Company, 26th Infantry, recipient of the Medal of Honor, posthumously. (Courtesy Colonel Robert R. McCormick Research Center of the 1st Infantry Division Museum at Cantigny)

great help to me. But he often became very homesick and wondered why, after North Africa, Sicily, and D-Day, the army would not let him go home. He often said he knew his luck could not hold out forever, and that he would never get home." He was right; Damsky's friend was killed near Hamich.[72]

Ralph Puhalovich, Anti-Tank Company, 26th Infantry, was wounded in the Hürtgen. "They sent me out with a bazooka to hunt tanks," he said. "I was laying under a tree and heard this little voice say, 'You'd better get out of here.' In combat, you learn to pay attention to the 'little voices.' So I got up and went over to another GI who was dug in about fifteen yards away. At that moment, a mortar round came in and hit the exact place where I had just been. Then another round came in and exploded in the trees above us. I got hit in the buttocks with shrapnel. Later, at the aid station, there was a captured German there who laughed when he saw my wound; one of the other guys in the aid station smashed the German in the head with the butt of a rifle for laughing."[73]

Private Robert T. Henry, C Company, 16th Infantry, recipient of the Medal of Honor, posthumously. (U.S. Army Photograph)

A few Americans managed to penetrate into Hamich. One of them, Private First Class Carmen Turchiarelli of K Company, 16th Regiment, climbed to the second story of a house and fired a bazooka round down through the open turret of a panzer, setting it ablaze. It was the kind of bravery and devotion to duty that had become an everyday occurrence within the division. But, while there was no shortage of courage, ammunition was again running low, and no one was sure how long the 1st would be able hold the line.[74] But hold they did, and when it appeared that their positions were about to be overrun, the 1st Division dogfaces burrowed deeply into their icy foxholes and called their own artillery down upon themselves. The German assault was stopped dead in its tracks, but not before the 1st sustained heavy casualties. Harley Reynolds recalled that after Hamich, his B Company, 16th Regiment, which had an authorized strength of 200 men, was down to just twenty-seven.[75]

During the division's drive to the Roer, another 1st Division soldier earned the Medal of Honor at the cost of his life. Twenty-one-year-old Private Robert T. Henry, of Greenville, Mississippi, volunteered to attempt to knock out five enemy machine-gun emplacements that were holding up the advance of C

Company, 16th Infantry, near the hamlet of Luchem, about four miles east of Eschweiler. Despite the frigid temperatures, he stripped off everything that might slow him down—pack, helmet, overcoat, overshoes—grabbed his rifle and as many grenades as he could carry, and sprinted across open ground in a one-man assault. Machine-gun bullets hit him, but he staggered on, forcing the Germans to abandon their position before he died. During the break in the firing, Henry's platoon swiftly moved up and captured seventy Germans.[76]

To fill the division's depleted ranks, green and frightened troops were rushed from replacement depots to the front lines. The 16th Regiment's historian wrote, "replacements outnumbered the experienced men and vigorous training was a necessity to bring the recruits up to fighting pitch." They needed to learn in a hurry, for, "once again, as had happened so many times recently, the companies were encountering paratroopers—hard, arrogant fighters who resisted with extreme courage and fanatacism."[77]

Try as they might, the hard, arrogant Germans could not sustain their furious counterattacks indefinitely. On 7 December 1944, three years to the day after Japanese bombs had rained down on Pearl Harbor, the battle for the Hürtgen Forest was officially declared over. Many of the surviving 1st Division veterans—their uniforms torn and dirty, their eyes red from lack of sleep, their feet frozen, their faces haggard and unshaven, their ears still ringing from the unceasing roar of battle—were convinced that the fighting in the forest had been even more harrowing and costly than the battle for Easy Red and Fox Green.

Since reaching the German border on 11 September, the 1st Infantry Division had spent three months to advance ten miles, at a cost of hundreds of dead, wounded, and missing. Somebody did the math—at this rate, it would take eight years for the 1st to travel the 330 miles between Aachen and Berlin. Would anyone still be alive by then?

CHAPTER TWELVE

"Today Is a Very Fine Day"

THE OPTIMISTIC predictions of the war being over by Christmas lay dead and frozen in the snow-shrouded fields of Western Europe and coagulating on the blood-soaked sands of tropical isles and atolls. The far-flung, fortified islands of Kwajalein, Truk, Hollandia, Saipan, Guam, Peleliu, and Leyte had all fallen to the Americans in 1944, shortening the road to Tokyo each day. Yet the fanatical Japanese were still holding out on many more islands, prepared to fight to the last man. And no matter how optimistically the newsreels and newspapers and magazine and radio commentators spun the facts, there seemed to be no end in sight to the awful carnage.

In Europe, too, there was little reason to hope that Hitler's Third Reich might suddenly collapse, as had Kaiser Wilhelm's regime in November 1918; each mile driven into Germany by the Allies was met with greater and greater resistance, like a fist being pushed into fast-setting concrete. Even an attempt on the Führer's life by rebel Nazi officers in July had been botched; nothing and no one seemed able to stop the hate-filled Austrian ex-corporal who had started the world's descent into madness.

As America's fourth Christmas season since the United States entered the war commenced, there was an oppressive sense that the war might drag on indefinitely. In the U.S., the holiday was being celebrated in subdued fashion. Instead of being joyous, the hearts in many families were heavy, filled either with fear or grief. While some servicemen were safe at home, either because they had been wounded in battle; had finished their tour of duty; or because they were awaiting deployment overseas (the official draft ceiling had just been raised to age twenty-six), millions of husbands, fathers, brothers, and sons were gone, their absence symbolized by a simple, empty stocking tacked to the mantel of the family fireplace. Millions of families, to be sure, had sent packages containing millions of Christmas presents to their loved ones overseas, and the military postal system struggled mightily to assure that the packages would reach the soldiers, sailors, marines, and airmen, no matter how remote or dangerous the address. So what if the cakes and cookies arrived crushed beyond recognition or if, like the dainty napkins, shoe whitening, and spats Eddie Steeg had received from home in July, they were incongruous, useless, and inappropriate in a war zone? The fact that they were remembered at all heartened even the most battle-hardened, gore-stained veterans.

Back home, Americans still intently kept abreast of developments on the battle fronts, especially where their loved ones were serving. Their hearts also ached for the Londoners who were again feeling the club of Hitler's wrath, this time in the form of huge V-2 rockets that plunged from the sky without warning and did terrible damage.

Americans craved information, and they pored over newspapers and magazines, searching for any scrap of news that might be a harbinger of victory, or anything that would put words to the inexpressible feelings they held inside. Advertising captured the heartbreak of the season. An ad from the automaker Nash showed a wistful GI and the headline, "When I Go Home . . . ." The copy was weighted with the same yearning that filled virtually every homesick serviceman at Christmastime: "The guns fade down. And it seems to me I hear a dog's sharp bark, and a girl's voice, and the shrill of my own clear whistle. And the next thing I know, I'm over the gate and out of the war and it's Christmas again and I'm home. And then, I'm walking into a room with the biggest and brightest tree in the world. . . . The music stops and the carols are stilled and the bombers come up and the fighters scream against the surfbeat of the guns and I'm back where there's still a war to be won. But I know when I go home, I'll go home sure that no kids of mine will ever spend their Christmases in jungles, in foxholes, or on beachheads. . . ."[1]

Unfortunately, there would be numerous Christmases ahead when the sons of World War II veterans would be spending their Christmases in jungles, in foxholes, and on beachheads. And there were plenty of soldiers in this war, too, just inside Germany's vestibule, that were hunkered down in snow-filled holes; or taking cover in the scant shelter of a half-demolished building that was once somebody's home or shop; or trying to warm their hands over a jeep's manifold

Brigadier General Clift Andrus replaced General Huebner as commanding officer of the 1st Infantry Division. (Courtesy Colonel Robert R. McCormick Research Center of the 1st Infantry Division Museum at Cantigny)

or a tank's exhaust, while longing for home and girls and decorated trees and the warmth of a real bed, without worrying about an incoming artillery round or a dive-bomber's screaming attack or a sniper's bullet.

Having taken all its objectives, the weary 1st Infantry Division was finally pulled off the line on 11 December and given a welcome relief by the 9th Infantry Division; three days later, General Huebner was relieved of command and replaced by his crusty Division Artillery commander, Clift Andrus. By then, Huebner was almost as beloved by his men as Terry Allen had been. Huebner was "bumped upstairs" to replace Leonard T. Gerow as V Corps commander when Gerow was promoted to command the newly created Fifteenth Army. Willard Wyman was also transferred out, and given the 71st Infanty Division to command; Colonel George A. Taylor, C.O. of the 16th Infantry, became the assistant division commander.

Andrus, born at Fort Leavenworth, Kansas, in 1880 into a military family, had graduated from Cornell University in 1912, then was commissioned a second lieutenant of artillery. In Andrus, who had been head of "Div Arty" since before the North Africa campaign, and Taylor, the men of the 1st knew they had two aggressive and capable leaders; the Big Red One's drive toward Berlin, it was felt, would not miss a beat.[2]

As tough as the battles for Aachen and the Hürtgen Forest had been, they were soon eclipsed by a battle of even greater proportions—the so-called "Battle of the Bulge." In his last-gasp effort to turn the tide of war in his favor, Hitler gambled everything he had in the west with an all-out blitz, code-named *Wacht am Rhein* ("Watch on the Rhein"), designed to crash through American lines, capture the Belgian port of Antwerp, into which hundreds of thousands of tons of Allied supplies were now pouring, and split the Allied armies along the seam between Montgomery's 21st Army Group and Bradley's 12th. The blow would be so severe and demoralizing, Hitler believed, that the Allies would sue for a separate peace; he could then turn his attention back to preventing a collapse of his armies facing the Soviets in the east.

In charge of the counteroffensive in the west was *Generalfeldmarschall* Gerd von Rundstedt, the aged but able commander of *Oberbefehlshaber West* (or, *OB West*). Beneath him was *Generalfeldmarschall* Walter Model's formidable Army Group B, consisting of the Seventh Army, Fifth Panzer Army, and Sixth SS Panzer Army. The axis of attack would be through the same forest from which the Germans had launched their surprise attack against France in 1940—the thickly wooded Ardennes, from Monschau on the north to Echternach on the south.[3] A military historian described the Ardennes as being "at once the nursery and the old folks' home of the American command. New divisions came there for a battlefield shakedown, old ones to rest after heavy fighting and [to] absorb replacements for their losses."[4] In spite of its history, the Ardennes was an area that the Allies continued to mistakenly believe was "impenetrable."

Just as the French were caught unawares in 1940, so too were the Americans at the end of 1944. Two recently arrived, unblooded American infantry divisions—Walter E. Lauer's 99th and Allen W. Jones's 106th, both of Troy Middleton's VIII Corps—were in the front line along the "quiet" Ardennes, with the 1st Infantry Division, and others, to the north, in reserve.[5] They would soon be given a rude introduction to battle by an initial German assault wave of some 250,000 men—some wearing American uniforms and driving captured Ameri-

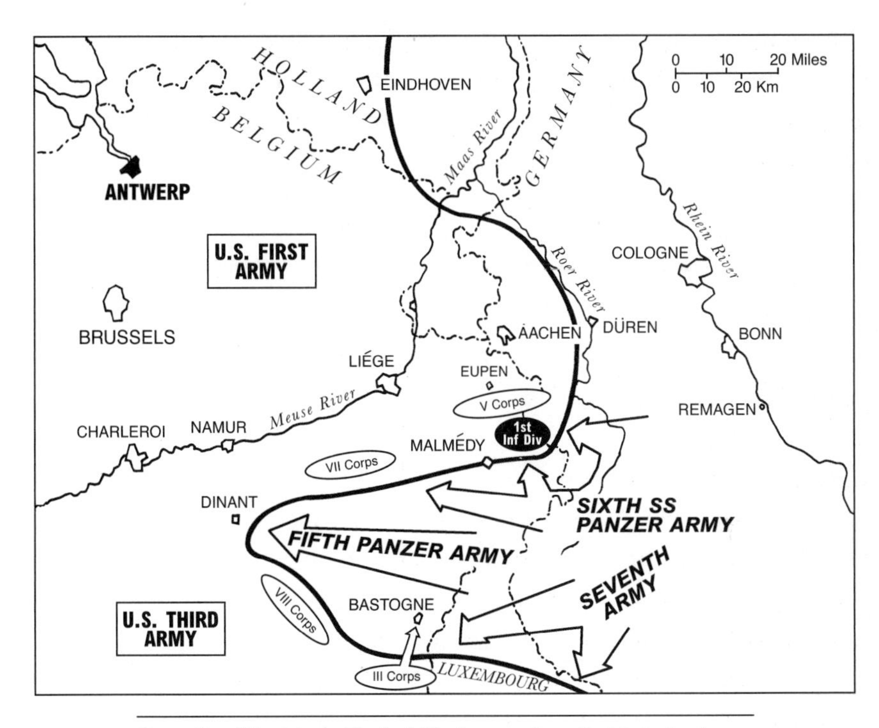

Operation *Wacht am Rhein*, Hitler's grandiose-but-failed scheme to split the American First and Third Armies and capture the port of Antwerp, became known as "the Battle of the Bulge."

can vehicles—with nearly 400 panzers and 335 self-propelled assault guns, and over 2,600 artillery pieces and rocket launchers. Another 55,000 troops and 561 armored vehicles stood in reserve, waiting for orders to move up and exploit the gains made by the first wave. Facing this force along the western front were only 83,000 Americans with 242 tanks, 182 tank destroyers, and 394 artillery pieces.[6]

On the frigid night of 15/16 December 1944, Hitler's uncompromising directive was issued to the keyed-up assault troops, who knew that their counteroffensive would spell either victory or defeat for the Third Reich: "Forward to and over the Meuse!"[7] Before dawn on 16 December, the spearhead of the twenty-five-division German assault burst out of the forest and slammed into the unsuspecting 99th and 106th Divisions, sending many of the green officers and troops fleeing in panic. Whole battalions melted in the face of the German onslaught, but calmer voices soon prevailed as elements of the Big Red One were quickly mobilized and trucked to the northern shoulder of the German penetration.

Captain Fred Hall, S-3 of the 16th Regiment's 2nd Battalion, noted, "On 16 December, we were sent near Robertville, Belgium, with a mission to defend a position along the northern shoulder of the Battle of the Bulge. . . . We had continual contact with the enemy, and several Germans wearing American uniforms were captured in our area. These soldiers were promptly interrogated to determine unit identification, strength and mission. . . . We had the unfamiliar task of preparing defensive positions using barbed wire and mines."[8]

Sergeant First Class Dorris H. Barickman, from Bowling Green, Kentucky, and a member of the 1st Recon Troop, noted the tenseness of that time: "We got word that the German armored was coming. . . . We were given orders to hold and not retreat under any circumstances. Hard on the nerve system!"[9]

In the Army's official history of the Battle of the Bulge, historian Hugh Cole wrote, "The 26th Infantry of the uncommitted 1st Infantry Division, then placed on a 6-hour alert, finally entrucked at midnight and started the move south to Camp Elsenborn [Belgium]. The transfer of this regimental combat team would have a most important effect on the ensuing American defense."[10] Arriving in the 99th Division's panicky command post at Elsenborn, an officer of the 26th Regiment declared, "You need worry no longer. The 1st Division is here. Everything is under control."[11]

The 26th Regiment began establishing defensive positions between the towns of Dom Butgenbach and German-held Büllingen on the night of 17 December to stop the Sixth Panzer Army from driving through that sector. It would not be easy. The weather was miserable; food and water froze; men were evacuated with frostbite; vehicles broke down; and weapons became all but inoperable in the bitter cold. (To quickly thaw the bolts on their weapons, some soldiers resorted to the only warm water they had—their urine.) Yet, none of this seemed to matter to the Germans who, in the early morning hours of 19 December, roared out of Büllingen and smashed into the 26th's positions. The 33rd Field Artillery Battalion, assigned to support Lieutenant Colonel Derrill Daniel's 2nd Battalion, 26th Regiment, still understrength from its ordeal in Aachen, fired illuminating rounds that exposed the charging panzers and infantry, then hammered the enemy with white-phosphorous and high-explosive shells until the assault lost its momentum and the German troops broke and retreated.

Later that morning, the Germans renewed their attack with fresh determination. Daniel's 2nd Battalion, reinforced by a mere five Shermans from the 745th Tank Battalion and four self-propelled guns of the 634th Tank Destroyer Battalion, took the brunt of a determined assault by SS-*Panzergrenadiers* and tanks from the 12th SS Panzer (*Hitlerjugend*) Division. Riflemen and artillerymen combined to stop every German attack; bodies clad in field-gray overcoats littered the snowy landscape, and flaming panzers were everywhere. Once again, the enemy fell back to regroup and await reinforcements. The American line, too, was strengthened by the timely arrival of the 16th Regiment.[12]

Al Alvarez, 7th Artillery, had been taking it easy before the fighting began, relaxing in a warm barn when, "Kaboom! A round came through an opening in the front wall and out the back wall with a startling, crackling explosion that showered us with debris. Straw flew everywhere, and we were covered with shards of wood, powdered stone, and animal droppings. No one was physically hurt, but someone had to change their laundry!"[13]

During the night of 19/20 December, German artillery and *Nebelwerfers* (multi-barreled rocket launchers) began to saturate the 2nd Battalion's positions. For three solid hours, the fire kept up, decimating an already-depleted G Company. As German infantry closed in under the cover of the barrage, Daniel called for all the artillery within range—twelve battalions—to hit the exposed enemy with an estimated 10,000 rounds. It was a slaughter, but the Germans would not give up.[14] At about 0600 hours on the frigid, foggy morning of 20 December, twenty German tanks and an infantry battalion struck American positions at Dom Butgenbach. The 1st Division countered with a mortar and artillery saturation that momentarily stopped the assault in its tracks, but the panzers came on and entered the village. A 57mm anti-tank unit, defending 2nd Battalion headquarters, went into action. Against the thick frontal armor of the German tanks the 57mm gun was generally worthless; the clever American gunners held their fire until the tanks had rolled past their positions and then fired point-blank at the lightly armored rear sections, sending the panzers up in flames.

Before dawn, another ten German tanks came roaring from Büllingen, heading straight for Company F at Dom Butgenbach, but heavy fire drove them off. The enemy then turned west and hit the line held by Company G; artillery fire again pushed the Germans back. The panzers continued probing to the west, next striking Company E. As the historian Hugh Cole wrote, "The 60mm mortars illuminated the ground in front of the company at just the right moment and two of the three tanks heading the assault were knocked out by bazooka and 57mm fire from the flank. The third tank commander stuck his head out of

Corporal Henry F. Warner, Anti-Tank Company, 26th Infantry, recipient of the Medal of Honor, posthumously. (Courtesy Colonel Robert R. McCormick Research Center of the 1st Infantry Division Museum at Cantigny)

the escape hatch to take a look around and was promptly pistolled by an American corporal."[15]

The American corporal was Henry F. Warner, of the 26th Infantry's Anti-Tank Company. Ralph Puhalovich, a member of Warner's unit, recalled, "[He] was a real quiet, unassuming, soft-spoken guy. He didn't drink and he didn't swear. You wouldn't suspect that he would be a hero."[16] According to Warner's Medal of Honor citation, "A third tank approached to within five yards of his position while he was attempting to clear a jammed breach lock. Jumping from his gun pit, he engaged in a pistol duel with the tank commander standing in the turret, killing him and forcing the tank to withdraw." The next morning, Warner was again in the thick of fighting. "Seeing a Mark IV tank looming out of the mist and heading toward his position, Cpl. Warner scored a direct hit. Disregarding his injuries, he endeavored to finish the loading and again fire at the tank, whose motor was now aflame, when a second machinegun burst killed him."[17]

On the 21st, another full-scale attempt by the 12th SS Panzer and 25th Panzer Grenadier Regiments to break through the 26th's lines was launched and, for several hours, the issue was seriously in doubt. Two platoons of the regiment's anti-tank company were thrown into the action and the 57mm guns accounted for two or three kills before being destroyed. A lone American tank destroyer rushed to the scene and knocked out seven panzers heading toward Dom Butgenbach. As the desperate battle raged, German panzers crushed American positions under their steel treads, only to be stopped by men with bazookas and rifles and hand grenades who refused to die.

By the afternoon of 22 December, the entire 1st Infantry Division was back on the line along the northern shoulder of the Bulge, along with the 2nd and 9th

Lieutenant Colonel Derril Daniel, commanding officer, 2nd Battalion, 26th Infantry. (Courtesy Colonel Robert R. McCormick Research Center of the 1st Infantry Division Museum at Cantigny)

Infantry Divisions. An official 26th Infantry Regiment report spoke of the ferocity of the fighting and the unbelievable bravery just days before Christmas: "Coming out of the mist which cloaked movements but seventy-five to a hundred yards away, the enemy tanks loomed up in front of the riflemen, who fought back with anti-tank guns, grenades, and rocket-guns. The massed tanks broke through the curtain of fire from infantrymen and the immediate supporting fires laid down by the artillery and tank and tank-destroyer elements, and overran the company main lines of resistance. Machine gunning the foxholes, the tanks sought to open a wedge for the following German infantry. Overrun and out-gunned, many riflemen died at their posts. Mortar crews left their weapons and joined the riflemen in repelling the German infantry. Machine gunners directed heavy and accurate streams of fire at the enemy. The smashing of machine-gun emplacements by the tanks that rode over the positions failed to halt the fire of the remaining machine gunners. . . . Ammunition bearers manned the weapons or fought as riflemen against the German tanks. The hostile armor rode back and forth across the gap, but failed to silence the riflemen who still fought off the German infantry. In the close fighting that followed, German tanks confidently made for the group of buildings housing the battalion CP and two company CPs. Locked in combat, the opposing infantry forces hurled every available man into the struggle."[18]

Only by summoning the last ounce of their strength, courage, and endurance were the Americans able to withstand the steel tide and prevent a German breakthrough. Giving the chilling order, "We stand and die here," Daniel rallied his troops. A platoon of self-propelled 90mm guns from the 703rd Tank Destroyer Battalion arrived at the last moment and turned German tanks into scrap-iron hulks. It was estimated that forty-seven German armored vehicles were destroyed and nearly 800 German soldiers lost their lives trying to drive Daniel's men out of Dom Butgenbach. The Americans lost nearly 250 men, five 57mm anti-tank guns, three tanks, and a tank destroyer.[19]

Eisenhower wasn't worried: "With these three proved and battle-tested units (the 1st, 2nd, and 9th Divisions) holding the position, the safety of our northern shoulder was practically a certainty."[20] It was only to the south, in a region known as the Schnee Eifel, east of St. Vith, that the American lines gave way and allowed for a deep, but temporary, enemy penetration. As the savage battle for the northern shoulder of the Bulge finally subsided, the Germans headed toward Bastogne and Malmédy, where the resistance was not quite as fierce, committing atrocities* and leaving scores of their own dead and dying comrades bleeding in the snow or burning inside their panzers. The German drive eventually sputtered and died less than halfway to Antwerp as the Allies recovered from their shock and punished von Rundstedt's armies severely; Hitler's last-gasp gamble to secure a vital victory in the west had failed. The end of the war was at last in sight, but it would not come quickly nor easily.

On 26 December 1944, the great Allied counter-counteroffensive began; the 1st Division's part in it did not commence until 15 January, but the violence of it shattered the soldiers' peaceful Christmas reveries. Hundreds of thousands of half-frozen GIs and British Tommies threw themselves at enemy positions all along the Siegfried Line in a maximum effort designed to gain ground and destroy German forces. When the 1st Division finally stepped off, Major General

---

* On 17 December, members of *SS-Obersturmbannführer* Joachim Peiper's spearheading *kampfgruppe* captured and executed eighty-six unarmed American soldiers at Baugnez, near Malmédy.

Troops from I Company, 16th Infantry, heading for the front on tanks near Schoppen, Belgium, during the Battle of the Bulge, 21 January 1945. (Courtesy Colonel Robert R. McCormick Research Center of the 1st Infantry Division Museum at Cantigny)

Andrus noted, "Most of the attacks were at night and the blizzards, rains, fogs, mud, ice, sleet, and enemy resistance did not let up as the division, with the 16th in reserve, fought ahead relentlessly." Steinbach fell the first day, and a passage was opened for the 7th Armored Division to drive toward St. Vith.

The weather was worsening. The 16th Infantry Regiment's historian recorded, "Snow was knee deep on the level and drifted to two and three times that depth where the wind could get at it. To make matters worse, it continued to snow so hard that it assumed the proportions of a blizzard. . . . Walking through the drifts was exhausting in the extreme and the troops halted frequently to rest. . . . The condition of the men was terrible. Wherever possible, men were in houses, but hundreds had to remain in the open. Wet clothes froze on them, there was a shortage of blankets, and it was impossible to keep socks dry. Men were coming down with bad colds, were developing trench feet, and when neither of these two illnesses occurred, they were so miserable in general that their continued determination to fight is one of the finest evidences of the quality of these American infantrymen."[21]

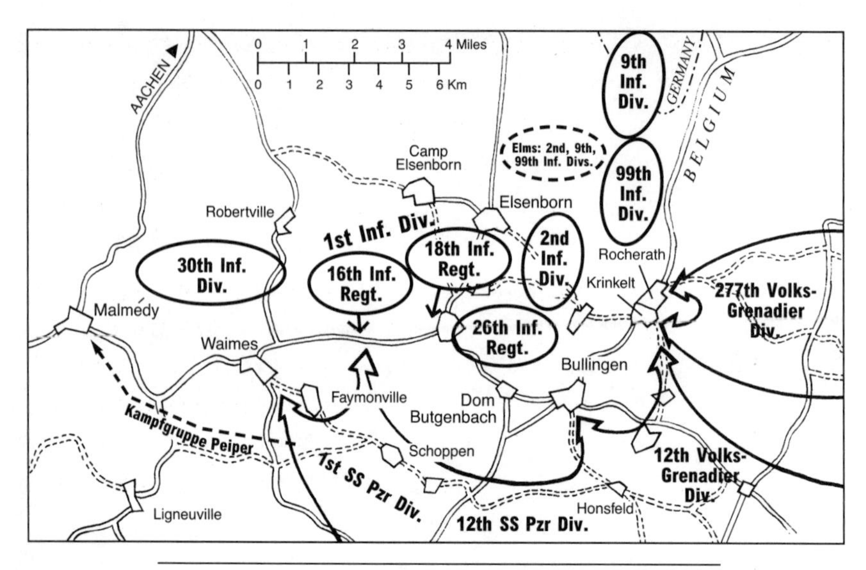

The Sixth Panzer Army attacks the northern shoulder of the "Bulge," 16–23 December 1944. (Positions approximate)

On at least one occasion, the bad weather actually worked to the advantage of the Yanks. On 19 January, while trying to take the town of Schoppen, less than three miles southwest of Dom Butgenbach, Lieutenant Colonel Charles Horner's 3rd Battalion, 16th Infantry, had been thrown back by determined German resistance and needed to come up with a better assault plan. According to the division's newspaper, "Col. Horner thought up some free-wheeling tactics, though there was a raging blizzard which had stopped all vehicular traffic, even couriers. Before daybreak, in the worst conditions that Americans ever fought under on this front, Col. Horner sent a company commanded by Captain Karl E. Wolf over a ridge and around the town to take it from the rear. It was a hazardous maneuver, storming an enemy-garrisoned town in pitch darkness. But the Americans found the entire enemy garrison sound asleep. Col. Horner's men are campaigning to rename Schoppen 'Horner's Corners.'"

About the same time that Horner and his men were taking Schoppen, another battalion, the 1st Battalion of the 26th Regiment, was also battling the elements and the enemy. The division's newspaper reported: "The battle of Learnard's Gulch is over, and American infantry, not supposed to be such great shakes at snow fighting, has added one for the books. Until two days ago,

Learnard's Gulch was an unnamed 2-mile-long defile. Germans were perched firmly atop a 5,000-foot-long rise commanding it, and a 1st Division battalion under Lt. Col. Henry G. Learnard was going nowhere trying to get through. Then Col. Learnard had an idea. He asked and received permission from the 30th Division on his right to swing around and pass through its lines to hit the Germans from the rear. . . . By night, through a marrow-chilling snowstorm, Col. Learnard's men made a forced march, going by truck part of the way, and trudged through drifts sometimes chest deep up the side of the rise. The Germans did not know what hit them. Those not killed were stunned, incredulous, and surrendered. Now the defile is down on 1st Division records as Learnard's Gulch."[22]

The 1st continued to push back the enemy and drive through a second line of *Westwall* fortifications and into the Buchholz Forest. On 28 January 1945, the British Broadcasting Corporation aired a tribute to the 1st Infantry Division by NBC war correspondent John McVane. He told his listeners:

> The American 1st Infantry Division has done it again. . . . We heard that in a situation where all seemed fluid and changing, two points held firm as a rock—the shoulders of the [German] drive and Bastogne. Without knowing, I was sure the 1st Division would be in one place or another—the roughest part of the battle. Well, Bastogne was the job of the 101st Airborne. But my guess was right; the 1st Division took over one shoulder of the drive, stopped the Germans cold, and turned what might have been a wide-open hole into a tight corridor that could be handled, cut into, chopped up when the time came. In this last exploit, the 1st has gone right on with the job it has been doing for more than two years—taking on the best German divisions, the cream of Hitler's army, and pinning their ears back. I think there's no doubt that the men with the Red One on their shoulders have broken the hearts of more German divisions than any other single unit in the American Army.
>
> This time it was a crack SS Panzer division. The 1st was resting when the action began. They went to work quickly and efficiently, as they always do. A forest area was cleared of German paratroops. Then the 1st hit the panzers. In two days, the 1st got forty-one tanks. A German infantry division came to the Panzer unit's support and together they attacked the 1st. The men of the 1st are used to having the Germans gang up on them. They just went on fighting their way ahead and retook Weismes.[23]

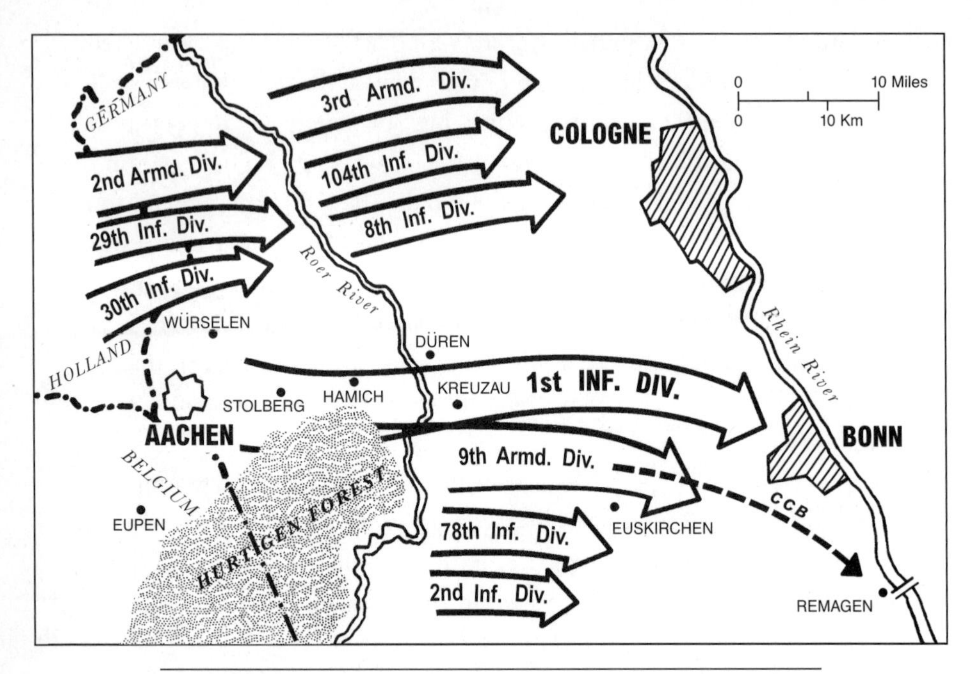

The 1st Division's drive from Aachen to Bonn. (Positions approximate)

January passed into February, and the 1st was given a few weeks off the line by the 99th Division, which had regained its equilibrium after the Battle of the Bulge.[24]

On 25 February 1945, the 1st relieved the 8th Infantry Division and was ordered to head for the university town of Bonn, on the southern edge of the heavily industrialized, densely populated Dortmund-Essen-Dusseldorf-Cologne metropolitan area. Once Bonn fell, the commanders decided the 1st would cross the Rhein River and drive for the Ruhr area. Harold Monica thought it sounded easier said than done. He remembered being told that, "The top-grade troops that might have opposed us now had been committed in the Battle of the Bulge, and we were advised only inferior troops of security and static level were between us and the Rhein. Maybe so, but somebody forgot to tell the Germans they were inferior troops."[25]

Besides an enemy that refused to give up, natural obstacles blocked the 1st's advance. Halfway between Aachen and Bonn flows the Roer River, which had risen nearly three feet in thirty-six hours, thanks to heavy rains and intentional flooding by the Germans who controlled the sluice gates upstream; the nor-

1st Infantry Division troops cross the Roer River on their drive into Germany, 25 February 1945. (Courtesy Colonel Robert R. McCormick Research Center of the 1st Infantry Division Museum at Cantigny)

mally sluggish current was clocked at twelve miles an hour, too swift for bridging. In the middle of February, the division started crossing the river in boats under cover of darkness. Meanwhile, to the north of the 16th's position, elements of the 8th Infantry Division were crossing the Roer near Düren. It was finally decided that throwing a bridge across the Roer in the 16th RCT's sector was too hazardous, and so the regiment was moved north and used the same bridge as the 8th Division.[26]

As with every kilometer in Germany, the road to Bonn—less than thirty miles away—was long, painful, and hampered by the delaying tactics of a retreating enemy. The 1st entered Bonn on the cold, overcast morning of 8 March 1945; unlike the bloody meat grinder at Aachen, the capture of Bonn was almost textbook in its execution. Yet, strange incidents took place. In one, a column of American soldiers marched side by side down a dark street in Bonn next to a column of German troops. "Lieutenant R. H. Smith, platoon leader of the First Platoon in column," wrote the 16th Regiment's historian, "quickly decided against a fire fight lest more enemy be aroused, so the German squad and the American flying column marched side by side down the streets of Bonn. It seems impossible that after a few yards, [the Germans] should not have realized they were marching with Americans. However, after a block or two, one of the Germans asked, 'What panzer division is this?'" The confusion was due to a Sherman tank armed with a new 76mm main gun that was at the head of the U.S. column; the gun had a muzzle brake on it that, in the predawn gloom, resembled the ones on German tanks. "At any rate, the two opposing forces marched side by side down Köln Strasse. At Rosental Strasse, the Americans turned left and the Germans continued down Köln Strasse."[27]

As the day became light, the city's defenders suddenly discovered Americans in their midst and the fight for Bonn erupted. The battle was sharp and, given the size of the city, exceptionally short; two days later Bonn was in 1st Division hands. American casualties had been blessedly light, especially when compared to Aachen.[28]

The division was given a few days to rest and recuperate. Harold Monica recalled that his company's CP was set up in an abandoned German house with, for a war-weary soldier, luxurious accommodations: soft beds, overstuffed chairs, a kitchen, even a wine cellar. "The best week of the war, for me, was NOW," Monica noted. Here the war seemed to stop; enemy resistance was nil, and the 1st enjoyed the opportunity to rest in place. And rest it did. "I established a very strenuous routine," he admitted. "Wake up call for breakfast, eat, then park in the chair next to the phone and smoke cigars, with a bottle of wine to keep me company. Once the bottle was empty . . . like magic, a full bottle would arrive. Then lunch and return to the above procedure. After dinner, cigars and wine until sleep time. Tomorrow, just like today. What a life. This is the way war should be. Would be nice to sit here and let someone, anyone else, finish the war. But someone upstream, the 9th Armored Division, got the Remagen Bridge intact and were across the Rhein." The good times in Bonn ended, and the Big Red One was soon back on the road to Remagen, where it crossed the

Troops from the 16th Infantry Regiment cautiously advance through Bonn past the body of a dead German defender, 8 March 1945. (Courtesy Colonel Robert R. McCormick Research Center of the 1st Infantry Division Museum at Cantigny)

river and headed into the heart of Germany, protecting the left flank of the 3rd Armored Division.[29]

Once the 1st was across the Rhein, resistance again stiffened. Tanks, artillery, and infantry seemed to be encountered at every bridge and crossroads, at every bend in the road, at every stand of trees, at every tiny hamlet along the way. Had Terry Allen still been at the head of the 1st, he would have undoubtedly been very proud, for the men were living up to the division's motto: "Nothing in hell will stop the 1st Infantry Division." Town after town fell to the Big Red One—Marenbach, Rimbach, Niederkumpel, Werkhausen, Kuchhausen, Koppingen—as the division headed for its next major objective, Hamm, northeast of Dortmund.

Medic Allen Towne reported that his aid station began to see a lot of casualties, including a number of African-American soldiers assigned to the 18th Regiment. As the American military would not be racially integrated until after the war, this was quite a noteworthy event. He wrote, "Up until a few weeks ago, there

Staff Sergeant George Peterson, K Company, 18th Infantry Regiment, recipient of the Medal of Honor, posthumously. (Courtesy Colonel Robert R. McCormick Research Center of the 1st Infantry Division Museum at Cantigny)

had been no black soldiers in the 18th Infantry and perhaps in the entire 1st Division. There was now one platoon in B Company of the 18th Infantry. They had been in a firefight and performed well. Several men had been wounded. Before this incident, I had not realized there were not any black soldiers in the regiment. I had never thought about it."[30]

A desperate struggle took place near Hamm on 30 March at the village of Eisern. Here, elements of the 18th Infantry Regiment were attacking a well-entrenched, battalion-size enemy force. During this action, two members of K Company performed actions so heroic on the same day that both were awarded the Medal of Honor. Staff Sergeant George Peterson of Brooklyn led a platoon in an attempt to outflank the German positions when he was severely wounded in the legs. Peterson continued to crawl forward and knocked out two machine-gun nests with grenades. Although wounded again, he went after another machine-gun nest and silenced it with a rifle grenade. Only then did he allow himself medical treatment. As his citation read, "He was being treated by the company aid man when he observed one of his outpost men seriously wounded by a mortar burst. He wrenched himself from the hands of the aid man and began to crawl forward to assist his comrade, whom he had almost reached when he was struck and fatally wounded by an enemy bullet."[31]

During this same attack, First Lieutenant Walter J. Will, although hurt and bleeding profusely, brought three wounded men to safety. He then led the rest of his platoon in an attack on two machine guns that had his men pinned down, and destroyed the first position. "He continued to crawl through intense enemy fire to within twenty feet of the second position," reads his citation, "where he leaped to his feet, made a lone, ferocious charge, and captured the gun and its nine-man crew." Will then noticed that another platoon was pinned down by two additional machine-gun nests. He led a squad and lobbed three grenades at the Germans, silencing one gun and killing its crew. "With tenacious aggressiveness, he ran toward the other gun and knocked it out with grenade fire. He then returned to his platoon and led it in a fierce, inspired charge, forcing the enemy to fall back in confusion. During this final charge, Lieutenant Will was mortally wounded."[32]

First Lieutenant Walter J. Will, K Company, 18th Infantry Regiment, recipient of the Medal of Honor, posthumously. (Courtesy Colonel Robert R. McCormick Research Center of the 1st Infantry Division Museum at Cantigny)

Once Hamm was captured, the 1st Division moved on, taking other hamlets, where resistance varied from none to fierce. They were just dots on the map, of no military, cultural, or political importance, but each one represented a place where more GIs would be wounded and where more American families would lose more sons.

On 31 March, elements of the division were rushed to Buren to participate in the closing of the "Ruhr Pocket," caught between the First and Ninth Armies; more than 300,000 of the enemy were taken prisoner in this pocket. In early April, the division crossed the Weser River, where strong enemy resistance was anticipated but failed to materialize.[33]

General Eisenhower noted in his memoirs, "During the First Army's advance, more than 15,000 of the enemy were cut off in the Harz Mountains. The defenders fought stubbornly and held out until April 21. The country was exceedingly difficult. The week-long fighting to reduce the pocket and to beat off other German troops who attempted to relieve the garrison was of a bitter character."[34]

The 1st Infantry Division could certainly relate to Eisenhower's words for, by 12 April, the 1st had reached the Harz Mountain region, and there was no sign that the Germans were on the verge of collapse. "The Harz Mountain campaign, while short, was a tough grind for the infantry," reads the 16th Regiment's history. "Some days the going was so hard over rough, mountainous terrain that 500 yards an hour was the limit for foot troops even when unopposed. In the heavily forested mountains, road blocks were particularly effective. Sometimes the enemy would have blown trees down across the road for hundreds of yards. The terrain offered perfect positions for hundreds of strongpoints. Had the enemy been well-organized instead of in a state of confusion, it might have taken weeks to dislodge him from these gloomy mountains."[35]

With his battalion temporarily detached from the 18th Regiment and attached to the 3rd Armored Division as part of Task Force Y, Harold Monica noted in his diary that the task force commander, a full colonel, called all the officers together and announced, "'Gentlemen, your objective is *Berlin!*' Then complete silence for a minute or so to let this sink in. What a feeling. . . . I started to tingle everywhere, the stomach tightened up; maybe not tears, but plenty moist eyes. After thirty months over here, the end of the war is now in sight."

The task force roared eastward, with troops riding atop Sherman tanks and in trucks through towns and villages where the retreating enemy now put up half-hearted resistance. However, Major General [Maurice] Rose, the 3rd Armored Division commander, was killed in an encounter with enemy tanks. In ten days, Monica's task force advanced 150–175 miles and was approaching Dessau on the Elbe River, some forty miles from the outskirts of Berlin.

"The Dessau area was home to three German officer-candidate schools; these guys were not about to give up without a fight," he said. "After a preparatory artillery barrage, two companies of tanks and infantry were deployed for the attack, one company in reserve. So 25–30 tanks and 400 infantry, all firing at the edge of town, crossed the 500 yards of open terrain. The tremendous machine-gun, rifle, and tank cannon fire kept the enemy down. . . . We were in the western edge of Dessau. As we proceeded to clean up the town, you never knew where a group of those young fanatics would show up. One of them got close enough to one of our tanks and knocked it out with a *panzerfaust*. . . . Still not far into town, Captain Jessie Miller, B Company commander, was shot and killed."

Monica noted that Miller had been with the division ever since its landing in North Africa and was engaged to marry an English girl. More tragedy was to follow. "My friend, Tommy Yarborough, who had been the B Company Executive Officer, took over command of B Company. Two days later the last enemy pocket had been squeezed up against the Elbe River and B Company, with a couple of tanks, was attacking them. Tommy was shot and killed during this action. In less than an hour, thirty-five or so Jerries surrendered and resistance in the 3rd Armored Division sector ceased. . . . Dessau was secure and we had been ordered not to cross the river.

"On occasion, the thought had occurred to me: who would be the last to die? Now we knew. . . . Tommy Yarborough was the last man from the 1st Battalion, 18th Infantry, to be killed in World War II. In fact, he may well have been killed by the last bullet fired at the Battalion. Why Tommy's luck ran out so late is anybody's guess. Dessau, Germany, to me was, and is, a terribly expensive piece of ground."[36]

Just as they did not get to Paris, the men of the 1st Infantry Division did not get to Berlin. The division was detached from the First Army and attached to Patton's Third Army, which was poised to enter Czechoslovakia. The Big Red One now encountered little resistance as it chased remnants of German units into Czechoslovakia. The "privilege" of taking the capital of the Third Reich was given to the Russians, which was probably just as well. Of all the World War II belligerents, it was the Soviet Union that had suffered the most: over 20 million dead.

The worst was saved for last. The battle for Berlin turned into a building by building, block by block meat grinder in which no quarter was asked and none given. On 30 April, as Russian troops closed in on his chancellery in Berlin, Adolf Hitler died by his own hand. Still, the fighting, sporadic though it was, continued. It is estimated that 300,000 Russians perished or were wounded in the battle of Berlin that lasted from 16 April to 2 May.[37] Had the 1st been required to assist in the taking of the sprawling city, the division's casualty lists would have, no doubt, reached catastrophic proportions.

American and Russian forces linked up at Torgau on the Elbe on 25 April. Two days later, the 16th Infantry Regiment made a long, deep plunge into enemy territory, bypassing recently captured Leipzig, and then thrusting toward Selb, on the German-Czechoslovak border. On 7 May, the 16th Regiment was in Kynsperk; the 18th was in Sangerberg and Mnichov; and the 26th was in Shönbach when the division received orders: "All troops halt in place and maintain defensive positions. Effective at once. Details to follow."[38]

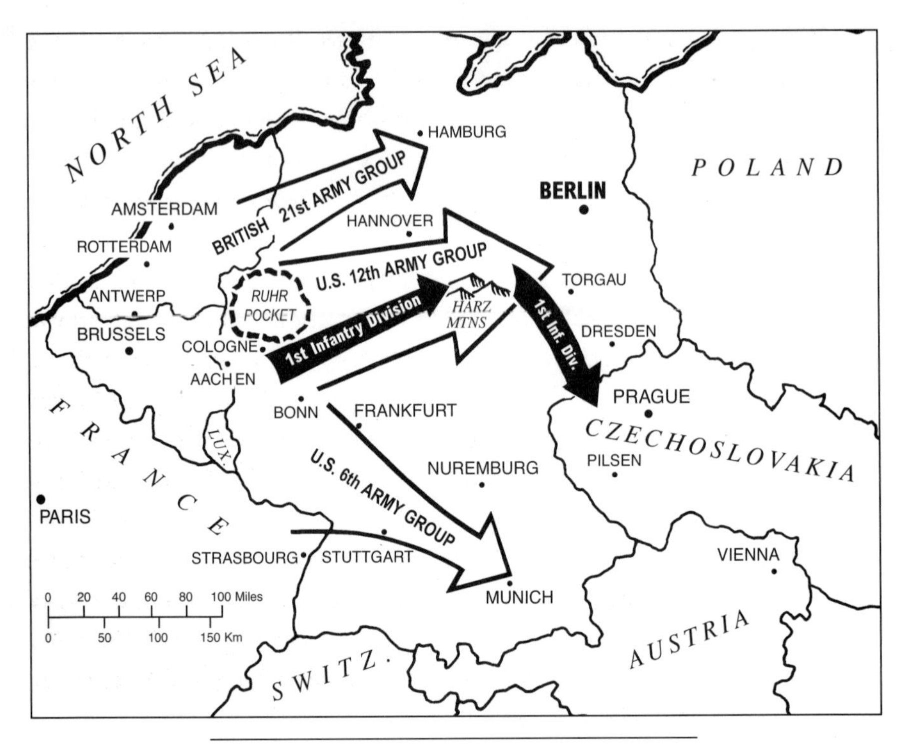

The final thrust into Germany by the Americans and British, April–May 1945. (Positions approximate)

The next day, the orders read: "Cease firing." A terse, bland message, conveying none of the pent-up emotion of a joyful, war-weary world, was broadcast from Eisenhower's headquarters: "The mission of this Allied force was fulfilled at 0241 local time, May 7, 1945."[39]

Hitler was dead, the Third Reich was defunct, and the war in Europe was, at long last, well and truly over. A very strange sound came over Europe: the sound of silence. It was as if the war switch had suddenly been turned to "Off." There was no more rattle of machine guns; no more *pop-pop-pop* of small arms; no more whistle of falling bombs; no more scream of incoming artillery and mortar shells; no more skull-splitting explosions. It was a deep and profound silence, punctuated only by church bells in the distance, tolling that peace, after nearly five years of continuous bloodshed, had finally returned to the Continent.

Captain Fred Hall, S–3 of the 2nd Battalion, 16th Regiment, noted in his diary on 9 May 1945: "Today is a very fine day in Franzenbad, Czechoslovakia.

Yesterday was announced as V-E Day, so they tell me. There has been little or no manifestation of victory hereabouts. In the first place, people are too busy and, in the second place, with everything as it is, it seems a little silly. After all that has taken place, I know the travesty of war is that it solves nothing."[40]

A Czech-born American warrant officer in the 1st Quartermaster Battalion, Paul Bystrak, took advantage of the cessation of hostilities to travel to his birthplace, the village of Sobotiste, which was in Soviet-controlled territory. After spending several days drinking and celebrating with his relatives in the town, Bystrak and his driver loaded their command car with enough booze to float a battleship. On the way back to American lines, Bystrak was stopped by Red Army troops in Prague; never having seen an American before, they thought Bystrak and the driver were Czech soldiers and were giving them a hard time. Finally convincing the Soviet troops that they were Americans, the Reds "became like children. They couldn't give me enough souvenirs. One of them gave me a cigarette lighter, and I don't even smoke. He said, 'You know how many German officers I had to kill before I found one who had a cigarette lighter?' So I took it, along with the souvenir money and that type of thing, and we drank all the slivovitz I had brought from the village."[41]

With the war over, accolades began to pour in for the men of the "Fighting First." One such came from Hal Boyle, a Pulitzer Prize–winning war correspondent, who noted in a broadcast on 14 May 1945, "All I can remember with any feeling of pride in the whole sorry business of war is the courage and fortitude of the men who fought it. I don't think the nation will ever forget the 1st, the 2nd, the 3rd Armored Divisions, not the 1st, the 2nd, 3rd, 5th, the 9th, 34th, 36th, and 45th Infantry Divisions, nor the 82nd and 101st Airborne Divisions. There is a real roll call of honor from Casablanca to Bastogne to Prague. But of them all, I think the best symbol of the American Army overseas is the Fighting First Infantry Division. They have fought their way more miles against more Germans than any other unit in the American Army. They left their dead by the hundreds in Tunisia, Sicily, France, Belgium, and Germany. And when the final surrender came, they were still killing Nazis. Their battle achievements dwarf their losses. But you can't forget these soldiers who died. We can reconvert our war factories for peace—that will be easy. But how can we ever reward these lost, magnificent men?"[42]

Forty-nine years later, Al Alvarez visits the 1st Infantry Division memorial at Omaha Beach, 6 June 1993. (Courtesy Al Alvarez)

When one stands today at the simple obelisk that rises above the silent, hallowed dunes of Omaha Beach—with its listing of the names of the Normandy dead of the 1st Infantry Division—it is impossible not to feel humbled by what these brave and frightened young men accomplished for the benefit of future generations.

The 1st Infantry Division in World War II compiled a combat record equaled or surpassed by very few of the fifty-two divisions that fought in Europe and the Mediterranean Theaters. It had endured 443 days in combat, marched over 2,300 miles (not counting sea voyages), and participated in some of the bloodiest campaigns of the war: North Africa, Sicily, Normandy, Aachen, the Hürtgen Forest, the Battle of the Bulge. The battle streamers on the division flag were not won cheaply; 4,280 men of the Big Red One died along the road to victory, and 15,208 were wounded. Only four other American Army divisions suffered more total casualties.[43]

Viewed from the perspective of six decades later, it is still impossible not to be awed by the achievements of the men of the 1st Infantry Division; by their self-sacrifice; by their loyalty; by their devotion to duty, honor, country. It is impossible to view their accomplishments as anything less than *heroic* in the truest sense of the word. It is impossible not to realize that, without the men of the 1st Infantry Division—from the generals and colonels and captains to the sergeants and corporals and privates—the invasion of the continent of Europe, and the war itself, might have turned out quite differently.

Although now bent with age, the veterans of the 1st Infantry Division still hold their heads proudly. Surprisingly few are willing to be labeled a "hero." "The real heroes are the guys who didn't make it back," seems to be the consensus. They were put to the test in a trial by fire that few Americans will ever know, and they passed the test. Very few of them came through whole. Almost everyone who returned home alive bore a scar—if not physically, then emotionally. Spending days, weeks, months, and years under fire takes its toll on one's nerves. Even six decades later, many of the veterans will admit to still having nightmares and other manifestations of psychological problems related to their traumatic combat experiences.

Many of those who survived the war often look back—and ahead—with sober reflection. James Watts, a lieutenant with the 81st Chemical Mortar Battalion attached to the 1st Division at Normandy, cautioned, "There must not be another Normandy. War is frightful enough. The destructiveness of the atomic bomb has changed the nature of warfare. Nuclear warfare is unthinkable; it must not happen. We could not have concentrated the men and ships of the invasion in the nuclear age. Mankind must find a way to prevent wars. War used to feed on the youth of the nations. Now it threatens our very existence."[44]

Private First Class William M. Lee, from Chicago, who served with D Company, 26th Infantry Regiment, from Kasserine to war's end, gave his thoughts in 1994: "We have still not attained the goal we seek—a perfect peace with our neighboring countries and all nations of the world. Most likely it will never come about. But that isn't to say we shouldn't seek it or try to make it so. We live in the greatest nation of all time. We are a good people, sharing our abundance even with the nations we defeated, and freed our Allies who were shackled by Hitler's legions. For fifty years now, we have kept our European cousins from killing each other, and that's never happened before. On the very day we defeated [the Germans], we took up the sword and beat it into a plowshare so that our enemy could clothe, feed, and provide for its people. There is no record elsewhere that any other conquering nation dealt so fairly with its enemy. We live in a precarious time, but with a well-equipped armed force, we will win the inevitable peace."[45]

This book began with Private First Class Louis Newman sitting atop a half-submerged truck off Omaha Beach, with the panorama of the invasion before him, so it is only fitting to give him the last word: "From my perch, I was completely detached from what I was seeing. I had come to the conclusion that, as an infantryman in a prolonged war, I could not survive. I had set my mind on the fact that I would be killed. Paradoxically, my fear and anxiety on top of the truck on June 6th was at a low ebb—I am going to get killed anyway, so why worry? From that point on, in battle after battle, I was able to carry on with a clear mind. I was fortified by the close comradeship taught to me by the peacetime army at Fort Wadsworth, New York, and later, on Organization Day of the 18th Infantry, on May 3, 1941. I served with three units within the regiment. First there was K company, who taught me that the *esprit de corps* meant not just *thinking* your unit was the best, but *being* the best. I also take great pride in having been part of the gallant men of A Company. My war was fought as a member of Cannon Company—of which I was a charter member—organized April 1942.

"Undoubtedly the war would have been won without the 1st Infantry Division, but victory would have probably taken longer and American casualties would have been much greater. I think the 1st set the standard by which the other divisions were measured. All we had to do was to look at the Big Red One patches on our sleeves. It said we were 'Number One,' so we had to live up to that designation."[46]

Epilogue

Following the outbreak of peace, the Big Red One survivors of the war began to put their lives back together, forge new careers, resume old ones, or continue to serve their country in uniform.

A few months after being relieved of command of the 1st Infantry Division, **Terry de la Mesa Allen** was put in charge of a new infantry division, the 104th "Timberwolf" Division, which he led in 195 days of combat, including the battle for Aachen, from the autumn of 1944 until Germany surrendered in May 1945. Greatly loved by the men under his command, Allen also received much praise from above. British General Sir Harold Alexander called him "the finest division commander I have seen in two world wars." Allen retired at war's end at age fifty-seven and returned home to El Paso, Texas, where he became an insurance man. Tragically, his son, Lieutenant Colonel Terry Allen Jr., a battalion commander with the Big Red One in Vietnam, was killed in action at Ong Thanh in October 1967—an emotional blow from which the elder Allen never recovered; he died in 1969 at age eighty-one, following a car accident.

Theodore Roosevelt Jr., who was the 1st Infantry Division's assistant division commander from 1942 until he and General Allen were relieved in August 1943, became the assistant division commander with the 4th Infantry Division during its D-Day landings at Utah Beach, and was the first American general to go ashore on 6 June 1944. A month later, the bandy-legged little general was picked by Bradley to take command of the 90th Infantry Division in Normandy. On the morning of 14 July 1944, an aide went to inform Roosevelt of his new appointment but discovered that the fifty-seven-year-old general had died of a heart attack in his sleep. He was posthumously awarded the Medal of Honor.

After the war, **Clarence R. Huebner** became the deputy commander in chief and chief of staff of EUCOM—the Army's European Command, which helped contain the growing Communist threat while providing a stable administrative power in shattered West Germany. In November 1947, he also became commanding general of USAREUR—U.S. Army, Europe. In 1949, he was the commander in chief of EUCOM and the U.S. Military Governor in Germany. He retired in 1950 and died in 1972.

Clift Andrus, who took command of the Big Red One in December 1944 when General Huebner was promoted to command of V Corps, retired in 1952. He died in September 1968.

Willard G. Wyman, after his steadying performance on Omaha Beach, was given command of the 71st Infantry Division in November 1944, which he led in action across southeastern Germany. His post-war career was distinguished by his command of IX Corps during the Korean War; he was later commander in chief of NATO Land Forces; commander in chief of Sixth Army in southeast Europe; and commander of the U.S. Continental Army Command (CONARC), during which time he was instrumental in advancing the concept of armed helicopters and the development of the M-16 rifle. He retired from the Army in 1958 and died in 1969.

George A. Taylor, who, as commander of the 16th Infantry Regiment, deserved great credit for his role in organizing the frightened, immobile troops on Omaha Beach into a cohesive fighting force, became a brigadier general and assistant division commander of the 1st Infantry Division in October 1944. He retired in 1946 with a disability and died in 1969.

Omar N. Bradley became a General of the Army, only the fifth officer to wear five stars. After the war, he served as Army Chief of Staff and was the first chairman of the Joint Chiefs of Staff. After retiring from the Army in 1953, he served as head of the Bulova Watch Company. On 8 April 1981, just minutes after receiving an award in New York, he collapsed and died. He was eighty-eight years old. He is buried at Arlington National Cemetery.

George S. Patton Jr., who felt that the only honorable way for him to die was by the last bullet fired in the last battle of the war, was denied that death. Instead, he died on 21 December 1945 from complications following an accident in which his staff car smashed into an Army truck near Mannheim, Germany, on 9 December. He is buried at the American Military Cemetery at Hamm, Luxembourg.

Dwight D. Eisenhower was elected thirty-fourth president of the United States (1953–1961). He previously had been awarded a fifth star and served as Army Chief of Staff. He retired from active duty in 1948 and became president of Columbia University. In 1950, he left academia and became head of NATO, the North Atlantic Treaty Organization. Initially reluctant to be drafted by the Republicans as their presidential candidate, Ike gave in to the party's demands and handily defeated

Adlai Stevenson in the election. He served two terms, during which time he presided over the end of the Korean War; the race for outer space between the United States and the Soviet Union; an intensification of the Cold War; and the racial integration of public schools. He died in 1969 at age seventy-nine and was buried in his home town of Abilene, Kansas.

Al Alvarez, the communications specialist in the 7th Artillery Battalion, reenlisted in the Army; earned a commission; saw combat with the 82nd Airborne Division during the Korean War; spent a year under fire in Vietnam; engaged in operations in Bolivia and the Dominican Republic; and retired as a lieutenant colonel after thirty-two years in uniform. After his military career was over, he served as North Carolina state regional director of human resources and Cumberland County CETA master planner and later managed local department stores. As of 2003, he lived in Fayetteville, North Carolina, with his wife, Florence; they had four children and eight grandchildren.

Ted Aufort served with Headquarters, 1st Battalion 16th Infantry, in North Africa and Sicily, where he suffered a concussion injury. He earned the Silver Star and the Bronze Star with Oak Leaf Cluster and deserved (but didn't receive) the Purple Heart. After the war, he was called up to serve in the Korean Conflict. In 2003, he was living in El Cajon, California.

Medal of Honor recipient **Carlton Barrett**, member of Headquarters Company, 18th Infantry, fell on hard times twenty years after the war. His marriage broke up and a leg was amputated at the Veterans' Administration Hospital in Los Angeles. He moved to the Veterans' Home in Yountville, California, was reunited with his wife, and died in 1986. His Medal of Honor was donated by his family to the 1st Infantry Division Museum in Wheaton, Illinois.

William D. Behlmer, who served with the 16th Infantry's Anti-Tank Company from North Africa to Normandy, was wounded on D-Day and lost a leg. After recovering, he attended Georgia Tech and became an industrial engineer. In 2003, he resided in Marietta, Georgia.

The D-Day experiences of **John Bistrica**, C Company, 16th Infantry, have appeared in several books and television documentaries, and he has presented numerous speeches on World War II to various schools and groups in Ohio. Before the war, he built parts for the Army's Bailey bridges in a war plant; afterward, he became a carpenter and cabinet maker. As of 2003, he had been married for fifty-five years to Anne Marie and they had four children and four grandchildren. He was named a Distinguished Member of the Regiment by the Secretary of the Army in 1997. He lived in Youngstown, Ohio, and still enjoyed woodworking and maintaining friendships with his Army buddies and the families he met while stationed in England.

An accounting clerk before being drafted in 1941, **Everett Booth**, who commanded M Company, 16th Infantry, and was wounded in the arm coming ashore on D-Day, spent thirty-four years in the Army, and retired as a colonel. He was awarded the Distinguished Service Cross, Silver Star, Bronze Star, and Purple Heart. After his military service, he returned to the accounting field in Highland, Indiana.

Dan Curatola earned the Bronze Star with two Oak Leaf Clusters during his service with 3rd Battalion, 16th Infantry, In Normandy, he was seriously wounded by a mine. After the war, he used the G.I. Bill to obtain a college education, then retired to Bethlehem, Pennsylvania.

After surviving the Japanese attack on Pearl Harbor, and the battles of North Africa and Sicily, **William T. Dillon**, a lieutenant with A Company, 16th Infantry, was captured in France and escaped. After being discharged from a hospital in England, he joined the 101st Airborne Division but was injured in a practice jump and spent twenty-three months in Army hospitals. After the war, he became a pharmacist and worked for twenty-two years at the VA Hospitals in Memphis, Fayetteville (North Carolina), Palo Alto, and San Diego. He and his wife Frankye were married for twenty-nine years and had four children and seven grandchildren. He died in 1994.

Theodore L. Dobol, the Polish-born sergeant with K Company, 26th Infantry, badly wounded in the hedgerows, was honored with four Silver Stars and five Purple Hearts. He rose in rank to become the Sergeant Major of the 26th Regiment, then Command Sergeant Major of the 1st Infantry Division. He also instructed at West Point and spent time in Vietnam. In all, he served nearly thirty-two years in the Army. He passed away in 1996.

William B. Gara, commander of the 1st Engineer Combat Battalion, earned a Bronze Star for valor, two Silver Stars, and two Purple Hearts. After retiring from the Army, he was a plant engineering operations manager for several companies. He passed away in 2001 at the age of eighty-four.

Fred W. Hall Jr., operations officer of the 2nd Battalion, 16th Infantry, returned to New Hampshire; obtained his law degree from the University of Michigan; became an attorney with a Rochester, New Hampshire, law firm; was recalled to active duty during the Korean War; stayed in the Army Reserve; and retired as a lieutenant colonel in 1966. He and his wife, Jane, had three children, and were living in Rochester in 2003, where Hall still practiced law with the firm of which he was a partner.

After being evacuated for wounds received on Fox Green beach, **Steve Kellman**, L Company, 16th Infantry, recovered and married his sweetheart in August 1945; they were married for fifty-six years until her death in 2001, and had two sons and two grandchildren. A student at New York University before the war, he went into sales after the war, becoming vice-president of marketing and part owner of a shoe-manufacturing company in Wisconsin. In 2003 he was dividing his time between Wausau, Wisconsin, and Winter Haven, Florida, enjoying golf and travel and being active in the 16th Regiment Association. In 1999, he was named a Distinguished Member of the Regiment.

Ray Klawiter, D Company, 18th Infantry, lived in Philadelphia before the war, where he worked for Sears, Roebuck. After the war, he returned to Sears as a buyer, then worked for Edwards Shoes as a sales manager for twenty years. He and his wife Mae had five children and ten grandchildren. A widower, he moved to Ocean City, New Jersey. In 2003, he was honored by being named a Distinguished Member of the Regiment.

Using the example of his grandfather who had served in the Civil War, **William Lee**, D Company, 26th Infantry, volunteered for the Army and saw action in North Africa, Sicily (where he contracted malaria), France, Belgium, and Germany. After the war, he worked for the Postal Service in Mount Vernon, Illinois, then retired to Chicago.

Thomas R. McCann, a sergeant with 18th Infantry headquarters, went through North Africa, Sicily, Normandy, and the European campaign without a scratch. After the war, he earned his master's degree and taught school in Louisiana for forty years before retiring in 1986. He maintained contact with his buddies after the war and, in 1994 returned to England and Normandy for the fiftieth anniversary celebrations of the invasion. Although he traveled extensively, he maintained a fondness for Puddletown, England, and its people. "There is no place like England," he said, "and my favorite place is Puddletown."

Harold P. Monica, a lieutenant with D Company, 18th Infantry, and eventual company commander, returned to New Hampshire and built a career as a manufacturers' representative. He then moved to Concord, New Hampshire, and retired.

Robert E. Murphy, commanding officer of H Company, 18th Infantry, had twenty-eight years of service in the U.S. Army, including all of the 1st Division's campaigns—from North Africa to the end of the war. In 1955, he became senior American adviser to the commandant of the Vietnam Officers Candidate School. After staff positions in the United States and West Germany, he returned to Vietnam in 1966 and served as an inspector general. Following his retirement from the Army in 1968, Colonel Murphy was appointed clerk of the Superior Court of Hillsborough County, New Hampshire. He later was elected to nine two-year terms in the state legislature. He and his late wife, Greta, had three children; one son joined the Special Forces. As of 2003, he was living in Manchester, New Hampshire.

Louis Newman, Anti-Tank Company, 18th Infantry, who sat atop a truck and watched the invasion unfold before him, received a medical discharge after being wounded in combat. He married Kitty in 1947 and they were married for forty-nine years, until her death in 1996. Their son became a professor at the University of Guelph in Canada. Newman retired in 1973 from the General Accounting Office at the Brooklyn Post Office and moved to Tamarac, Florida.

A bellhop and cocktail waiter before enlisting in 1940, **Joseph Nichols**, I&R Platoon member in the 16th Infantry, won the Bronze Star and, after the war, entered the investment field, living in New York.

Nelson Park, a first lieutenant with C Company, 18th Regiment, had been an engineering student at the University of Idaho before the war, returned to school and received his engineering degree, then worked as an engineer in California, living in Whittier.

Ralph Puhalovich, an anti-tank gunner with the 26th Regiment, earned two Purple Hearts and two Bronze Stars. He returned to California to pursue his degree and a career in engineering with several firms in the Oakland-San Leandro area. He married his wife, Louise, in 1952 and they had two children and two grandchildren. They moved to Twain Harte, California.

Harley Reynolds, a sergeant in B Company, 16th Infantry, took advantage of the educational opportunities offered by the G.I. Bill of Rights following his discharge. As a result, he studied engineering and worked as a tool design engineer in St. Petersburg, Florida, for forty-seven years before retiring in 1996. Twice a widower, he moved to St. Petersburg with his third wife, Dorothy.

Kimball R. Richmond, the commanding officer of I Company, 16th Infantry, remained in the Army, retiring in 1961. One of the most highly decorated 1st Division soldiers, he was awarded the Distinguished Service Cross, Silver Star with two Oak Leaf Clusters, Bronze Star with two Oak Leaf Clusters, and Purple Heart with two Oak Leaf Clusters. His brother, Deane, an Army lieutenant, was killed in action near Metz, France, in November 1944. After retiring from active duty, he entered civilian life and became a self-employed insurance agent in Mariposa, California. He died in 1976 at age fifty-nine, but because of his exploits in helping organize the 3rd Battalion's drive off Omaha Beach, he has been immortalized; a building at Fort Riley, Kansas, home of the 1st Infantry Division, was named Richmond Hall in his honor. Furthermore, in 1991 he was inducted into the Fort Benning, Georgia, Officer Candidate School's Hall of Fame.

Edward Sackley, C Company, 16th Infantry, made it through the war without being wounded and earned the Bronze Star in March 1944. After the war, he graduated from the University of Wisconsin, raised six children, and moved to Skokie, Illinois.

Before entering the service, **Eddie Steeg**, the diminutive, fun-loving mortarman with D Company, 18th Infantry, grew up in Camden, New Jersey. After the war, he attended Temple University on the G.I. Bill, making a career as a heating/ventilation/air conditioning specialist in the Camden area. He enjoyed skiing, playing tenor sax in several small combos, marching in the Philadelphia Mummer's Parades and, late in life, arranging reunions with his Army buddies. He died in 1999, proud of the fact that his son, Harold, daughter Chyrl, a grandson, and a granddaughter all also served in the armed forces. Unfortunately, he was unable to finish his delightful memoirs.

Allen N. Towne, the combat medic, returned to school following the war and earned a degree in chemical engineering; received a master's in industrial administration; worked for General Electric for nineteen years; then served as the director of United Technologies' Insulation Plant. He was awarded three U.S. patents. During his forty-seven-year marriage, he and his wife Camelia had three children and eight grandchildren. In 2000, he published his memoirs in *Doctor Danger Forward*, which is being used by the Joint Armed Forces Medical School in Bethesda, Maryland. He retired to Midlothian, Virginia.

Jess E. Weiss suffered from post-traumatic shock after the war. Badly wounded at Aachen, he recovered to become an insurance agent in New York, but was beset by physical and mental problems caused by combat. His many brushes with death brought out an intense interest in near-death experiences, and he wrote four books on the subject which, besides helping others, helped him gain a new perspective on life and spirituality. He and his wife, Joyce, had four children and three grandchildren. He called Jericho, New York, home.

Karl E. Wolf, a lieutenant with HQ Company, 3rd Battalion, 16th Regiment, later commanded I Company as well as the 3rd Battalion; spent twenty years in the Army; retired as a lieutenant colonel; became an attorney; and worked as a legal counsel for Philco Corporation and, later, at Ford Aerospace for twenty-five years. His military awards include the Silver Star, Bronze Star, Purple Heart, and Belgian Croix de Guerre. In 2003, he and his wife, Lola, had been married for fifty-four years and had three children and three grandchildren. The Wolfs lived in Corona del Mar, California.

Walter D. Ehlers, L Company, 18th Infantry, who earned the Medal of Honor in the hedgerows of France, spent thirty-four years after the war working for the Veterans' Administration in California as a benefits counselor, retiring in 1980. He then worked for the Disabled Americans Veterans for eight years. A modest man, most of the people with whom he came in contact did not even know of his wartime achievements. In 1964, on the twentieth anniversary of the invasion, he was invited by President Lyndon Johnson to attend a special gathering at the White House; he flew to Washington, D.C., with General Omar Bradley.

The weight of the Medal is heavy with responsibility. "It's kept me honest my whole life," he said. "When you have a distinction like that, you don't want to dishonor it. We've had some Medal recipients who have ruined their lives, drank too much. But I have too much respect for it to do anything that would dishonor it."

He often thought of his late brother, Roland, who died on D-Day. "He was the bravest man I ever knew. My hero. Not a day goes by that I don't think about him."

The principal speaker at the fiftieth anniversary commemorations in Normandy, he launched a new career as a public speaker at schools, civic organizations, and veterans' groups in Southern California and around the world. His message to schoolchildren is simple: get an education. "When you have a job to do, whatever it is, you need as much training as possible to accomplish it successfully—whether it's fighting a war, becoming a professional athlete, movie star, or schoolteacher." (*Los Angeles Daily News,* 29 March 2003)

He and Dorothy, his wife of forty-eight years, had three children and eleven grandchildren; one son became an Army major in the Kansas National Guard and served in Bosnia with the peacekeeping forces. In 2003, the Ehlers were living in Buena Park, California.

AUTHOR'S POSTSCRIPT

Although I was an officer with the U.S. Army in Germany in the mid–1960s, I did not visit Normandy until 6 June, 1994—the fiftieth anniversary of the invasion. I was struck by the fact that, in many parts of Europe, most traces of the war had been irrevocably erased, leaving the visitor to wonder if the war had ever passed through this town, or if great armies had ever marched across this plain, or if whole battalions were slaughtered for a seemingly insignificant piece of real estate.

In Normandy, there is no worry that the struggle and the sacrifices will be forgotten any time soon. All along the sixty-mile stretch of coastline—from Utah Beach at La Madeleine to Sword Beach at La Brêche de Hermanville—artifacts and reminders of the great struggle remain in great profusion. The British and Canadian beaches are replete with mementos of British and Canadian resolve and courage. Behind the beachheads, where brave, glider-borne or airborne infantrymen came down to earth, there are pieces of hallowed ground—Ste.-Mère-Eglise, Ste. Marie Dumont, Pegasus Bridge over the Orne Canal, and the Merville Battery, to name but four. At Arromanches, numerous hulks that once formed part of the artificial "Mulberry" harbor still punctuate the seascape, and everywhere—in Caen, Bayeux, Arromanches, and in virtually every little Norman town and village—there are markers and museums dedicated to the monumental battle. Studded along the dunes of Utah Beach are the silent remains of scores of German bunkers, pillboxes, and casemates, along with rusting tanks, half-tracks, and artillery pieces. At the spectacular site of Point du Hoc, atop a sheer cliff climbed by American Rangers, huge concrete bunkers have been upturned as though by a giant's careless hand and grassed-over shell holes still deeply dent the landscape.

But it is the stark serenity of Omaha Beach that is most compelling. Standing on the round stones of the shingle at the water's edge and gazing up at the heights, it is not difficult to visualize the overwhelming chaos of 6 June 1944, to realize that, no matter where one steps, one is standing on sacred ground where young American soldiers were wounded or killed. It is not hard to imagine the awful sounds that filled the air that day—the concussion of shells, the scream of shrapnel, the snapping of bullets, the pitiful cries of the wounded, the shouted commands of officers and NCOs, the prayers of chaplains over the bodies of the fallen.

Today, a visitor need not brave bullet and shell and minefield to make the journey from the beach to the heights; even the few ominous bunkers that remain pose no threat. A paved pathway that passes by the 1st Division memorial obelisk erected atop Resistance Nest 62 provides easy access. At the top of the bluff, one can look down upon the vast stretch of coastline and see with the mind's eye the countless individual acts of courage that once took place there.

In the vast U.S. cemetery above Omaha Beach, where 9,386 Americans were interred—men who purchased victory and the peace that followed with their lives—one is moved by the enormity of the human cost of war. Here, rank after precisely aligned rank of marble gravestones, giving the name and unit of the deceased who rest for all time "in honored glory," recall the boys who gave everything in a war none of them wanted, but in which duty and loyalty compelled them to take part. Red-headed 1st Lieutenant Jimmie Monteith is buried here, as is the former assistant commanding general of the 1st Infantry Division, Teddy Roosevelt Jr.—at rest beside his brother, Quentin, an aviator who perished in World War I and was later reburied here.

One also cannot help but be moved by the sight of elderly men wandering through the stunted forest of white marble headstones, searching for the final resting place of buddies who died on 6 June or in the days and weeks that followed. Sometimes, the elderly men are seen to kneel before a headstone, touch the engraved name, and whisper a silent greeting or prayer. They rise, wipe away a tear, come to attention, and salute, their pilgrimage to Normandy concluded.

A short distance from the cemetery is the edge of the bluff up which the men of the 1st Infantry Division climbed. When you stand on the edge, if the wind through the trees is just right, you can hear the faint, plaintive sound of a lone bugle playing "Taps." You look out over the beachhead and at the English Channel stretching to the horizon, and you can see the ghosts of ships that once spread themselves as far as the eye can see. You can see those young, scared boys of the 1st Infantry Division struggling in the surf down below, trying to break through the curtain of lead and barbed wire, failing, then trying again. You see them now, coming up the hill, fire in their eyes at the impertinence of an enemy who had dared to get in their way, who had the temerity to shoot at them, who stood between them and victory—and going home. You are filled with awe at what they accomplished—not only here, but for a year before and another year after.

You turn back for one last look at the profusion of white marble headstones. The cemetery at Omaha Beach is a place of great solemnity and sadness—and of great pride—pride in a generation that overcame unbelievable obstacles, demonstrated courage and stamina far beyond that asked of ordinary individuals, and sacrificed itself for higher ideals: the overthrow of tyranny and the re-establishment of peace and freedom in Europe.

This pride is encapsulated in a simple, twelve-word inscription within the chapel at the American cemetery:

Think not only upon their passing.
Remember the glory of their spirit.

Appendix

1st Infantry Division Medal of Honor Recipients (WWII)

(in chronological order)

(P) denotes posthumous award

INDIVIDUAL	DATE OF ACTION	LOCATION
(P) Reese, James W.	5 August 1943	Near Troina, Sicily
(P) Monteith, Jimmie W., Jr.	6 June 1944	Omaha Beach, France
(P) Pinder, John J., Jr.	6 June 1944	Omaha Beach, France
Barrett, Carleton W.	6 June 1944	Omaha Beach, France
(P) DeFranzo, Arthur F.	10 June 1944	Vaubadon, France
Ehlers, Walter D.	10 June 1944	Goville, France
Merli, Gino J.	4–5 September 1944	Sars la Bruyere, Belgium
Schaefer, Joseph E.	24 September 1944	Stolberg, Germany
Brown, Bobbie E.	8 October 1944	Aachen, Germany
Thompson, Max	18 October 1944	Haaren, Germany
Lindsey, Jake W.	16 November 1944	Hamich, Germany
(P) McGraw, Francis X.	19 November 1944	Schevenhutte, Germany
(P) Henry, Robert T.	3 December 1944	Luchem, Germany
(P) Warner, Henry F.	20–21 December 1944	Dom Butgenbach, Germany
(P) Peterson, George	30 March 1945	Eisern, Germany
(P) Will, Walter J.	30 March 1945	Eisern, Germany

Notes

Chapter One

1. Louis Newman interview by author, February 24, 2000.

2. Gordon A. Harrison, *U.S. Army in World War II: The European Theater, Cross-Channel Attack* (Washington, DC: GPO, 1951), pp. 129–130.

3. Tony Hall, ed., *D-Day: Operation Overlord—From Its Planning to the Liberation of Paris* (London: Salamander, 1993), p. 11.

4. William M. Hammond, *Normandy* (Washington, DC: Center for Military History, 1994), p. 3.

5. Harrison, p. 5.

6. Harrison, p. 8.

7. Samuel Eliot Morison, *The Invasion of France and Germany, 1944–1945,* Volume II of *History of United States Naval Operations in World War II* (Boston: Little, Brown, 1959), pp. 4–5.

8. Martin Gilbert, *The Second World War: A Complete History* (New York: Henry Holt, 1989), pp. 353–354; and Hall, pp. 16–19.

9. John W. Baumgartner, *16th Infantry Regiment* (Privately published. Bamberg, Germany: 1945), pp. 1–6; John F. Votaw and Steven Weingartner, eds., *Blue Spaders: The 26th Infantry Regiment, 1917–1967* (Wheaton, IL: Cantigny First Division Foundation, 1996), pp. 5–45; and Shelby L. Stanton, *World War II Order of Battle* (New York: Galahad Books, 1984), p. 205.

10. Hans Habe, "The American Army Is Different," in Karl Detzer, ed., *The Army Reader* (New York: Bobbs-Merrill, 1943), pp. 41–47.

11. Henry Rowland memoir, USAMHI.

12. George J. Koch, USAMHI questionnaire.

13. Cornelius Ryan, *The Longest Day* (New York: Popular Library, 1959), pp. 1,204–1,209.

14. James C. Bradford, ed., *The Atlas of American Military History* (New York: Oxford University Press, 2003), pp. 157–158.

15. Terry Allen papers, USAMHI.

16. Allen N. Towne, *Doctor Danger Forward* (Jefferson, NC: McFarland & Co., 2000), p. 25.

17. Gilbert, pp. 375–376; and Gerald Astor, *Terrible Terry Allen: Combat General of World War II—The Life of an American Soldier* (New York: Presidio/Ballantine, 2003), p. 124.

18. Terry Allen papers, USAMHI; and Baumgartner, p. 15.

19. Bradford, p. 158.

20. Gilbert, pp. 375–392.

21. Astor, *Terrible Terry Allen*, pp. 141, 144–145; Baumgartner, pp. 21–23; and Stanley P. Hirshson, *General Patton: A Soldier's Life* (New York: HarperCollins, 2002), p. 323.

22. Chandler and Ambrose, pp. 1,006–1,007.

23. Richard Collier, *The War in the Desert* (Alexandria, VA: Time-Life Books, 1977), p. 168; Carlo D'Este, *Patton: A Genius for War* (New York: HarperCollins, 1995), pp. 642–643; and Alfred D. Chandler and Stephen Ambrose, eds., *The Papers of Dwight David Eisenhower, The War Years* (Baltimore: Johns Hopkins, 1970), p. 1,007.

24. Harold P. Monica, unpublished memoir: *The War Years.*

25. D'Este, *Patton,* p. 466.

26. Ibid., pp. 471–474.

27. Collier, pp. 169–171; D'Este, *Patton,* p. 474; and Chandler and Ambrose, p. 1,059.

28. Ernie Pyle, *Here Is Your War* (New York: Henry Holt, 1945), p. 210.

29. Ibid., p. 153.

30. D'Este, *Patton,* pp. 480–487.

31. Baumgartner, pp. 26–32; and Collier, pp. 191–192.

32. Fred W. Hall Jr., "A Memoir of World War II." (unpublished).

33. Omar N. Bradley, *A Soldier's Story* (New York: Henry Holt, 1951), pp. 109–110.

34. Astor, *Terrible Terry Allen,* pp. 83–88, 170.

35. Quentin Reynolds, radio script, June 8, 1944 (USAMHI).

36. Harrison, pp. 48–59.

37. Albert N. Garland and Howard M. Smyth, *U.S. Army in World War II: The Mediterranean Theater. Sicily and the Surrender of Italy* (Washington, DC: GPO, 1965), pp. 88–111.

38. D'Este, *Patton,* p. 506; and Carlo D'Este, *Bitter Victory: The Battle for Sicily, 1943* (New York: E.P. Dutton, 1988), p. 468.

39. *This Is Sicily,* War Department pamphlet, date unknown, pp. 5–6.

40. Flint Whitlock, *The Rock of Anzio* (Boulder: Westview, 1998), p. 36.

41. Leonard E. Jones, USAMHI questionnaire.

42. Garland and Smith, pp. 300–315.

43. D'Este, *Bitter Victory,* pp. 428–440; and Garland and Smith, pp. 406–425, 435–553.

44. D'Este, *Bitter Victory,* pp. 457–458.

45. James M. Reese Medal of Honor Citation, McCormick Research Center (MRC).

46. D'Este, *Bitter Victory,* pp. 457–458; and Garland and Smith, pp. 324–347.

47. D'Este, *Bitter Victory,* p. 470.

48. Bradley, pp. 154–157.

49. Harry C. Butcher, *My Three Years with Eisenhower* (New York: Simon and Schuster, 1949), p. 376.

50. Allen papers, USAMHI.

51. Bradley, pp. 156–157.

Chapter Two

1. Bradley, pp. 156–157.

2. Adrian R. Lewis, *Omaha Beach: A Flawed Victory* (Chapel Hill, NC: University of North Carolina Press, 2001), pp. 259–261.

3. Votaw and Weingartner, *Blue Spaders,* p. 47.
4. Ibid., p. 70.
5. Joseph Dawson papers, USAMHI.
6. Joseph Dawson interview by John Votaw, April 16, 1991, McCormick Research Center.
7. James K. Woolnough papers, USAMHI.
8. George Pickett interview by John Votaw, May 31, 1994, MRC.
9. Fred Hall memoir.
10. Towne, p. 77.
11. Whitlock, pp. 68, 82.
12. Towne, p. 81.
13. William Faust, USAMHI questionnaire.
14. Monica memoir.
15. Newman interview by author, February 24, 2000.
16. Stephen E. Ambrose, *D-Day, June 6, 1944—The Climactic Battle of World War II* (New York: Simon and Schuster, 1995), pp. 69–70; Harrison, pp. 112–116; and Norman Albert, *Operation Overlord: Design and Reality* (Harrisburg, PA: Military Service Publishing Co., 1952), pp. 70–71.
17. Harrison, pp. 53–57; and Morison, p. 32.
18. John Keegan, *Six Armies in Normandy* (New York: Viking Press, 1982), p. 71.
19. Hammond, pp. 3–13; and Morison, pp. 4–17.
20. Bradley, pp. 236–237.
21. William B. Gara interview by author, June 25, 2000.
22. Fred Hall memoir.
23. Monica memoir.
24. Stanhope B. Mason memoir, USAMHI.
25. Monica memoir.
26. Baumgartner, p. 68.
27. Edward J. Sackley, USAMHI questionnaire.
28. Harley A. Reynolds memoir, USAMHI.
29. Monica memoir.
30. Edward Steeg memoir.
31. Steve Kellman interview by author, June 17, 2000.
32. William M. Lee, USAMHI questionnaire.
33. Kellman interview by author, June 17, 2000.
34. Al Alvarez memoir.
35. Votaw and Weingartner, *Blue Spaders,* p. 47.
36. Jones, USAMHI questionnaire.
37. Thomas R. McCann memoir, USAMHI.
38. Raynes Minns, *Bombers and Mash: The Domestic Front, 1939–45* (London: Virago Press, 1980, reprinted 1999), p. 166.
39. Robert F. Hilbert interview by author, February 24, 2000.
40. Newman interview by author, February 24, 2000.
41. McCann memoir.
42. Minns, pp. 166–173.
43. Monica memoir.
44. Jim Hunt, *Bridgehead Sentinel,* spring 2000

45. Towne, p. 88.
46. Monica memoir.
47. Whitlock, pp. 137–314.
48. Butcher, pp. 491, 502.
49. D'Este, *Decision in Normandy* (New York: E. P. Dutton, 1983), pp. 71–104.
50. Hall, p. 75.
51. *Omaha Beachhead (6 June–13 June 1944).* "American Forces in Action" Series (Washington, DC, 1945, reprinted 1984), p. 30.
52. *Omaha Beachhead,* p. 30; and Morison, p. 31.
53. Towne, p. 176; and *Omaha Beachhead,* pp. 8–20.
54. Tim Kilvert-Jones, *Omaha Beach: V Corps' Battle for the Normandy Beachhead* (Conshohoken, PA: Combined Publishing, 1999), pp. 139–141.
55. Morison, pp. 58–65.
56. Butcher, p. 531.
57. Morison, p. 58.
58. Harrison, pp. 183–187.
59. Gilbert, p. 350.
60. John Miller Jr., *U.S. Army in World War II: The War in the Pacific. Cartwheel: The Reduction of Rabaul* (Washington, DC: Center of Military History, 1990), p. 267.
61. Philip A. Crowl and Edmund G. Love, *U.S. Army in World War II: The War in the Pacific. Seizure of the Gilberts and Marshalls* (Washington, DC: Center of Military History, 1990), passim.

Chapter Three

1. Christopher J. Cornazzani, USAMHI questionnaire.
2. Daniel Curatola, USAMHI questionnaire.
3. Dawson interview by John Votaw, April 16, 1991, MRC.
4. Baumgartner, p. 68.
5. Kellman interview by author, June 17, 2000.
6. Walter Halloran address to the Dr. Harold Deutsch Memorial Minnesota World War II Roundtable: "The Role of the Combat Photographer," January 11, 1996.
7. Butcher, pp. 533–535.
8. Monica memoir.
9. Roger L. Brugger memoir, MRC.
10. Fred Hall memoir.
11. Baumgartner, p. 69.
12. Ambrose, *D-Day,* pp. 43–46.
13. Gara interview by author, June 25, 2000.
14. Steeg memoir.
15. Lawrence Johnson Jr., *The Cannoneer*, April 1994.
16. Alvarez memoir.
17. Watts memoir and letter to author, May 4, 2000.
18. Gara interview by author, June 25, 2000.
19. Jerome Alberts memoir, MRC.
20. Richard Borden memoir, MRC.
21. Francis J. Murdock interview by John Votaw, October 23, 1995, MRC.

22. Kellman interview by author, June 17, 2000.
23. Newman interview by author, February 24, 2000.
24. Kellman interview by author, June 17, 2000.
25. Gara interview by author, June 25, 2000.
26. Theodore G. Aufort, USAMHI questionnaire.
27. Dawson interview by John Votaw, April 16, 1991, MRC.
28. Raymond J. Klawiter interview by author, June 10, 2000.
29. Steeg memoir.
30. Nelson G. Park letter to author, June 16, 2000.
31. Gara interview by author, June 25, 2000.
32. Alvarez letter to author.
33. Steeg memoir.
34. Joseph E. Nichols, USAMHI questionnaire.
35. Hilbert interview by author, June 15, 2000.
36. William D. Behlmer, USAMHI questionnaire.
37. Newman interview by author, February 24, 2000.
38. William T. Dillon memoir, USAMHI.
39. Ralph A. Berry Sr., USAMHI questionnaire.
40. Simon Hurwit memoir, USAMHI.
41. Everett L. Booth, USAMHI questionnaire.
42. Lyme *Star,* October 25, 1991.
43. Towne, p. 90.
44. Fred Hall memoir.
45. Aufort memoir.
46. John B. Ellery memoir, MRC.
47. Newman interview by author, February 24, 2000.
48. Dillon memoir, USAMHI.
49. Alberts memoir.
50. Robert E. Murphy interview by author, October 12, 2002.
51. Klawiter interview by author, June 10, 2000.
52. Monica memoir.
53. Harrison, pp. 270–272.
54. Monica memoir.
55. Ed Ireland interview by John Votaw, February 29, 1992, MRC.
56. Bradley, p. 250.

Chapter Four

1. Edward Ellsberg, *The Far Shore* (New York: Dodd, Mead, 1960), pp. 124–127, 140, 171–173.

2. Martin Blumenson, "Rommel," in Correlli Barnett, ed., *Hitler's Generals* (New York: Grove Weidenfeld, 1989), pp. 293–299; and Erwin Rommel, *The Rommel Papers,* Basil H. Liddel-Hart, ed. (New York: Harcourt, Brace, Jovanovich, 1953), pp. 3–87.

3. Rommel, p. 191.
4. Ibid., pp. 295–296.
5. Ibid., pp. 304–326, 359–369.
6. Ibid., pp. 408–422.

7. Morison, pp. 39–42; and D'Este, *Fatal Decision: Anzio and the Battle for Rome* (New York: HarperCollins, 1991), pp. 13, 15–16, 31, 87.

8. Rommel, p. 451.

9. Ibid., pp. 457–458.

10. "Translation of Field Marshal Rommel's Report After His Inspection of Defenses of the Atlantic Wall, 22 April 1944," MRC.

11. Rommel, pp. 454–455.

12. Tonie and Valmai Holt, *Major & Mrs. Holt's Battlefield Guide to the Normandy Landing Beaches* (Barnsley, South Yorkshire: Pen and Sword Books, 1999), pp. 22–23; and Samuel W. Mitcham Jr., *The Desert Fox in Normandy: Rommel's Defense of Fortress Europe* (Westport, CT: Praeger, 1997), p. 57.

13. Morison, pp. 113–114; and Ambrose, pp. 112, 322–323, 517–518, 532.

14. *Omaha Beachhead,* p. 26; and Katherine V. Dillon et al., *D-Day Normandy: The Story and the Photographs* (Herndon, VA: Brassy's, 1999), p. 23.

15. Paul Carell, *Invasion—They're Coming! The German Account of the Allied Landings and the 80 Days' Battle for France* (New York: E. P. Dutton, 1963), pp. 9–10, 84.

16. Harrison, p. 319n.

17. Carelll, pp. 9–10, 84.

18. Gara interview by author, June 25, 2000.

19. Carell, p. 89.

20. Morison, pp. 55–56; and Ambrose, pp. 257–258.

21. Ambrose, *D-Day,* p. 251.

22. Klawiter interview by author, June 25, 2000.

23. Ellsberg, pp. 129–130.

24. Morison, pp. 114–116.

25. Ellsberg, pp. 144–145.

Chapter Five

1. *New York Times,* June 5, 1944.

2. *United States News,* May 5, 1944.

3. Morison, p. 72.

4. Ibid., p. 110.

5. Dillon memoir, USAMHI.

6. Newman interview by author, February 24, 2000.

7. Tony Hall, p. 71.

8. Klawiter interview by author, June 10, 2000.

9. Towne, p. 96.

10. Cornazzani, USAMHI questionnaire.

11. Towne, p. 96.

12. John F. Dulligan file, MRC; and Ryan, pp. 68–69.

13. Dawson interview, MRC.

14. McCann memoir, USAMHI.

15. Morison, p. 83.

16. Ambrose, *Eisenhower, Vol. 1,* New York: Simon and Schuster, 1983, p. 305.

17. Fred Hall memoir.

18. Monica memoir.

19. Chester B. Hansen diary, USAMHI.
20. Monica memoir.
21. Alvarez memoir.
22. Chester B. Hansen diary, USAMHI.
23. Harrison, pp. 273–274.
24. Stephen Badsey, *Normandy 1944: Allied Landings and Breakout* (London: Osprey, 1997), p. 66.
25. H. R. Knickerbocker and Don Whitehead et al., *Danger Forward: The Story of the First Infantry Division in World War II* (Washington, DC: Society of the First Division, 1947), p. 207.
26. Carell, p. 14.
27. Ryan, pp. 81–83; Keegan, p. 145; and Ambrose, p. 567.
28. Knickerbocker and Whitehead, p. 208.
29. Aufort memoir.
30. Johnson, *The Cannoneer,* April 1994.
31. William H. Lynn memoir, USAMHI.
32. G Company, 16th Infantry Regiment report, June 15, 1944, USAMHI.
33. Ralph Puhalovich interview by author, June 12, 2000.
34. Brugger memoir, MRC.
35. Keegan, p. 15.

Chapter Six

1. Holt, pp. 12–14.
2. *Omaha Beachhead,* p. 19.
3. Harrison, pp. 305–311; and Morison, p. 119.
4. Kellman interview by author, June 17, 2000.
5. Halloran address.
6. Ryan, p. 193.
7. G Company, 16th Infantry Regiment report, June 15, 1944, USAMHI.
8. Park, letter to author, June 16, 2000.
9. Gara interview by author, June 25, 2000.
10. Hurwit memoir, USAMHI.
11. Robert A. Giguere, "My Personal History of 6th Beach Battalion," MRC.
12. Harley Reynolds memoir.
13. Ernest Hemingway, "Voyage to Victory," *Collier's,* July 22, 1944.
14. *United States News,* June 19, 1944.
15. Brugger memoir, MRC.
16. Watts interview by author, June 13, 2000.
17. Kellman interview by author, June 17, 2000.
18. Jess E. Weiss, *The Vestibule* (New York: Pocket Books, 1972), pp. xxvi–xxvii.
19. Halloran address.
20. Lynn memoir, USAMHI.
21. Harley Reynolds memoir, USAMHI.
22. Fred Hall memoir.
23. Ellsberg, pp. 222–224.
24. Carell, p. 82.

25. Ellsberg, pp. 234–237; and Morison, p. 134.
26. Alvarez memoir.
27. Gara interview by author, June 25, 2000.
28. Alvarez memoir.
29. Henderson letter to author.
30. Kellman interview by author, June 17, 2000.
31. Curatola, USAMHI questionnaire.
32. Morison, pp. 138–140.
33. Thomas B. Allen, "Untold Stories of D-Day," *National Geographic*, June 2002.
34. Carell, p. 80.
35. William Manchester, *Goodbye, Darkness* (New York: Bantam Doubleday Dell, 1980), p. 272.
36. Halloran address.
37. E Company, 16th Infantry Regiment report, USAMHI.
38. F Company, 16th Infantry Regiment report, USAMHI.
39. Blythe F. Finke, *No Mission Too Difficult! Old Buddies of the 1st Division Tell All About World War II* (Chicago: Contemporary Books, 1995), pp. 191–192.
40. Dawson interview by John Votaw, April 16, 1991, MRC.
41. 16th Infantry Regiment report of June 6, 1944, MRC.
42. Ellsberg, pp. 222–224.
43. Kellman interview by author, June 17, 2000.
44. *Omaha Beachhead*, pp. 48–49.
45. Kellman interview by author, June 17, 2000.
46. *Omaha Beachhead*, p. 75; and Baumgartner, p. 96.
47. Kimball Richmond Citation for Distinguished Service Cross, July 1, 1944, USAMHI.
48. Booth, USAMHI questionnaire.
49. Finke, p. 196.
50. Fred Hall memoir.
51. Eldon Wiehe memoir, USAMHI.
52. Brugger memoir, MRC.
53. Isadore R. Berkowitz, USAMHI questionnaire.
54. Baumgartner, p. 99.
55. Behlmer, USAMHI questionnaire.
56. Murray Hackenburg memoir, USAMHI.
57. Karl Wolf memoir.
58. *Omaha Beachhead*, pp. 45–47.
59. Baumgartner, p. 88; and Knickerbocker and Whitehead, p. 219.
60. 16th Infantry Regiment report, MRC; and Knickerbocker and Whitehead, p. 219.
61. CBS interview transcript, USAMHI.
62. Dawson interview by John Votaw, April 16, 1991, MRC.

Chapter Seven

1. Knickerbocker and Whitehead, p. 210.
2. 16th Infantry Regiment official report, USAMHI.
3. 16th Infantry Regiment Intelligence & Reconnaissance Diary, USAMHI.

4. Harley Reynolds memoir, USAMHI.
5. John E. Bistrica, USAMHI questionnaire.
6. Merle Miller, "The Red One," *Yank,* May 25, 1945.
7. Aufort memoir, USAMHI.
8. Harley Reynolds memoir, USAMHI.
9. Dillon memoir, USAMHI.
10. Watts memoir and interview by author, June 13, 2000.
11. Johnson, "The Cannoneer," April 1994.
12. Alvarez memoir.
13. John B. Carroll, USAMHI questionnaire.
14. Lynn memoir, USAMHI.
15. Knickerbocker and Whitehead, pp. 212–213.
16. Morison, pp. 140–148.
17. Kenneth P. Lord memoir, USAMHI.
18. Gara interview by author, June 25, 2000.
19. Morison, pp. 149, 152.
20. Ibid., p. 154.
21. Bradley, pp. 270–271.
22. Hansen diary, USAMHI.
23. Knickerbocker and Whitehead, pp. 212–213.
24. Bistrica memoir, USAMHI.
25. Knickerbocker and Whitehead, p. 213.
26. Harley Reynolds memoir, USAMHI.
27. *Omaha Beachhead,* p. 58.
28. Hackenburg memoir, USAMHI.
29. Ellery memoir, MRC.
30. John J. Pinder Medal of Honor Citation, MRC.
31. Aufort memoir, USAMHI.
32. Bradley, p. 273.
33. Knickerbocker and Whitehead, p. 214.
34. Lynn memoir, USAMHI.
35. Gara interview by author, June 25, 2000.

Chapter Eight

1. *Omaha Beachhead,* p. 82.
2. G. C. Burch and T. T. Crowley, *Eight Stars to Victory: Operations of the First Engineers' Combat Battalion in World War II* (Publisher and place unknown, 1947, reprinted 1987), p. 130.
3. *Omaha Beachhead,* p. 82.
4. Ralph "Andy" Anderson interview by author, September 11, 2002.
5. Jack Bennett interview by author, September 15, 2002.
6. *Omaha Beachhead,* pp. 84–85.
7. Murphy interview by author, October 12, 2002.
8. Borden memoir, MRC.
9. Alberts memoir, MRC.

10. Murphy interview by author, October 12, 2002.
11. *Omaha Beachhead*, pp. 82–85; and Robert Baumer letter to author, September 3, 2002.
12. Hansen diary, USAMHI.
13. Monica interview by author, June 8, 2000.
14. Steeg memoir.
15. Lewis C. Smith memoir, USAMHI.
16. Walter D. Ehlers interview by author, April 27, 2002.
17. Carlton Barrett Medal of Honor Citation, MRC.
18. Newman interview by author, February 24, 2000.
19. Klawiter interview by author, June 10, 2000.
20. Steeg memoir.
21. Alberts memoir.
22. Cornazzani, USAMHI questionnaire.
23. Theodore Dobol memoir, MRC.
24. *Miami Daily News*, August 6, 1944.
25. Giguere memoir, MRC.
26. Cornazzani, USAMHI questionnaire.
27. McCann memoir, USAMHI.
28. Hilbert interview by author, June 15, 2000.
29. Towne, pp. 99–101.
30. Aufort memoir.
31. *Omaha Beachhead*, p. 75; and Baumgartner, p. 96.
32. Harley Reynolds memoir, USAMHI.
33. Dillon memoir, USAMHI.
34. Johnson, "The Cannoneer," April 1994.
35. Baumgartner, p. 97.
36. Brugger memoir, MRC.
37. Baumgartner, pp. 96–97.
38. Jimmie Monteith Medal of Honor Citation, MRC.

Chapter Nine

1. Badsey, pp. 69–71.
2. Bradley, pp. 271–272.
3. Fred Hall memoir.
4. John Finke interview by John Votaw, August 9, 1989, MRC.
5. Watts memoir.
6. Murphy interview by author, October 12, 2002.
7. Park letter to author, June 16, 2000.
8. Ehlers interview by author, April 27, 2002.
9. Ellery memoir, USAMHI.
10. Carell, pp. 86–88.
11. Dwight D. Eisenhower, *Crusade in Europe* (New York: Doubleday, 1948), p. 253.
12. Butcher, p. 565.
13. Dawson interview by John Votaw, April 16, 1991, MRC.
14. Ireland interview by John Votaw, February 29, 1992, MRC.

15. *Omaha Beachhead,* pp. 113–114.

16. Carell, p. 95

17. Gordon Williamson, *SS: The Blood-Soaked Soil* (Osceola, WI: Motorbooks International, 1995), pp. 148–149.

18. Chester Wilmot, *The Struggle for Europe* (London: Collins, 1952), p. 329; and "A Crack German Panzer Division and What Allied Air Power Did to It Between D-Day and V-Day" (USAMHI).

19. Votaw and Weingartner, *Blue Spaders,* p. 57; and Finke, p. 201.

20. Ralph Puhalovich interview by author, July 9, 2000.

21. Finke, p. 200.

22. Dobol memoir, MRC.

23. *Miami Daily News,* August 6, 1944.

24. Correspondence from Andrew Woods, MRC.

25. *Omaha Beachhead,* p. 101.

26. Wolf memoir.

27. Kellman interview by author, June 17, 2000.

28. Bennett interview with author, September 15, 2002.

29. Anderson interview by author, September 11, 2002.

30. Newman interview by author, February 24, 2000.

31. Wolf memoir.

32. Gerald Astor, *June 6, 1944: The Voices of D-Day* (New York: St. Martin's Press, 1994), p. 282.

33. Harley Reynolds memoir.

34. Klawiter interview by author, June 10, 2000.

35. Steeg memoir.

36. Dillon memoir, USAMHI.

37. Towne, pp. 103–104.

38. Ellery memoir, MRC.

39. 1st Infantry Division G-1 Report, June 1944, MRC.

40. V Corps History, p. 64.

41. Mitcham, pp. 93–94.

Chapter Ten

1. Butcher, p. 567.

2. Doris Kearns Goodwin, *No Ordinary Time. Franklin and Eleanor Roosevelt: The Home Front in World War II* (New York: Touchstone/Simon & Schuster, 1994), p. 509.

3. *New York Times,* June 7, 1944.

4. *Chicago Tribune,* June 6, 1944.

5. *Time,* June 12, 1944.

6. Keegan, p. 146.

7. "FDR's Prayer" in *Vital Speeches of the Day,* Vol. X, November 15, 1944, p. 514.

8. Ernie Pyle, *Here Is Your War* (New York: Henry Holt, 1945), pp. 440–442.

9. Johnson, *The Cannoneer,* April 1994.

10. Monica memoir.

11. Watts memoir.

12. Ellery memoir.
13. Brugger memoir.
14. Dillon memoir.
15. Hirshson, p. 494; and Belton Y. Cooper, *Death Traps: The Survival of an American Armored Division in World War II* (Novato, CA: Presidio Press, 1998), pp. 44–47.
16. Hilbert interview by author, June 15, 2000.
17. *Miami Daily News,* August 6, 1944.
18. *Omaha Beachhead,* p. 110; and Harrison, pp. 333–335.
19. Harrison, pp. 333–335.
20. *Omaha Beachhead,* pp. 134–135; and Harrison, pp. 330–335.
21. Mitcham, pp. 94–99; and Carell, pp. 112–115.
22. Brugger memoir, MRC.
23. Newman interview by author, February 24, 2000.
24. Pyle, *Brave Men,* pp. 365–368.
25. Ehlers interview by author, April 27, 2002.
26. *Omaha Beachhead,* p. 121.
27. Butcher, p. 570; and Eisenhower, p. 253.
28. Butcher, pp. 570, 571–572.
29. *Omaha Beachhead,* pp. 127, 136.
30. Harrison, p. 350; and *Omaha Beachhead,* pp. 136–137.
31. Towne, pp. 105–106.
32. *Omaha Beachhead,* p. 136.
33. Ehlers interview by author, April 27, 2002.
34. Anderson interview by author, April 27, 2002.
35. *Miami Daily News,* August 6, 1944.
36. Votaw and Weingartner, pp. 55–56.
37. Baumgartner, p. 115; and Knickerbocker and Whitehead, p. 194.
38. Harrison, pp. 339–340.
39. Monica memoir.
40. Ireland memoir, MRC.
41. Monica memoir.
42. Harrison, p. 340.
43. Hansen diary, USAMHI.
44. *Omaha Beachhead,* p. 116.
45. Hansen diary, USAMHI.
46. Newman interview by author, February 24, 2000.
47. Dobol memoir, MRC; and Votaw and Weingartner, pp. 56–58.
48. 3rd Battalion, 26th Infantry Regiment Journal, June 9, 1944, MRC.
49. Puhalovich interview by author, July 9, 2000.
50. Ehlers interview by author, April 27, 2002.
51. Arthur DeFranzo Medal of Honor Citation, MRC.
52. Votaw and Weingartner, p. 58.
53. Harrison, pp. 348–350.
54. Monica memoir.
55. Towne, pp. 106–107.
56. Harley Reynolds memoir, USAMHI.

57. Bradley, p. 292; and Votaw and Weingartner, p. 60.
58. Alvarez memoir.
59. Votaw and Weingartner, p. 60.
60. Fred Hall memoir.
61. Steeg memoir.
62. *Miami Daily News,* August 6, 1944.
63. Monica memoir.
64. Dillon memoir, USAMHI; and *Army Times,* September 21, 1946.
65. Fred Hall memoir.
66. Puhalovich letter to parents, June 16, 1944.
67. Quentin Reynolds radio script, June 8, 1944, USAMHI.
68. Quentin Reynolds letter to Mary Frances Allen, June 20, 1944.

Chapter Eleven

1. Baumgartner, pp. 112–144.
2. Harrison, p. 408; Carell, pp. 152, 181, 222; and Rommel, pp. 503–506.
3. Martin Blumenson, *U.S. Army in World War II: The European Theater of Operations. Breakout and Pursuit* (Washington, DC: Center of Military History, 1993), pp. 214–223.
4. Ibid., pp. 228–260.
5. Monica memoir.
6. Blumenson, *Breakout and Pursuit,* pp. 257–259.
7. Monica memoir.
8. Blumenson, *Breakout and Pursuit,* pp. 257–259.
9. Towne, p. 118.
10. Blumenson, *Breakout and Pursuit,* pp. 230–263.
11. Towne, p. 120.
12. Baumgartner, p. 127.
13. Blumenson, *Breakout and Pursuit,* pp. 344–345.
14. Towne, p. 122.
15. Bradley, p. 371.
16. Blumenson, *Breakout and Pursuit,* pp. 506–527.
17. Bradley, p. 372.
18. Blumenson, *Breakout and Pursuit,* pp. 516, 535, 557–558.
19. Bradley, pp. 385–396.
20. Monica memoir.
21. Steeg memoir.
22. Monica memoir.
23. "Commemorative History of the 18th Infantry Regiment."
24. Blumenson, *Breakout and Pursuit,* p. 684.
25. Hall memoir.
26. Monica memoir.
27. Gino Merli Medal of Honor Citation, MRC; and *New York Times,* June 17, 2003.
28. Steeg memoir.
29. MacDonald, *U.S. Army in World War II: The European Theater. The Siegfried Line Campaign* (Washington: GPO, 1951), p. 36.
30. Votaw and Weingartner, p. 76.

31. Baumgartner, pp. 155–157.
32. Monica memoir.
33. Charles Whiting, *Bloody Aachen* (New York: Stein & Day, 1976), pp. 27–28; and MacDonald, *Siegfried Line Campaign,* pp. 70–71, 81–82, 87, 283.
34. *Blue Spaders*, pp. 76–77; and MacDonald, *Siegfried Line Campaign*, pp. 285–288.
35. Wolf memoir.
36. Harley Reynolds letter to author, September 2, 2002.
37. Steeg memoir.
38. Monica memoir.
39. Votaw and Weingartner, pp. 77–78.
40. Baumgartner, p. 157.
41. Wolf memoir.
42. Harley Reynolds letter to author, September 2, 2002.
43. Bistrica memoir, USAMHI.
44. Joseph E. Schaefer Medal of Honor Citation, MRC.
45. Bradley, pp. 431–432.
46. Baumgartner, p. 165.
47. Wolf memoir.
48. MacDonald, *Siegfried Line Campaign,* p. 286.
49. Bobbie Brown Medal of Honor Citation, MRC.
50. Murphy interview by author, October 12, 2002.
51. MacDonald, *Siegfried Line Campaign,* pp. 309–310.
52. Darrell M. Daniel, monograph, "The Capture of Aachen" (Combined Arms Research Library, Fort Leavenworth, KS), pp. 6–11.
53. Harley Reynolds letter to author, September 2, 2002.
54. Bennett interview by author, September 15, 2002.
55. William C. Heinz, quoted by Andrew Woods, MRC, (from an article in the *Fort Worth Star-Telegram,* October 22, 1944).
56. Dawson interview by John Votaw, April 16, 1991, MRC.
57. MacDonald, *Siegfried Line Campaign,* pp. 286–290; and Baumgartner, pp. 165–171.
58. Dawson interview by John Votaw, April 16, 1991, MRC.
59. MacDonald, *Siegfried Line Campaign,* p. 316.
60. Max Thompson Medal of Honor Citation, MRC.
61. Baumgartner, pp. 157–172.
62. Daniel, p. 11; and MacDonald, *Siegfried Line Campaign,* p. 316.
63. Votaw and Weingartner, pp. 87–88.
64. Towne, p. 144.
65. Butcher, pp. 691–692.
66. Monica memoir.
67. Website: Triumph & Tragedy, www.webbuild.net/BeforeTaps/Triumph.html.
68. Astor, *Terrible Terry Allen,* p. 269.
69. MacDonald, *Siegfried Line Campaign,* pp. 417–421.
70. Jake W. Lindsey Medal of Honor Citation, MRC.
71. Francis X. McGraw Medal of Honor Citation, MRC.
72. Bert Damsky memoir, USAMHI.

73. Puhalovich interview by author, June 12, 2000.
74. Baumgartner, p. 181.
75. Harley Reynolds letter to author, September 2, 2002.
76. Robert T. Henry Medal of Honor Citation, MRC.
77. Baumgartner, pp. 180–183.

Chapter Twelve

1. *Newsweek,* December 25, 1944.
2. Baumgartner, p. 184; and Votaw and Weingartner, pp. 89–90.
3. Danny S. Parker, *Battle of the Bulge: Hitler's Ardennes Offensive, 1944–1945* (Philadelphia: Combined Books, 1991), p. 67.
4. MacDonald, *A Time for Trumpets,* p. 83.
5. Bradley, pp. 449–462.
6. Parker, p. 85.
7. Hugh M. Cole, *U.S. Army in World War II: The European Theater of Operations. The Ardennes: Battle of the Bulge* (Washington, DC: Center of Military History, 1994), p. 75.
8. Fred Hall memoir.
9. Dorris H. Barickman, USAMHI questionnaire.
10. Cole, p. 86.
11. Votaw and Weingartner, p. 99.
12. Ibid., pp. 104–107.
13. Alvarez memoir.
14. Cole, pp. 129–131; and MacDonald, *A Time for Trumpets,* pp. 403–407.
15. Cole, pp. 130–131.
16. Puhalovich interview by author, June 12, 2000.
17. Henry F. Warner Medal of Honor Citation, MRC.
18. Votaw and Weingartner, p. 106.
19. MacDonald, *A Time for Trumpets,* pp. 407–408.
20. Eisenhower, p. 348.
21. Baumgartner, pp. 197–199.
22. *American Traveler,* June 6, 1945.
23. Burch and Crowley, p. 230.
24. Votaw and Weingartner, pp. 111–118.
25. Monica memoir.
26. Baumgartner, pp. 205–209.
27. Ibid., pp. 235–236.
28. Ibid., p. 243.
29. Monica memoir.
30. Towne, p. 166.
31. George Peterson Medal of Honor Citation, MRC.
32. Walter J. Will Medal of Honor Citation, MRC.
33. Baumgartner, p. 255.
34. Eisenhower, p. 410.
35. Baumgartner, pp. 256–257.
36. Monica memoir.

37. Albert Axell, *Russia's Heroes—1941–45* (New York: Carroll & Graf, 2001), p. 245.
38. Stanton, p. 77.
39. Butcher, p. 834.
40. Fred Hall memoir.
41. Finke, pp. 257–258.
42. *American Traveler,* June 6, 1945.
43. Stanton, p. 75.
44. Watts memoir.
45. Lee memoir, USAMHI.
46. Newman interview by author, February 24, 2000.

Selected Bibliography

Oral Histories

Anderson, Ralph "Andy". Interviewed by author, September 11, 2002.
Bennett, Jack. Interviewed by author, September 15, 2002.
Dawson, Joseph. Interviewed by John Votaw, McCormick Research Center (MRC), April 16, 1991.
Ehlers, Walter. Interviewed by author, April 27, 2002.
Finke, John. Interviewed by John Votaw, MRC, August 9, 1989.
Gara, William B. Interviewed by author, June 25, 2000.
Hilbert, Robert F. Interview by author, June 15, 2000.
Ireland, Ed. Interviewed by John Votaw, MRC, February 29, 1992.
Kellman, Steve. Interviewed by author, June 17, 2000.
Klawiter, Raymond J. Interviewed by author, June 10, 2000.
Monica, Harold P. Interviewed by author, June 8, 2000.
Murdoch, Francis J. Interviewed by John Votaw, MRC, October 23, 1995.
Murphy, Robert E. Interviewed by author, October 12, 2002.
Newman, Louis. Interviewed by author, February 20, 2000.
Pickett, George. Interviewed by John Votaw, MRC, May 31, 1994.
Puhalovich, Ralph. Interviewed by author, July 9, 2000.
Smith, Albert H. Interviewed by Ed Aymar, Ft. Riley, Kansas, February 28, 1983.
Watts, James H. Interviewed by author, June 13, 2000.

Unpublished Sources

Alberts, Jerome. Memoir. (MRC)
Alvarez, Alfred A. Memoir and letters to author.
Aufort, Theodore G. U.S. Army Military History Institute (USAMHI) questionnaire.
Barickman, Dorris H. USAMHI questionnaire.
Beach, John B. USAMHI questionnaire.
Behlmer, William D. USAMHI questionnaire.
Berkowitz, Isadore R. USAMHI questionnaire.
Berry, Ralph A., Sr. USAMHI questionnaire.

Bistrica, John E. USAMHI questionnaire.
Booth, Everett L. USAMHI questionnaire.
Borden, Richard. Memoir. (MRC)
Brugger, Roger L. Memoir. (MRC)
Carroll, John B. USAMHI questionnaire.
Cole, Richard H. USAMHI questionnaire.
Cornazzani, Christopher J. USAMHI questionnaire.
Curatola, Dan. USAMHI questionnaire.
Damsky, Bert. Memoir. (USAMHI)
Davey, Kenneth C. "Navy Medicine on Omaha Beach." (MRC)
Dillon, William T. Memoir. (USAMHI, and information provided to author by his widow, Frankye Dillon)
Dobol, Theodore L. Memoir. (MRC)
Donofrio, William G. USAMHI questionnaire.
Ellery, John B. Memoir. (MRC)
Evans, Rupert L. USAMHI questionnaire.
Faust, William. USAMHI questinnaire.
Gast, Loren W. USAMHI questionnaire.
Giguere, Robert A. "My Personal History of 6th Beach Battalion." (MRC)
Hackenburg, Murray. Memoir. (USAMHI)
Hall, Fred W., Jr. "A Memoir of World War II."
Hansen, Chester. Diary. (USAMHI)
Henderson, Allen. *Wartime Diary*.
Henry, Robert T. Medal of Honor Citation. (MRC)
Holmes, Roy W. USAMHI questionnaire.
Hurwit, Simon. Memoir. (USAMHI)
Johnson, Lawrence, Jr. USAMHI questionnaire.
Jones, Leonard E. USAMHI questionnaire.
Koch, George J. USAMHI questionnaire.
Lee, William M. USAMHI questionnaire.
Lord, Kenneth P. Memoir. (MRC and USAMHI questionnaire)
Lynn, William H. Memoir. (USAMHI)
Mason, Stanhope. Memoir. (USAMHI)
McCann, Thomas R. Memoir. (USAMHI)
Monica, Harold P. Memoir: "The War Years."
Moretto, Rocco J. Letter, March 25, 1996. (MRC)
Newman, Louis. Letter to author, November 3, 2002.
Nichols, Joseph E. USAMHI questionnaire.
Park, Nelson G. Letter to author, June 16, 2000.
Pilck, Joseph W. USAMHI questionnaire.
Reynolds, Harley. Memoir. (USAMHI)
Rowland, Henry C. Memoir. (USAMHI)
Sackley, Edward J. USAMHI questionnaire.
Smith, Albert H. Memoir.
Smith, Lewis C. USAMHI questionnaire.

Spalding, John. Interviewed by Forrest C. Pogue, February 9, 1945. (National Archives)
Steeg, Edward. Memoir. (Provided to author by his daughter, Chyrl Zickgraf)
Wiehe, Eldon. Memoir. (MRC)
Wolf, Karl E. Memoir: "The War Years of Karl E. Wolf."
Zerfass, Raymond E. USAMHI questionnaire.

Published Sources (Books)

Allied Landing Craft of World War Two. Annapolis: Naval Institute Press, 1989.

Ambrose, Stephen E. *D-Day, June 6, 1944—The Climactic Battle of World War II*. New York: Simon & Schuster, 1994.

______. *Eisenhower, Volume I*. New York: Simon and Schuster, 1983.

Astor, Gerald. *June 6, 1944: The Voices of D-Day*. New York: St. Martin's Press, 1994.

______. *Terrible Terry Allen: Combat General of World War II—The Life of an American Soldier*. New York: Presidio/Ballantine, 2003.

Axell, Albert. *Russia's Heroes—1941–45*. New York: Carroll & Graf, 2001.

Badsey, Stephen. *Normandy 1944: Allied Landings and Breakout*. London: Osprey, 1997.

______, ed. *The Hutchinson Atlas of World War II Battle Plans: Before and After*. London: Fitzroy Dearborn, 2000.

Baumgartner, John W. *16th Infantry Regiment*. Privately published. Bamberg, Germany: 1945.

Belchum, David. *Victory in Normandy*. London: Chatto & Windus, 1981.

Blumenson, Martin. "Rommel," in *Hitler's Generals*, Correlli Barnett, ed. New York: Grove Weidenfeld, 1989.

______. *U.S. Army in World War II: The European Theater of Operations. Breakout and Pursuit*. Washington, DC: Center of Military History, 1993.

Bradford, James C., ed. *The Atlas of American Military History*. New York: Oxford University Press, 2003.

Bradley, Omar N. *A Soldier's Story*. New York: Henry Holt, 1951.

Burch, G.C., and T.T. Crowley. *Eight Stars to Victory: Operations of the First Engineers' Combat Battalion in World War II*. Publisher and place unknown, 1947 (reprinted 1987).

Butcher, Harry C. *My Three Years with Eisenhower*. New York: Simon & Schuster, 1946.

Carell, Paul. *Invasion—They're Coming! The German Account of the Allied Landings and the 80 Days' Battle for France*. New York: E. P. Dutton, 1963.

Chandler, Alfred D., and Stephen Ambrose, eds. *The Papers of Dwight David Eisenhower. The War Years*. Baltimore: Johns Hopkins, 1970.

Churchill, Winston S. *The Second World War: Triumph and Tragedy*. Boston: Houghton Mifflin, 1953.

Cole, Hugh M. *U.S. Army in World War II: The European Theater of Operations. The Ardennes: Battle of the Bulge*. Washington, DC: Center of Military History, 1994.

Collier, Richard. *The War in the Desert*. Alexandria, VA: Time-Life Books, 1977.

Cooper, Belton Y. *Death Traps: The Survival of an American Armored Division in World War II*. Novato, CA: Presidio Press, 1998.

Crowl, Philip A., and Edmund G. Love. *U.S. Army in World War II: The War in the Pacific. Seizure of the Gilberts and Marshalls*. Washington, DC: Center of Military History, 1990.

Dank, Milton. *Turning Points of World War II: D-Day*. New York: Franklin Watts, 1984.

D-Day: The Normandy Invasion in Retrospect. Lawrence, KS: University Press of Kansas, 1971.

D'Este, Carlo. *Decision in Normandy.* New York: E.P. Dutton, 1983.

______. *Bitter Victory: The Battle for Sicily, 1943.* New York: E.P. Dutton, 1988.

______. *Fatal Decision: Anzio and the Battle for Rome.* New York: HarperCollins, 1991.

______. *Patton: A Genius for War.* New York: HarperCollins, 1995.

Detzer, Karl, ed. *The Army Reader.* "The American Army Is Different," by Hans Habe. New York: Bobbs-Merrill, 1943.

Dillon, Katherine V., Donald M. Goldstein, and J. Michael Wenger. *D-Day Normandy: The Story and the Photographs.* Herndon, VA: Brassy's, 1999.

Eisenhower, Dwight D. *Crusade in Europe.* New York: Doubleday, 1948.

Ellis, John. *The Sharp End: The Fighting Man in World War II.* New York: Scribner's, 1980.

Ellsberg, Edward. *The Far Shore.* New York: Dodd, Mead, 1960.

Foote Finke, Blythe. *No Mission Too Difficult! Old Buddies of the 1st Division Tell All About World War II.* Chicago: Contemporary Books, 1995.

Ford, Harvey S. *What You Should Know About the Army.* New York: W. W. Norton, 1941.

Garland, Albert N., and Howard M. Smyth. *U.S. Army in World War II: The Mediterranean Theater. Sicily and the Surrender of Italy.* Washington, DC: GPO, 1965.

Gilbert, Martin. *The Second World War: A Complete History.* New York: Henry Holt, 1989.

Goodwin, Doris Kearns. *No Ordinary Time. Franklin & Eleanor Roosevelt: The Home Front in World War II.* New York: Touchstone/Simon & Schuster, 1994.

Hall, Tony, ed. *D-Day: Operation Overlord—From Its Planning to the Liberation of Paris.* London: Salamander, 1993.

Hammond, William M. *Normandy.* Washington, DC: Center for Military History, 1994.

Harrison, Gordon A. *U.S. Army in World War II: The European Theater. Cross-Channel Attack.* Washington, DC: GPO, 1951.

Hastings, Max. *Overlord: D-Day and the Battle for Normandy.* New York: Simon & Schuster, 1984.

Heavey, William F. *Down Ramp: The Story of the Army Amphibian Engineers.* Washington, DC: Infantry Journal Press, 1947.

Heidenheimer, Arnold. *Vanguard to Victory: History of the 18th Infantry.* 1954.

Hirshson, Stanley P. *General Patton: A Soldier's Life.* New York: HarperCollins, 2002.

Holt, Tonie and Valmai. *Major & Mrs. Holt's Battlefield Guide to the Normandy Landing Beaches.* Barnsley, South Yorkshire: Pen and Sword Books, 1999.

Howarth, David. *D-Day—The Sixth of June, 1944.* New York: Bantam, 1959.

Howe, George F. *U.S. Army in World War II: The Mediterrean Theater. Northwest Africa: Seizing the Initiative in the West.* Washington, DC: GPO, 1991.

Katcher, Philip. *U.S. 1st Infantry Division, 1939–45.* London: Osprey, 1978.

Keegan, John. *Six Armies in Normandy.* New York: Viking Press, 1982.

Kilvert-Jones, Tim. *Omaha Beach: V Corps' Battle for the Normandy Beachhead.* Conshohoken, PA: Combined Publishing, 1999.

Knickerbocker, H.R., and Don Whitehead et. al. *Danger Forward: The Story of the First Infantry Division in World War II.* Washington, DC: Society of the First Division, 1947.

Lewis, Adrian R. *Omaha Beach: A Flawed Victory.* Chapel Hill, NC: University of North Carolina Press, 2001.

Liddell-Hart, Basil H., ed. *The Rommel Papers.* New York: Harcourt, Brace, Jovanovich, 1953.

MacDonald, Charles B. *U.S. Army in World War II: The European Theater. The Last Offensive.* Washington, DC: GPO, 1951.

______. *U.S. Army in World War II: The European Theater. The Siegfried Line Campaign.* Washington, DC: GPO, 1951.

______. *A Time For Trumpets: The Untold Story of the Battle of the Bulge.* New York: Bantam Books, 1984.

Manchester, William. *Goodbye, Darkness.* New York: Bantam Doubleday Dell, 1980.

Matloff, Maurice. *U.S. Army in World War II: The European Theater. The Last Offensive.* Washington, DC: GPO, 1973.

McManus, John C. *The Deadly Brotherhood: The American Combat Soldier in World War II.* Novato, CA: Presidio Press, 1998.

Miller, John, Jr. *U.S. Army in World War II: The War in the Pacific. Guadalcanal: The First Offensive.* Washington, DC: Center of Military History, 1989.

______. *U.S. Army in World War II: The War in the Pacific. Cartwheel: The Reduction of Rabaul.* Washington, DC: Center of Military History, 1990.

Minns, Raynes. *Bombers and Mash: The Domestic Front, 1939–45.* London: Virago Press, 1980 (reprinted 1999).

Mitcham, Samuel W., Jr. *The Desert Fox in Normandy: Rommel's Defense of Fortress Europe.* Westport, CT: Praeger, 1997.

Morison, Samuel Eliot. *The Invasion of France and Germany, 1944–1945.* (Volume II of *History of United States Naval Operations in World War II.*) Boston: Little, Brown, 1959.

Norman, Albert. *Operation Overlord: Design and Reality.* Harrisburg, PA: Military Service Publishing Co., 1952.

Omaha Beachhead (6 June–13 June 1944). "American Forces in Action" Series. Washington, DC, 1945 (reprinted 1984).

Parker, Danny S. *Battle of the Bulge: Hitler's Ardennes Offensive, 1944–1945.* Philadelphia: Combined Books, 1991.

Pöppel, Martin. *Heaven and Hell: The War Diary of a German Paratrooper.* Staplehurst, England: Spellmount, 1988.

Prange, Gordon W. *At Dawn We Slept: The Untold Story of Pearl Harbor.* New York: Penguin Books, 1981.

Pyle, Ernie. *Brave Men.* New York: Henry Holt, 1944.

______. *Here Is Your War.* New York: Henry Holt, 1945.

Ryan, Cornelius. *The Longest Day.* New York: Popular Library, 1959.

Shirer, William L. *The Rise and Fall of the Third Reich.* Greenwich, CT: Crest, Fawcett, 1960.

Stanton, Shelby L. *World War II Order of Battle.* New York: Galahad Books, 1984.

Towne, Allen N. *Doctor Danger Forward.* Jefferson, NC: McFarland & Co., 2000.

Tute, Warren, John Costello, and Terry Hughes. *D-Day.* New York: Collier Books, 1974.

Votaw, John F., and Steven Weingartner, eds. *Blue Spaders: The 26th Infantry Regiment, 1917–1967.* Wheaton, IL: Cantigny First Division Foundation, 1996.

______. *The Greatest Thing We Have Ever Attempted: Historical Perspectives on the Normandy Campaign.* Wheaton, IL: Cantigny First Division Foundation, 1998.

Weiss, Jess E. *The Vestibule.* New York: Pocket Books, 1972.

Werstein, Irving. *The Battle of Aachen*. New York: Thomas Y. Crowell, 1960.
Whiting, Charles. *Bloody Aachen*. New York: Stein & Day, 1976.
______. *Kasserine*. New York: Stein & Day, 1984.
Whitlock, Flint. *The Rock of Anzio*. Boulder: Westview, 1998.
Williamson, Gordon. *SS: The Blood-Soaked Soil*. Osceola, WI: Motorbooks International, 1995.
Wilmot, Chester. *The Struggle for Europe*. London: Collins, 1952.
Young, Peter. *D-Day*. New York: Galahad, 1981.

Published Sources (Newspapers and Periodicals)

Allen, Thomas B. "Untold Stories of D-Day." *National Geographic*, June 2002.
American Traveler, The (U.S. 1st Infantry Division newspaper), June 6, 1945.
Army Times, September 21, 1946.
Bridgehead Sentinel, April, July, October 1956.
Cannoneer, The (7th Artillery Battalion newsletter).
Chicago Tribune, June 6, 1944.
Hemingway, Ernest. "Voyage to Victory." *Collier's*, July 22, 1944.
Keegan, John. "D-Day: History's Greatest Invasion." *U.S. News & World Report*, May 23, 1994.
Life, December 25, 1944.
Los Angeles *Daily News*, March 29, 2003.
Lyme (England) *Star*, October 25, 1991.
Martin, Ralph G. "This Was D-Day." *Yank* magazine, June 30, 1944.
Miami Daily News, August 6, 1944.
Miller, Merle. "The Red One." *Yank* magazine, May 25, 1945.
______. "The Men of the Fighting First." *Argosy*, January 1951.
Morris, Roy, Jr. "Papa's Two-Front War." *WWII History* magazine, January 2003.
New York Times, June 5, 1944.
Newsweek, December 18 and 25, 1944.
Press The, (Atlantic City, New Jersey), June 6, 1994.
Ramsey, Winston G., ed. "Normandy." *After The Battle*, No. 1, 1973.
______. *Jupiter Courier-Journal* (Jupiter, Florida), interview of Allan B. Ferry, October 9, 1983.
Small, Collie. "The Big Red One Wrote the Book." *Saturday Evening Post*, February 2, 1946.
Time, June 19, 1944.
United States News, The , May 5, 1944.
Vital Speeches of the Day. "FDR's Prayer." Vol. X, November 15, 1944.
Woods, Andrew. "Captain Joseph T. Dawson." *Bridgehead Sentinel*, August 25–26, 1998.

Films and Videos

D-Day: The Great Crusade. War Stories series. ITN Productions, 1984.
D-Day: The Total Story. Greystone Productions, 1994.
Morning: June–August 1944. The World at War series. Thames Television, 1968.
Normandy to the Rhine. The Century of Warfare series. Time-Life Video; Nugus/Martin Productions, 1994.
The True Story of the Big Red One. Greystone Productions. 1994.

Other Sources

"A Crack German Panzer Division and What Allied Air Power Did To It Between D-Day and V-Day." USAMHI.

Allen, Terry. Personal papers. USAMHI.

Army Field Manual FM 100-5, "Operations," June 15, 1944.

Barrett, Carlton W., Medal of Honor Citation, MRC.

Baumer, Robert. Letter to author, Sept. 3, 2002.

Beach, John B. Personal papers. USAMHI.

Brown, Bobbie, Medal of Honor Citation, MRC.

CBS Television audio transcript (unaired): Interview by Andy Rooney of Joe Dawson, Albert H. Smith, Bill Washington, Charles Horner, and Max Zera, April 29, 1984. (copy in USAMHI)

"Commemorative History of the 18th Infantry Regiment." Copy in MRC.

Constable, John W. Personal papers. USAMHI.

Daniel, Darrell M. Monograph: "The Capture of Aachen." Combined Arms Research Library, Fort Leavenworth, Kansas.

DeFranzo, Arthur, Medal of Honor Citation, MRC.

1st Infantry Division G-1 Report, MRC.

Gabel, Dr. Christopher R. Monograph: "Military Operations on Urbanized Terrain: The 2nd Battalion, 26th Infantry, at Aachen, October 1944." (MRC)

Halloran, Walter. Address to the Dr. Harold Deutsch Memorial Minnesota World War II Roundtable, January 11, 1996: "The Role of the Combat Photographer."

Heinz, William C., quoted by Andrew Woods, MRC, from an article in the Fort Worth *Star-Telegram,* October 22, 1944.

Hendrick, Harten W. Personal papers. USAMHI.

Lindsey, Jake W., Medal of Honor Citation, MRC.

McGraw, Francis X., Medal of Honor Citation, MRC.

Merli, Gino, Medal of Honor Citation, MRC.

Monteith, Mimmie W., Jr., Medal of Honor Citation, MRC.

Peterson, George, Medal of Honor Citation, MRC.

Pinder, John J., Medal of Honor Citation, MRC.

Reams, Quinton F. Personal papers. USAMHI.

Reese, James M., Medal of Honor Citation, MRC.

Reynolds, Harley, letter to author, September 2, 2002.

Reynolds, Quentin. Radio script, June 8, 1944. USAMHI.

Reynolds, Quentin. Letter to Mrs. Terry Allen, June 20, 1944. USAMHI.

Richmond, Kimball R. Personal papers. USAMHI.

Richmond, Kimball, Citation for Distinguished Service Cross, July 1, 1944, MRC.

Schaefer, Joseph E., Medal of Honor Citation, MRC.

16th I&R Diary.

Skogsberg, Paul. Personal papers. USAMHI.

Thompson, Mas, Medal of Honor Citation, MRC.

"This Is Sicily." War Department pamphlet, date unknown.

"Translation of Field Marshall Rommel's Report after His Inspection of Defenses of the Atlantic Wall, 22 April 1944." USAMHI.

V Corps History, MRC.
Votaw, John, MRC. Correspondence with author.
Warner, Henry F., Medal of Honor Citation, MRC.
Website: www.mwci.org (History of the USS *Augusta*).
Website: www.webbuild.net/BeforeTaps/Triumph.htm: "Triumph and Tragedy."
Will, Walter J., Medal of Honor Citation, MRC.
Woods, Andrew, MRC. Correspondence with author.
Woolnough, James K. Personal papers. USAMHI.

Index

Italicized page numbers indicate photographs.